*The book* First the Kingdom of God: Global Voices on Global Mission *honors Peter Kuzmič and his contribution to global Christianity in a fitting manner. As one of the contributors states, Kuzmič articulated the vision and exemplified the praxis of the Kingdom of God as transcending denominational, ethnic, and national interests. I am particularly pleased to see the two emphases come through strongly. One is that of the Kingdom of God, which is the most dominant point of reference in Jesus' message. The other is the holistic and integrated understanding of the gospel and its relevance to the entire life and mission of the church. These emphases are much needed in the definition of the Gospel in our world today. The editors have done an admirable job, reflecting their experience and passion for global Christianity in editing this book. I commend William Carey International University Press for releasing such a quality publication.*
Ken Gnanakan
Chairman, International Council for Higher Education

*This collection represents some of the best thinking today on the Church's mandate to proclaim the gospel of the Kingdom to all nations. It is filled with both excellent biblical scholarship and practical understanding of how the kingdom of God relates to our modern world and the Church's mission within it.*
David Taylor
Research Director, U.S. Center for World Mission

*As a scholar from the former Yugoslavia, Peter Kuzmic is uniquely positioned to both understand and offer perspective on global Christianity. First, he is a genuine product of a multi-traditional context in which Catholics, Orthodox, and Evangelicals had to learn to get along under the worst of conditions. Second, he is a student of Christianity around the world, and he maintains an extensive network of friends and colleagues from virtually every country. Drawing from this wealth of experience and relationships, this wonderful book offers a broad view of God's kingdom both ecclesiastically and culturally.*
Todd M. Johnson
Co-editor, *World Christian Encyclopedia* and *Atlas of Global Christianity*

# First the Kingdom of God:
# Global Voices on Global Mission

Daniel K. Darko
and
Beth Snodderly, Editors

William Carey International University Press
1539 E. Howard Street, Pasadena, California 91104
wciupress@wciu.edu
www.wciupress.org

Daniel Darko and Beth Snodderly, editors
*First the Kingdom of God: Global Voices on Global Mission*

Copyright © 2014 by Darko and Snodderly

Except as provided by the Copyright Act, no part of this publication may be reproduced, stored in a retrieval system or transmitted in any form or by any means without the prior written permission of the publisher.

All rights reserved

ISBN: 9780865850774

Library of Congress Control Number: 2013952358

Unless otherwise noted, Scripture verses are from the New International Version.

# Contributors

Corneliu Constantineanu
*Institutul Teologic Penticostal, Bucureşti-Romani, Rector/President*

Barry H. Corey
*Biola University, President*

Daniel K. Darko
*Gordon College, Associate Professor of Biblical Studies*

Ruth Padilla DeBorst
*Latin American Theological Fellowship, President*

Scott Hafemann
*University of St. Andrews, Reader in New Testament*

Peter Kuzmič
*Gordon-Conwell Seminary, Distinguished Professor of World Missions and European Studies; Evangelical Theological Seminary (Osijek, Croatia), Founder and President*

Gregory M. Mundis
*Assemblies of God World Missions, Executive Director*

Bruce J. Nicholls
*Asia Theological Association, Senior Advisor*

C. René Padilla
*Micah Network, President Emeritus*

Ronald J. Sider
*Palmer Theological Seminary, Distinguished Professor of Theology, Holistic Ministry & Public Policy*

Beth Snodderly
*William Carey International University, President*

Timothy C. Tennent
*Asbury Theological Seminary, President and Professor of World Christianity*

Miroslav Volf
*Yale Divinity School, Professor of Theology and Founding Director of Yale Center for Faith & Culture*

Christopher J.H. Wright
*Langham Partnership International, International Director*

Hwa Yung
*Malaysian Methodist, Bishop*

# Contents

**Introduction - 1**

Seeking the Kingdom of God in a Changing Landscape
*Daniel K. Darko*

**The Kingdom of God and the Spread (and Distortion) of the Gospel**

The Church and the Kingdom of God: A Theological Reflection - 9
*Peter Kuzmič*

The Gospel in Historic and Cultural Transmission - 41
*Timothy C. Tennent*

**Connectedness and Mutual Submission under God's Rule**

Honor Everyone!" Christian Faith and the Culture of Universal Respect - 65
*Miroslav Volf*

Paul's Legacy of Cooperation for Twenty-First Century Missiology and
  Missions Practice - 87
*Daniel K. Darko*

"Unlikely" Contributions Toward a Global Social Ethic: Can Anything Good
Come from There? – 105
*Ruth Padilla DeBorst*

John Sung Revisited - 113
*Hwa Yung*

Hermeneutics: Christian-Muslim Perspectives - 125
*Bruce J. Nicholls*

Christendom, Christianity and Islam—Does Europe Need to Hear the Gospel?:
  A Brief Reflection from a Pentecostal Perspective - 147
*Gregory M. Mundis*

## The Integration of All of Life under Christ's Reign

Faith and Life: A Pauline Perspective on the Integration of Faith and Everyday Life - 167
*Corneliu Constantineanu*

Pentecostalism and the Collegiate Institution: A History and Analysis of This Strained Alliance - 193
*Barry H. Corey*

Contextual Scripture Engagement and Transcultural Mission - 215
*C. René Padilla*

## The Kingdom of God in Conflict with the Kingdoms of the World

Divine Judgment and the Completion of the Missionary Task: Paul's Motivation for Ministry in 1–2 Thessalonians—A Response to Thor Strandenæs - 225
*Scott Hafemann*

"The Obedience of Faith among the Nations": Old Testament Ethics in Covenantal and Missional Perspective - 235
*Christopher J.H. Wright*

Evangelicals and Structural Injustice: Why Don't They Understand It and What Can Be Done? - 257
*Ronald J. Sider*

Conclusion: "He Will Reign Forever and Ever" – 265
*Beth Snodderly*

**Index** - 273

# Acknowledgments

The breadth of scholarship and depth of content of this book are due in part to the initial work of Corneliu Constantineanu, Marcel Marceralu, Krešimir Šimić, and Miroslav Volf who edited a larger (894 pages) multi-lingua *festschrift* for Peter Kuzmič. To a selection from this earlier work we have added three chapters, including one by Peter Kuzmič on his life theme, "seek first the Kingdom of God." We are grateful also to the contributors for making the time to share their invaluable insights and experience with our readers.

Beth Snodderly (one of the editors) showed real enthusiasm and went beyond the usual task of an editor to devote more time to copyediting. Beth's experience and passion for global Christianity contributed significantly to the quality of this project. William Carey International University Press (WCIU Press) has been gracious in working with us to make the dream for this publication a reality. Heather Holt of WCIU Press was particularly helpful in this regard. To Jessica Rhodes, we say thank you for compiling the bibliography during a busy examination week for you at Gordon College, MA. There are many others that deserve a word of gratitude but the brevity of space would not permit us to name them all.

Peter Kuzmič is both a contributing author and the one we wish to honor with this book. We are all blessed to know him and appreciate his contribution to global Christianity. We hope that this volume featuring his former students, protégés, and colleagues becomes a useful tool in the hands of scholars, students, and Christians interested in trends in global Christianity. Thus it is to Peter Kuzmič that we dedicate this work. Thank you, Peter, for your work in advancing the Kingdom of God.

DANIEL DARKO

# Introduction:
# Seeking the Kingdom of God in a Changing Landscape

Daniel K. Darko

World Christianity in our century engenders exciting yet challenging prospects in non-Western countries where there is neither "separation of church and state" nor a concept of "Christianity as a movement for the marginalized." In a recent visit to Africa, I attended an event honoring a pioneer in one Pentecostal movement in which two members of parliament from opposing parties and a cabinet minister shared their faith unreservedly as Pentecostal Christians. The country's President and a high percentage of parliamentarians profess to be Christians. Beyond politics, the financial and industrial sectors also comprise a large proportion of "movers and shakers" who are Christians, and positively engage with their Islamic and African Traditional counterparts in the public arena. It soon became apparent that the cordiality between Christians, Muslims an African Traditionalists differ significantly from what one may find in some Christian settings in the United States. Some of these African leaders shared stories about how they as Christians shared rooms with Muslim friends at the University and currently work side by side with Muslims and animists. This is not only an African phenomena but it is also a growing trend in Asian and South American countries.

Global Christianity and globalization present us with an opportunity to seize in the quest to evince the faithful presence of the Kingdom of God in our broken world. World conflict is unfortunately tied to world religions as much as poverty and a wide array of social challenges are present in the majority world. One example is the ethno-religio conflict in former Yugoslavia during the 1990s. Serbians and Croats assumed a "national Christian identity" both during and in the aftermath of the war. God was supposedly with both sides even as grenades were being shelled and inconceivable forms of abuse were visited on teenage girls. The Orthodox Serbs believed God was on their side while the Catholic Croats felt empowered by God to gain victory over their enemies. Christians versus Christians! Ironically, it would take Christian leaders who espoused a vision of *Missio Dei* that transcends denominational boundaries, ethnic divide, and social status to mobilize "Kingdom" missionaries in a decisive effort to bring hope, reconciliation, and to garner socio-political forces for transformation. I encountered Professor Peter Kuzmič in Croatia in the mid-1990s doing just that. At the nearest available time, Peter gave a few of us one unforgettable tour of Vukovar (an entire city reduced to rubbles), and a couple of mass gravesites in the area. The last visit on the trip was to a Catholic monastery where he lamented evil for what it is and shared about the dedication of Catholic monks resident in the monastery during the siege and invasion of Vukovar. Peter was the President of the Evangelical Churches in Croatia as well as the Evangelical Theological Seminary yet he spoke about the priests as fellow ministers and sharers in Kingdom service. He later seized the opportunity to challenge us to reflect on the embodiment of the Kingdom of God and our part in *Missio Dei*; our role in fostering reconciliation, healing, and training for Christian leaders to serve the post-war former Yugoslavia.

The war had split Yugoslavia into the smaller countries of Bosnia and Herzegovina, Croatia, Macedonia, Montenegro, Serbia, and Slovenia. A new sense of identity and nationalism filled the air, yet a gaze beyond the surface would underline hopelessness and bitterness as fairly accurate descriptors of the plight of most people. As a prophet of peace, a champion of social justice, and pastor of all people, Peter Kuzmič articulated the vision and exemplified the praxis of the Kingdom of God as transcending denominational, ethnic, and national interests.

We may recall Jesus announcing the scope of his mission to include proclamation of the good news to the poor, recovery of sight to the blind, release to the oppressed, and proclaiming the year of the Lord's favor (Luke 4:18; cf. Isa. 61:1-2). This book is a collection of essays from experts who share this vision of the Kingdom, who have worked with Peter Kuzmič in related tasks and who write as a tribute to a colleague dedicated to world missions. Using the legacy of Peter Kuzmič as a starting point, contributors elevate the discussion on how we may be responsible "Kingdom" servants in the changing context of modern Christianity. The essays (except the chapter by Peter himself and the concluding chapter) are taken from a multi-lingua *festschrift* for Professor Kuzmič, originally edited by Miroslav Volf, Corneliu Constantineanu, Marcel V. Măcelaru, and Krešimir Šimić, here shortened and edited to make it easily accessible to the English readership.

## The Changing Landscape and the Unchanging Gospel

The demarcation between the *ecclesia* versus the academy, and church versus society in the ongoing discourse in world missions seems inconsistent with both the biblical framework of the Kingdom of God and praxis in early Christianity. Modern trends in world Christianity, be it the shift in the majority of the Christian population from the West to the rest of the world, or the task of Western missionaries in the non-Western world, are prompting a renaissance of faithful witness in a world without Christ. *Missio Dei* is being unwrapped from the image of the Church as "the kingdom of the West." In fact, gone are the days when Western norms were equated with Christian values. The worldwide church is international, ecumenical, and increasingly cross-cultural in its outlook. Today's Christians are increasingly comfortable with a hybrid of traditional hymns, contemporary songs, and lyrics in foreign languages that worshippers may not even understand. The twenty-first century has embraced diversity as beauty, and a hybrid of Calvinist-Arminian theology as a sound theological framework. Moreover, there are more people of different races, nationalities, and languages professing Jesus as Lord today than any other time in human history.

It is worth noting that the rise of immigrant churches in the Western hemisphere, often replicating the style of their home churches in Korea, Nigeria, Brazil, or China, is a popular trend. These churches often show little or no desire to integrate other people groups if it requires the need to alter some cultural aspects of the worship services. The positive side is that they provide space to harness social connectedness and keep religious interests alive in diaspora. Conversely, they become social ghettos fencing off the richness of multi-cultural and multi-ethnic interaction. Undoubtedly, immigrant churches are thriving from Flushing to San Francisco, from London to Birmingham and from the Bronx to Boston. Europe's two largest churches (Kiev and London) were founded and are led by Nigerian natives. The traditional Caucasian evangelical churches and the press seem oblivious of these groups of evangelicals in the United States and elsewhere. It is quite interesting to observe how talking points about evangelicals during electoral seasons in America appear to ignore the presence of immigrant Christian movements.

Multiple factors account for the changing trends in global Christianity. Prayer, biblical orthodoxy, and social involvement are significant factors. Christian devotion and discipline is a common feature in places where churches are growing. For example, prayer meetings of Korean Presbyterian members may be mistaken for a Pentecostal revival meeting elsewhere. Testimonies on miracles and exorcism are regular features in Presbyterian and Baptist churches in some countries. Catholic charismatic renewal movements operate literally like charismatic churches and share similar experiences. Rigid doctrinal barriers are tumbling down while we find some missionaries confused or afraid to share their experience with their sending churches for fear of losing support. In England, it is indisputable that any significant growth in the Church of England is most likely to happen through the work of its charismatic wing, being spearheaded by the Holy Trinity Brompton (London) and its church plants. Prayer, singing, and dancing are replacing the frigid upstanding and reflective style previously prevalent in mainline churches.

Numbers could be misleading since numerical growth is not tantamount to spiritual growth. Sound biblical teaching is a rarity today. Prayer-full churches are seeing great results yet even local leaders in these churches have expressed the need for moderation, good discipleship, and a place for common sense in religious praxis. It may be exaggerating to suggest that Western churches may be good in discipleship and organizational structures while their non-Western counterparts appear more disciplined and devoted in the areas of prayer, fasting, and evangelism. The crux of the matter is that the rest of the world needs the West as much as the West needs the rest to revive the dying churches, in the quest for healthy spiritual growth within, faithful presence (good moral examples) in the world, and responsible social engagement.

Consequently, modern trends in Christianity call for salient questions that require serious consideration: How may Western Christians embrace unfamiliar developments in their sister churches overseas? Do the West and East have something to learn from each other? What about the social responsibility of thriving churches in poverty-stricken countries? Do Christians have a role in peace and reconciliation in a world marred by religious conflicts? Does the spreading of the gospel have anything to do with social involvement—feeding orphans, clothing the naked or freeing sex-slaves? Should Christians whose neighbors and work colleagues are Muslims, African Traditionalist, Hindus, and Buddhists relate to them and engage them for the common good of society? In other words, how may Christians be the salt of the earth and light of the world? To what extent may Western Christians work in concert with their non-Western counterparts to provide good theological education, leadership training, and mutual support?

The interface of cultures and value systems in the emergence of globalization shows traces of what we find in global Christianity. The contrast between an individual-centered Christian framework and community-centered value systems are but one such paradox. The Church today meets where old pillars of cultural, racial, and tribal prejudice once stood. Denominations that have their origins rooted in the desire to be separate from other races now constitute mixed-race leadership and congregations. Tribalism in Africa and elsewhere is gradually giving way to a sense of belonging in one family of God's people. It is however misleading to surmise that all is going well. No! Christians still face the challenge to engage non-Christians meaningfully and respectfully in the pursuit for just society. Opportunities come at no better time for dialogue and reflection if the worldwide Christian community is poised "to seek first the Kingdom of God" so that "all" national and denominational causes for anxiety may subside, *Deo volente*.

## A Look at the Rear View Mirror:
### Origins of the Mission of the Kingdom of God

The inauguration of the Kingdom of God was marked by the advent of Christ in our human history. His teachings, life, and miraculous deeds were misconstrued, misread, and misappropriated by even his own disciples due to their personal and cultural biases. This became evident in the post-resurrection encounter with Jesus when the question was posed, "Lord, would you at this time restore the kingdom back to Israel?" Note the desire to meet ethnic or national interest. This was soon after [...] about the Kingdom of God (Acts 1:3-8). Jesus unders[...] of the mission, commencing from Jerusalem and [...] world (Acts 1:8). The global and cross-cultur[...] ssment and readjustment of cultural and [...]

Luke provides us with [...] God in relation to global mi[...]d Temple Judaism as a [...] comes as a Jew bu[...] when the discipl[...] gathered from [...] who are spea[...] native languag[...] Mesopotamia, Jude[...]ia, Egypt and the part of [...]ome" (Acts 2:7b-10 ESV). Tho[...] in turn took the message to variou[...] the Jesus movement at its post-Pentecost i[...]th challenges of preferential treatment in the distri[...] of nationalism (Acts 6) and theological concerns link[...] elations (Acts 10, 11). The leaders however responded by cho[...]ers to address these problems (Acts 6). The Early Church perseve[...] aring for one another, living in unity and devotion to commendable spir[...]al disciplines (Acts 2:42-47; 4:32-37), but their ability to engage non-Jews and converts from pagan cultures remained untested at the early stage.

The subsequent conversion of Saul of Tarsus brought early Christianity face to face with cultures, religious practices, and socio-political issues that were not always compatible with Jewish conventions. In other words, the mere expansion of the Church did not curtail personal biases or prejudices. For example, Paul later expressed his disappointment with Peter's judgment on ethno-race relations (Gal. 2:12-13). Luke records a major move in global mission during Paul's time in Antioch (Acts 13:1-3), the city from which the disciples had first been called Christians (Acts 11:26). Unlike Pentecost, here the Holy Spirit visited gifted leaders from diverse ethnic and socio-economic backgrounds at a prayer meeting at which Paul and Barnabas would be appointed for global assignment. There was a black man called Simeon, an aristocrat named Manaen, an African (possibly Greek) from Cyrene, called Lucius, and two Jews—a former Pharisee by the name of Saul and another one called Barnabas. Paul's and Barnabas' commission to the Gentiles eventually led to cross-cultural and inter-ethnic questions about circumcision and pagan practices as they relate to salvation and community membership. Later, we find leaders in Antioch working together with their counterparts in Jerusalem to address these issues (Acts 15).

Today the Church continues to face similar challenges requiring similar approaches to resolution. Christians from different denominations and nations may do well to work together in addressing issues facing the movement and exploring the way to be real light—be it spiritual, social, ethical, or political. This book does not seek to address all challenges of global missions but it is evident that it makes a significant contribution to the conversation to refocus our attention to the holistic scope of the Kingdom of God and its commensurate praxis.

**Rising to the Charge: Global Voices on the Mission of the Kingdom of God**

As noted earlier, *First the Kingdom of God* assembles a collection of essays from renowned Christian leaders of diverse cultures at the frontiers of global Christianity to elevate the conversation and to address key aspects of the changing trends aforementioned. This volume offers unique perspectives from multiple disciplines, ethno-racial diversity, and confessional affiliations. The lay person, clergy, or scholar is invited to re-examine his/her theological and social framework of missions afresh in the light of a global and interconnected geo-political global landscape. There are four parts to the discussion: Beginning with a seminal work of Professor Kuzmič, the first section provides a biblical and historical framework of the good news of the Kingdom of God, as the Church seeks to carry out its mission. The second section underscores the necessity for mutual interdependence in how Christians work together as Kingdom citizens and in the manner in which Christians may engage the wider society, especially in Islamic cultures. The third section flags a blind spot—the frequent divorcing of Christian mission from Christian praxis—and shows how this has been or may be bridged in "daily life," Christian education, and faithful witness across cultures. The final section (fourth) is self-explanatorily entitled "The Kingdom of God in Conflict with the Kingdoms of the World." Here, the modus operandi is grounded in Scripture and responsible social engagement. The concluding chapter reflects on the victory of the Kingdom of God through the surprising submission of the Lamb to the Father's will.

Our contributors have aptly married first class scholarship with accessible style for general readership to inform, ignite a new passion, and refocus mission praxis on the Master's vision—to "seek first his Kingdom and his righteousness" (Matt. 6:33). As you prepare to delve into this book, may you brace yourself for stimulating discourse, broader perspective of missions, and personal challenge to the effect that "all our powers may engage to do the master's will." May God keep your eyes fixed on him, renew your heart, and grant the openness to be a faithful "Kingdom citizen."

# The Kingdom of God and the Spread (and Distortion) of the Gospel

# The Church and the Kingdom of God: A Theological Reflection[1]

Peter Kuzmič

## Introduction

The Kingdom of God and the Church of Jesus Christ are two key New Testament concepts, both crucial for the understanding of God's plan for humanity and central to the fulfillment of his redemptive purpose. While the Church cannot be identified with the Kingdom, for (as we shall show later) the latter is a larger and more comprehensive term, the two are nevertheless in close correlation and cannot be separated either. It may be significant to point out that the very saying of Jesus from which the theme, "I will build my Church," is taken brings the Church and the Kingdom together. Peter's divinely revealed confession that Jesus is Messiah and God's Son provides the context in which Jesus for the first time reveals his intention to build "my Church" (*ekklesia mou*) and promises the keys of the "Kingdom of heaven" (*basileia ton ouranon*). This intention of Jesus is stated in connection with apostolic authority which is to be determinative for the spiritual destiny of mankind, as his plan "to build" is carried out on the basis of his work and their apostolic ministry.

### The Church in Relation to the Kingdom

What exactly is the relationship between the Kingdom of God that Jesus preached and the Church he founded? It is of immense importance for us as we discuss the nature and the mission of the Church to understand the intentions of Jesus. I am somewhat concerned that in our evangelical and evangelistic activism we are tempted to put the cart before the horse. We must understand who we are before we can know what we are to do. It is imperative for us to examine both our conscious and our hidden assumptions in the full light of the divine plan and purpose, taking into account the totality of scriptural teaching, so that our task may first of all be our obedient understanding of his task and

---

[1] *Editors' Note: This seminal article originally appeared in a book that is now out of print, edited by Bruce Nichols,* The Church: God's Agent for Change, *published by Paternoster Press, and used here by permission of the author. It is also translated into Korean and other languages.*

that our mission may naturally proceed from the quality of our spiritual nature and being. Acting must be a natural outgrowth of being. The mission of God carried out in our world requires the people of God. The shining of the light in the world presupposes light, and the salty effect on the earth results from the quality of the salt.

We gratefully acknowledge the growth of the Church around the globe and joyfully celebrate the redeeming victories of Christ and his people in diverse contexts of our needy world. At the same time, we must face up to the fact that in many places the credibility of the Church is seriously undermined, that the Church is questioned, criticized, attacked, and here and there even brutally persecuted. The Church is seriously challenged in its mission and even in its very existence by the highly competitive and militant resurgence of Islam. It is criticized by the Marxists as an "opiate" to the people that thereby fosters the enslavement of the exploited masses who would otherwise work for the social and political liberation which they certainly deserve. Many in the Third World still see the Church as an export of Western civilization and culture and as an instrument of the powerful and superior. In the West, the working classes, the young, and the intellectuals have (by and large) long been alienated from the churches, which tend to be predominantly either bourgeois or peasant-type, and the very make-up of a society supposedly built on Christian principles is undergoing a cultural and moral disintegration of unprecedented proportions.

The Church known to the world appears to have lost the keys to the Kingdom of God. As a result many, especially the young, seem to be saying, "Jesus Yes, church No."

Was the Church a mistake? Or as Hans Kung phrased it, was it "a rather poor substitute for the Kingdom"?[2] Those who think so, because of the discrepancy they see between Jesus' life and proclamation and the empirical reality of most Christian communities, tend rather unfairly to cite the oft-quoted formula of A. Loisy: "Jesus proclaimed the Kingdom of God, and what came was the Church."[3]

Evangelicals rightly emphasize the authority and reliability of the Scriptures and the importance of the teaching of Jesus as recorded in them. This logically leads to searching the Scriptures and striving for faithful obedience to Jesus. Given such a commitment, it is clear that a proper understanding of the Church is possible only when the framework of Jesus' teaching on the Kingdom of God is its primary point of reference and central concern. For the Kingdom of God is "both the starting point and the goal of the Church."[4]

---

[2] Daniel Harrington, *God's People in Christ: New Testament Perspectives on the Church and Judaism* (Philadelphia: Fortress Press, 1980), 28.

[3] Alfred Loisy, *L'Evangile et l'Eglise* (Paris, 1902), III.

[4] Rene Padilla, "The Kingdom of God and the Church," *Theological Fraternity Bulletin*, No. 1 and 2 (1976): 1.

Speaking of the Kingdom as related to the Church means primarily to speak of the reign of Christ exercised over and through the community called by his name. That reign of Christ in the present has, however, two most important points of reference. The first is a foundational one, the past Christ-event, encompassing the Incarnation, the earthly life and ministry of Jesus, and their culmination in his substitutionary death and victorious resurrection. The Kingdom came in the person of Jesus, and the Church is the result of that coming of the King.

The second point of reference is still in the future and will find its fulfillment in the return of Christ, which will bring about the completion of the Kingdom and the absorption of the Church into it. What was already begun when Jesus inaugurated the Kingdom is yet to be fully realized when he comes in power and glory.

It is within this two-advent structure of salvation history that the Church exists "between the times." It has always to *look back* as it is built on the foundation laid by Christ and the apostles while it also *looks forward*, fully cognizant of the fact that while it "builds," it is *his* Church and he will come both to complete and to judge it (cf. 1 Cor. 3:10-15).

The Church has to learn to work because of what Christ has already done and wait for what he will yet do. As soon as it loses one of these perspectives it has become unfaithful. It must learn to live in the present tension produced by the overlapping of the old and the new age, knowing that although it works within the old it belongs to the new, and its work in the old is on behalf of the new.

The parameters of this Christological understanding of salvation history, scripturally based, provide the framework for a right understanding of the nature and mission of the Church as related to the central concern of Jesus—the Kingdom of God. They will therefore serve as the basic outline of this chapter. However, before we proceed to the main body of the chapter, let us briefly, and of necessity only partially, review the treatment of the topic in the post-apostolic history of the Church.

### *The Kingdom in Post-Apostolic History*

In the first two centuries the Kingdom of God was largely interpreted in eschatological and millenarian terms, in terms of the inner spirituality of individual believers. The Church was the present reality while the Kingdom was viewed as a hope belonging almost exclusively to the eschatological future for an individual's enjoyment of God's blessings. While the Christian church, despite its advances, was still a minority suffering persecution at the hands of imperial powers, it strove to be the "pure church"[5] withdrawing from the world and awaiting the future coming of the Kingdom of God to vindicate its cause.[6]

The Constantinian reversal provided the religio-political context within which it became possible to think of the Church and the Kingdom in more closely correlated terms. The theologians of the Byzantine court developed the theology of the Christian *imperium* under the slogan, "one God, one Logos, one Emperor, one Empire." The Kingdom of God came to be seen as the *Corpus Christianum*, ruled by the *regnum* and *sacerdotum*. The Church became a state church, the servant of the interests of the Empire. Both the Eastern imperial theology and the Western Episcopal theocracy reduced the Kingdom of God to the terrestrial realities of role and power by Pope and Emperor. Although Augustine's thinking is more profound and more discerning, even he, in his *De Civitate Dei,* was tempted to identify the Kingdom of God with the Church. Not only the Church triumphant, but also the church militant, became almost synonymous with the Kingdom. Augustine explicitly stated that "the Church even now is the Kingdom of Christ and the Kingdom of heaven.[7] The medieval church indiscriminately followed Augustine in identifying the visible ecclesiastical system with the Kingdom of God and in applying such views to sanction the unholy alliance of throne and altar. Such thinking and the subsequent alliance of church and state led to tragic consequences, such as when serious attempts were made to create by force a "pure" Holy Christian Empire in which there was room for neither non-Christians nor Christian heretics. At worst the "holy" Crusades replaced the mission of the Church totally, and at best they were seen as equally important to the extension of the Kingdom of God.

The Reformers identified the Kingdom of God with the invisible Church. Ladd summarizes the view of the Reformers, although at some risk of oversimplification, by saying: "The Kingdom was to them the reign of God in the hearts of the redeemed and was therefore essentially a religious concept and primarily a present reality."[8] Yet it needs to be noticed that there is considerable divergence between the view of the Reformers with respect to the Kingdom. Zwingli's view is colored by his humanist conception of it. Luther varies, drawing heavily upon some aspects of Augustine's thinking, elaborating

---

[5] The extreme case was the Donatists' attempts to create a perfectionist ecclesiology; see Augustine's polemic against their views.

[6] There are striking similarities in the doctrinal emphasis and behavioral patterns between the Jewish apocalypticists (see "The Jewish Hopes and Expectations" section of this chapter), certain segments of the Early Church, and the modern apocalyptic sects. Parts of the evangelical movement of our day come dangerously to the last named group.

[7] Augustine, *The City of God*, XX, 9.

[8] George Eldon Ladd, *Crucial Questions about the Kingdom of God* (Grand Rapids: Eerdmans, 1952), 25. The Reformers are followed by some contemporary evangelical reformed scholars such as G. Vos and O.T. Allis.

the christocentric emphasis of his own teaching, depending on the state for protection, and suiting his theological polemics to his own struggles against the more radical segments of the Reformation. Calvin has a well-developed theology of the Kingdom of God, pointing to a christocracy characterized by (Geneva-style) church control over the State.[9]

Christians following the Reformation tradition viewed the Church as it is defined in the Augsburg Confession: "the congregation of saints in which the gospel is rightly taught and the Sacraments are rightly administered."[10] This definition of the Church as merely *congregatio sanctorum* (and *fidelium*) has rightly been criticized as partial and defective on two basic grounds.[11] First, it fails to relate the Church to its foundation in the Kingdom of God. Second, it leads to an ecclesiocentricity which forgets that the Church has a missionary function in the world. No wonder we find little emphasis on world mission in the period of Protestant orthodoxy. A full biblical ecclesiology knows no *congregatio* without mission.

### The Modern Debate

The debate about the Kingdom of God over the last 150 years has been largely academic and in most cases somewhat divorced from the ecclesiological issues. Albrecht Ritschl (1822–1889) understood the Kingdom-concept in terms of the prevalent evolutionary understanding of history, and interpreted it as a present reality and force behind the progress which would find its full realization in this world. In the latter part of the nineteenth century Ritschl's thinking, presented within the framework of Neo-Kantian philosophy, was the most influential view. Skydsgaard summarized this period as follows:

> An immanent and spiritualistic conception of the Kingdom of God prevailed, which corresponded well with the optimistic view of man and of our world so typical of that period. Christianity was turned into a glorified *Kulturprotestantismus*, in many ways essentially a bourgeois phenomenon, which suited well the religious ideology of humanism.[12]

---

[9] For more extensive and reliable discussions of Reformers' views see: Thomas F. Torrance, *Kingdom and the Church: A Study in the Theology of the Reformation* (Edinburgh and London: Oliver and Boyd, 1956); T. F. Torrance, "The Eschatology of Reformation," *Scottish Journal of Theology Occasional Papers* no. 2 (1957): 36-62; and Heinrich Quistorp, *Calvin's Doctrine of the Last Things* (London: Lutterworth Press, 1955).

[10] *Augsburg Confession*, VII.

[11] For more recent criticisms see W. Pannenberg, *Theology and the Kingdom of God* (Philadelphia: Westminster Press, 1969), 75-76; Carl Braaten, *The Future of God* (New York: Harper and Row, 1969), 112-16.

[12] K.E. Skydsgaard, "Kingdom of God and the Church," *Scottish Journal of Theology* 4, no. 4 (1959): 386.

A revolution in New Testament studies at the turn of the 20th century generated a strong reaction against this basically non-eschatological Ritschlian view of the Kingdom of God. Johannes Weiss,[13] Albert Schweitzer,[14] and others rediscovered the eschatological element of Jesus' teaching on the Kingdom of God. Their view (which later came to be known as "consistent eschatology") discounts the concept of an already present Kingdom in Jesus' teaching, claiming that he points only to an entirely future, apocalyptic reality which is to arrive by a cataclysmic in-breaking during Jesus' own life time.

C.H. Dodd,[15] the father of "realized eschatology," represents the opposing view to that of Weiss and Schweitzer, arguing that the apocalyptic elements in Jesus' teaching are to be taken as merely symbolic (the Early Church having been mistaken in interpreting them literally), for the Kingdom of God is already a present fact with no future fulfillment. "The *eschaton* has moved from the future to the present, from the sphere of expectation into that of realized experience."[16]

The school of liberal Protestant exegesis that flourished until recently generally considered the Church to be a latter creation with no relation to the historical Jesus and his teaching on the Kingdom of God. Such a negative attitude toward the Church resulted from an unhistorical interpretation of the work and mission of Jesus himself. (Catholic ecclesiology responded to such liberal challenges with the affirmation that "Jesus of Nazareth did found a clearly defined ecclesiastical organization and put Peter at its head as a kind of replacement for Jesus.")[17]

A number of serious exegetical and theological studies have attempted to recover the biblical balance and have synthesized the views of "thoroughgoing eschatologists" (like Weiss and Schweitzer) and the "realized eschatologists" (like Dodd and his followers).[18] We mention in passing especially the name of Oscar Cullmann,[19] who has been very influential in evangelical circles.

---

[13] J. Weiss, *Die Predigt Jesu vom Reich Gottes*, 2nd ed. (Gottingen: Vandenhoeck und Ruprecht, 1900; ET 1971).

[14] Albert Schweitzer, *The Quest of the Historical Jesus*, 1st ET. (London: 1919), many subsequent editions.

[15] See especially Dodd's *The Parables of the Kingdom* (London: Nisbet, 1935). Dodd acknowledges his indebtedness to Rudof Otto, *The Kingdom of God and the Son of Man* (ET, London: Lutterworth, 1943).

[16] Dodd, *Parables*, 50.

[17] Harrington, *God's People*, 27.

[18] See Ladd, *Crucial Questions*, 35-39; *Jesus and the Kingdom: The Eschatology of Biblical Realism* (Waco: Word, 1964), 23-38.

[19] See especially Cullmann's *Christ and Time* (Philadelphia: Westminster Press, 1950) and *Salvation in History* (New York: Harper and Row; London: SCM, 1967). Of great relevance to the topic of this paper is also Cullmann's study, "The Kingship of Christ and the Church in the New Testament," published in *The Early Church* (London: SCM, 1956).

The recent renaissance of evangelical New Testament scholarship has much for which to be commended. The late George Eldon Ladd must be credited for bringing back to the evangelical agenda the topic of the Kingdom of God.[20] This has been unduly neglected in reaction to the one-sided approach to the topic typical of the "social gospel" movement and other liberal and secularized abuses of the theme.[21] Though there is still much confusion and lack of theological precision, evangelical thinkers are beginning to explore with great urgency the theme of the Kingdom of God and how it relates to both the Church and the world. Much study needs yet to be done in this area.

The most significant ecumenical treatment of the topic was at the World Council of Churches conference, "Your Kingdom Come," held in May 1980 in Melbourne. The findings of that important gathering have been widely publicized. Evangelicals have discussed them extensively, and though evaluations vary, the Melbourne Conference has been criticized for its lack of biblical foundation, for one-sided (socio-political) thinking and activism, and for insufficient concern for the billions who yet need to hear the saving gospel of the Kingdom of God.

**The Church and the Community of the King: The Past Christ-event**

The announcement of the nearness of the Kingdom of God, first by John the Baptist and then by Jesus, sounds strange to our modern ears. We are not used to this monarchical concept or the manner of its introduction and are unsure of its meaning. It is obvious from the Gospel accounts, however, that the contemporaries of Jesus were acquainted with the concept and were not initially surprised or unclear as to its meaning. They had awaited the message and longed for the messenger for some time.

---

[20] See Ladd, *Crucial Questions*. Since 1974 the revised edition of the same work has been issued by the same publisher as *The Presence of the Future*, and there are popular expositions of the theme in *The Gospel of the Kingdom: Scriptural Studies in the Kingdom of God* (London: Paternoster, 1959) and *A Theology of the New Testament* (Grand Rapids: Eerdmans, 1974), especially pp. 45-134. Another significant evangelical treatment of the theme is Herman Ridderbos, *The Coming of the Kingdom* (Philadelphia: Presbyterian and Reformed, 1962).

[21] For some historical descriptions of the evangelical reactions see the following: George M. Marsden, *Fundamentalism and American Culture* (New York: Oxford University Press, 1980); E. R. Sandeen, *The Roots of Fundamentalism* (Chicago: University of Chicago Press, 1970); Donald W. Dayton, *Discovering an Evangelical Heritage* (New York: Harper and Row, 1976); David O. Moberg, *The Great Reversal: Evangelism Versus Social Concern* (Philadelphia and New York: Lippincott, 1972); Timothy P. Weber, *Living in the Shadow of the Second Coming* (New York and Oxford: Oxford University Press, 1979).

## The Jewish Expectations of the Kingdom

Having suffered at the hands of foreign oppressors for several centuries the Jews of the inter-testamental period clung to the Old Testament promises of the deliverance to come. They expected a Messiah who would bring about an apocalyptic reversal, defeating the forces of evil and restoring justice to the chosen people of God. They pictured a Davidic King, a mighty conqueror over the enemies of Israel, a heavenly supernatural Son of Man who would come with "authority, glory, and sovereign power" and whose dominion "will not pass away," and his kingdom never be destroyed (Dan. 7:14). This idea of the coming Kingdom with its great reversal of evil and restoration of justice fired the imagination of the oppressed Jews and inspired their political hopes. They were looking for the Kingdom of God (cf. Luke 2:25, 38; 23:51) and the time was ripe when John the Baptist appeared with his preparatory and prophetic message, "Repent, for the Kingdom of heaven is near" (Matt. 3:2).

The same message was adopted and further elaborated by Jesus (Matt. 4:17) and, upon his commission, proclaimed by the apostles (Matt. 10:7). The Kingdom truly came in the very person of Jesus, who was the Son of Man of Daniel's vision. It was clear, however, that the popular expectations of the Jews were not met by what Jesus had to offer. He did perform miracles; and there were moments like the feeding of the five thousand when they were certain that he was the one for whom they were waiting; and so in their zealous impatience they even tried to make him a King by force (John 6:15). Even his disciples were not immune to these false hopes, both before and after the resurrection (cf. Luke 24:21, Acts 1:6). But he did not come as a mighty king with glory and splendor, but rather as a man among men, in humility, poverty, and weakness. His mission was different from their expectations. He was not to be their political liberator and king, nor was he to fulfill their nationalistic hopes and bring them material blessings.

Because of a special covenantal relationship, the Jews were expected to be the natural subjects of the Kingdom (Matt. 8:12).[22] Jesus was mindful of this and the Kingdom was at first offered only "to the lost sheep of Israel" (Matt. 10:5-7). But they rejected it and he made it clear to their religious leaders that "the Kingdom of God will be taken away from you and given to a people who will produce its fruit" (Matt. 21:43). The blessings and privileges along with the responsibilities that earlier belonged to Israel were to be inherited by a new people of God, the Church of Jesus Christ.

## The Kingdom of God and Eternal Life

The public ministry of Jesus begins with the proclamation that God's appointed time has come—"the Kingdom of God is near"—and the call to repentance and faith in this good news (Mark 1:15). In the first three Gospels the term

---

[22] The NIV translates inexactly *huioi tes basileias* as "the subjects of the Kingdom."

"Kingdom" is used 121 times. Strictly speaking, *basileia* and the Aramaic *malkuth* should not be translated as "kingdom," but rather more exactly as "reign," or "rule," "sovereignty," or "kingship." For it is not primarily a question of the *place* of God's rule but rather of *his reign itself*. We shall use these terms interchangeably, always referring to the general reign of God, in particular as exercised by the Lord Jesus Christ over and through the messianic community—his Church.

The idea of the Kingdom of God—this "master-thought" of Jesus, as it has been called—occupies a place of supreme importance in his teaching and mission. It is *the* theme; it is the gospel, the good news of forgiveness, joy, and peace; it is the *summum bonum*, "the pearl of great value" (Matt. 13:45-46) for which everything is to be sacrificed; it is to be sought above everything else and it brings with it everything else (Matt. 6:33). Thus it is to be not only sought after but also prayed for. "Your Kingdom come" is a prayer that God may reign and his will be done on earth as it is in heaven.

The Kingdom focuses on the King, for it is his person and work that are the heart and center of the gospel. With him and in him the new age of salvation has come and the gift of life and forgiveness is freely offered. The only conditions for entrance into this new realm of blessings are repentance (change of mind and lifestyle) and faith (personal trust) in the One who is King. Such receptivity to the redemptive activity of God's rule working among men in Christ brings new life with new values.

In the discourse following the encounter with the rich young ruler Jesus makes it clear that "the Kingdom of God" and "eternal life" are interchangeable terms.[23] John the Evangelist picks up the concept of the Kingdom under the theme of "life" or "life eternal," another thoroughly eschatological concept. Except for twice in the conversation with Nicodemus (John 3:3, 5), he regularly replaces the Synoptic term "Kingdom of God" with "life" or "life eternal." It is beyond the scope of this chapter to argue that there is no difference in meaning between the two forms, and that what we find here is a superb example of contextualization by one who skillfully and responsibly adapts Jewish eschatology for broader Christian use. We will give only one example by comparing John 3:3, 5 with 3:36:

| 3:3, 5 | "Unless a man is born again [from above], he cannot [see] … enter the Kingdom of God" [*ou dunatoi eiselthein eis ten basileian tou theou*] | with | 3:36 | "whoever believes in the Son has *eternal life* [*zoen aionion*], but whoever rejects the Son will not see life [*zoen*]." |

---

[23] Compare Mark 10:23-24 and 30.

Both refer to the age to come which has broken into the present, offering its blessings to those who are receptive and bringing a judgment upon those who reject the free gift of life in the new age. George Ladd has summarized the relation of *life* and *Kingdom* in the eschatological perspective of God's rule as follows:

> If Kingdom is the gift of life bestowed upon his people when he manifests his rule in eschatological glory, and if God's Kingdom is also God's rule invading history before the eschatological consummation, it follows that we may expect God's rule in the present to bring a preliminary blessing to his people.[24]

Jesus understood it as his mission to preach the Kingdom of God, and the days of his ministry are characterized as the time in which "the good news of the Kingdom of God is being preached" (Luke 16:16). When shortly after his inaugural and programmatic sermon in Nazareth the people of Capernaum, impressed by his miracles, "tried to keep him from leaving them," he told them, "I must proclaim the good news of the Kingdom of God to other towns also, because that is why I was sent' (Luke 4:42-43).

In Jesus, then, we see the Kingdom manifested in two ways: in the Kingdom preaching-teaching and in the Kingdom's working miraculously (healings, exorcisms). The entrance of the new age into the present old age is verbally announced and powerfully demonstrated by his person in acts of mercy defeating the powers of evil. The same pattern is evident as Jesus sends out his disciples with the twofold task of proclaiming the Kingdom and performing the signs that are characteristic of its arrival—healing the sick and casting out demons (see Luke 10:9, 11, 17). In obedience to his command and empowered by his kingly authority, the disciples carried the message and demonstrated the power of the Kingdom in the same way that he did. And yet he reminds them that this is only an inauguration and that what is even more important is the full consummation of his rule in heaven where their "names are written" (Luke 10:20).

On one occasion within the controversy that arose from a victorious power-encounter, he explicitly announced that his victory over demons was the evidence that "the Kingdom of God has come to you" (Luke 11:20; Matt. 12:27). And to the question of the Pharisees as to "when the Kingdom of God would come," he replied, "The Kingdom of God is in your midst" (Luke 17:20-21).

### The Church and the Keys of the Kingdom

"I will build my Church" (Matt. 16:18) is one of the only two cases in the Gospels where the word, *ekklesia,* appears. It is no wonder that the authenticity of this saying of Jesus has been questioned by many who attempt to explain it

---

[24] Ladd, *Jesus and the Kingdom,* 201-02.

away as a later ecclesiastical addition. There are, however, 114 occurrences of *ekklesia* in the New Testament, mostly referring to Christian community, either universal or local. Does that mean that in the teaching of Jesus the "Kingdom" concept was central while the "Church" occupied only an insignificantly small place? Does it further suggest that in the apostolic age the Kingdom was relegated to a less important place and actually replaced by the Church as a sociologically identifiable body of believers? Did early Christians fail to comprehend Jesus' teaching about the Kingdom and so dilute it by substituting for it a more easily manageable human institution? Or did they invent the Church because of their embarrassment over the delay of the expected *parousia*?

Here it is important to note that, while the term *ekklesia* is not often on Jesus' lips, the community of believers is implied throughout his message and is referred to in other forms. As F. A. Hort warned long ago, "This is one of the cases in which it is dangerous to measure teaching about things by the range of the names applied to things."[25] The very concept of a Messiah implies the messianic community. The Great Commission's command to disciple and baptize clearly points to Jesus envisioning the continuation and growth of the *ekklesia*. The technical term "the Twelve" may be taken simply to mean "disciples," and the whole concept of discipleship is certainly central to Jesus' teaching and to the conception of the Church. It is safe to conclude that "wherever we find disciples and discipleship in the Gospels, there we are dealing with what was a direct preparation for the founding of the *Ecclesia*."[26]

What is the relationship between the statement of Jesus, "I will build my Church" and the following promise, "I will give you the keys of the Kingdom of heaven"? The very fact that Jesus speaks of the Church and the Kingdom in a logical sequence of thought must imply that the two are closely associated. Some will go so far in interpreting Matthew 16 as to claim a complete identification of the Church and the Kingdom. Others will point out that they are mentioned together because they are closely related as "two aspects of the same institution which Jesus will 'build'."[27] O.T. Allis states that "the expressions 'Kingdom of heaven' and 'Church' are in most respects at least equivalent, and that the two institutions are co-existent and largely co-extensive."[28] In further elaborating this thought, Allis then arrives at a debatable theological conclusion. He affirms, "The Kingdom and the Church are institutions which are both present in the world today; and they are so

---

[25] Renton J. A. Hort, *The Christian Ecclesia* (London: MacMillan and Co., 1898), 18.

[26] Hort, *Christian Ecclesia*, 19-20.

[27] Oswald T. Allis, *Prophecy and the Church* (Philadelphia: Presbyterian and Reformed, 1945), 82.

[28] Allis, *Prophecy*, 83.

closely related, so nearly identical, that it is impossible to be in the one and not in the other."[29]

The question of the text can be properly settled only by looking at the context. The immediate context is Peter's confession of Jesus' Messiahship at Caesarea Philippi. The broader context, as provided by Matthew, is the preceding demand of the Pharisees and Sadducees (prompted by their expectations and doubts) that Jesus authenticate himself by "showing them a sign from heaven" and Jesus' subsequent warning against them. The confession itself is the beginning of the disclosure of the "messianic secret," namely that the true nature of Jesus' mission would lead him not to a national restoration of Israel and political crowning, but rather to his own death in Jerusalem. From now on it is not the crowds that hear his message, but the select group of disciples who are instructed as to his purpose—an outcome very different from the popular expectations of Israel.

The keys of the Kingdom have something to do with the announcement of the Church. From now on the Kingdom is no longer active through Israel. A new people has been entrusted with the keys to the Kingdom. The Church is to take over the role of God's witness and redemptive agent in the world. The keys which are to open or close the doors leading to the enjoyment of the blessings of the new age are now taken away from the leaders of the Jewish religion and entrusted into the hands of the apostles of Christ. The words, "bind" and "loose," are actually rabbinical *termi technici* used to describe the rabbi's authority in doctrinal matters and simply mean, "decide with authority." (It is beyond the intention of this chapter to provide a detailed exegesis of this passage or to speculate as the further meaning of either of these terms—or for that matter of the term *petra* ["rock"]).[30]

Whatever our view, the Church is actually "built on the foundation of the apostles and prophets with Christ Jesus himself as the leader and chief cornerstone" (Eph. 2:20). Peter, in confessing the Messiahship of Jesus, speaks as a representative of the apostles who became the foundation on which the Church in its initial stages was to be erected. The intention of Jesus was certainly not—as traditional Catholicism interpreted it—to determine ecclesiastical power structures, "but rather to indicate the connection between the Church and the Kingdom and the conditions under which the one might be identified with the other."[31] In addition, the promise of the keys to Peter meant

---

[29] Allis, *Prophecy*, 84.

[30] See Commentaries on Matthew; the extensive discussion in Oscar Cullmann, *Petrus: Junger, Apostel, Martyrer* (Munich and Hamburg: Sibenstern, 1967), available also in ET; P. Hoffmann, "De Petrus-Primat im matthaus-evangelium" in J. Gnilka, ed., *Neues Testament und Kirche: Fur Rudolf Schnackenburg* (Herder, 1974), 94-114; R. E. Brown, k. L. Donfried, J. Reumann, *Peter in the New Testament: A Collaborative Assessment by Protestant and Roman Catholic Scholars* (London: G. Chapman, 1974).

[31] A. B. Bruce, *The Kingdom of God* (Edinburgh: T. and T. Clark, 1890), 264.

that in "calling Jesus Lord by the Holy Ghost, was the ideal of the Kingdom realized."[32]

Our interpretation of the meaning of the text is aided and clarified by comparing it to Luke 11:52 where we find a somewhat similar context in Jesus' condemnation of the Pharisees and Scribes. Because "you have taken away the key to knowledge. You yourselves have not entered, and you have hindered those who were entering."[33] The Jews had the keys of the knowledge that leads to the reign of God (cf. Rom. 3:2, "the Jews have been entrusted with the very words of God"), but now they have rejected the King himself. Therefore the Church becomes "a chosen people, a royal priesthood, a holy nation, God's special possession" (1 Pet. 2:9).

### The Mid-Point of the Old and New Ages

As we have already pointed out, the Jewish expectations of a Messiah who was to be a political liberator, apocalyptic Son of Man, and Davidic King were not met by Jesus. His final journey to Jerusalem ended not on David's throne, but on a scandalous cross. All four evangelists record the inscription of the title on the cross, *ho basileus ton Ioudaion*, "the King of the Jews." When questioned by Pilate, Jesus made it clear, however, that his "Kingdom is not of this world" (John 18:36). The Jews chose Caesar (John 19:12, 15) and had the spiritual King crucified. His death, however, was divinely purposed so as to establish the basis of a new covenant for a new people of God, who by his merit, by his grace, and by their subsequent response of faith, would experience the forgiveness of sins and enter the "[eternal] life" or blessings of the Kingdom. The redeemed people are now "purchased people," the way to life leads through his death, and he has the full right on the basis of the price paid to call this new people "my Church."

The Church is an eschatological community because it is a Christological reality. The central point in God's redemptive activity is the cross of Jesus Christ accompanied by his victorious resurrection. It is the mid-point of salvation history in which previous anticipations find their fulfillment and which is decisively determinative for the end-point of human history.

---

[32] Bruce, *Kingdom*, 264.

[33] G.E. Ladd comments: "The key of knowledge which should open the door of the Kingdom of God had been entrusted to the leaders of the Jewish people. This key was the correct understanding and interpretation of the Old Testament which should have led the Jews to recognize in our Lord's person and ministry the presence of the Kingdom of God and the fulfillment of the Old Testament promises ... However, the scribes had taken away the key of knowledge; they so interpreted the Scriptures that they pointed away from Christ rather than to Him as the One who had come to fulfill the prophets. Thus they refused to enter into the realm of Kingdom blessings which Jesus brought, and they hindered those who wanted to enter." (*The Gospel of the Kingdom*, 193).

The "gospel of the Kingdom" is inseparable from the "word of the cross" (*logos tou staurou*), for it is the message of the cross that brings salvation. For Paul, it is the cross that represents both the power (*dunamis*) and wisdom (*sophia*) of God (1 Cor. 1:18-24).

It is at the cross that we see Jesus as "our High Priest" (cf. Hebrews). All the aspects of his threefold office of Prophet, Priest, and King are foundational for the Kingdom of God as it finds its expression in the community of believers who are called by his name. He is not only the Prophet proclaiming the Kingdom. He is the King himself. He is not only the Priest who administers "once for all" (Heb. 10:10) and "always lives to intercede for them" (Heb. 7:25). He is also the Head of his Church and the Ruler of the universe.

We shall do well to listen to the admonition of Comenius, who well understood the need for the "total Christ" to be present among his followers. In his *Bequest of the Unity of Brethren*, he says, "Christ must find among you not only a pulpit for his prophetic office; not only an altar for his office as priest and bishop, but likewise a throne and a scepter for his kingly office."[34]

The unique Christ-event of the cross and resurrection mark the beginning of the new age and the beginning of the end of the old age. The disobedience of the first Adam brought the sentence of death upon humanity; the obedience unto death on the cross of the second Adam brings about the defeat of the powers of death and makes him the Head of a new humanity, gathered in his Church.

The Early Church expressed its faith in Christ the King and pledged its allegiance to him in that short yet powerful confession, "Jesus is Lord." The early Christological hymn brings Christ's pre-existence, Incarnation, crucifixion, resurrection, and the final consummation together as a short history of God's redemptive activity and rule recognized in the acknowledgement of his lordship:

> Who being in very nature God, did not consider equality with God something to be used to his own advantage; rather, he made himself nothing by taking the very nature of a servant, being made in human likeness. And being found in appearance as a man, he humbled himself by becoming obedient to death—even death on a cross! Therefore God exalted him to the highest place and gave him the name that is above every name, that at the name of Jesus every knee should bow, in heaven and on earth, and under the earth (Phil. 2:6-10), NIV).

The King is thus at the same time the Suffering Servant (cf. the four "Servant Songs" of Isaiah) who gives his life functioning as the Priest and the supreme sacrifice, and by defeating the powers of death, becomes the "firstfruit" and guarantee of the life to come. He becomes the Lord. Thus he, the risen Lord, in the context of the Great Commission declares, "All authority

---

[34] Johann Amos Comenius, *The Bequest of the Unity of Brethren*, English ed. (Chicago: The National Union of Czechkoslovak Protestants in America, 1940).

in heaven and on earth has been given to me" (Matt. 28:18). His ascension ended the short period of the post-resurrection appearances and placed him in the royal position "at the right hand of God" (Col. 3:1).

The theme of the Kingdom of God, although used less frequently than in the Synoptic Gospels, is not totally absent from the apostolic proclamation.[35] The term *basileia* appears eight times in Acts and fourteen times in the Pauline writings, and the context reveals that the concept of Kingdom is of major importance in the preaching of Paul, and essentially synonymous with its use by Jesus. It is clear, however, that Paul took the original messianic language of the Kingdom of God as used by Jesus, with which the Jews were familiar, and translated and expressed it with a "dynamic equivalent," with which his new audience of the wider mission field was acquainted. We have seen that John more or less replaced the form, "Kingdom of God," with "eternal life," retaining a continuity of meaning. Paul finds the best expression in a term that was widely used in a number of convergent areas: the Septuagint Greek Old Testament in which Yahweh is *Lord*, Roman politics marked by Caesar's claim to be the sole *Lord*, the heathen temple, and the slave market. The baptismal confession that "Jesus (Christ) is Lord"[36] becomes the equivalent of the acknowledgment of Christ's Kingship and the point of entrance into the Kingdom of God.

K.L. Schmidt summarizes this aspect of the proclamation of the Early Church as follows:

> We can see why the apostolic and the post-apostolic Church of the New Testament did not speak much of the *basileia tou theou* explicitly, but always emphasized it implicitly by its reference to the *kurios Iesous Kristos*. It is not true that it now substituted the Church (*ekklesia*) for the Kingdom as preached by Jesus of Nazareth. On the contrary, faith in the Kingdom of God persists in the post-Easter experience of Christ.[37]

The Apostle Paul brings the whole spectrum of different aspects of the lordship of Christ into focus and relates it to the Church as he prays for the Ephesians "that the God of our Lord Jesus Christ" may give them "the Spirit of wisdom and revelation" so that they might know him better and have enlightened hearts to "know the hope, ... the riches ... and his incomparably great power." "That power is the same as the mighty strength he exerted when he raised Christ from the dead and seated him at his right hand in the heavenly realms, far above all rule and authority, power, and dominion, and every name that is invoked, not only in the present age but also in the one to come. And God placed all things under his feet and appointed him to be head over

---

[35] See Acts 17:7; 19:8; 20:25; 28:23, 31; Rom. 14:17; 1 Cor. 4:20, etc.

[36] See Rom. 10:9; 1 Cor. 12:3; 2 Cor. 4:5; Phil. 2:11; Acts 16:31, etc.

[37] K.L. Schmidt, "*Basileia*," *Theological Dictionary of the New Testament*, ed. G. Kittel (Grand Rapids: Eerdmans, 1964), 1: 589.

everything for the Church which is his body, the fullness of him who fills everything in every way" (Eph. 1:17-23).

## The Church as the Community of the Spirit

The resurrection of Jesus was the key event ushering the powers of the age to come into the present age by transforming the finality of the death of Jesus into a triumph over it. It was a significant event that marked off the disciples of Jesus as the community who believed in the risen Lord. The Risen One has, however, announced another "end-time" event to follow shortly—the outpouring of the Spirit, promised for the "last days" (Acts 2:17). However we interpret the "Johannine Pentecost" (John 20:22), it is clear that John emphasizes a theological continuum between the cross, resurrection, ascension, and the outpouring of the Spirit. The Spirit is to "replace" Jesus as the "other advocate" (*parakleton*) (John 14:16) and is given as a guarantee of the efficacious continuity of Christ's work in the community of his believers.

The representative group of 120 disciples was gathered in Jerusalem in direct obedience to the command of the risen Lord and bound together by their common belief in him. The fulfillment of his promise was the experience of the mighty, visible, and audible manifestation of the divine power as "all of them were filled with the Holy Spirit" (Acts 2:4). The Pentecost-event was crucial for the launching and constitution of the Christian church, the new eschatological community bound together by their loyalty to the risen Lord and the common experience of the Spirit. The beginning of the age of the Spirit is coterminous and coextensive with the age of the Church, the community of the Spirit. Like the resurrection of Jesus, Pentecost was seen by early Christians "as the precursor of the end" and as "the beginning of a whole new epoch of salvation-history."[38] The early Christian community itself tasted the power of the age to come, and it is not impossible that the outpouring of the Holy Spirit and the beginning of the Church was at first seen by them as a fulfillment of Jesus' words about the coming of the Kingdom of God. It is this Kingdom that is now predominantly manifested in and through the Church as the community of the Spirit.

The power of the Spirit was to make the new community a witnessing, missionary-oriented movement (cf. Acts 1:8). The book of Acts shows that a church is essentially a community of the Spirit, experiencing at its very inception a last-day-like harvest and taking the gospel to the ends of the world. This mission of the Church is not something that is carefully planned and executed according to a preconceived strategy of the apostolic leadership of the Jerusalem church. It is a spontaneous Spirit-driven and Spirit-controlled movement proceeding from the nature of the Spirit-filled community. The mission of the Early Church energized by the Holy Spirit universalizes the

---

[38] J.D.G. Dunn, "Pentecost," in *New International Dictionary of the New Testament*, ed. C. Brown (Exeter: Paternoster, 1976), 2: 783-88.

mission of Jesus, using the "keys of the Kingdom" to open the gates of divine promise to the people of the new covenant from all nations and races.

## The Church Participates in the Kingdom: The Present Reign of Christ

### *The Church Is Not the Kingdom*

In the previous section we have shown that the Church is the result of the coming of the King, the Lord Jesus, who is its founder. The Kingdom of God which Jesus announced and brought is of central importance for a right understanding of the Church and is its most dominant point of reference within God's redemptive economy. "The dogma of the Kingdom ought to be the main dogma of the Church, and the main dogma for every individual member of it."[39] Or, as W. Pannenberg puts it, "the doctrine of the Church begins not with the Church but with the Kingdom of God."[40] The Church owes its existence to the Kingdom of God and "both conceptions belong closely together, so that it is hardly possible to reach a clear understanding of the nature of the Church without relating it to the basic New Testament conception of the Kingdom of God."[41]

A.M. Fairbairn states:

> The Kingdom is the immanent Church and the Church is the explicated Kingdom, and nothing alien to either can be in the other ... The Church is the Kingdom come into living souls and the society they constitute. ... The Kingdom is the Church viewed from above; the Church is the Kingdom seen from below.[42]

But while it is true that the biblical Church has to be defined in terms of its relationship to the rule of Christ, it is nonetheless impossible to identify the two as Fairbairn does. The Kingdom is a broader and more comprehensive concept and cannot be contained by the Church; nor has the Church any right to claim the Kingdom as its present possession.

However inseparable their relationship may be, the Church is not the Kingdom of God. The regenerate Church in which Christ is acknowledged as Lord and the life and power of the Holy Spirit are operative is at its ultimate, only the nearest approximation and the most authentic communal expression of the Kingdom of God in history.

The apostles were sent, like Jesus himself, to preach the gospel of the Kingdom. Several times the book of Acts summarizes their proclamation with

---

[39] Clutton Brook, *What Is the Kingdom of Heaven?*, 126, cited by L. Berkhof in *The Kingdom of God* (Grand Rapids: Eerdmans, 1951), 10.
[40] Pannenberg, *Theology and the Kingdom*, 39.
[41] Skydsgaard, "Kingdom of God," 385.
[42] A.M. Fairbairn, *Christ in Modern Theology*, 1893, 528ff., cited in *Expository Times*, XLVII (May, 1936): 370.

this term. The content of the proclamation of the Kingdom of God is usually identified with the saving name of Jesus, but never with the Church. In Samaria "they believed Philip as he proclaimed the good news of the Kingdom of God and the name of Jesus Christ" (Acts 8:12). In the synagogue at Ephesus we find Paul "arguing persuasively about the Kingdom of God" (19:8). At the very end of the book Luke gives two summaries of Paul's ministry in Rome as he ministered to Jewish leaders he explained and declared to them the Kingdom of God and tried to convince them about Jesus (28:23), and in the final verses, "for two whole years Paul ... welcomed all who came to see him. He proclaimed the Kingdom of God and taught about the Lord Jesus Christ—with all boldness and without hindrance!" (28:30-31).

Here we see how the proclaimer and bringer of the Kingdom in the Early Church became the subject of proclamation. The Early Church did not preach itself; it preached the gospel of the Kingdom, that is, the good news about Jesus Christ. In none of these passages, nor in others, is it possible to substitute "Church" for "Kingdom"!

The attempt to identify the Church with the Kingdom is not only unbiblical, but also highly dangerous. The history of the Church provides ample evidence for this, from the Constantinian era to the present. It teaches us that whenever and wherever the Church equates itself with the Kingdom of God, it will be tempted to grasp, hold, and abuse earthly power. In this connection we do well to listen to W. Pannenberg's "prophetic" insight:

> The theological identification of the Church with the Kingdom of Christ has all too often served the purposes of ecclesiastical officials who are not attuned to the Kingdom of God. Many Christians, especially church leaders, like to think they are in possession of the truth, or at least that they possess the ultimate criterion of the truth. Because they feel themselves to be so indispensably related to the very Kingdom of Christ, they fail to recognize the provisional character of all ecclesiastical organizations. They are unable to stand humbly before the coming Kingdom of God that is going to bring about the final future of the world. They are blinded to the ways in which even now, proleptically, the future manifests itself in the world (and not just in the Church, nor even always through the Church). Precisely because the Church mistakes herself for the present form of the Kingdom, God's rule has often had to manifest itself in the secular world outside, and frequently against, the Church.[43]

The Church is the *result* of the preaching of the Kingdom of God, the fellowship of those who have experienced the power and tasted the blessings of the Kingdom. The Kingdom is its beginning, its foundation, but the Kingdom of God also remains its goal. For the Church is "the fellowship of aspirants of the Kingdom of God," as Hans Kung said, adding that "belonging to the church is no guarantee, in this era of temptation, of belonging to the final Kingdom of

---

[43] Pannenberg, *Theology and the Kingdom*, 78.

God."[44] The meaning of the Church does not reside in itself in what it is, but in what it is moving towards.[45]

## The Cost of Entering into the Kingdom

Biblical history is the story of God's redemptive acts directed toward the creation of a new humanity, a people who rightfully belong to him and authentically represent him among the nations. It is the people who recognize God as their King and constitute his royal priesthood on earth. In the Old Testament they are called the *kehal Yahweh*, the "community [assembly] of God." The corresponding Greek term denotes the New Testament people of God as *ekklesia tou theou* "The Church of God."

This community, addressed as "the people of God," the "body of Christ," etc., is always a visible and identifiable company of believers on this earth. It is unfortunate and misleading that the words "Kingdom" and "Church" are nowadays frequently used as if they were autonomous entities. These concepts cannot stand on their own and if we are to understand the true nature and mission of the believing community we call "the Church," we must carefully adhere to the use of this terminology in the Scriptures. When we speak of the "Kingdom of God," the emphasis is on God, on his kingly power and reign, on his redeeming acts and sovereign authority. The operative word in the phrase, "the Kingdom of God," is *theou*.[46]

> The phrase "is telling something about God" (the fact that he reigns), not describing something called "the kingdom" ... Reduction in modern usage to merely "the Kingdom" is therefore questionable not only because it departs in fact from biblical usage, but primarily because it betrays a basic misunderstanding which takes "the Kingdom of God" as a description not of God in his sovereignty, but of an identifiable "thing."[47]

We run a similar risk of emptying or reducing its biblical content when we speak of "the Church" without properly emphasizing that it is "the Church of God" (or "Christ"). Here the operative word is *theou* or *Christou*. The Church can rightfully be called so only if and when it recognizes the lordship of Christ and submits to it. It is "the body of Christ" consciously living under his headship. This new community of redeemed and forgiven people is "the elect" (*eklekton*), called and chosen by God to be "the saints" (*hagioi*). Their origin, their very nature, and their whole character are derived from the One to whom

---

[44] Hans Kung, *The Church* (New York: Sheed and Ward, 1967), 95-96.
[45] Kung, *The Church*, 96.
[46] See Kittel, "*Basileia*,"; L. Newbigin, *The Household of God* (London: SCM, 1953), 28.
[47] R.T. France, "The Church and the Kingdom of God: Some Hermeneutical Issues" (an unpublished paper, read at the WEF's Theological Commission study unit, "Faith and Church," Cambridge, 1982).

they belong, God himself. Their character is an expression of God's character, for their life flows from the life God gives; and their mission is an extension of the mission of God's Son.

The proclamation of the good news of the arrival of the Kingdom of God in the person of Jesus of Nazareth demands a response of repentance and faith (Mark 1:15). Such a response results in the new life which God bestows. It means "being saved" or "born again," to use the most common evangelical parlance of our day. It demands a radical decision, a change of mind (*metanoia*), a transfer from the kingdom of darkness into the Kingdom of the light of God's Son (Col. 1:13). Such a response to the message of the King and the subsequent change of life entailed means *entering the Kingdom of God*. This entry into the realm of the blessings of God's Kingdom is a gift; it comes at God's initiative and depends on his grace which is freely available to the sinful and undeserving. However, it is not so cheap as some evangelistic propaganda of Western evangelicalism superficially seems to suggest.

Jesus does not minimize the cost and difficulties of entering into the Kingdom of God. It is true that the response to his message is made on an individual basis and in terms of personal acceptance. Its result, however, is not just the salvation of that individual's soul for heaven or a present sweet communion with Jesus expressed in almost private terms. Becoming a Christian, entering into the Kingdom of God, is a prospect open only to those who are willing to deny themselves and their own interests in order to acknowledge God's sovereign rule over the totality of their lives and relationships. It may entail giving up family (cf. Matt. 10:34-37) and wealth, as clearly demonstrated by the story of the rich young ruler (Mark 10:17ff.). These demands of the King Jesus can hardly be understood by believers who live in societies where Christian faith is culturally acceptable and respectable. It is in such contexts that the message of the Kingdom of God with all its demands is seldom heard, often diluted and frequently denied by those who claim to "know Jesus." In the proclamation the demands are usually replaced by promises, as if the two were not inseparably and conditionally related. "But seek first his kingdom and his righteousness, and all these things will be given to you as well" (Matt. 6:33).

Those followers of Jesus who live under totalitarian political regimes, or amongst militant Muslims, or wherever they are a faithful minority, know that belonging to Jesus the King, living under his lordship, exacts a price. They know, as the Early Church knew, that serving Jesus means indifference towards the treasures and values of this world, abandoning all anxiety for trustful confidence in the heavenly Father, the King who rules even in the midst of adverse circumstances. The Church of Jesus Christ today needs to be reminded that persecution is a biblical sign of belonging to the Kingdom of God. "In fact, everyone who wants to live a godly life in Christ Jesus will be persecuted" (2

Tim. 3:12).[48] Faithful witness to Christ today does not in every case necessarily result in suffering, but H. Berkhof rightfully reminds us that suffering

> could well be a significant criterion for judging the genuineness of our words and deeds. Words that do not cost anything and deeds that are meant to make us popular have nothing to do with the apostolary firstfruit character of the people of God.[49]

The Church of Jesus Christ fulfills its mission in a fallen and antagonistic world, living in a tension produced by the overlapping of two ages, between the "already" and "not yet fully" of the Kingdom of God. Along with the present-day experience of the Church globally, this leads us to a realistic assessment of our situation.

> In the world in which we live, in which every successful act of cooperation or reconciliation can be matched by cruelty and persecution on a very large scale, it is becoming very doubtful whether Christianity can register any worthwhile advance in the near future without suffering.[50]

This statement was made in 1968 and its truthfulness has been already proven in the meantime, while we are and shall increasingly become witnesses to its relevance in our own days and in days to come.

Entering the Kingdom of God means joining the believing community, for "the spirit of the kingdom is love, and impels to fellowship."[51] Belonging to Jesus Christ means being part of that organic and authentic community which is the closest expression of the Kingdom of God on earth. It means being a member of his Church, built by him and ruled by him. It is in this new community of disciples of Jesus that the presence of God is experienced, his sovereignty acknowledged, his rule obeyed and his will carried out.

The Church is that community which God gathers by the Holy Spirit to be his own people and to be sent into the world to announce and live out the message of the King, who is the Lord Jesus. It is the company of men and women who by the very nature of their special calling are distinctively people of God, grounded in the redemptive purposes of God and sustained by his presence and power. The nature and mission of the Church are determined by this special relationship between God and his people, Christ and the Church.

---

[48] See also 1 Pet. 2:20-21; 4:12-17; Matt. 5:10-12; 10:16-23; 24:9; Mark 13:9-13; Luke 21:12-17.

[49] H. Berkhof, *Christian Faith* (Grand Rapids: Eerdmans, 1979), 419.

[50] C.S. Duthie, *Outline of Christian Belief* (Nashville: Abingdon, 1968), 87.

[51] Bruce, *Kingdom,* 60.

### The Church as the Servant of the King

In the Incarnation, the King Jesus, very God, humbled himself by "taking the very nature [form] of a servant (*doulos*)" (Phil. 2:7). Speaking of the new kind of relationship between those who belong to his Kingdom, he emphasizes his own example which they are to follow, for he "did not come to be served, but to serve (*diakonesai*)" (Matt. 20:28; par Mark 10:45). At the Last Supper he washes the disciples' feet to challenge them to servanthood (John 13:1-17) and warns them not to be like "the kings of the Gentiles"; rather their leaders should be servants, even as "I am among you as one who serves" (Luke 22:25, 27). Jesus is saying this in fellowship around the table which is itself one of the signs of the arrival of the Kingdom and a pointer to its ultimate fulfillment in the *eschaton* "at my table in my kingdom." The crucial line in this discourse is "I confer on you a kingdom, just as my Father conferred one on me" (Luke 22:29, 30).[52]

The ministry of Jesus was marked by the threefold service of preaching, teaching, and demonstrating the good news of the Kingdom of God. He performed the signs pointing to its arrival in his own person, culminating in the ultimate act of service when he gave "his life as a ransom for many" (Mark 10:45). His exemplary ministry and the sacrifice of his life became a summons to service for all of his followers. John draws the conclusion from the sacrifice of Jesus that "we ought to lay down our lives for our brothers and sisters" (1 John 3:16).

The Church is not the Kingdom, neither can it claim a monopoly on the Kingdom of God. It will approximate the Kingdom and enjoy its blessings only in proportion to its submission to the King, as his servant. The contemporary evangelical movement, with its emphasis on individualism, its striving for measurable success, and its spirit of worldly competition in both the expansion of its programs at home and its missionary endeavors abroad, stands in grave danger of being permeated by the spirit and values of this world. To me, an outsider,—and to many of my brethren—some of the Western-sponsored missionary and evangelistic enterprises come across as self-serving organizations baptized with a Christian name, rather than an expression of the servant spirit of the Kingdom of God. May the Lord of the Church grant that I am wrong and forgive me if I speak unfairly.

The fact remains, however, that the true nature and mission of the Church are marked by humble service, and recognition that we can claim no ownership of the things and people that belong to God alone. He is the King. We are to be his humble servants, always ready to obey his command and to do his will. Whatever exists outside this attitude has no right to be called the Church of Jesus Christ for it is out of tune with the Kingdom of God. The Kingdom demands commitment and obedience in service, following the model of the

---

[52] Note carefully the whole discourse, especially vv. 24-30 and the fact that the following admonition is to Peter.

Servant-King. The nature and mission of the Church can be rightly understood, lived, and practiced only in right relation to its founder and head, Jesus Christ, and in accordance with his central message about the Kingdom of God. Only the Church that is deeply rooted in—and wholly faithful to—the divine purposes disclosed in Christ will be sustained by the power of his Spirit, and effectively able to reach out in service and mission to the needy world.

The servant is known not only by his service humbly rendered to others, but also by his attitude of simple unquestioning trust and receptivity. Jesus elaborates this attitude in the Sermon on the Mount, and in his teaching that it is impossible to "receive the kingdom of God" or to "enter it" unless we are like little children (Mark 10:13-16). What a shock to find out that a great many evangelicals who adhere to the verbal inspiration of Scripture, and verbally acknowledge the lordship of Christ, by some unbelievable exegetical gymnastics and the imposition of a foreign interpretive scheme upon the biblical record, have relegated a large part of the ethical teaching of Jesus to a future eschatological form of the Kingdom of God. May the Lord Jesus forgive us for lording it over his Word in such an unfaithful way, for perverting the holy intentions he has for his followers, and for disobedient evasion of the most central, demanding, and challenging part of his teaching.

## The Call to Repentance

When we seriously consider the intentions of Jesus and examine the visible expressions of the Christian faith in light of the biblical revelation, we may at times be tempted to despair over the empirical church. We realize that "not even in the regenerate Church is the reign of God perfectly manifest."[53] At such a point we humbly recognize that although the Church must be defined in terms of its relationship to the Kingdom of God in its "already" of Jesus' life and message, the Kingdom is "not yet" its present possession. The Church is not yet *in patria*, but is still in *via*; it is "already," but is still on the way and has "not yet" arrived at its final destiny and completion. In pointing out this difference, Skydsgaard warns:

> She is the *ecclesia viatorum*, always exposed to the temptation of Antichrist to apostasy and emancipation. The moment the Church forgets that, when she establishes herself as the highest authority in the world, she ceases to be the Church of Jesus Christ and becomes renegade.[54]

We evangelicals would automatically assume such a statement to apply to the Roman Catholic Church and to some more or less liberal Protestant church bodies. It is true that one of the gravest errors the medieval Catholic Church

---

[53] Carl F. Henry, "Evangelism and Social Action," *Crux* 16, no. 3 (Sept. 1980): 27.

[54] Skydsgaard, "Kingdom of God," 92-93.

committed (with the help of Augustine) was to identify itself with the Kingdom of God. Thus the reign of Christ was perverted into the reign of the church; christocracy became ecclesiocracy. The distinction between the two was blurred, to say the least. Some modern-day ecumenical endeavors run the same risk as they rush to identify their own programs with the program of the Kingdom of God.

But are we evangelicals innocent in this area? Are we humble enough to recognize that despite our rich Reformation heritage and scriptural orthodoxy, and in spite of our present-day successes in missions, evangelism, and church growth, we still need to say to our Master: "We are unworthy servants; we have only done our duty" (Luke 17:10)? Have we? Do we recognize that our distinction between the visible and the invisible Church is hardly a biblical one and that we frequently use it only as a cover for our sins and disobedience to the Lord of the Church? Does reality affirm that we believe in the *ecclesia semper reformanda*, or have we become so fossilized in our structures, so immobile in the ways in which we "serve the Lord," so dogmatic in some of our doctrinal formulations, that even the Lord Jesus himself is unable to evoke the response and reform he desires from us? Is our understanding of the Church and its ministry so static that even the dynamic reign of the Kingdom of God is prevented from breaking in anew with a spirit of renewal and revival? Are not the evangelical churches along with all the others tempted to boast like the Laodicean church that we are rich, that we have acquired wealth and need nothing, when in reality such a declaration itself betrays the sad fact that we are "wretched, pitiful, poor, blind, and naked" churches (Rev. 3:17), who feel self-satisfied and self-sufficient only because we have lost the touch of the Lord and the sense of his kingly presence? The church (or mission or other Christian agency) that begins to glory and boast in its own achievements, while it stops repenting for its shortcomings and crying for the sins of the needy world, shows signs of backsliding which—unless there is repentance—will cause it to be rejected by the King Jesus. We may ponder Pascal's description of the Church: "*Bel etat de l'Eglise quand elle n'est plus soutenue que le Dieu.*" (The Church is in good condition when it is supported by God alone.)[55]

Unless the first public command of the King Jesus —"Repent ye"—resounds again clearly, unmistakably, and unapologetically as part of the Good News about the Kingdom of God, and unless we humbly take the servant role in submission to the King Jesus, many of our evangelical churches are in danger of ending up on the road that leads away from the Kingdom.

The first of Luther's 95 Wittenberg Theses, and thus the first public word of Reformation, was: "Our Lord and Master Jesus Christ desires that the whole life of the faithful should be a life of repentance." Visser't Hooft comments in this regard:

---

[55] Quoted by W.A. Visser't Hooft, *The Kingship of Christ: An Interpretation of Recent European Theology* (London: SCM, 1948), 70.

But the tragedy of the Reformation churches is that this explosive truth, which was destined to give birth to a constantly reformed Church in daily renewed communication with Christ, was considered as an achievement and a ground for glorying. These churches of dynamic repentance became churches of arrested repentance. They dug themselves in, instead of remaining on the move. They fought battles for sterile victories.[56]

The rapid expansion of evangelical churches, their striving for numerical strength and respectability in the wider Christian and secular world, makes them easily susceptible to the same spiritual sicknesses and decay. We too are in danger of becoming secular and self-sufficient, lacking in the love, faith, and courage by which the people of the King of Kings are known. We too are prone to think up "profound reasons for a profitable compromise with paganism." Our church also needs to be "reminded how little it can count on itself and how easily it falls from reformation into deformation."[57]

Let us beware of the subtle temptation to mistake the Church for Christ. The Church of Jesus Christ is only that to the degree in which the people called by his name are faithful to him and live under his kingship. *Ubi Christus, ibi ecclesia!*

### The Church Open to the Power of the Holy Spirit

"For the Kingdom of God is not a matter of talk but of power" (1 Cor. 4:20). The Kingdom of God is a dynamic concept. Jesus not only preached the gospel of the Kingdom but also demonstrated its power and his kingly compassion through the miracles he performed. His miracles signaled his sovereign authority which neither illness, demons, nor death were able to withstand. He sent the apostles to preach the Kingdom of God and gave them power to heal the sick and cast out demons (Matt. 10:1, 7-8). It is clear that in the New Testament Church the Christ-given commission to preach the good news of the Kingdom of God is linked with the equipping power of the Holy Spirit to overcome the forces of evil. The apostles did not regard preaching and healing as disparate tasks. To them the gift of the Spirit was not just a sign of the coming of the new age, but also the present manifestation of the power of the Kingdom. The Holy Spirit was the very life of the Church, not replacing but rather centralizing and always exalting Christ—which is the Spirit's primary mission. Christ rules where the Spirit moves, for the coming of the Kingdom in the convicting, cleansing, and enabling power of the Holy Spirit is the beginning of the end of everything that opposes the rule of God.

In the theological thinking of the past, Christology has usually been considered the basis for ecclesiology. The connection of the two was often seen in ontological terms, which has not infrequently led to a very static view of the

---

[56] Visser't Hooft, *Kingship*, 70.
[57] Visser't Hooft, *Kingship*, 71.

Church. Such a view was further fostered by institutionalization of the church whose sole concerns were its own doctrine, order of worship, and self-serving organizational structures. The powerlessness and sterility of such churches became evident as soon as they lost the support of worldly powers and had to stand on their own. Such negative developments, along with the more positive recent Pentecostal-charismatic renewal, led to an increasing recognition that the doctrine of the Church must also be founded on pneumatology. The pneumatological aspect of the Church brings into focus the dynamics and power of the Kingdom of God, especially when the Spirit's role in energizing the believing community for its mission in her world is acknowledged. It is now increasingly and rightly recognized that in the Church the charismatic must have priority over the purely institutional.[58] Fossilized institutionalism, lifeless sacramentalism, and narrowminded legalism can all be signs of the absence of the Spirit of Christ. Such churches are without power and without joy. "For the Kingdom of God is not a matter of eating and drinking, but of righteousness, peace, and joy in the Holy Spirit" (Rom. 14:17).

When believers give the Spirit of God freedom to move, the Church moves away from the unbiblical dichotomy between clergy and laity and a process of "democratization" takes place, leading to the discovery of the gifts of the Spirit by the members of the congregation and to the ministry of the whole body of Christ. To churches that give no freedom to the Spirit of God to work, the following description often applies: "The spiritual gifts of the laity have atrophied, while the responsibilities of ministers and administrators have hypertrophied."[59] Such congregations are impoverished with respect to two of the basic components of a biblical Church—the priesthood of all believers and the true sense of Christian fellowship. Both their mission and their nature are incapacitated. Their assembling turns out to be the private show of the pastor for his private audience and often the result is that instead of mutual care for the well-being of each and all, growing into a fellowship of the Spirit, they have "degenerated until they consist of unrelated individuals who attend church services for private reasons."[60] The Christian church which takes the kingship of Christ seriously will be a church continually filled, renewed, and controlled by the Holy Spirit. Otherwise it will easily become "the prey of secular social forces ... influenced by the inexorable laws of sociology rather than by the creative force of the Holy Spirit."[61]

Lesslie Newbigin argued for a three-cornered understanding of the Church, which, in addition to emphasis on right teaching, i.e. apostolic witness (the

---

[58] See, for example, Howard A. Snyder, *The Community of the King* (Downers Grove: InterVarsity, 1977).

[59] Richard F. Lovelace, *Dynamics of Spiritual Life* (Downers Grove: InterVarsity, 1979), 171.

[60] Visser't Hooft, *Kingship*, 76.

[61] Visser't Hooft, *Kingship*, 76.

emphasis of Protestantism), and true order, i.e. continuation of the apostolate (as stressed in Catholicism), must also include the Pentecostal emphasis on the role of the life-giving Spirit of God. He illustrates his criticism of the distortion and deficiency of the first two views by contrasting scriptural and church-traditional criteria and practice.

> The apostle asked the converts of Apollos one question: "Did you receive the Holy Spirit when you believed? And got a plain answer. His modern successors are more inclined to ask either "Did you believe exactly what we teach?" or "Were the hands that were laid on you our hands?" and—if the answer is satisfactory—to assure the converts that they have received the Holy Spirit even if they don't know it. There is a world of difference between the two attitudes.[62]

The beginning of the Pentecostal movement in the West, and its rapid spread and phenomenal growth in the countries of the Third World, also witness unmistakably to the fact that the Holy Spirit is not synonymous with the bourgeois spirit for which much of the Christian establishment seemed to have mistaken him in their monopolizing approach to the Kingdom of God. The spirit (like wind) moves (blows) wherever he (it) pleases (John 3:8). The underdogs of any society, the poor and the oppressed, the working class and the despised and uneducated peasantry are nowadays recipients of the saving grace of Christ and participants in the powerful manifestations of the Holy Spirit's working. This truly is the sign of the Kingdom, for our Lord himself was anointed by the Spirit "to proclaim good news to the poor ... to set the oppressed free ..." (Luke 4:18). If our mission is to be modeled after the mission of Jesus, as we evangelicals have rightly emphasized (especially since Lausanne), then we must be consistent and face up to the challenge of the supernatural aspects of Jesus' and the apostles' ministry and the role of "signs and wonders" in the mission of the Church. Spiritualizing such passages as the above inaugural statement of Jesus, so as to suggest, for example, that Jesus "was talking about healing blinded hearts in captivity to sin," does not do justice to the plain meaning of the text. Countless numbers of examples could be cited of hermeneutical abuses and unbelievable exegetical misconstructions, all obvious twisting of the scriptural text in order to avoid the clear challenge of the full gospel and justify the powerlessness of much of the contemporary Christian church. The sad fact is that many evangelicals who swear their allegiance to an authoritative and inerrant Bible often were (and are) guilty of the most gross abuses of Scripture in this respect.

We are to beware of all sensationalism, superficial charismatic triumphalism, and selfish searching for miracles. We are to be critical whenever and wherever miracles are sought after without the obedient acknowledgement of the lordship of Christ and his sovereignty. We are also to distrust those who

---

[62] Lesslie Newbigin, *The Household of God* (London: SCM, 1953), 104.

speak more about the gifts than the Giver. At the same time, however, we must face the totality of the biblical teaching on the mission of the Church, including the role of the supernatural in the spreading of the gospel (especially in frontier and pioneering situations), and acknowledge the importance of the full range of the gifts of the Spirit for the proper understanding and healthy functioning of the Church.

Evangelicals still have to realize that "preaching the Word" alone is not enough. Many evangelical churches are known for excellent biblical preaching and yet they are impotent in evangelism. My experience in the Pentecostal movement, where preaching has regrettably often been poor in both content and form, has nonetheless convinced me that the presence of the Spirit is, as Wolfhart Pannenberg would say, "much more suggestive and inspiring than dozens of sermons delivered by inhibited preachers."[63] Donald Gee, one of the better known Pentecostal pioneers and Bible teachers, known for his balance and ability to express it, aphoristically pointed the way: "The Word alone will make you dry up, the Spirit alone will make you blow up, the Word and the Spirit together will make you grow up."[64]

"Without the *pneuma* there is no *soma*."[65] Let us, however, humbly recognize that the Holy Spirit is not our possession and can be neither controlled nor confined by the Church. He is never called "the Spirit of the Church" and no church body (not even Pentecostal or charismatic!) has any right to boast that it "has the Spirit." He is nobody's property! Let us confess that the whole Church needs a new infusion of the Holy Spirit in order to be renewed in its nature and empowered for the end time harvest in its mission both at home and abroad. Let us humbly recognize that the Church of Jesus Christ is dependent on the Holy Spirit for its very life and that he is the chief and powerful executor of Christian mission.

We sum up discussion of this section with the relevant admonition of David Watson:

> There is no guaranteed bestowal of the Spirit at baptism, confirmation or ordination. ...The Spirit will not be tied to the church, nor to any ecclesiastical office within the church. ... The church which tries to tie the Spirit to its institutionalized forms, to its traditional patterns, or to its doctrinal statements, will quickly find itself moribund and powerless. True spiritual life and freedom will come only insofar as the church submits to the Spirit, listens to the Spirit and obeys the Spirit. At every stage we must learn to hear what the Spirit is saying to

---

[63] Pannenberg, *Theology and the Kingdom of God*, 90.

[64] Donald Gee, quoted in *Beyond Canberra*, ed. Bruce Nicholls and Bong Rin Ro (London: Regnum Books, 1993), 143.

[65] Padilla, "The Kingdom of God and the Church," 7.

the churches, even if that word is sometimes a word of rebuke, or a warning of judgment. God gives the Spirit to those who obey him.[66]

## The Church Will Inherit the Kingdom:
## The Future Coming of Christ

The Church looks back to its beginnings in the first coming of Christ and forward to its completion at his second coming. While it enjoys the blessings of the "already" of the Kingdom of God it is also aware that the kingly rule of Jesus is "not yet" fully actualized. This recognition makes the Church both humble and hopeful, grateful and longing. While it believes that the Kingdom has in Christ already arrived in history, it faithfully works on behalf of its greater realization within history and expectantly prays, "Thy Kingdom come," waiting for its full consummation at the end of history.

The Kingdom of God is from above; it is supernatural and cannot be produced by human effort nor realized without God. As David Bosch in his comparison of Melbourne and Pattaya stated:

> Unless our salvation is grounded in the yesterday of God's normative revelation in Christ crucified and risen, and unless it stretches out towards the tomorrow of our ultimate salvation, we are engaged in the futile effort of building God's Kingdom with our own hands.[67]

Evangelicals are known for upholding the doctrine of the return of Christ and for their emphasis on eschatology. Unfortunately, however, the knowledge and experience of this author with evangelical "eschatologizing" is a very negative one. It seems to me that evangelicals have almost universally traded the Kingdom of God for divisive millenarian debates and idle speculations about end-time chronology and related world events. In some Western countries, especially in the USA, "end time" teaching is a growing type of industry and a flourishing business. Sensational eschatology with its speculative guesswork, often popularized in the form of science fiction and made relevant by dubious yet dogmatic references to the political and economic events of our very day, seems to serve for millions of naïve Bible-believing Christians as a religious substitute for astrology. Worse yet, much of this apocalypticism leads to "eschatological paralysis," passive withdrawal from the world and fatalistic despair, rather than to Christian hope that engenders ethical action and responsible involvement, which should be the result of a truly

---

[66] David Watson, *I Believe in the Church* (Grand Rapids: Eerdmans, 1978), 166-67.

[67] David J. Bosch, "Melbourne and Pattaya: The Left Foot and the Right Foot of the Church?" (a paper available to this author only its unpublished form), 7.

biblical eschatology.[68] Such perversion of scriptural teaching is a theological heresy with far-reaching implications. This preoccupation with apocalypticism ends in attempts to de-eschatologize history and de-historicize eschatology, importing an unbiblical dualism into supposedly biblical teaching and thereby divorcing eschatology from ethics. Carl Henry is right in his criticism of dispensational theology which in its extreme forms

> Evaporates the present-day relevance of much of the ethics of Jesus. Eschatology is invoked to postpone the significance of the Sermon on the Mount and other segments of New Testament moral teaching to a later Kingdom age. Dispensationalism erects a cleavage in biblical ethics in the interest of debatable eschatological theory. Dispensationalism holds that Christ's Kingdom has been postponed until the end of the Church age, and that Kingdom-ethics will become dramatically relevant again only in the future. New Testament theology will not sustain this radical repudiation of any present form of the Kingdom of heaven.[69]

We must remind ourselves that with Jesus Christ the eschatological future has already invaded our historical present. It is true that we are emphasizing the third and tending to ignore the first two. We evangelicals are tempted toward just the reverse. Let us resist this temptation by committing ourselves both to fervent prayer that the King(dom) may come, and to active involvement on behalf of its coming; to obedient living and service under the Kingship of Christ by the enabling power of the Holy Spirit. Let us acknowledge his sovereignty, obey his rule, and carry out his will. May the motto of Wheaton College be the motto for all followers of Jesus: "For Christ and His Kingdom"—*Christo et regno eius*!

## Bibliography

Allis, Oswald T. *Prophecy and the Church: An Examination of the Claim of Dispensationalists that the Christian Church Is a Mystery Parenthesis which Interrupts the Fulfillment to Israel of the Kingdom Prophecies of the Old Testament.* Philadelphia: Presbyterian and Reformed, 1945.

Berkhof, Hendrikus. *Christian Faith: An Introduction to the Study of the Faith.* Grand Rapids: Eerdmans, 1979.

---

[68] For a more extensive treatment of the future aspect of the Kingdom of God and how it relates to the present Christian responsibility see my CRESR paper, "Eschatology and Social Responsibility: An Evaluation of Evangelical Views and Attitudes," in *Word and Deed*, ed. Bruce Nicholls (Exeter: Paternoster Press, 1985), 135-64.

[69] Carl F. Henry, *Christian Personal Ethics* (Grand Rapids: Eerdmans, 1957), 551.

Berkhof, Louis. *The Kingdom of God: The Development of the Idea of the Kingdom, Especially Since the Eighteenth Century.* Grand Rapids: Eerdmans, 1951.

Brown, Raymond E., K. L. Donfried, and J. Reumann. *Peter in the New Testament: A Collaborative Assessment by Protestant and Roman Catholic Scholars.* London: G. Chapman, 1974.

Bruce, A. B. *The Kingdom of God; Or, Christ's Teaching According to the Synoptical Gospels.* 4th ed. Edinburgh: T&T. Clark, 1891.

Comenius, John Amos. *The Bequest of the Unity of Brethren.* Chicago: The National Union of Czechoslovak Protestants in America, 1940.

Cullmann, Oscar. *Christ and Time.* Philadelphia: Westminster, 1950.

──────. "The Kingship of Christ and the Church in the New Testament." In *The Early Church.* London: SCM, 1956.

──────. *Petrus: Junger, Apostel, Martyrer.* Munich and Hamburg: Sibenstern, 1967.

──────. *Salvation in History.* New York: Harper and Row; London: SCM, 1967.

Dayton, Donald W. *Discovering an Evangelical Heritage.* New York: Harper and Row, 1976.

Dodd, C. H. *The Parables of the Kingdom.* London: Nisbet, 1935.

Dunn, J.D.G. "Pentecost." In *New International Dictionary of the New Testament*, edited by C. Brown. Vol. 2, 738-88. Exeter: Paternoster, 1976.

Duthie, Charles S. *Outline of Christian Belief.* Nashville: Abingdon Press, 1968.

Fairbairn, A. M. "Christ in Modern Theology." *Expository Times* 47, no. 8 (1936): 370.

Harrington, Daniel. *God's People in Christ: New Testament Perspectives on the Church and Judaism.* Philadelphia: Fortress Press, 1980.

Henry, Carl F. H. *Christian Personal Ethics.* Grand Rapids: Eerdmans, 1957.

──────. "Evangelism and Social Action." *Crux* 16, no. 3 (1980): 27.

Hoffman, P. "De Petrus-Primat im matthaus-evangelium." In *Neues Testament und Kirche: Für Rudolf Schnackenburg,* edited by Joachim Gnilka. Herder, 1974.

Hooft, DD W. A. Visser't. *The Kingship of Christ: An Interpretation of Recent European Theology.* London: SCM, 1948.

Hort, Renton J. A. *The Christian Ecclesia.* London: MacMillan, 1898.

Kung, Hans. *The Church.* New York: Sheed and Ward, 1967.

Ladd, George E. *Crucial Questions about the Kingdom of God.* Grand Rapids: Eerdmans, 1952.

_____. *The Gospel of the Kingdom: Scriptural Studies in the Kingdom of God.* London: Paternoster, 1959.

_____. *Jesus and the Kingdom: The Eschatology of Biblical Realism.* Waco: S.P.C.K., 1966.

_____. *A Theology of the New Testament.* Grand Rapids: Eerdmans, 1974.

Lovelace, Richard F. *Dynamics of Spiritual Life: An Evangelical Theology of Renewal.* Downers Grove: InterVarsity, 1979.

Marsden, George M. *Fundamentalism and American Culture: The Shaping of Twentieth-Century Evangelicalism: 1870–1925.* New York: Oxford University Press, 1980.

Moberg, David O. *The Great Reversal: Evangelism Versus Social Concern.* Philadelphia and New York: Lippincott, 1972.

Newbigin, Lesslie. *The Household of God.* London: SCM, 1953.

Otto, Rudolf. *The Kingdom of God and the Son of Man.* London: Lutterworth, 1943.

Padilla, Rene. "The Kingdom of God and the Church." *Theological Fraternity Bulletin.* no. 1&2, (1976).

Ribberbos, Herman N. *Coming of the Kingdom.* Philadelphia: The Presbyterian and Reformed Publishing Company, 1962.

Sandeen, Ernest R. *The Roots of Fundamentalism: British and American Millenarianism, 1800–1930.* Chicago: University of Chicago Press, 1970.

Schweitzer, Albert. *The Quest of the Historical Jesus.* London: 1919.

Skydsgaard, K.E. "Kingdom of God and the Church." *Scottish Journal of Theology* 4, no. 4 (1959): 386.

Snyder, Howard A. *The Community of the King.* Downers Grove: InterVarsity, 1977.

Watson, David. *I Believe in the Church.* Grand Rapids: Eerdmans, 1978.

Weber, Timothy P. *Living in the Shadow of the Second Coming: American Premillennialism, 1875–1925.* New York and Oxford: Oxford University Press, 1979.

Weiss, J. *Die Predigt Jesu vom Reich Gottes.* 2$^{nd}$ ed. Gottingen: Vandenhoeck und Ruprecht, 1900; ET 1971.

# The Gospel in Historic and Cultural Transmission
Timothy C. Tennent

One of the most important, but often neglected, phrases in the Apostles' Creed is the statement, "he suffered under Pontius Pilate." Some have wondered why the Early Church would include in this very ancient confession of faith the name of the very Roman governor who presided over Jesus' trial and ordered his crucifixion. Upon reflection, however, it is clear that this phrase is a strategic ongoing reminder that the gospel intersects real human history. This is the only phrase in the Apostles' Creed which roots the gospel in a particular time and a particular place. As Andrew Walls has noted, "the Incarnation is not just that God became a man, but that he became a particular man."[70] There is no generic Incarnation. There is only the very specific one in which God in Jesus Christ took on particular flesh and lived in a particular culture and spoke a particular language. He didn't just walk on the vague sands of time, he walked on the real sands by the Sea of Galilee. In the same way, there is no such thing as a generic gospel which safely inhabits some a-cultural space. The gospel is rooted in a particular history and, through cross-cultural transmission, must take form and shape in living cultural contexts. The Church is not merely instrumental in proclaiming the gospel as a static historical event which took place in the distant past, but the Church is an ontological reality established by God himself, not only to proclaim and herald the gospel, but to embody the gospel in a potentially infinite number of new historical and cultural contexts.

This essay will fall into two major sections. The first section will provide a historical framework to help the reader understand how the gospel has been received within historical cultures through the ages. Given the limitation of space, this cannot be a full survey of Christian history. Instead, this essay will focus on a few key themes and key moments in Christian history to help us better understand our context today. The second section will address how the wide variety of cultural receptions and embodiments of the gospel has shaped and changed how evangelicals have understood the term "the gospel."

---

[70] Andrew F. Walls, "The Translation Principle in Christian History," in *The Missionary Movement in Christian History: Studies in the Transmission of Faith* (Maryknoll: Orbis, 1996), 26-42 (27).

## A Framework for Understanding Christian History

One of the great contributions of Lausanne to the larger ecumenical movement has been the focus on Christian history, not merely Church history. Church history tends to focus on particular denominations and confessional movements identified by various churches through the ages. Christian history, in contrast, seeks to capture a larger perspective and examines the overall movement of Christianity as a world movement. To understand this perspective, three key themes will be addressed: the advance and recession motif, the cross-cultural transmission of the gospel, and the shift in the center of Christian gravity.

### *Advance and Recession*

One of the peculiar features of the spread of Christianity is that it has been characterized primarily by serial, not progressive, growth. In other words, Christianity has not had an even, steady growth beginning with a central, cultural and geographic center from which it subsequently spread to its present position as the largest, most ethnically diverse religion in the world. Instead, Christian history has been one of advance and recession. Christian history has witnessed powerful penetrations of the gospel into certain geographic and cultural regions, only to later experience a major recession in that region and, sometimes, even wither away almost to extinction. However, just as Christianity was waning in one quarter, it was experiencing an even more dramatic rebirth and expansion in another.

This advance-and-recession theme is such a major feature in Christian history that the eminent Church historian Kenneth Scott Latourette uses it as a major organizing theme for his famous multivolume work, *A History of Christianity*.[71] The important point is to recognize that despite what it feels like when a Christian is living in the midst of a particular cultural and geographic advance, if you step back and look at the whole picture of Christian history then you must be forced to conclude that there is no such thing as a particular Christian culture or Christian civilization.

This picture is in stark contrast to what one observes, for example, in Islam or in Hinduism, the next two largest religions after Christianity. Islam initially emerged in Saudi Arabia and from that geographic and cultural center has spread all over the world. Today there are far more non-Arab Muslims than Arab Muslims. Yet, despite its diversity, Islam retains a distinctly Arab orientation. Devout Muslims insist that the *Qur'an* is untranslatable into any

---

[71] Kenneth Scott Latourette, *A History of Christianity*, rev. ed. (Peabody, MA: Prince, 2000), 1. Latourette uses as his heading for A.D. 500–950, "The Darkest Hours: the Great Recession." The next section, for A.D. 950–1350 he titles "Four Centuries of Resurgence and Advance." The next section, 1350–1500 is titled "Geographic Loss and Internal Lassitude, Confusion, and Corruption, Partly Offset by Vigorous Life." Many of the subheadings also reflect this theme as, for example, chapter 28, "Western Europe: Decline and Vitality" and chapter 40, "Stagnation and Advance: The Eastern Churches."

language other than Arabic. The call to prayer goes out in Arabic, regardless of the national language of the surrounding Muslims. All Muslims face towards Mecca when they pray. All of these are important indicators that Islam has had a progressive, not serial, growth. It has always enjoyed a single cultural and geographic center in Saudi Arabia and has never been forced to fully embrace cultural translatability.

Hinduism emerged in the Ganges plain of North India over three thousand years ago, making it one of the oldest religions in the world. Yet Hinduism has never lost its cultural and geographic center in North India. Just as Islam can hardly be imagined apart from Saudi Arabia, the home of the holy city of Mecca, the Ka'ba, the black stone and the tomb of Muhammad in Medina, so it is difficult to imagine a Hinduism which withers away in India, but finds a new center in, say, sub-Saharan Africa. Yet this is precisely what has happened repeatedly in the history of the Christian movement. As Christians in the 21st century, we are experiencing the most dramatic advance and recession in the history of the world Christian movement. However, in order to understand this phenomenon, we need to see it within the historical context of the second major theme; namely, the cross-cultural transmission of the gospel. Within this theme, three examples will be highlighted.

## *The Cross-cultural Transmission of the Gospel*

FROM JEWISH BIRTH TO GENTILE HOME.

Christianity began as a Jewish movement fulfilling Jewish hopes, promises and expectations. Indeed, the continuity between Judaism and Christianity seemed so seamless to the earliest believers that they would never have thought of themselves as changing their religion from Judaism to something else. They understood Christianity as the extension and fulfillment of their Jewish faith. Yet right in the pages of the New Testament we read the story of those unnamed Jewish believers in Antioch who took the risky—and very controversial—move to cross major cultural and religious barriers and share the gospel with uncircumcised pagan Gentiles. Acts 11:19 begins by recounting how, after the persecution in connection with Stephen, these scattered believers began to share the gospel "as far as Phoenicia, Cyprus, and Antioch, spreading the word only among Jews." The very next verse records one of the most important missiological moments in the entire New Testament: "Some of them, however, men from Cyprus and Cyrene, went to Antioch and began to speak to Greeks also, telling them the good news about the Lord Jesus." This is the beginning of a new cultural frontier which, though radical at the time, would soon become so prominent that it would be considered normative Christianity. At the time that these unnamed believers from Cyprus and Cyrene began to preach the gospel to Gentiles, the Church comprised Jewish believers and a few Gentile God-fearers like Cornelius and the Ethiopian eunuch who had accepted the Torah. In other words, the Gentile God-fearers had accepted the Jewish

Messiah as their Messiah and were living out their new faith on Jewish terms. The cultural center of this young fledgling movement, known simply as "the Way" (Acts 9:2; 19:23; 24:14), was based in Jerusalem under apostolic leadership. Jerusalem was the first geographic center of the Christian movement, and Judaism was its first religious and cultural home.

The importance of Jerusalem is underscored by what happened when news got back to Jerusalem about this surprising turning to Christ among Gentiles. The apostles in Jerusalem sent Barnabas down to Antioch to investigate this new movement. Later Paul and Barnabas entered into such a sharp disagreement with some Judaizers who strongly opposed the Gentiles coming to Christ apart from Judaism (including circumcision, submission to the Torah, dietary restrictions, etc.) that Paul traveled to Jerusalem to make his case before the apostles. The Jerusalem Council met to debate and to discuss the basis for accepting Gentiles into the Church. The group decided, of course, that Gentiles did not need to come to Jesus Christ on Jewish cultural and religious terms. They were not asked to submit to or to keep the many intricacies of the Jewish Law, but only to respect a few broad guidelines which would clearly separate the Gentiles from their pagan past, while still affirming that sinners are saved not by keeping the Law but by faith in Jesus Christ. The Jewish "center" formally recognized the presence of Christ in these new Gentile brothers and sisters. Since this "Way" now included Gentiles on their own cultural terms, it could no longer regard itself as a curious subset of Judaism. The faith had successfully traversed its first major cross-cultural transmission.

THE FALL OF THE EMPIRE AND THE BIRTH OF "BARBARIAN" AND BYZANTINE FAITH.

The turn of the fourth century in the Roman Empire was marked by the most brutal persecution the Church had ever experienced. Emperor Diocletian ordered the destruction of church buildings and Bibles, and he imprisoned many Christian leaders. However, all of this changed when his successor Constantine issued an edict of toleration in 313. In the decades which followed, Christianity experienced dramatic expansion among Hellenistic Gentiles until Christianity soon became the "professed faith of the overwhelming majority of the population of the Roman empire."[72] In fact, Christianity became almost conterminous with the empire.[73] Greek-speaking peoples with Hellenistic cultures and pagan backgrounds were now the best example of representative

---

[72] Latourette, *History of Christianity*, vol. 1, 97.

[73] Latourette, *History of Christianity*, vol. 1, 269. Stephen Neill tentatively estimates that the number of Christians in the Empire on the eve of the Edict of Toleration (313 CE) was approximately 5 million (10% of the population of the Empire). By the time Emperor Justinian officially closed the School of Athens in 529 the number of Christians was closer to 25 million. See Stephen Neill, *A History of Christian Missions* (London: Penguin, 1990), 39, 41.

Christianity. Indeed, by the fourth century, Jewish Christians represented only a tiny percentage of the Church.

Throughout the fourth century the Roman Empire increasingly showed signs of weakness and disintegration. Tragically, the moral and spiritual climate of nominal Christianity generally mirrored that of the declining empire.[74] Christianity might have shared the same demise as the empire, symbolized best by the famous sacking of Rome by the Goths in the year 410.[75] Remarkably, however, Christianity found new vitality outside the empire, among new people groups westward in Ireland and Scotland and eastward into Arabia, Persia, and beyond.[76] Many of the invading Germanic peoples were also brought to faith in Jesus Christ. In a matter of a few decades the Church was facing another new cultural shock with the entrance of Visigoths (Spain), Ostrogoths (Italy), Franks (northern Gaul), Burgundians (southern Gaul), Vandals (North Africa), Angles and Saxons (Britain), all entering the church in significant numbers. Centuries later this pattern would repeat itself. The relatively stable Carolingian empire, which had been substantially Christianized, eventually disintegrated, and a new wave of invasions began with the arrival of the Scandinavians, who were also, in turn, evangelized.

Not only was Christianity continually making cultural gains on one hand while suffering losses on the other, but the geographic center was also shifting. By the end of the second century, Rome, as capital of the empire, was the most important city for Christians. Indeed, even in the structure of the book of Acts, we are already beginning to see the strategic and cultural importance of Rome for Christians. However, in 330 Constantine relocated the capital to Byzantium, which he renamed Constantinople (modern-day Istanbul). By the time Rome was sacked in 410, Constantinople was the undisputed geographic center of the Christian faith. Christianity experienced some remarkable advances in the East during this time, including important progress among the Slavic peoples. During the ninth and tenth centuries, when Christianity in the West had reached dangerously low levels of faith and practice, Constantinople represented the most vibrant expression of Christianity in the world. In fact, the Russian ruler Vladimir was so moved by what he experienced in Constantinople that he sponsored the propagation of Eastern Christianity throughout Russia. Christianity, it seems, was becoming accustomed to reinvigorating its life through cross-cultural transmission to new people groups and adapting to new cultural and geographic centers.

---

[74] During this period the Church was either focused on internal, doctrinal disputes as reflected in the ecumenical councils, or they had become part of monastic communities which were not interested in revitalizing Roman civilization.

[75] The official conquest of the Empire is generally dated as 378, the year the Goths killed the Emperor in the battle of Adrianople.

[76] St. Patrick arrived in Ireland around 432 CE, Columba founded his famous monastery in Iona in 563, and Aidan founded Lindisfarne in Northumbria in 635.

A FAITH FOR THE WORLD: MISSIONARIES AND MIGRATIONS.

The Protestant Reformation led by Luther (1483–1546), along with the Roman Catholic Counter-Reformation led by Ignatius Loyola (1491–1556), represent renewal movements which helped to stimulate new vitality among previously Christianized peoples who had become largely nominal. Christianity in the Middle Ages was still confined primarily to Europe, which remained the geographic center. However, a revitalized European Christianity eventually led to dramatic missionary endeavors which brought the gospel to many new people groups, including most in Latin America and many in Asia. Fueled by missionary activity in the wake of the *Padroado* (1493),[77] the Roman Catholic Church founded the *Sacra Congregatio de Propaganda Fide* in 1622 to assist in training new missionaries, to oversee all Roman Catholic missionary work, and to coordinate major new missionary initiatives in non-Roman Catholic regions of the world. Eventually the Protestants, beginning with the Moravians and later the creation of dozens of new mission-sending societies, followed with their own missionary initiatives. The 19th century missionaries would plant the seeds for a future 21st-century Christian harvest beyond anything they could have imagined during their lifetimes. However, quite apart from missionaries committed to sharing their faith across cultural and geographic lines, Europe itself was engaged in the largest ocean-based migration in the history of the world. From 1500 until the middle of the 20th century, millions of Europeans relocated to the New World, bringing their faith with them and spawning the birth of massive new populations, largely Christian. The gospel, once again, proved that it was culturally and geographically translatable. Soon the English-speaking world, including Britain and North America, became the most important new center of vibrant Christianity.

### *Living on the Seam of History*

The purpose of these brief snapshots is to underscore the fact that the lifeblood of Christianity is found in its ability to translate itself across new cultural and geographic barriers and to recognize that areas which once were the mission field can, over time, become the very heart of Christian vitality, while those areas which were once at the heart can lose the very faith they once espoused. Jerusalem, Antioch, North Africa, and Constantinople were all at one time at the center of Christian vibrancy. Yet all of these places have only a very tiny remnant of Christianity remaining and, with the exception of Jerusalem, are

---

[77] The *Padroado* was the Papal decree which divided the world between Spain and Portugal, initially giving Spain exclusive rights to the New World in the West and Portugal the rights to the East. Later the line was moved to give Portugal access to the New World (modern-day Brazil).

almost completely Islamic.[78] In contrast, places like Lagos, Nigeria, and Seoul, South Korea, where the presence of Christianity at one time seemed almost unimaginable, are today vibrant centers of Christian faith.

If you happen to live right in the middle of one of these great cultural expansions, it is all too easy to be left with the impression that your experience and expression of Christianity is somehow normative for all Christians everywhere. It is also clear from the writings of Christians who happened to live in places which, in their day, were at the very center of global Christianity, that they fully expected that Christianity would always be dominant where they lived. The mission field would always be in other places and with other people. Indeed, during the height of such a major cultural and geographic expansion it is difficult to imagine the day when Christianity might wither away in such a place. One hundred years ago it would have seemed incredible if someone told you that before the end of the 20th century the historic William Carey Memorial Church in Leicester, England, would be a Hindu temple. One hundred years ago it would have seemed highly unlikely that by the dawn of the 21st century there would be more evangelicals in Nepal than in Spain.[79] One hundred years ago few would have believed you if you said that on a typical Sunday at the threshold of the 21st century only around 1 million Anglicans would attend church in Great Britain compared to over 17 million Anglicans who are in Sunday worship in Nigeria.[80] Many people firmly believed that the presence of these new Christians was only an unfortunate by-product of Western imperialistic colonialism and that in the wake of colonialism it would wither and die.[81] Others agreed, insisting that the forces of globalization would secularize the world, and religion would become marginal to 21st-century life. In fact, precisely the opposite is unfolding. During the postcolonial period, the Church outside the Western world is experiencing the most dramatic growth in

---

[78] For an excellent study of the decline of Christianity in the East, see, Bat Ye'or, *The Decline of Eastern Christianity Under Islam: From Jihad to Dhimmitude* (London: Associated University Press, 1996).

[79] According to David Barrett, there were 120,000 evangelicals in Spain in 2000, whereas Nepal had 185,000. By the year 2025 Spain is projected to have 131,000 evangelicals compared with Nepal's 405,000. This figure does not count the 1.3 million Pentecostals in Nepal. David B. Barrett, George T. Kurian and Todd M. Johnson, *World Christian Encyclopedia*, 2nd ed (New York: Oxford University Press, 2001), 527, 687.

[80] Bill C, "Worship Numbers Fall Again," *Church Times,* November 2, 2006, http://www.churchtimes.co.uk/articles/2004/16-january/news/worship-numbers-fall-again. In fact, there are more Anglicans in Nigeria alone than in the whole of Europe. See Ruth Gledhill, "Archbishop Thanks Africa for Lessons on Faith," *Times (London)*, July 26, 2003; Charlotte Allen, "Episcopal Church Plays Russian Roulette on the Gay Issue," *Los Angeles Times*, August 10, 2003; Dianne Knippers, "The Anglican Mainstream: It's Not Where Americans Might Think," *Weekly Standard*, August 25, 2003.

[81] Dana Robert, "Shifting Southward: Global Christianity Since 1945", *International Bulletin of Missionary Research* 24, no. 2 (April 2000): 53.

history. The modern world has not turned into a secular city, and modernization has not led to the predicted collapse of religious faith. Indeed, even the eminent sociologist Peter Berger has noted that "secularization theory is essentially mistaken" because "the assumption that we live in a secularized world is false." Berger goes on to say that the key assumption of secularization theory, which insisted that "modernization necessarily leads to a decline of religion, both in society and in the minds of individuals... turned out to be wrong."[82]

It is a special opportunity to live during a period in history when you are able to witness firsthand one of these great cultural and geographic transmissions of the gospel. Since I hold a faculty position in two seminaries, one in the USA and one in India, I have had the privilege over the last 20 years to teach every year in India as well as in the USA. My constant movement back and forth between North America and Asia has been very instructive for me. Despite the very tiny percentage of Christians in North India, I always leave that country with a sense of excitement and encouragement. The reason is that I see many signs that they are experiencing the sunrise of a major move of God in their land. It is true that a number of my Indian students have been beaten and even imprisoned for their faith in Jesus Christ, but I cannot shake the impression that India is moving toward a more profoundly Christian future. In contrast, despite the rather large percentage of Christians in North America, I always leave the USA with the troubling impression that apart from a new Great Awakening, Christianity in North America is in the throes of a precipitous decline. I see many signs of the erosion of authentic Christian life and vitality in the West. In Western Europe, where I also lived for three years, the situation is even more beleaguered.[83] All of this inevitably has the effect of stimulating theological reflection about what it means to be a Christian in the West and how we are to live out our faith within the context of the new realities of global Christianity. It also gives fresh insight into what it means to be a Christian in a land which was formerly designated pejoratively as "pagan" but is quickly emerging as a new Christian heartland, the new "normative" Christianity.

Augustine witnessed the barbarian invasions, realized their significance, and produced his classic *City of God*. William Carey lived at one of these seams of history and produced his influential *Enquiry*. We now live at another one of these great junctures in the history of the world Christian movement, and God is raising up new voices who will move beyond merely lamenting the emergence of a post-Christian West, and will be able to articulate the

---

[82] Peter L. Berger, "The Desecularization of the World: A Global Overview," in *The Desecularization of the World: Resurgent Religion and World Politics*, ed. Peter L. Berger (Grand Rapids: Eerdmans, 1999 and Washington, D.C.: Ethics and Public Policy Center, 1999), 2, 3.

[83] See George Weigel, *The Cube and the Cathedral: Europe, America and Politics without God* (New York: Basic Books, 2005).

significance of the remarkable rediscovery of Christianity: the rediscovery of a Christianity which is simultaneously more ancient and more shockingly fresh; a Christianity which is both post-Western and trans-Western. Christianity is being rediscovered apart from the West, but due to dramatically changing immigration patterns into North America and Europe and the growth of Christianity in so many different parts of the world, even the term "Southern Christianity" may yet be inadequate to describe what is happening.

### The Seismic Shift in the Center of Christian Gravity

The most evident sign that we are living on a "seam" of some new historical epoch of Christian history is the rise of the Majority World Church and the signs of the possible, although once unthinkable, demise of Western Christianity. Therefore, this deserves more careful scrutiny. Evidence of this development is seen, for example, when we observe where the majority of Christians are now located around the world. This is often referred to as a shift in the "center of gravity" of the world Christian movement. The statistical center of gravity refers to that point on the globe with an equal number of Christians living north, south, east and west of that point. After its birth in Asia, Christianity had its most vigorous growth as it moved steadily westward and northward. As more and more people in the West embraced Christianity, the statistical center of gravity moved north and west. However, beginning in 1900, the statistical center began to shift dramatically southward, and in 1970 it began to move eastward for the first time in 1,370 years (see Chart A)! Today the statistical center of Christianity is located in Timbuktu! This means that for the first time since the Reformation, the majority of Christians, (approximately 67 percent), are now located outside the Western world. Some specific examples of how the Church is changing will, perhaps, help to illustrate this shift better. At the turn of the 20th century, the Christian Church was predominately white and Western. In 1900 there were more than 380 million Christians in Europe and fewer then 10 million on the entire continent of Africa.[84] Today there are over 367 million Christians in Africa, comprising one-fifth of the entire Christian Church. Throughout the 20th century a net average gain of 16,500 people were coming to Christ every day in Africa. From 1970 to 1985, for example, the Church in Africa grew by more than 6 million people. During that same time, 4,300 people per day were leaving the Church in Europe and North America.[85]

---

[84] The World Christian Database notes that there were 380,641,890 Christians in Europe and 9,938,588 Christians in Africa. See worldchristiandatabase.org.

[85] Lamin Sanneh, *Whose Religion Is Christianity?: The Gospel Beyond the West* (Grand Rapids: Eerdmans, 2003), 15. Elizabeth Isichei says that the number leaving the church in the West is 7,500 per day. See Elizabeth Isichei, *A History of Christianity in Africa* (Grand Rapids: Eerdmans, 1995), 1.

Chart A[86]

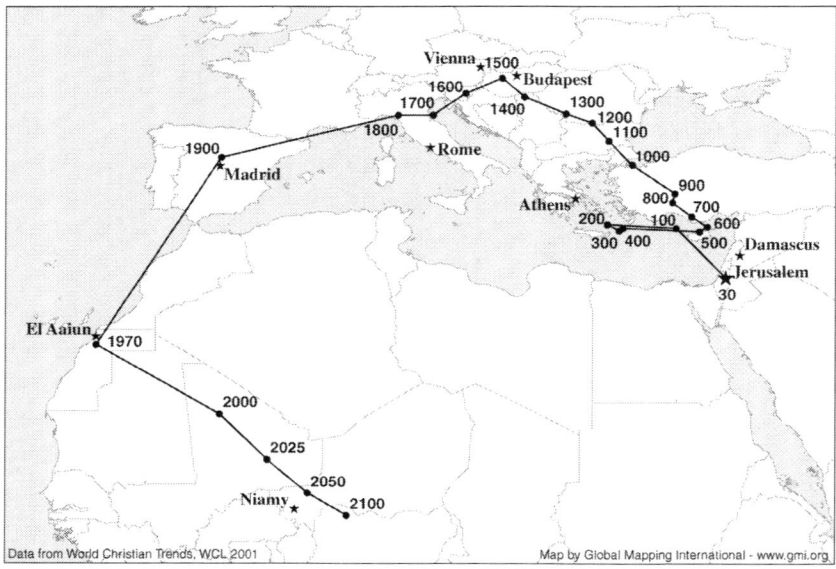

The Church is not just moving southward, it is also moving eastward. In Korea, for example, despite the fact that Christianity was not formally introduced within the country itself until the 18th century, it is staggering to realize that today there are over 20 million Christians in South Korea alone. In fact, South Korea is widely regarded as the home of the modern church growth movement, which is exemplified by the remarkable story of the Yoido Full Gospel Church pastored by Dr. David Cho. Founded in 1958 with only five people in a small living room, the church now claims over 700,000 members, making it easily the largest church in the world.

India has been called the cradle of the world's religions, having given birth to Hinduism, Buddhism, Jainism, and Sikhism. Yet today this land of exotic eastern religions is also the home of over 60 million Christians.[87] Church

---

[86] Todd Johnson and Sun Young Chung, "Tracking Global Christianity's Statistical Centre of Gravity, A.D. 33–A.D. 2100," *International Review of Mission*, 95, no. 569 (April 2004): 167.

[87] Todd M. Johnson, Sarah Tieszen, and Thomas Higgens, "Counting Christians in India, A.D. 52–2200," unpublished research report from the Center for the Study of Global Christianity, the research center at Gordon-Conwell Theological Seminary which produces the *World Christian Encyclopedia*. This represents 6.15% of the population of India, far above the official 3% figure given by the government. However, the official

planting in India, particularly in the traditionally Hindu north, is taking place at a blistering pace, so that many missiologists are predicting that by the year 2050 India will have over 126 million Christians.[88] However, even Korea and India cannot match the dramatic rise of the Chinese Church. Even as recently as Mao Zedong's famous Cultural Revolution in China (1966–1976) there were only about 1 million Christians in China. Today the Chinese church comprises more than 90 million believers and is the fastest growing church on the planet.[89]

Western scholars and liberal Christians have long predicted the demise of historic Christianity and the rise of the "secular city."[90] Their solution has been to call the church to abandon faith in the supernatural and the historic confessions of the Christian faith. They have argued that doctrines such as the deity of Christ, the Trinity, and the authority of the Bible are no longer credible or believable in the modern world. Therefore Christianity should conform to the norms of Western secularism. However, it seems that rather than saving Christianity, secular relativistic forces are quickly turning 21st-century mainline liberal Protestantism into a curious aberration, a mere footnote, in the larger story of the advance of global Christianity.

In contrast, the dramatic rise of Majority World Christianity is to a large extent morally and theologically conservative. These new Christians believe the Bible, are Christ centered, and are supernaturalistic. Philip Jenkins' study of Majority World Christianity found, in contrast to their Western counterparts, that they have a "much greater respect for the authority of Scripture" and "a special interest in supernatural elements of Scripture, such as miracles, visions, and healings." They also believe in the "continuing power of prophecy."[91] As

---

figures disenfranchise millions of Christians who are counted as "tribals" or who remain within Hindu communities.

[88] This is the current projection of the Center for the Study of Global Christianity. This will represent 8.94% of the population of India.

[89] Barrett, et al., *World Christian Encyclopedia*, 2nd ed., 191.

[90] John Spong carefully outlines his understanding of the slow demise of historic Christianity in a section of his book entitled "Exile of the Present." See John Spong, *Why Christianity Must Change or Die* (San Francisco: HarperCollins, 1999), 29-42. Harvey Cox advocated the demise of traditional faith and the rise of the "secular city." See Harvey Cox, *The Secular City: Secularization and Urbanization in Theological Perspective* (New York: MacMillan, 1966). Cox later courageously admitted that he was wrong. Indeed, he said, "before the academic forecasters could even begin to draw their pensions, a religious renaissance of sorts is under way all over the globe." See Harvey Cox, *Fire from Heaven: The Rise of Pentecostal Spirituality and the Reshaping of Religion in the Twenty-first Century* (Reading, MA: Addison-Wesley, 1995), xvi.

[91] See Philip Jenkins, *The New Faces of Christianity: Believing the Bible in the Global South* (New York: Oxford University Press, 2006), 4. Jenkins makes several remarkable discoveries about some of the differences in how Majority World Christians read the Bible as compared to their Western counterparts. For example, African believers venerate the Old Testament as an ongoing, living source of authority in a way which far exceeds the way it is used in the West. Furthermore, the Book of James

Peter Berger has said, "To put it simply, experiments with secularized religion have generally failed; religious movements with beliefs and practices dripping with reactionary supernaturalism have widely succeeded."[92] The French writer Gilles Kepel has aptly called this dramatic turnaround the "revenge of God" (*la revanche de Dieu*).[93] As Harvey Cox has noted, "if God really did die, as Nietzsche's madman proclaimed, then why have so many billions of people not gotten the word?"[94] There is a global Christian revolution happening outside the Western world, and most Western Christians are only gradually beginning to realize the full implications of this shift.

## The "Gospel" and Cultural Embodiments

If the gospel does not exist in a vacuum, but must become manifest in particular contexts, then it raises the question as to how the very word, "gospel," has undergone change in the midst of the emerging new cultural receptions and embodiments. Have Christians changed their understanding of what the word, "gospel," means, and, if so, what is the nature of these transformations? This is the focus of this second part of the essay. There are three cultural embodiments which must be examined, with an emphasis on how these embodiments have influenced our understanding of the word, "gospel." The first will be how the gospel was understood within the context of "Christendom" and how it is understood now in a new "post-Christendom" context. The second compares how the gospel is understood differently within the contexts of modernity and postmodernity. Finally we will examine how the gospel is understood differently within the context of the rise of global Christianity.

### *The "Gospel" as Understood in Christendom and Post-Christendom: Moving from "Jerusalem" to "Athens"*

Christendom refers to a political and ecclesiastical arrangement that reinforces a partnership between the church and the state. The state strengthens the church by promoting Christian hegemony over religious and cultural life. The church, in turn, gives legitimacy to the state by supporting the ruler and tacitly implying divine sanction on the actions of the state. In the context of Christendom, Christianity receives protection from the civil authorities (the King/Queen of England has the title "Defender of the Faith") and receives many privileges because it is the "established" religion of the realm. The classic phrase was *Cuius regio, eius religio*, broadly meaning, the faith of the ruler, was the

---

appears to be the most quoted book of the New Testament. See Jenkins, *The New Faces of Christianity*, 53, 54, 60-62.

[92] Berger, *Desecularization of the World*, 4.

[93] As quoted in Cox, *Fire from Heaven*, xvii. See Gilles Kepel, *The Revenge of God* (Cambridge, MA: Polity, 1994).

[94] Cox, *Fire from Heaven*, 103.

religion of the realm. The ruler was responsible for the spiritual welfare of the people; the ruler decided how they would worship, and in his or her dominion uniformity of faith and practice was considered normal. To embrace a different faith was to be a "dissenter" with all of the explicit and implicit sanctions that term implied. Because of the connection with the state, Christendom often (even unconsciously) regarded the Christian faith in territorial ways. To belong to the "realm" meant, by definition, that you shared the faith of the "realm." Particular embodiments of the gospel were, therefore, linked to specific geographic regions. There are few places whose histories have been shaped more by this dynamic than the countries of the former Yugoslavia. To be a Croat is to be Roman Catholic, to be a Serb is to be Eastern Orthodox, to be a Bosnian is to be a Muslim, and so forth.

Christendom has existed in official, explicit ways as well in unofficial, implicit expressions. In certain regions, most notably Europe and Latin America, Christianity was constitutionally granted special status and, therefore, we find Christendom it its most explicit expression. In other regions, such as the United States, church and state are officially kept separate. The US Constitution does not sanction a particular version of Christianity but nevertheless has found innumerable ways to extend special status to Christianity over other non-Christian religions. State funerals take place in the National Cathedral, God's name is invoked in public speeches, biblical texts are quoted on public occasions, and so forth. Even in unofficial Christendom, society is frequently committed to a civil religion as a kind of societal consensus that affords Christianity a privileged status within the broader society.

Protestantism originated as a movement within the larger context of European Christianity and therefore was born in the context of Christendom. This profoundly influenced the way the word, "gospel," was understood. To be a Christian within a Christendom arrangement is to see Christianity at the center of all public discourse. Evangelism occurs passively because Christianity is the prevailing plausibility structure. Christianity is the normative expression of religious faith and ethical action, and there are no major dissenting voices or alternative religious worldviews. Therefore, the "gospel" does not need to defend itself robustly against, for example, either secular atheism or some alternative religious worldview such as Islam or Hinduism. Islamic or Hindu counter-claims are virtually non-existent in Christendom. The most frequently found encounters between Christendom-type Christianity and non-Christian faiths are when it has engaged them as a cultural "other" in military campaigns (such as the Crusades) or has sponsored missionaries who, often unwittingly, have transmitted the gospel and the host culture in a single package.

Today the "gospel" has to be rediscovered in the West apart from Christendom. The Balkans will not be able to truly hear the gospel until they hear it as a post-Christendom faith. We can learn much from many of our Majority World brothers and sisters who have learned over many centuries how to live out their faith as a minority faith or, often, in the context of a state-sponsored religion other than Christianity.[95] Many countries, like Bosnia, with a predominately Islamic population, have their own version of "Christendom." However, rather than calling it something like "Islamicdom," it is often best observed by the presence of Islamic Sharia as the governing arrangement and which effectively merges "mosque and state." Even in a place like India, which is governed by a secular constitution, Hinduism consistently receives special recognition and protection. Similar examples could be given with countries like Bhutan, Nepal, or Thailand.

What are the implications of this for how the "gospel" is understood? Several examples can be given. First, the gospel must be invested with a renewed capacity to critique culture, not just accommodate it. Only when the gospel is freed from the chains of Christendom can it provide the necessary critique of the state and the prevailing culture that is required when the kingdoms of this world clash with the lordship of Jesus Christ. Second, the gospel must become more robust in responding to very specific challenges that hitherto went unnoticed. In a Christendom context, the challenges of unbelief or from other religions are distant and remote. Therefore, the gospel gradually becomes domesticated and weakened. Today we are witnessing the rise of many new challenges all around us: postmodern relativistic secularism, the rise of Islamic fundamentalism, the seeping pluralism of Hinduism, to name a few. These challenges will inevitably force faithful Christians to become far more articulate about what constitutes genuine Christian identity. Third, evangelism has to become more intentional, and one cannot assume that any of the dominant Christian paradigms of the last century are widely understood. Even basic religious categories like "God" or "sin" or "faith" which once sat very comfortably within the security of a mono-religious discourse must now be explained and clarified.

Tertullian famously once asked, "What has Athens to do with Jerusalem ... what has the academy to do with the Church?"[96] Tertullian envisioned a culture with the revelation of God's Word at the center. Divine self-disclosure is seen to trump all other knowledge and discourse. In this sense "Jerusalem" represents a society framed by revelation and therefore theological and cultural stability. "Jerusalem" represents a congregation of the faithful gathered to hear God's Word, the centrality of the pulpit, and the one-way pronouncements which are issued "six feet above contradiction." In contrast, "Athens" represents dialogue and speculation. "Athens" is the place of religious pluralism and dialogic speculation. Today, we must recognize that we are no longer proclaiming the gospel from the "Temple Mount" of our "Jerusalem." Instead, we are seeking to persuade the gospel into people's lives in the midst

---

[95] For example, Nepal has traditionally been a "Hindu kingdom," Bhutan a "Buddhist kingdom," and Saudi-Arabia an "Islamic kingdom."

[96] Tertullian, *De Praescriptione Haereticorum* 7.9.

of the raucous, pluralistic, experimental, skeptical environment of the "Mars Hill" of their "Athens." There are competing deities and revelations which clamor for attention. The gospel which we proclaim is largely "unknown," and our witness may need to find collaborative help from general revelation to gain a hearing for the gospel.

### The "Gospel" as Understood in Modernity and Postmodernity: Proclaiming Truth, Meaning, and *Telos* in a Culture that Has Lost Its Moorings

The second cultural embodiment which must be examined is how the "gospel" is understood in the context of modernity and postmodernity. Peter Kuzmič, the internationally renowned leader from Eastern Europe, and plenary speaker for Lausanne 2 in Manila, once commented that the most defining word of our time is the word, "post." We live in a post-communist, post-Christendom, post-denominational, post-Western, post-Enlightenment, and postmodern world. The prominence of the word, "post," is yet another signal that we are living in this seam between two epochs of history discussed earlier. There seems to be a growing consensus that there is a crisis occurring within modernity which may signal the end of, or a major modification in, the Enlightenment project. This crisis has been described as postmodernism and is already having a profound influence on how the gospel is being understood and communicated by evangelicals.

One of the earliest writers to recognize the collapse of modernity and the movement towards a post-Enlightenment world was the French philosopher Jean-François Lyotard in his 1979 work *The Postmodern Condition: A Report on Knowledge*.[97] In this work he coined the word, "postmodern," in the way that it is used in today's discourse. He stated that the fundamental shift of our time as Western civilization is a growing crisis of truth.[98] In the modern world there was a belief in an overarching truth, whether informed by a Christian worldview or even a secular belief in progress and the perfectibility of humanity. Lyotard argued that modern societies produced order and stability by generating what he called "grand narratives" or "master narratives." These grand narratives provide a clear sense of *telos* of destiny. Intellectual reflection was the embarking on a journey with a clear destination: the pursuit of truth.

In contrast, the postmodern context is marked by a collapse of all grand narratives. Postmodernism marks the movement away from claims to

---

[97] Jean-Francois Lyotard, *The Postmodern Condition: A Report on Knowledge* (Minneapolis: University of Minnesota Press, 1985).

[98] This trend and the implications of it for the contemporary church has been expounded brilliantly by David F. Wells. See especially his *No Place for Truth* (Grand Rapids: Eerdmans, 1993) and *Above All Earthly Pow'rs: Christ in a Postmodern World* (Grand Rapids: Eerdmans, 2005).

objectivity and a greater emphasis on fragmented forms and discontinuous narratives. In short, the very notion of truth as Truth has begun to collapse. There is no longer a cohesive "canopy of truth" or metanarrative which gives meaning and purpose to our civilization. We are left only with our personal narratives. The only "truth" which remains is what is true "for me," and little courage or confidence remains to state with certainty that anything is true for everyone, or to speak about objective truth. To use the language of Lesslie Newbigin, in postmodernism there are no more "public facts," all we have left are "personal preferences."[99]

Looking back from this perspective, we can easily see how the evangelical understanding of the gospel has been influenced by Enlightenment thinking. On the positive side, the gospel benefited from the notion of a metanarrative and the idea of a final, all encompassing *telos* to which all of human history was moving. The Christian metanarrative and final goal of history may have been different from that of the Enlightenment, but at least the paradigm was there to build on. On the negative side, the overemphasis on reason sometimes produced hyper-rational expressions of Christianity. Furthermore, the deeply imbedded notions of human progress often caused evangelicals not to take sin seriously enough and to render the "gospel" as nothing more than the greatest "self-help" plan.

How is postmodernism influencing the evangelical understanding of the gospel? What implications does this have for Christian mission? How do we inhabit a postmodern world where Christianity is regarded as merely one local story among many? How do we respond to the postmodern lack of confidence about any claim to a universal story which gives a "canopy of meaning" to the entire human race, or that gives insight into the origin, the purpose, and, indeed, the destiny of the human race?

It is clear that postmodernism poses a number of serious challenges to the gospel. First, postmodernism erodes the very concept of objective truth rooted in God's self-revelation. Therefore, the authority of the Bible, the trustworthiness of expository preaching, and the call to repentance, to name just a few, all suffer. Second, postmodernism's emphasis on personal narrative, separate from any overarching metanarrative, has further pushed the Church towards a privatized understanding of the gospel. Under the sway of postmodernism, the gospel loses its historical, missional, and cosmic dimensions, and through a radical kind of reductionism it becomes merely a prescription for obtaining personal peace. Third, postmodernism's emphasis on the autonomy of personal choices has further pushed the Church towards a full acceptance of marketing strategies for attracting new believers, business models for long-term planning and strategy, and a general entertainment orientation because in this new world the "consumer is king." Once the gospel

---

[99] This is one of the central arguments in Lesslie Newbigin's *Foolishness to the Greeks* (Grand Rapids: Eerdmans, 1986).

must be made "fun," then there is little room for the prophetic imagination, the cost of discipleship, or the call to repentance.

In response, the Church must regain confidence in the truth of the gospel of Jesus Christ. We need a fresh understanding of the rule and reign of God as the great eschatological fact to which all history is moving. The wonderful thing about the biblical vision of the *eschaton* is that it simultaneously trumps the modernist notions of human progress as well as the postmodern malaise about any ultimate meaning at all. We need a renewed call to repentance, a *metanoia* about what it means to be the people of God called to mission. Finally, and this is one of the great contributions of the Lausanne movement, we need to discover that deeper ecumenism which looks beyond our own institutional aggrandizement and discovers that overarching evangelical unity which can move the Church forward in the face of the challenges of our day.

## The "Gospel" as Understood When it Comes from One Center to What Happens When It Is Transmitted from Multiple Centers of Universality

One of the most enduring features of Christian history has been the persistent tendency for each of the major Christian traditions to draw from a single locus of cultural vitality. Roman Catholicism, Eastern Orthodoxy, and Protestantism have each been dominated by a single center of universality. Roman Catholicism has been dominated by a worldview which sees Western Europe in general and Rome in particular as the center of gravity for the Christian movement. It is not surprising that every single pope in history has been from Western Europe. Eastern Orthodoxy throughout its history has been dominated by the central importance of Byzantine tradition, history, and culture. Protestantism, while far more diverse, has nevertheless been dominated by Western culture since its inception until the early decades of the 20th century.

As pointed out earlier in the essay, we are now witnessing the dramatic decline of European Christianity. This in itself is not unique. We have seen the gospel wither and decline in areas of previous vitality before, as in North Africa. We have seen the gospel emerge with new vitality in a new cultural center, as in Byzantium. However, we are now observing something unique in Christian history. John Mbiti has called the emergence of multiple new "centers of universality."[100] This means that for the first time in history, the gospel is simultaneously emerging with strength in multiple different cultural centers. It is not as if the gospel is only emerging with vitality in sub-Saharan Africa. It is also emerging with renewed vitality in Korea, China, India, and even Latin America. We now have multiple centers of universality. For the first time, this means that the gospel can no longer be identified primarily with one cultural center. This will inevitably enhance the universality of the gospel, since the

---

[100] As quoted in Kwame Bediako, *Christianity in Africa: The Renewal of a Non-Western Religion* (Maryknoll: Orbis, 1995), 157.

gospel will no longer be tied to a particular cultural center. It will also simultaneously enhance the need for greater cultural sensitivity, global partnerships, and cooperation, all things which are the hallmarks of the Lausanne movement. The day has finally arrived when we can say that the Church of Jesus Christ on every continent is both sending missionaries and receiving missionaries. This new reality has been captured well by Samuel Escobar in his book *The New Global Mission: The Gospel from Everywhere to Everyone*.[101] The phrase "from everywhere to everyone" precisely describes the new situation we are in.

The other major development is that the demographics are transforming even the former heartlands of Christianity. Immigration patterns are slowly transforming the face of Christianity even in North America and Europe. The fastest growing Christian groups in North America and Europe are the non-white, non-European peoples. African, Chinese, Korean, Indian, and Hispanic churches, to name a few, are springing up all across America in unprecedented numbers. John Wesley famously said, "the world is my parish." Today we must say that the world is in my parish. The former phrase envisions a single cultural center and implies implicitly a "West reaches the Rest" worldview. The latter phrase more accurately captures that the mission field is now everywhere, and all Christians in all places can participate in effective cross-cultural ministry.

What are the implications of this for the "gospel"? First of all, the gospel must be rediscovered as a post-Western faith. The gospel has been overly identified with the West for so long that we cannot even imagine all the ways the gospel has been unwittingly domesticated by its long sojourn with Western culture. The Church all over the globe (even in the so-called post-Christian West) must rediscover the gospel as a post-Western faith.

Second, even though the geographic center of Christian gravity has moved, this has not dramatically changed the fact that in terms of theological training, finances, and book publications, to name a few, the West continues to play a central and vital role. Nevertheless, the very places which boast the strongest educational centers for theological education (namely, Western Europe and North America) are also the very cultural centers where Christianity is declining the fastest. This is another new situation the Church is facing. We have no real precedent for a situation where the geographic center of Christian gravity is so dramatically different from the centers of theological education, the center of mission financing, or the center of book production. All of this has profound implications for missions in the 21st century.

---

[101] Samuel Escobar, *The New Global Mission: The Gospel from Everywhere to Everyone* (Downers Grove: InterVarsity, 2003).

We are in danger of becoming what John Mbiti calls "kerygmatically universal" while remaining "theologically provincial."[102] In other words, the global centers of the Church's vibrant proclamation are becoming increasingly diverse, whereas theological reflection continues to be dominated by Western scholarship. Mbiti's point was that even though "the centers of the Church's universality are no longer in Geneva, Rome, Athens, Paris, London, or New York" but are now in "Kinshasa, Buenos Aires, Addis Ababa, and Manila," there has not been the corresponding shift towards "mutuality and reciprocity in the theological task facing the universal Church."[103] This means that the Church in the West must re-think its missionary role beyond first-generation gospel work of evangelism and church planting and also think about its role in helping to stimulate theological training institutions, encouraging indigenous theological writing, and so forth. The West itself will be increasingly in need of first-generation gospel work, and the Majority World will increasingly need second- and third-generation gospel work.

Finally, we must learn to re-think how the gospel is transmitted to new people groups. This is another unique feature in the history of Christian expansion. There are precious few examples in Christian history where a people group with less power and economic strength have brought the gospel to a people group with greater power and economic strength. Throughout Christian history, the gospel has almost uniformly been shared by people with greater economic and political power with those of less power and resources. To this day the very word, "missions," in the minds of many people is synonymous with economic assistance and various ministries of mercy. However, today the emerging dominant paradigm is that people groups from underdeveloped countries are likely to produce the greatest number of cross-cultural missionaries. This means that the traditional ways in which missions has been supported will no longer be viable. It will likely mean a dramatic rise in self-supporting and/or bi-vocational missionaries from around the world, closer to the 18th-century Moravian model than the 20th-century faith missions model.

## Conclusion

This essay has provided a broad historical framework for helping us to understand the nature of our time. It is clear that the Church is undergoing another major "advance and recession" motif and we are caught in the middle (or on the seam) between a "Western recession" and a "non-Western advance."

---

[102] John S. Mbiti, "Theological Impotence and the Universality of the Church," in *Mission Trends No. 3: Third World Theologies*, ed. Gerald H. Anderson and Thomas F. Stransky (New York: Paulist; Grand Rapids: Eerdmans, 1976), 6.

[103] Mbiti, "Theological Impotence," 9, 10; and Bediako, *Christianity in Africa*, 154.

Living during the transition between two major historical epochs is always fraught with a sense of disequilibrium and special challenges. The Lausanne movement is uniquely poised to reflect on these changes and to serve as a bridge between important conversations going on by Christians all over the world.

This essay has also sought to understand how these historical changes are influencing how Christians, particularly evangelicals, have understood the gospel. We have seen that the gospel is, to use the language of Andrew Walls, both the "prisoner" and the "liberator" of culture. On the one hand, the gospel's transformative work transcends any cultural particularities. On the other hand, it is clear that the gospel message has often been domesticated because of its long sojourn within a particular cultural context. This essay has highlighted three major shifts in how the word, "gospel," is now being understood in a post-Christendom, postmodern, multi-centered Christian movement.

## Bibliography

Barrett, David B., George T. Kurian, and Todd M. Johnson, eds. *World Christian Encyclopedia: A Comparative Survey of Churches and Religions in the Modern World*. 2nd ed. 2 vols. New York: Oxford University Press, USA, 2001.

Bediako, Kwame. *Christianity in Africa: The Renewal of a Non-Western Religion*. Maryknoll: Orbis, 1995.

Berger, Peter L. "The Desecularization of the World: A Global Overview." In *The Desecularization of the World: Resurgent Religion and World Politics*, edited by Peter L. Berger. Grand Rapids: Eerdmans, 1999.

Cox, Harvey. *Fire from Heaven: Pentecostalism, Spirituality, and the Reshaping of Religion in the Twenty-first Century*. Reading: Addison-Wesley, 1995.

Cox, Harvey. *The Secular City: Secularization and Urbanization in Theological Perspective*. New York: MacMillan and Company, 1966.

Escobar, Samuel. *The New Global Mission: The Gospel from Everywhere to Everyone*. Downers Grove: InterVarsity, 2003.

Isichei, Elizabeth. *A History of Christianity in Africa: From Antiquity to the Present*. Grand Rapids: Eerdmans, 1995.

Jenkins, Philip. *The New Faces of Christianity: Believing the Bible in the Global South*. New York: Oxford University Press, 2006.

Johnson, Todd and Sun Young Chung. "Tracking Global Christianity's Statistical Centre of Gravity, A.D. 33–A.D. 2100." *International Review of Mission* 95, no. 569 (2004): 167.

Kepel, Gilles. *The Revenge of God.* Cambridge: Polity, 1994.

Latourette, Kenneth Scott. *A History of Christianity.* Rev. ed. Peabody: Prince, 2000.

Lyotard, Jean-Francois. *The Postmodern Condition: A Report on Knowledge.* Minneapolis: University of Minnesota Press, 1985.

Mbiti, John S. "Theological Impotence and the Universality of the Church." In *Mission Trends No. 3: Third World Theologies,* edited by Gerald H. Anderson and Thomas F. Stransky. Grand Rapids: Eerdmans, 1976.

Neill, Stephen. *A History of Christian Missions.* London: Penguin, 1990.

Newbigin, Lesslie. *Foolishness to the Greeks: The Gospel and Western Culture.* Grand Rapids: Eerdmans, 1986.

Robert, Dana. "Shifting Southward: Global Christianity Since 1945." *International Bulletin of Missionary Research* 24, no. 2 (2000).

Sanneh, Lamin. *Whose Religion Is Christianity?: The Gospel Beyond the West.* Grand Rapids: Eerdmans, 2003.

Spong, John. *Why Christianity Must Change or Die: A Bishop Speaks to Believers in Exile.* San Francisco: HarperCollins, 1999.

Walls, Andrew F. "The Translation Principle in Christian History." In *The Missionary Movement in Christian History: Studies in the Transmission of Faith.* Maryknoll: Orbis, 1996.

Weigel, George. *The Cube and the Cathedral: Europe, America and Politics without God.* New York: Basic Books, 2005.

Wells, David F. *Above All Earthly Pow'rs: Christ in a Postmodern World.* Grand Rapids: Eerdmans, 2005.

Wells, David F. *No Place for Truth or Whatever Happened to Evangelical Theory?* Grand Rapids: Eerdmans, 1993.

Yeor, Bat. *The Decline of Eastern Christianity under Islam: From Jihad to Dhimmitude.* London: Associated University Press, 1996.

# Connectedness and Mutual Submission under God's Rule

# "Honor Everyone!":
# Christian Faith and the Culture of Universal Respect

Miroslav Volf

### Disclosure

I grew up under an anti-religious regime of intolerance. Mild intolerance it was, compared to what many, especially religious groups, suffered in the 20th century and continue to suffer in many places around the world today. But I know from firsthand experience what it means to live in bugged quarters, receive surreptitiously opened mail, and talk on tapped phone lines; "security agents" have threatened and interrogated me for months running.[104] I have also many times heard the story of my father's horrendous trials. An innocent man, he was, literally, nearly starved to death during months of detainment in a concentration-camp hell because the "powers that be" assumed his guilt without making even the slightest effort to check out his case—indeed, without even asking for his name!

At the level of my early and formative experiences, I associate irreligion with intolerance. But also in my experience, religion has not fared any better than irreligion. My grandfather was a Baptist minister and my father a Pentecostal one. They agreed that their communities had it easier under the rule of Communists than under the cultural and political dominance of Catholics and the Orthodox. My longing for the open horizon of respect grew in the constricted space of both religious and secular intolerance. The faith that my parents handed down to me—the faith that as a teenager I found too difficult a burden to bear—would not buckle under the pressure to abandon its own truth, while it struggled against becoming infected by intolerance suffered at the hands of those who identified with the red star or the cross.

But is the cross a symbol of an intolerant religion the way the red star has become a symbol for an intolerant social and political project?

---

[104] For an autobiographical account, see Miroslav Volf, *The End of Memory* (Grand Rapids: Eerdmans, 2006).

## And the Intolerance Prize Goes to...

Imagine an international prize for the most intolerant religion. Which one would win? As a jury, also imagine critics of religion, past and present. In the minds of the majority of such critics, all religions would be candidates for the prize because all are blindly irrational and therefore intolerant. Judaism, Christianity, and Islam, Abrahamic faiths that affirm the undisputed rule of one sole God and insist on one universal truth,[105] would likely emerge as the top contenders, embodying as they do what is sometimes called the "imperialism of the universal."[106] Christianity might be pronounced the winner for seeking to impose itself relentlessly on everyone under the guise of general benevolence. Or maybe the perverse prize might go to Islam, a religion that many of today's critics envisage as a blindfolded man with scimitar in hand.[107]

Religious people, prone to disparage their rivals, often join the critics. I've heard Christians insist that whereas Christianity is a religion of love, Islam is a religion of violence, with a fierce and irrational deity demanding unconditional submission at its center. And I've heard Muslims return the compliment. None lesser than the former president of Malaysia, Mahathir Mohammad, who has said in my presence that, as the divinely commanded genocide of the ancient Canaanites attests, both Judaism and Christianity are clearly more violent than Islam.

If the critics (and rival advocates) are correct about the intolerance of the Abrahamic faiths, a major storm looms on our horizon. First, ours is an interconnected and interdependent world in which many religions inhabit a common space within single states. Second, Christianity and Islam today are the fastest growing religions and claim the greatest number of members; taken together, their adherents account for more than half of living humanity. It is these two religions which, in critics' opinions, vie for first prize in intolerance. Third, since religious people, including Muslims, for the most part embrace democratic ideals, they will continue to push for their vision of the good life in the public square. Intertwined, growing, and assertive, religions will make life intolerable for millions—if the critics are correct.

But are the critics correct? In one respect, they are. Followers of all three Abrahamic faiths, but especially of Christianity and Islam, have often been intolerant, even gruesomely violent. The history of their intolerance is long and their path through time is littered with demeaned, displaced, and destroyed

---

[105] See the relation between monotheism, exclusivism, and intolerance in Jan Assmann, *Moses the Egyptian: The Memory of Egypt in Western Monotheism* (Cambridge, MA: Harvard University Press, 1997); *Die Mosaische Unterscheidung, Oder der Preis des Monotheismus* (Munich: Carl Hanser, 2003).

[106] This phrase is from Pierre Bourdieu, *Firing Back: Against the Tyranny of the Market 2* (London: Verso, 2003), 86; *Pascalian Meditations* (Stanford: Stanford University Press, 2000), 71.

[107] One of the twelve famous Danish cartoons portrayed Muhammad in this way.

people. Perhaps surprisingly to some, many followers of these religions agree with critics on this point (though followers add that their religions have an even more impressive history of generosity and the struggle for justice). So critics and advocates are united on this point: in practice, Abrahamic religions have often been and continue to be intolerant.[108] The dispute between them is primarily about whether intolerance is a defining characteristic of these faiths or a profound distortion of them.

Applied to the Christian faith, the faith that I embrace and about which I write here, the dispute is about what it means to be a consistent Christian—a Christian who lives in line with the letter and the spirit of basic Christian convictions. To take two contrasting examples, is a Crusader, exclaiming "Christ is the Lord" while cleaving the head of an infidel, a consistent Christian?[109] Or is a Trappist monk serving the Muslim poor while living under the threat of death from violent extremists a consistent Christian?[110] Is the Crusader misusing faith in his lust for economic, political, or cultural domination, or is he unflinchingly enacting authentic Christian convictions? Is the Trappist monk moderating his fierce religion with generic human kindness, or is he consistently practicing the Christian faith? Put more generally, the dispute is this: Are intolerant Christians bastardizing their own religion, or is the Christian faith itself an intolerant religion? Critics argue for the second position and insist that all impulses toward any toleration the Christian faith may contain must have come to it from secular sources and are in deep tension with the faith itself.

The issue is critical, and I don't mean just for the self-image and good reputation of Jews, Christians, and Muslims (though if the critics are correct, such people live in what is a religious equivalent of North Korea[111]). In a globalized world with resurgent religions, world peace itself greatly depends on religious tolerance. Religions are not going away. If intolerance is in their DNA, religiously inspired and legitimized conflicts are inevitable. In today's intermingled and interdependent world with vibrant and assertive religions, apart from genuinely religious motivation for tolerance, we can expect cold disrespect, zealous intolerance, and fierce violence to be the order of the day.

Are there genuinely religious reasons for tolerance? In this essay I will argue that authentic Christian convictions foster not just tolerance but genuine respect

---

[108] By "practice" here I mean not just intolerance in the violent action of Christians but also intolerance in the very way they have formulated Christian convictions, intolerance in "deed" and in "word."

[109] The example comes from George Lindbeck, *The Nature of Doctrine* (Louisville, KY: Westminster John Knox, 1984), 64.

[110] For an account of seven Trappist monks who were beheaded in Algeria in 1996, see the movie, "Of Gods and Men."

[111] So Christopher Hitchens in a debate with Tony Blair about whether or not religion is a force for good ("Is Religion a Force for Good in the World?," The Munk Debates, November 26, 2010, video http://www.c-spanvideo.org/program/Blairan).

for all human beings. The idea of respect for all makes sense only if we distinguish between respect due to persons on account of their achievement or status (as in "I respect her for her integrity!"), and respect due to them simply on account of their humanity (as in, "human beings must respect one another in all their diversity").[112] More on this fundamental distinction later.

## Tolerance—the Chief Mark of the True Church

A specifically Christian argument for tolerance is not new. In what is likely the most influential text on tolerance ever written, *A Letter Concerning Toleration* (1689), John Locke, the progenitor of political liberalism, states in the very first sentence that toleration is "the chief characteristic mark of the true Church."[113] His argument in support of this claim rests mainly on two key Christian convictions.

### *Tolerance and Freedom*

The first conviction concerns the centrality of freedom in coming to faith. The nature of faith is such that no one can be forced to believe. To embrace (or reject) Christian faith is to reorient all the fundamental commitments of one's life. If we are forced to believe, we will believe insincerely and thereby both dishonor God[114] and violate our own conscience.[115] "True and saving religion," writes Locke, "consists in the inward persuasion of the mind, without which nothing can be acceptable to God."[116] Such faith can grow only in the soil of freedom.

A critic may raise an eyebrow out of suspicion that Locke might be importing "inward persuasion" into the Christian faith from outside, from his modern sensibilities. Locke has in mind a lone individual, before God, heeding the voice of his conscience alone. But such a person, a critic might contend, is a product of an individualistic age whose ways of understanding the human person and social relations have been brought about by secular developments.

---

[112] "United Nations Millennium Declaration," No. 6 (http://www2.ohchr.org/english/law/millennium.htm).

[113] John Locke, *A Letter Concerning Toleration*, in *Two Treatises of Government and a Letter Concerning Toleration*, ed. Ian Shapiro (New Haven: Yale University Press, 2003), 215.

[114] "Whatsoever is not done with that assurance of faith is neither well in itself, nor can it be acceptable to God. To impose such things, therefore, upon any people, contrary to their own judgment, is, in effect, to command them to offend God; which, considering that the end of all religion is to please him, and that liberty is essentially necessary to that end, appears to be absurd beyond expression" (Locke, *A Letter*, 233).

[115] "No way whatsoever that I shall walk in against the dictates of my conscience will ever bring me to the mansions of the blessed" (Locke, *A Letter*, 233).

[116] Locke, *A Letter*, 219.

After all, the argument about freedom in coming to faith flows from the pen of a philosopher dubbed the progenitor of Western "possessive individualism."[117]

The eyebrow can safely come down. Cultural novelty and the character of Locke's own individualism need not concern us here. From the very beginning, Christians have insisted on the need to embrace faith freely. The apostle Paul wrote that "one believes with the heart," which is to say not by mere outward conformity to ambient influences or explicit dictates, but with the very core of one's being (Rom. 10:10). Similarly, around 300 CE, during the Diocletian persecution, Christian apologist Lactantius insisted that "nothing is so much a matter of free-will as religion; ... if the mind of the worshipper is disinclined to it, religion is at once taken away, and ceases to exist."[118] A century earlier Tertullian made the same point: "It is unjust to compel freemen against their will" to engage in religious rituals, for the gods "can have no desire of offerings from the unwilling."[119] Faith is essentially a free and personal act. Coerced faith is no faith at all. Both early and contemporary Christians agree on this point.[120]

## Tolerance and Love

The second reason why Locke thinks that tolerance is a chief mark of the true Church concerns the centrality of love in the exercise of the Christian faith. The apostle Paul wrote famously that, no matter how deep is my knowledge of the tenets of my faith, no matter how impressive are my moral achievements, if I "do not have love, I am nothing" (1 Cor. 13:2). Echoing the apostle Paul, Locke argues that even if a person has a true claim to orthodoxy, to moral excellence or to liturgical correctness, "yet if he be destitute of charity, meekness, and goodwill in general towards all mankind, even to those that are not Christians,

---

[117] See C. B. Macpherson, *The Political Theory of Possessive Individualism: Hobbes to Locke* (Oxford: Clarendon, 1962).

[118] Lactantius, *Divine Institutes*, V, 20, as quoted by John R. Bowlin, "Tolerance Among the Fathers," *Journal of the Society of Christian Ethics* 26, no. 1 (2006): 27.

[119] Tertullian, *Ad Scapulum* II, as quoted in Bowlin, "Tolerance among the Fathers," 18. How Augustine, with his own interpretation of "Compel people to come in" (Lk. 14:23; see "Concerning the Correction of the Donatists," *St. Augustine: Letters 156-210* [trans. Roland Teske; Hyde Park, NY: New City, 2004], 185), and the whole tradition that followed him comport with this account of faith must remain unexamined in this short essay (see Bowlin, "Tolerance among the Fathers," 28-31).

[120] This was one of the main points of Pope Benedict XVI's remarks on Islam and violence in his infamous Regensburg address. Significantly, he makes his point by quoting a Byzantine emperor who argued that "faith is born in the soul, not the body. Whoever would lead someone to faith needs the ability to speak well and to reason properly, without violence and threats" (see "Faith, Reason and the University – Memories and Reflections," *The Holy See*, September 12, 2006, http://www.vatican.va/holy_father/benedict_xvi/speeches/2006/september/documents/hf_ben-xvi_spe_20060912_university-regensburg_en.html; for the discussion, including Muslim reactions, see Miroslav Volf, *Allah: A Christian Response* [San Francisco: HarperOne, 2011], 19-39).

he is certainly yet short of being a true Christian himself."[121] Intolerance is incompatible with genuine love because it is implausible that "infliction of torments and exercise of all manner of cruelties" is an expression of love[122]—a stance that advocates of fierce love from Augustine on have disputed.[123] For Locke, intolerance is therefore incongruous with authentic faith. An intolerant faith is a seriously compromised faith.

Locke's two Christian arguments for tolerance—from how one comes to faith and from how one should live as a person of faith—are compelling.[124] The first is an argument for specifically religious toleration, Locke's primary concern; the second is comprehensive and grounds all other kinds of toleration. A consistent Christian is a tolerant Christian, Locke argues.

We can strengthen his case. We could argue that all Christian convictions about the self, social relations, and the good are governed by the claim that God, far from being a domineering despot, is self-giving love (as I have done in my book, *Free of Charge*).[125] We could demonstrate that Christians should love neighbors and honor their personal and communal integrity precisely in circumstances rife with potential for intolerance—when they face "others" who are different and whose behavior they disapprove of, or at whose hands they have suffered violence (as I have demonstrated in my book, *Exclusion and Embrace*).[126] We could show that the neighbors whom Christians should love and respect include their chief religious rivals, Muslims (as I have shown in my book, *Allah: A Christian Response*).[127] We could also make the case for Christian public engagement's being guided by the "Golden Rule," which obliges us to grant to others the same rights we seek for ourselves (as I have done in *A Public Faith*).[128] All these would be important, specifically religious arguments for tolerance and respect.

But in the present essay I will take a different approach. I will zero in on the grounds for respect found in the Christian Holy Scriptures. In fact, I will concentrate on a single command. It is found in 1 Peter, a text that speaks more

---

[121] Locke, *A Letter*, 215.

[122] Locke, *A Letter*, 216.

[123] See, for example, the medieval figures discussed in Jonathan Riley-Smith, "Crusading as an Act of Love," in *Medieval Religion: New Approaches* (ed. Constance H. Berman; New York: Routledge, 2005), 49-67.

[124] For a comprehensive discussion of the whole range of Locke's arguments for tolerance, see Susan Mendus, *Toleration and the Limits of Liberalism* (Atlantic Highlands, NJ: Humanities Press International, 1989), 22-43.

[125] Miroslav Volf, *Free of Charge: Giving and Forgiving in a Culture Stripped of Grace* (Grand Rapids: Zondervan, 2006).

[126] Miroslav Volf, *Exclusion and Embrace: Theological Exploration of Identity, Otherness, and Reconciliation* (Nashville: Abingdon, 1996).

[127] Miroslav Volf, *Allah: A Christian Response* (San Francisco: HarperOne, 2011).

[128] Miroslav Volf, *A Public Faith: How Followers of Christ Should Serve the Common Good* (Grand Rapids: Brazos, 2011).

explicitly and comprehensively than any other in the New Testament on how Christians ought to live in socially pluralistic settings laden with tensions. The command is terse and direct: "Honor everyone" (1 Pet. 2:17 ESV).[129] For Christians who consider the Holy Scriptures to be the Word of God, to honor everyone is not a mere suggestion or a counsel of prudence, but a strictly religious duty. In what does this duty consist?

## Honor

Let's first take up the idea of "honoring," and then turn to the more surprising, even radical part of this command, namely, that Christians should honor everyone. I'll use "honoring" and "respect" as synonyms.

### *Honor, Period!*

In discussing toleration, philosophers sometimes speak of the "circumstances of toleration." They describe conditions under which we are called to show tolerance. Three such conditions are crucial: (1) diversity, (2) disapproval, and (3) disparity in power.[130] 1 Peter addresses Christian communities living in a setting in which all three of these conditions obtain. First, these communities embarked on a markedly different way of life from the surrounding culture, and even different from their ancestors; these Christians saw themselves as "a chosen race" and "a holy nation" (2:9). Second, they felt "maligned" as "evildoers" (2:12), and they in turn believed that their compatriots' lives were marked by "futility" (1:18). Finally, they were a small and powerless minority, a network of insignificant communities scattered throughout the Roman Empire (1:1-2). Different, disliked and marginal, they faced abuse and mild persecution (1:6; 3:9). These were exactly the circumstances that cry out for toleration.

Surprisingly, 1 Peter contains no demand—not even a plea—for Christians to be tolerated. Later Christian writers, starting with Tertullian (b. 160 CE), will issue such demands. Even before Tertullian, theologians had argued for toleration without demanding it. Justin Martyr (100–165 CE) noted in his *Apology* that people of diverse religions "all are profane in the judgment of one another, on account of their not worshipping the same objects."[131] If Rome tolerates such religions, it should tolerate Christians as well, rather than putting

---

[129] As I expound the command here, I will not be able to relate it to biblical texts in which it seems that Jesus and Christians are described as doing exactly the opposite of what obeying this command seems to require, such as when Jesus tells "the Jews" who seek to kill him, "your father [is] the devil" (John 8:44). On this issue see Miroslav Volf, *Captive to the Word of God: Engaging the Scriptures for Contemporary Theological Reflection* (Grand Rapids: Eerdmans, 2010), 105-10.

[130] For a discussion of "the circumstances of toleration," see Mendus, *Toleration*, 8-9.

[131] Justin Martyr, *Apology*, I, 24 (http://www.earlychristianwritings.com/text/justinmartyr-firstapology.html).

them "to death as sinners" even though they "do no wrong."[132] Being religiously different, Justin Martyr argued, is no ground for intolerance.

Justin Martyr's and Tertullian's stances are what we would expect: the weak and marginal preach tolerance to the strong and dominant who oppress them. First Peter is different. This text does not address the strong and dominant at all. It demands nothing of others, but much of the Christian communities themselves. Instead of insisting that the persecuting non-Christians tolerate Christians, it commands the persecuted Christians to honor non-Christians!

If we focus on the regime of intolerance under which Christians were suffering, such a command makes little sense and might imply internalized oppression and servility. It seems strangely misdirected—addressed to those who suffer intolerance rather than directed against social arrangements that foster intolerance and the individuals who perpetrate it. But if we shift attention to the mindset of intolerance,[133] then the command that they honor everyone makes sense, and a more profound sense than would their legitimate demand to be tolerated. For intolerance suffered engenders intolerance perpetrated. Intolerance suffered seeks to infect the mind of the persecuted, as I know from firsthand experience and as studies in social psychology attest.

The command to honor everyone blocks you from perpetrating the kind of intolerance you yourself are forced to endure. Even more, it impresses on you that respecting a person is not a matter of the reciprocal exchange of equivalents: I'll respect you if you respect me, and I'll respect you to the extent that you respect me. Instead, respecting a person is a matter of a moral stance, an unconditional imperative:[134] I'll respect you whether you respect me or not. The command is not, "Honor, if you are honored!" or "Honor, if you want to be honored!" The command is, "Honor, period." The hope is, of course, that others will do the same and that the respect will be mutual. But that outcome is neither the reason nor condition of my honoring.

As a moral stance and a command of the one God of all people, the injunction to honor everyone has universal validity. It's not simply what Christians ought to do; it's what everyone ought to do. And so the command issued to weak and persecuted Christian communities is, implicitly, a demand—a moral demand—binding on their abusers as well: They, too, ought to honor everyone, including Christians. The text has planted a seed from which the explicit demand for tolerance will sprout. It has also countered a prevalent tendency of victims of intolerance (a tendency to which the ancient

---

[132] Justin Martyr, *Apology*, I, 24.

[133] For the distinction between "regimes of intolerance" and the "mindset of intolerance" see Michael Walzer, *On Toleration* (New Haven: Yale University Press, 1997), 8-13.

[134] Socrates was famous for having advocated the unconditional validity of moral commands: when injured, we should not "injure in return, as many imagine; for we must injure no one at all," it being the case that "injustice is always an evil" (Plato, *Crito* 49b).

Christians themselves will succumb after Christianity has been established as the religion of the empire): the weak issue demands to the strong but conveniently forget those demands when they themselves achieve a position of power.[135] "Honor everyone" is valid for all, the marginal and not just the dominant, and maybe especially for the marginal once they have become the dominant.

### *Honor, not Tolerate!*

The command is to honor or respect, not merely to tolerate. I write, "merely to tolerate," well knowing that for many even mere tolerance would mean life rather than death, or at least a sheltered space to be oneself without exclusion and abuse. So it was for me growing up as a minister's kid in a country ruled by communists committed to atheism as a social good. "You tall one! Get out of the classroom, and never show up again with that thing around your neck!" This was my biology teacher bellowing. She disliked the cross I was wearing. A fierce atheist, she could not abide the display of religious symbols in the classroom. I would have been grateful for mere tolerance—a resigned acceptance that a student deluded enough to commit himself openly to a religious faith has a right to learn biology in a public school. Respect would have been too much to ask for.

Tolerance may be our best hope in some situations, but there is still something mere about it. "To tolerate someone else is an act of power," writes Michael Walzer in *On Toleration*. He continues: "to be tolerated is an acceptance of weakness."[136] Moreover, toleration can go hand in hand with a stance of affective and moral exclusion. After the communist regime has been toppled, I can commit myself to tolerate old-style Marxist teachers intolerant of me and my faith while projecting utter disdain and disgust every time I encounter them or speak of them.

No such power dynamic is implied in "honoring," at least not in the way 1 Peter employs the term, and, obviously, disdain is excluded. I can honor my superiors ("the emperor" [2:17], in the monarchical political order of 1 Peter), I can honor my subordinates ("wives" [3:7], in the patriarchal cultural setting of 1 Peter), and I can honor my equals (the majority included in "everyone"). The outsiders, all of them, writes one commentator, "are not to be despised because

---

[135] John Locke commented on the tendency for persecution and tolerance to become a function of relative power: "Where they have not the power to carry on persecution and to become master, there they desire to live upon fair terms and preach toleration" (Locke, *A Letter*, 217).

[136] Walzer, *On Toleration*, 52. He references Stephan Carter's claim that "the language of tolerance is the language of power" (*The Culture of Disbelief* [New York: Basic Books, 1993], 96).

they are not believers, nor hated because they are persecutors, nor treated with contempt because they are of lower rank or status, but treated with honor."[137]

But in what does honoring a person, every person, consist? First Peter is silent on the matter. The text implies that honor is due to people on account of their social station ("the king," "wives"), as well as that honor is due to all ("everyone"), presumably on account of their humanity. But what precisely is the honoring due to all? We won't go wrong if we assume that to honor persons as human beings (as distinct from honoring them for status or achievement) means to treat them as beings created and loved by God. Since they are created by God, we need to refrain from violating their integrity as human beings; since they are loved by God, we need to help nurture their capacities and powers.[138]

One way to articulate a Christian account of respect is to compare it with that of Immanuel Kant, a German philosopher pivotal in developing the Western concept of respect. He famously distinguished between "respect" and "love." To "respect" means not to debase a person as a mere means to one's own subjective ends; to "love" means to make the ends of another person my own ends.[139] Understood Christianly, in honoring or respecting people we, in a sense, combine Kant's respecting and loving without completely identifying them: We don't treat people as a means to our own ends, and we do seek to further other people's ability to pursue their own ends. Respect, then, is a mode of love. That's different from tolerance, though not less than tolerance.

### *Honor, Even While Disapproving!*

Tolerance, it is sometimes said, is close to blithe indifference, even casual acceptance. Respect, it is claimed, is virtually identical with full approval, even strong endorsement. If that were true, 1 Peter would be a text of intolerance and disrespect. A note of strong disapproval runs through it—disapproval not only of the abuse Christian communities were suffering, but also of the outsiders' very way of life. True, 1 Peter does not establish the difference between insiders and outsiders primarily by rejecting what is outside, but rather by affirming the communities' core convictions. "Soft difference" is what I have called this stance elsewhere.[140] Still, the text draws bold boundary lines between Christian and non-Christian ways of living, and does so in religious

---

[137] I. Howard Marshall, *I Peter* (Downers Grove: InterVarsity, 1991), 85. See also Leonard Goppelt, *A Commentary on 1 Peter* (trans. John E. Alsup; Grand Rapids: Eerdmans, 1993), 190 and Joel B. Green, *I Peter* (Grand Rapids: Eerdmans, 2007), 76.

[138] I draw here on David Kelsey, *Eccentric Existence: A Theological Anthropology* (Louisville, KY: Westminster John Knox, 2009), 279-80.

[139] See Immanuel Kant, *The Metaphysics of Morals* (ed. Mary Gregor; Cambridge: Cambridge University Press, 1996), 155-56 [6:393-4]. On respect in Kant, see Gene Outka, "Respect for Persons," in *Westminster Dictionary of Christian Ethics,* ed. James F. Childress and John MacQuarrie (Philadelphia: Westminster, 1986), 540-45.

[140] On the difference between insiders' and outsiders' being "soft" in 1 Peter, see Volf, *Captive to the Word of God,* 65-90.

and moral terms. Is that very act of critical demarcation a mode of intolerance and disrespect?

It is not. If we were unable to tolerate and respect notwithstanding disapproval, the consequences would be grave. Here is what follows from two premises I believe are uncontested.

Premise One: Differences in ways of life among religions and secular worldviews run deep and stubbornly persist; chances of erasing them are slim.

Premise Two: People consistently (and rightly) refuse to accept what they find unacceptable.

Conclusion: If acceptance were required for tolerance, the pervasive mindset of intolerance would persist as well.

Consequence: To prevent the world from sinking into intractable conflicts, we would need to counter pervasive mindsets of intolerance with regimes of intolerance. Some form of totalitarianism is the inevitable consequence of the inability to tolerate while disapproving.

Summary: If tolerance means acceptance, intolerance rules.

As it turns out, the idea of tolerating despite disapproving is built into the very logic of tolerance. Tolerance would undo itself if it were incompatible with disapproval. For, by definition, tolerance is needed in situations of disapproval, when we judge a person or a group to be morally wrong.[141] Take disapproval away, and tolerance disappears as well because there is nothing to tolerate.

It is similar with respect. What would happen if, out of respect for someone whose views or behavior I disapprove, I changed my opinion? Respect would turn into a condescending lie and cancel itself out. For I cannot change my considered opinions at will.[142] Respect requires judgment rendered truthfully, whether that judgment is positive or negative. Commitment to truthfulness—and therefore to standing by one's considered negative judgment—is a condition of the possibility of both tolerance and respect.

### *Honor, and Call It as You See It!*

"Every man has commission to admonish, exhort, convince another of error, and, by reasoning draw him to truth," wrote Locke in *A Letter Concerning Toleration*.[143] He did not dwell much on how to respect people as one draws them to truth. It sufficed for him to note: "it is one thing to persuade, another to

---

[141] What is sometimes called "the paradox of toleration" involves explaining "how the tolerator might think it good to tolerate that which is morally wrong" (Mendus, *Toleration*, 20).

[142] See on this point (in the context of the discussion of the equal worth of diverse cultures), Charles Taylor, "The Politics of Recognition," in *Multiculturalism and the Politics of Recognition* (ed. Amy Gutmann; Princeton: Princeton University Press, 1994), 68-72.

[143] Locke, *A Letter*, 219.

command; one thing to press with arguments, another with penalties."[144] His topic was tolerance. If you persuade and press with arguments, you tolerate; if you command and press with penalties, you don't. But 1 Peter calls for respect, not mere tolerance. How then do you engage respectfully those with whom you disagree, those whose views you disapprove of?

In describing how Christians should commend their way of life to non-Christians—how they should give "an accounting for the hope" they have—1 Peter uses two nouns: "gentleness" and "respect" (3:15-16).[145] Gentleness is a servant of respect. A gentle person foregoes aggressiveness, open or hidden, and grants others time to come to their own judgment. When truth is at stake, respecting others requires more than simply not violating the integrity of their search for truth. Respecting them means (1) we don't distort them. Instead, we take pains to get to know them accurately, also including how they understand and experience themselves and how they understand and experience us.[146] Respecting them means (2) we treat them as possible sources of insight, not merely as "beneficiaries" of our instruction. Facing them, we are aware of our likely lack of understanding and remain open for a surprise in regard to who they are and what insights their convictions may contain.[147]

Friedrich Nietzsche's philosophy is as far from the way of Jesus Christ as Dionysus, god of libidinal revelry, is from the Crucified, the God of sacrificial love.[148] When I taught a course on "Nietzsche for Theologians" at an evangelical institution, I laid down a rule: In the class we were not allowed to tear down Nietzsche's philosophy but only to discuss what's right about it. Most students were predisposed to think that Nietzsche was utterly wrong, and the rule was designed to help them learn from him; if they attacked too soon, they would close themselves off from his insights.

But the rule was not merely a pedagogical tool. Its goal was also to facilitate respect. I granted from the start that Christians find much to disagree with in Nietzsche's philosophy. For instance, I myself disagreed even with his setting libidinal revelry in complete opposition to sacrificial love, let alone with his

---

[144] Locke, *A Letter*, 219.

[145] The word for "respect" is literally "fear." Scholars debate whether it refers to reverence for God (so Goppelt, *1 Peter*, 237 [German edition]) or to the respect for people (so Norbert Brox, *Der erste Petrusbrief* [Zürich/Neukirchen-Vluyn: Benzinger/Neukirchener, 1979], 160). The use of "fear" elsewhere in the epistle suggests reverence for God (1:17; 2:18; 3:2), but the present context favors respect for people.

[146] On this section, see on combating prejudice in Volf, *Allah*, 203-7.

[147] On this point, see the reflections on "Evangelism" in Volf, *Allah* (207-13) and on witness in Volf, *A Public Faith* (chapter 6).

[148] The last line of Nietzsche's autobiography, *Ecce Homo* (an allusion to Pilate's words of Christ at the end of John's Gospel) reads, "Have I been understood? – *Dionysus against the Crucified*..." (Friedrich Nietzsche, *Ecce Homo: How One Becomes What One Is* [trans. R. H. Hollingdale; London: Penguin, 1992], 104).

celebration of "hard" power[149] and his unqualified denial of God.[150] But disagreeing with persons, even arguing with them strenuously, is not a form of disrespect; treating them from the start as either benign simpletons or sly purveyors of error from whom no insight can come is a form of disrespect. Notwithstanding his heavy-handed, anti-Christian polemics—especially in his late book, *The Anti-Christ*[151]—Nietzsche deserves respect, including the respect of treating him as a potential source of insight.[152]

And so does everyone else.

## Everyone

Everyone? Really everyone? Even those who, unlike Nietzsche at the height of his powers, cannot formulate a single, half-baked thought? Even those who, very much unlike Christ, crucify others on the cross of the crucifiers' own utter selfishness?

### *Indiscriminate Respect*

After Jared Lee Loughner shot at point-blank range U.S. Representative Gabrielle Giffords, killed six people, and wounded nineteen, I posted on my Facebook wall: "1 Peter says: 'Honor everyone.' 'Honor'—not merely 'don't demean' or 'tolerate,' but honor. And 'everyone'—not only 'those in our political camp' or 'with our moral persuasions,' but everyone." I meant the comment as a reminder that in a polarized and vociferous political and cultural climate we ought to respect our opponents. To me, the shooting was a warning, an enactment of the inhumane depth to which we may sink if we fail to sustain a culture of respect even for those with whom we profoundly disagree.

One of my Facebook friends pushed the comment to its conclusion. He asked: "Does this also mean: 'honor' the shooter?" "Yes, honor the shooter as well," I responded without flinching. "We should honor all folks whom God loves and for whom Christ died, and who, whatever else they are, are neighbors we are commanded to love as we love ourselves." The reach of God's love is the scope of our respect. As the first is universal, the second must be as well. Just as God's love is utterly indiscriminate, is embracing of people of all colors,

---

[149] See Friedrich Nietzsche, *Thus Spoke Zarathustra* (eds. Adrian Del Caro and Robert Pippin; Cambridge: Cambridge University Press, 2006), 172.

[150] See Friedrich Nietzsche, *The Gay Science* (trans. Walter Kaufmann; New York: Vintage, 1974), Nos. 108, 125, 343.

[151] Friedrich Nietzsche, *Twilight of Idols/The Anti-Christ* (trans. R. J. Hollingdale; London: Penguin, 1990).

[152] Shortly after he completed *The Anti-Christ*, Nietzsche fell into permanent insanity. In that state also, he deserved respect. But of course at that point, by definition he ceased to be a potential source of insight; and treating him as a potential source of insight *then* would have, in a condescending sort of way, been to disrespect him as a person.

creeds, and credentials, whether they are the most admirable saints or the most deplorable evildoers, so also our respect should be indiscriminate.

This seems a radical stance—and from one angle it is. We should respect absolutely everyone on account of nothing else but the mere reality of their humanity! When it comes to respect, the only relevant question is: "Is this a human being?" If the answer is, "Yes," respect is due.[153] From another angle, the idea that we should respect everyone seems almost trite. It is so much a self-evident truth in contemporary modern culture that it feels more like a tacit cultural-background assumption—more like the cultural air we breathe—rather than an explicit moral conviction. But when a killer puts a bullet through the head of a citizen who belongs to a different political party, embraces a different religion, or lives by a different moral code, we realize how fragile that assumption is. Why should we respect the killer? How can we respect him? Even more radically, how can we claim that the worst human being has the same dignity and demands the same respect as the noblest one?[154] For this is what the belief in equal dignity entails.

## *Person and Work*

Christian theologians distinguish between "persons" and their "deeds," or between "person" and "work." We ought to respect all persons, but not necessarily all their deeds; some of their convictions, actions, or practices may deserve the very opposite of respect. But they themselves still deserve undiminished respect.

Advocates of the "politics of equal dignity" make a similar distinction. Immanuel Kant, who gave the idea of human dignity its "most impressive and systematic expression,"[155] is a good example. All human beings have equal dignity and therefore deserve equal respect because they are all capable of directing their lives guided by rational principles. He did not mean that they have dignity because they actually make rational choices. Instead, they have it because of their capacity for doing so. "This potential," writes Charles Taylor explicating Kant, "rather than anything a person may have made of it, is what ensures that each person deserves respect."[156] With regard to the capacity for rational action ("person," in my sense), devils and deacons, the vicious and the virtuous have equal dignity and deserve equal respect. With regard to the exercise of this capacity ("work," in my sense), they don't deserve equal

---

[153] A form of respect can be due also to beings other than humans. But I am here referring to the particular kind of respect due to human beings.

[154] Explicating Kant's position on human dignity, Allen Wood writes: "... the worst human being (in any respect you can possibly name) has the same dignity or absolute worth as the best rational being in that respect (or any other)" (*Kant's Ethical Thought* [Cambridge: Cambridge University Press, 1999], 132).

[155] Steven Lukes, *Individualism* (Oxford: Blackwell, 1973), 45.

[156] Taylor, "The Politics of Recognition," 41.

respect; I must not respect a vicious man as a moral agent though I continue to respect him as a human being.

Many people feel that there is something artificial and strained—something "academic" and "philosophical," in a derogatory sense—about the distinction between person and work. Persons are responsible for their deeds. Deeds—especially misdeeds—are not like water that slides off a duck's back without leaving a trace; instead, they "stick" to the doers and qualify their identities. Equally significantly, deeds shape the character of doers; repeated deeds create habits, and habits form character.

With some such reasons, a friend of mine resolutely resisted the idea of respecting the "shooter." She could not see how Mr. Loughner's deed could rightly elicit our disgust and merit utter condemnation, while Mr. Loughner as a person would deserve respect. His deed, she sensed, somehow is his person. A noble or successful person could be respected; respect for her moral or professional achievement redounds to her, and we respect the person on account of her achievements. Correspondingly, it would seem, we should despise an ignoble person on account of her despicable deeds; a person who commits evil deeds is an evildoer (even if it is true that she is also more than merely an evildoer).

Though the distinction between person and work sits uneasily with us, most of us in fact make it, and we do so in the case of those we love. In Shakespeare's *Measure for Measure*, Isabella pleads before the judge for the life of Claudio, her brother, by urging the judge to condemn Claudio's fault but not Claudio himself.[157] She wants clemency, and to grant it is to separate the doer from the deed, the person from the work. Similarly, all those who want to be truly loved make the distinction as well. When my older son was three, he expected (and told me so in unmistakable terms) that I would love him even if he were to become a donkey, let alone if he misbehaved! Love is love, he insisted rightly, and if the father loves, he will love irrespective of what the son does. My son separated the doer from the deed.

This basic insight about the nature of love lies at the heart of the general distinction in Christian theology between "person"—any person—and his "work." Martin Luther, a fierce German Protestant reformer, believed that it would be unworthy of God to love us because of our noble deeds or fail to love us because of our dastardly ones. God loves and therefore creates human beings; and God loves created human beings just because they exist. At the same time, just because God loves each human being unconditionally, God

---

[157] William Shakespeare, *Measure for Measure*, in *Riverside Shakespeare* (ed. G. Blakemore Evans; Boston: Houghton Mifflin, 1974), 560.

cannot love that which harms human beings. Hence God condemns sin, and does so on account of love for all human beings, saints and sinners alike.[158]

That God's love grounds the distinction between person and work makes it possible for Christians to respect everyone without thereby committing themselves to respecting everything. Without belief in the God who loves, is it plausible on purely secular grounds to distinguish between person and work and therefore to prescribe respect for everyone, no matter how evil their deeds? Maybe. But either way, this distinction is one important way in which the Christian faith underwrites respect for everyone. While condemning Mr. Loughner's deed, we ought to respect him as a person. We should abstain from violating his integrity as a human being and seek to nurture his capacities and powers.[159]

### Respecting What We Disagree With?

I respect a person on account of her humanity, but I respect her work on account of its excellence. Or, to put it with reference to myself as a recipient rather than as a giver of respect: I can simply claim respect for my self, but I must earn respect for my work. Clearly I, as an imperfect human being, cannot expect respect for everything that I believe or do, especially not in a world of pervasive differences in convictions and values; and I cannot give respect for everything another flawed person believes or does. So we seem to have arrived at a "rule of respect" analogous to the well known though disputed "rule of love": "Love the sinner, but hate the sin!"[160] The "rule of respect" is then, "Respect the person, but do not respect his mistaken convictions or misguided behavior!"

Might it be possible, however, to respect not just the person whose convictions we reject, but, in some cases, these mistaken convictions themselves? Cases in which respect for convictions is inappropriate are easy to find. If Mr. Loughner thought that his shooting rampage was justified, we could hardly respect his "moral stance"! Similarly, most of us agree that we ought to despise rather than respect the views of those who, like the Gaddafi regime in February 2011, believe that it is justifiable to shoot and bomb peaceful demonstrators. So it is with many moral stances of which we highly

---

[158] On the distinction between person and work in Luther, see Gerhard Ebeling, *Luther: An Introduction to His Thought* (trans. R. A. Wilson; Philadelphia: Fortress, 1970), 148-58.

[159] Clearly, respect in my sense of the term is compatible with punishing the offender. Indeed, under certain circumstances, punishment may be a way to respect the person as the doer of a morally abhorrent deed.

[160] Some object to the rule, but most who do so merely dispute that a given act for which respect is withheld is sinful rather than rejecting the rule itself. When there is agreement that the behavior in question is sinful or evil, most Christians at least accept the rule.

disapprove—we judge the character of the deed as evil, and we withdraw respect.

Should we do the same with overarching interpretations of life that markedly differ from ours? The issue is acute in relations between religions, especially when monotheists are involved.[161] To believe in one God is to affirm a single religious truth, and therefore to reject all other religions as at least in some significant way false.[162] If we apply the "person-work" distinction to the world of monotheist religions, it seems that a monotheist would respect all adherents of other religions, but not these religions themselves, since he would consider them significantly mistaken. We could then believe, as some Christians do, that Muhammad was demonically inspired and that Islam is an evil religion, while still respecting individual Muslims. Not surprisingly, most Muslims don't feel that such Christians respect them even when those Christians are committed to tolerating Muslims. Neither do Christians when the roles are reversed. For religious beliefs are ultimate; they are the most basic convictions a person can hold. Most people crave being respected not just for their bare humanity, but also in the basic orientation of their being.

There is no compelling reason why monotheists must withdraw respect from religions with which they disagree. In fact, it is likely that it would be a mistake not to respect these religions. Recall my earlier discussion of teaching Nietzsche, a thinker whose overarching interpretation of reality is, from a Christian standpoint, markedly more mistaken than a religion such as Islam. I asked my students—with the help of a rule!—to respect Nietzsche by treating him as a potential source of insight. But long before teaching that class, I myself came actually to respect his work. His philosophy was imaginative, his thinking stringent, his writing rhetorically powerful, some of his insights deep, and his overall position seductively compelling—all extraordinary achievements demanding respect. For a while, one of his books was on my nightstand; I was reading him before turning off the light, as a spiritual exercise of sorts.

I respect Nietzsche's thought, not just Nietzsche as a person, and I do so while continuing to embrace, happily and fully, all the major Christian convictions that Nietzsche set out to annihilate! I respect in a similar way the

---

[161] I make an assumption for which I am unable to argue here: all religions are not fundamentally the same. In this I differ from many contemporaries, scholars and laypeople alike, who unthinkingly embrace the idea of the basic sameness of all major religions, so that the choice between them is a matter of an accident of birth or of a preference for a certain way of life, but not a matter of truth. In contrast, I believe that religions, among the other things they do, make claims to truth, and that these claims sometimes overlap among religions (as when both Jews and Muslims say that they believe in one God), but sometimes also contradict one another (as when Christians claim that Jesus Christ was God incarnate and Muslims claim that he was a special prophet).

[162] For a discussion of this issue, see Volf, *Allah*, 221-24.

interpretations of reality put forward by Socrates, Buddha, and Muhammad—all seminal visionaries who advocated less radical alternatives to the Christian faith than did Nietzsche. My conviction that God is one, that truth is one, and that religions make truth claims in no way hinders me from respecting either the philosophies of Nietzsche and Buddha (who did not believe in God) or the thought of Socrates and Muhammad (who believed in God, though each in his own way and both somewhat differently from the way I do).

I implied that the attitude toward the visions of the founders of religions (Buddha, Muhammad) should be similar to the attitude toward the thought of major philosophers (Nietzsche, Socrates). Is the comparison between the two—founders of religions and philosophers—fair, however? It is.

How did I come to respect Nietzsche's work? The process had three elements: openness, presumption, and judgment. First, I was open to Nietzsche as a source of insight—a consequence of respecting him as a person, as I have argued earlier. Second, I was nudged to take him seriously by having a presumption that Nietzsche's work in fact does contain important insights—a presumption I adopted because he is considered a major thinker in the Western intellectual tradition. Finally, I studied his writings and formed a judgment that his thought warrants respect, even though I profoundly disagree with him.

I suggest that we come to respect (or not to respect) the vision of a founder of a religion in a similar way: we assume a stance of openness to insights, we grant the presumption of worth, and we make a judgment that either results in respect or does not. With regard to the presumption of worth, Charles Taylor writes:

> It is reasonable to suppose that cultures [and religions] that have provided the horizon of meaning for large numbers of human beings, of diverse characters and temperaments, over a long period of time—that have, in other words, articulated their sense of the good, the holy, the admirable—are almost certain to have something that deserves our admiration and respect, even if it is accompanied by much that we have to abhor and reject ... it would take a supreme arrogance to discount this possibility a priori.[163]

Just because so many diverse people have found different world religions compelling, we should presume that they deserve respect. Now, presumption is not yet a considered judgment that respect is in fact due. But such a judgment is, I believe, likely to follow.

What if a person's considered judgment does not result in respect for other religions, however? For instance, the person finds the treatment of women in a particular religion deplorable, and she cannot respect a religion that abuses women so egregiously. If that conclusion were an informed and considered judgment rather than a merely negative reaction, she would find herself back to

---

[163] Taylor, "The Politics of Recognition," 72-73.

respecting persons—all persons—without respecting their beliefs or practices. She would be acting no differently from robust atheists, committed to equal dignity and respect for all—from those who respect people who hold what they consider to be archaic and dangerous beliefs that merit only ridicule and reprimand.

In sum:

Respect for all people? That's an unconditional moral obligation!

Respect for world religions? That's a likely result of a considered judgment, notwithstanding deep disagreements!

The Christian faith, with its belief in the one God of love, demands the first attitude and is compatible with the second. When it comes to respect, that's the upside of embracing the Christian faith.

There is more to the upside. To examine it, I return to the respect for persons as distinct from their views and inquire about the spaciousness of the "circle of respect."

## *God, Dignity, and Respect*

Absent the God of love, I wondered previously whether we would have sufficient grounds to respect those whose deeds we seriously condemn— evildoers. Absent the God of love, there is a category of people who would most certainly fall out of the circle of respect.

Once again, recall Kant on dignity and respect (respect being the appropriate response to a person's dignity). He grounded human dignity on a particular capacity of human beings: their ability to set ends and direct their lives through reason. For Kant this capacity, and nothing else, gives human beings dignity.[164] Like Kant's, secular accounts of human dignity and respect are all built on a foundation of some human capacity. But what about human beings who are incapable of rationally directing their lives? Taylor describes what we tend to do in such cases:

> Our sense of the importance of potentiality reaches so far that we extend this protection [i.e. the claim that they have dignity and deserve respect] even to people who through some circumstance that has befallen them are incapable of realizing their potential in the normal way—handicapped people, or those in a coma, for instance.[165]

This is what we tend to do. But can we adequately justify such expansion of the "circle of dignity"?[166] What if someone were to argue, adhering to Kant strictly, that a person with Alzheimer's disease (or an infant) does not have dignity since she lacks the capacity of directing her life rationally? She then

---

[164] See Wood, *Kant's Ethical Thought*, 132-33.

[165] Taylor, "The Politics of Recognition," 41-42.

[166] For the phrase see Nicholas Wolterstorff, *Justice: Rights and Wrongs* (Princeton: Princeton University Press, 2008), 333.

would not deserve respect. If you ground human dignity in a capacity, those with the relevant capacity will deserve respect and those without it will not. You can affirm equal respect for those who have the capacity, but not equal respect for everyone. No capacity of human beings can ground universal human dignity. Absent God, some human beings inevitably fall out of "the circle of respect."

What difference does God make? If God created all human beings and loves each one of them, then all human beings—all those who have been born of a human being[167]—have dignity and deserve respect. God's relation to them as the Creator who loves them, not any of their capacities, grounds their dignity.[168] Affirmation of the existence of the one God of all people, critics argue, leads inevitably to intolerance. Affirmation of the existence of the one Creator who loves each human being, I contend, is not only compatible with universal respect but provides the only compelling reason for such respect.

## The Prize for Intolerance

Which religion gets the intolerance prize? In a sense, this essay does not help answer this broad question. First, I have written here only about the Christian faith, and exclusively about authentically Christian convictions, rather than about actual practices of flesh-and-blood Christians. Second, I have made no comparative judgments, no claims regarding either the superiority or inferiority of Christianity with regard to tolerance and respect. In its march through history, has Christianity been more or less intolerant than other religions (and secular philosophies of life), as some have argued?[169] I don't know what the answer is. I don't even know how I would go about finding the answer, what the proper method of assessing the relative intolerance of various religions might be. I would never accept the dubious honor of sitting on a jury deciding the prizewinner.

But I did try to answer a related and more important question: Is the Christian faith itself intolerant, or are intolerant Christians bastardizing their own religion? I have argued, negatively, that the practice of intolerance and disrespect strains against fundamental Christian convictions and violates an

---

[167] German theologian Dietrich Bonhoeffer, who worked in the time of Nazi disregard for human life (especially damaged human life), suggested this "definition" of a human being. He writes: "The question of whether life, in the case of persons severely retarded from birth, is really *human* life at all is so naïve that it hardly needs to be answered. It is disabled life, born of human parents, which can be nothing else than *human life*" (*Ethics,* vol. 6 of *Dietrich Bonhoeffer Works* [ed. Clifford J. Green; Minneapolis: Fortress, 2005], 195).

[168] In different ways both Wolterstorff (*Justice,* 323-61) and Kelsey (*Eccentric Existence,* 276-9) make that argument.

[169] See Naveed Sheikh, *Body Count: A Quantitative Review of Political Violence across World Civilizations* (Amman: The Royal Islamic Strategic Studies Centre, 2009).

explicit Christian command. I have argued, positively, that the Christian faith offers significant resources to foster a culture of universal respect. This culture, I believe, is what we need in today's intermingled and interdependent world, all awhirl with rapid change and alive with vibrant and assertive religions.

# Bibliography

Assmann, Jan. *Die Mosaische Unterscheidung, Oder der Preis des* Assmann, Jan. *Moses the Egyptian: The Memory of Egypt in Western Monotheism.* Cambridge, MA: Harvard University Press, 1997.

Bourdieu, Pierre. *Firing Back: Against the Tyranny of the Market 2.* London: Verso, 2003.

_____. *Pascalian Meditations.* Stanford: Stanford University Press, 2000.

Bowling, John R. "Tolerance Among the Fathers." *Journal of the Society of Christian Ethics* 26, no. 1 (2006): 27.

Carter, Stephen L. *Culture of Disbelief: How American Laws and Politics Trivialize Religious Devotion.* New York: Basic Books, 1993.

Ebeling, Gerhard. *Luther: An Introduction to His Thought.* Translated by R.A. Wilson. Philadelphia: Fortress Press, 1970.

Goppelt, Leonard. *A Commentary on 1 Peter.* Translated by John E. Alsup. Grand Rapids: Eerdmans, 1993.

Green, Joel B. *1 Peter.* Grand Rapids: Eerdmans, 2007.

Kant, Immanuel. *The Metaphysics of Morals.* ed. Mary Gregor. Cambridge: Cambridge University Press, 1996.

Kelsey, David. *Eccentric Existence: A Theological Anthropology.* 2 vols. Louisville: Westminster John Knox, 2009.

Lindbeck, George. *The Nature of Doctrine: Religion and Theology in a Postliberal Age.* Louisville: Westminster John Knox, 1984.

Locke, John. "A Letter Concerning Toleration." In *Two Treatises of Government and a Letter Concerning Toleration*, edited by Ian Shapiro. New Haven: Yale University Press, 2003.

Lukes, Steven. *Individualism.* Oxford: Blackwell, 1973.

Macpherson, C. B. *The Political Theory of Possessive Individualism: Hobbes to Locke.* Oxford: University Press, 1962.

Marshall, I. Howard. *I Peter (Tyndale New Testament Commentaries)*. Downers Grove: InterVarsity, 1991.

Mendus, Susan. *Toleration and the Limits of Liberalism*. Atlantic Highlands, NJ: Humanities Press International, 1989.

Naveed, Sheikh. *Body Count: A Quantitative Review of Political Violence across World Civilizations*. Amman: The Royal Islamic Strategic Studies Centre, 2009.

Nietzsche, Friedrich. *Ecce Homo: How One Becomes What One Is*. trans. R. H. Hollingdale; London: Penguin, 1992.

———. *The Gay Science*. Translated by Walter Kaufmann; New York: Vintage, 1974.

———. *Thus Spoke Zarathustra*, edited by Adrian Del Caro and Robert Pippin. Cambridge: Cambridge University Press, 2006.

———. *Twilight of Idols/The Anti-Christ*. Translated by R. J. Hollingdale. London: Penguin, 1990.

Outka, Gene. "Respect for Persons." In *Westminster Dictionary of Christian Ethics*, edited by James F. Childress and John MacQuarrie. Louisville: Westminster John Knox, 1986

Riley-Smith, Jonathan. "Crusading as an Act of Love." In *Medieval Religion: New Approaches*, edited by Constance H. Berman. New York: Routledge, 2005.

Taylor, Charles. "The Politics of Recognition." In *Multiculturalism and the Politics of Recognition*, edited by Amy Gutmann. Princeton: Princeton University Press, 1994.

Volf, Miroslav. *Allah: A Christian Response*. San Francisco: HarperOne, 2011.

———. *A Public Faith: How Followers of Christ Should Serve the Common Good*. Grand Rapids: Brazos, 2011.

———. *Captive to the Word of God: Engaging the Scriptures for Contemporary Theological Reflection*. Grand Rapids: Eerdmans, 2010.

———. *Exclusion and Embrace: Theological Exploration of Identity, Otherness, and Reconciliation*. Nashville: Abingdon Press, 1996.

———. *Free of Charge: Giving and Forgiving in a Culture Stripped of Grace*. Grand Rapids: Zondervan, 2006.

———. *The End of Memory*. Grand Rapids: Eerdmans, 2006.

Wolterstorff, Nicholas. *Justice: Rights and Wrongs*. Princeton: Princeton University Press, 2008.

# Paul's Legacy of Cooperation for Twenty-First Century Missiology and Missions Practice

Daniel K. Darko

Modern trends in Christian missions show a rapid increase in success among indigenous churches and presents increasing challenges to the role of Western missionaries in the global south. Traditionally, missionaries came from the rich West with better resources to serve in underdeveloped nations where the good news was unknown. Today, a majority of the world's two billion Christians do not reside in or come from Western countries. Amidst all this, some imperialist attitudes or tendencies in matters of doctrine and praxis among some missionaries have rather evoked colonial or anti-Western sentiments on the mission field. However, one cannot deny the shared commitment and compassion of both the West and South to reach the unreached. If the Kingdom of God would go forward to make a real difference in our hurting world, then some reflection is needed regarding the cooperation of the Christian workers of developed and underdeveloped worlds to keep the flame of missions unquenched.

The scope of this essay does not extend to every aspect of Paul's mission[170] but focuses on the challenges facing the Church in the area of partnership between the West and South and what Paul has to teach us about cooperation in the mission of God. I hope to explore Paul's self-understanding and attitude towards others and missions as a suitable model for 21st-century missions. I will make (a) some observations from the perspective of an African who served in Europe and currently presides over the missions program of a local church in the United States and (b) offer a brief account of some noteworthy legacies of Paul on this subject matter. The conclusion will put forward some proposals in light of aspects of the Pauline legacies under consideration. I will reflect on some questions that are often raised among senders and host nations such as,

---

[170] These authors provide elaborate discussion on Paul's mission and ministry, sometimes with significant difference in emphasis: L. J. Lietaert Peerbolte, *Paul the Missionary* (Leuven: Peeters, 2003); Christopher R. Little, *Mission in the Way of Paul: Biblical Mission for the Church in the Twenty-First Century* (NY: Peter Lang, 2005); Gerd Lüdemann, *Paul: The Founder of Christianity* (Amherst, NY: Prometheus, 2002); Eckhard J. Schnabel, *Early Christian Mission: Paul & the Early Church* (vol. 2; Downers Grove: InterVarsity, 2004).

what do Western missionaries have to contribute when church growth under indigenous leadership far exceeds what they find in the sending churches? Do indigenous churches need Western partners in ensuring sustainable growth in Christian formation and leadership development? In what ways has economic development garnered courage and conflict in the partnership? What is the way forward for partnership in global missions?

Paul was the missionary par excellence and authored about half of the New Testament. His ministry was fashioned around the Kingdom of God (Eph. 5:5) and the lordship of Christ. Since Jesus did not start or run a local church, the models we have for church growth and praxis have come mainly from pioneer missionaries like Paul. Over half of Luke's account on the formation of the Early Church in Acts is devoted to Paul's missionary endeavors. Arguably, there is no better model for cooperation in missions than that modeled by Paul of Tarsus. Undoubtedly, the trends in modern missions and the need for pragmatic overtures for cooperation between the West and South is more exigent now than at any other time.

## Changing Trends in World Missions

In this section I will cursorily present four well-known but often unstated challenges to the work of Christ—the one who reconciles the world to himself and charges the Church with a ministry of reconciliation.

### *More Christians in the Global South—So Who Has What to Offer Whom?*

Church growth in the second half of the last century in Asia, Africa, and Latin America has left an indelible mark on how we view world missions. It is no longer true to find Western missionaries going to remote areas where the gospel is unknown, to study languages, evangelize the unreached, and plant churches. This generalization, however, excludes dedicated Bible translators, such as Wycliffe translators, some of whom I have met in remote places under conditions that even native Africans like me would find unbearable. My observation is that the contribution of the West is changing to that of a supporting role and leadership development, while indigenous leaders step into the frontiers of evangelism and church planting. The need for foreign missionaries and their skill sets is hardly disputable, whether in Africa, Latin America, or Asia. However, the prevailing clash of wills and power struggles are being counterproductive in the quest "to make disciples of all nations."

It seems that the greatest threat for cooperation resides in the pursuit of personal interests and perceptions emerging from the ugly shadows of colonialism. This misplaced emphasis undercuts and undermines the true vision of the Kingdom of God and ostracizes invaluable partners in the process. The task is not only preaching and leading crowds of people into the church but also making disciples of the converts. For numerical growth to match spiritual growth, all gifted partners ought to recognize their place and appreciate what each brings into effective missionary undertakings. Here, Paul's example is worth emulating as we shall see below.

*The Clash of Values as Real Challenge to Outreach in the Global South*

Family values and issues relating to human sexuality pose challenges to the willingness of non-Western partners to host missionaries from denominations that ordain or show readiness to accommodate homosexual priests. I recall an incident in Eastern Europe where some local leaders directed their displeasure on the Presbyterian Church USA's stance on ordination of gays toward a missionary whose convictions and values were previously accepted without suspicion. Another area of contention is the clash of the "ultra" feminist agenda in the patriarchal cultures of Latin America or Africa and what some consider a threat to their fundamental values.

Moreover, missionary support and "suspect reporting" is a common point of reference and continues to pose questions of credibility. For example, if the reports of some of these Western missionaries were accurate, then all Africans would have given their lives to Christ or become Christians a couple of times over. Adding to this, the credibility of missionaries is tarnished by some "bad apples" that went ahead of the good ones. Host nations have resented "extravagant" living conditions of certain missionaries, sometimes without fully understanding the sacrifices involved in living abroad. But what the hosts deem high standards still fall below the familiar conditions of these missionaries. Should monetary support prompt envy and undermine missions?

*Economic Imperialism and Development as Fuel for a New Voice*

While missionaries are often accompanied by funding for assigned projects, traditional Western notions of power associated with money have surfaced in world missions. Money power becomes the basis for which the missionaries would want to have their way. In some quarters, locals have compromised their objectives and values for fear of losing support. In some African countries, Christian leaders are embarrassingly mocked by outsiders and labeled as puppets of their Western counterparts. This is currently changing as developing countries see more economic stability and local churches become self-supporting. Leaders who have a lesser price to pay or find no need for Western support are gathering courage to express their frustrations and disagreements in no polite terms. I recall a meeting in 2001 at the offices of Church of Pentecost International in Ghana (a fast growing church in Africa) where our offers to assist financially were refused on the basis that the African church has a policy not to accept Western support.[171] Unfortunately, economic development and geopolitics are advancing disparity and lack of will to work together. For

---

[171] As a native of Ghana, I was with the then Africa Director of Mustard Seed Foundation, Elizabeth Campbell, to explore if the organization could assist the good work of the church in any way.

example, the debate in the Anglican Communion about gay priesthood has seen assertions from non-Western leadership calling for radical distancing and rejection of financial support from certain Dioceses in the Communion. Accept or deny! Economics and power struggles are prominent bones of contention in today's West-South mission partnership.

*Immigration, Immigrant Churches, and Reversal of the Sent and Senders*

The growth of immigrant churches and the influence of their spirituality in developed nations are shaping the face of missions. For example, the two largest churches in Europe were pioneered and led by Nigerian natives (in Ukraine and London). Roman Catholics may have more concrete data to show on this matter in the United States. The United States census bureau projects that every fourth person in the country will be Hispanic by 2050. Hispanics currently form over 50 percent of all Catholics under 25 years old, and the average age for Catholics now is over 50. The Hartford Institute of Religion Research follows trends that show increase in attendance of Hispanics and Asians in US churches across denominational lines.[172] Moreover, non-Western leaders are becoming more instrumental in traditional Western churches in bringing about vibrancy and attracting increased attendances.[173] Should we start thinking in realistic terms about how to design partnership models for "reversed missions" in order to revitalize some of the "sleeping churches" of the West? Change agents may be a great need in the West, while the South may need skills and resources for leadership development and sustainable Christian formation.

The above cursory observations show that global missions have real prospects and challenges. I do not claim to have answers to all these challenges, but I hope Paul's legacy of commitment to the God who called him to service, and his willingness to work with others, will serve as a model for effective and biblically grounded missions practice. I have observed some of these outstanding qualities in Peter Kuzmič in his passion to promote Christian

---

[172] Dana L. Robert, "Shifting Southward: Global Christianity Since 1945," *International Bulletin of Missionary Research* 24/2 (2000): 56. It is indisputable that the fast growing churches today have adopted some aspects of Pentecostal experience or contemporary worship style with some emphasis on the power of God. The immigrants bring differences in approach to how services are conducted. For example, most of these members like to sing, clap, or lift hands and even dance in worship. They have also brought the subject of spiritual gifts and spiritual warfare into congregations that found them uncomfortable or strange spiritual matters. It is no longer rare, for example, to find a Spanish or African Catholic that identifies himself/herself as a Spirit-filled born again Christian with routine Bible studies regime. The fast emerging group is "evangelical Catholics."

[173] In the midst of all these developments, black churches (mostly Baptist) are doing well in the United States but it is also true that they have not been very interested in sending missionaries, supporting missions or engaging mission endeavors at expected levels.

missions as global mission from Europe to America, Africa to Asia, and Latin America to Australia, breaking the barriers of race, ethnicity, and denominations in order to advance the Kingdom of God. I could locate Pauline legacies here partially because my senses were sharply activated when I studied world missions under Peter at the Evangelical Theological Seminary at Osijek in Croatia. I hope this discussion will be a fitting tribute to the man I call a friend, mentor, and fellow minister (Peter), whose global vision made him reach out to me (an African) and offered me numerous opportunities to develop as a better scholar and Christian leader with a Kingdom vision. Paul will certainly be proud of who Peter is, what he has stood for in post-communist and post-war Eastern Europe, and what he does to advance the work of Christ. Let us now turn to make some observations in Paul's life and writings.[174]

## Paul's Legacy #1 – Mission as a Calling

This section is not an extensive discussion on whether Paul converted from Judaism or simply received a call for a new mission. It is assumed that the Apostle converted from an ideological/theological framework underpinning his zeal to persecute the Church and received a call simultaneously to witness about his encounter with the Lord Jesus. In other words, conversion does not necessarily exclude continuity with the past (Rom. 9–11). Paul makes personal assertions to the effect that he is called by grace to become an apostle (Rom. 1:1; Gal. 1:15). "His apostolic authority, about which we hear a good deal when it is challenged, as in Galatians and 2 Corinthians, is rooted not in himself but in the one who called him and sent him, and in awareness of a vocation to do specific, unique, and irreplaceable job."[175] The dramatic nature of this call and its emphasis on proclamation has been likened to that of Old Testament prophets.[176] "When it was least expected, this Saul, who was breathing threats and murder against the disciples of the Lord, becomes a brother to Ananias and to the very disciples whom until then he persecuted."[177]

The Lukan narrative in Acts 22 indicates three dimensions to his call and commission: first, to know the will of God experientially and second to see and hear the voice of the Righteous One (Acts 22:14; cf. Phil. 3:10). The third is a purpose clause that charges him to be a witness (Acts 22:15). It is this personal calling that would subsequently set the direction of his ministry. The missionary's personal calling and relationship with Christ is integral to one's

---

[174] The sources referred or alluded to include all of the biblical accounts on Pauline legacy, including disputed letters and Luke's account in Acts.

[175] N. T. Wright, *Paul: In Fresh Perspective* (Minneapolis: Fortress, 2005), 162.

[176] Johannes Munck, *Paul and the Salvation of Mankind* (Richmond, VA: John Knox, 1959).

[177] Justo L. Gonzalez, *Acts: The Gospel of the Spirit* (Maryknoll: Orbis, 2001), 127.

responsibility to God and attitude towards others whom God sends. Else how can one bear witness to what he/she did not see, hear or experience with Christ? The accusation of hypocrisy becomes warranted only when missions becomes a self-serving agenda. How often does conflict in the mission field revolve around personal interest? Paul describes himself as one who is called, sent, and as a slave to his master. His calling is received with humility and gratitude (Eph. 3:8). As Wright notes, "Paul even glimpsed of the dark humor of God through which a fanatical right-wing nationalistic Jew should be the one to take to the pagans the news that the Jewish Messiah welcomed them on equal terms."[178]

### Paul's Legacy #2 – Missions as God's Mission

God who calls to missions is the custodian and the one to whom the missionary is accountable. Paul is an apostle by "the will of God" (1 Cor. 1.1), through "God the Father" (Gal. 1.1), and his gospel is of God as well. Dunn argues that we cannot talk about Paul's theology, life, or ministry without observing his frequent reference to God (548 times in undisputed letters alone).[179] Paul was self-conscious about deviation and reminds his readers in almost every letter about this self-understanding. He is an ambassador carrying out God's ministry of reconciliation to the sinful world of humanity.[180] This "is an act of God prior to and independent of any abandonment of enmity to God on our part, and equally prior to and independent of any human endeavor to secure a standing with him on the grounds of legal righteousness or effort."[181] For Paul, he is simply a legate representing God and discharging his assigned duty. Thus, authentic missionaries understand that they are called and sent by God—"It is God who commissions the preachers, and their start out as a 'mission': they are sent by God."[182] Christian mission is *Missio Dei* and requires a relationship, dependence, and obedience to God. It is not a personal project, lest we fight for territories.

### Paul's Legacy #3 – Missions as Spirit-Directed and Empowered Service

Pauline mission is marked by spiritual encounters, not only on the road to Damascus. He understood his ministry as that which is enabled by the Holy Spirit. At Paul's (then Saul's) initial contact with a follower of Christ, Ananias

---

[178] Wright, *Paul*, 162.
[179] James D. G. Dunn, *The Theology of Paul the Apostle*, 28. See Gal. 1:15; 2:21; Rom. 15:15; 1 Cor. 3:10.
[180] See Hans Conzelmann, *An Outline of His Theology of the New Testament* (London: SCM, 1969), 208.
[181] Ralph P. Martin. "New Testament Theology: A Proposal—The Theme of Reconciliation," *The Expository Times* 9, no. 12 (1980): 367.
[182] Lietaert Peerbolte, *Paul the Missionary*, 208.

prayed for him to be "filled with the Holy Spirit" (Acts 9:17). The focus here is not the manner or form by which the Spirit expressed itself but that mission has a spiritual dimension and thereby requires spiritual sensitivity. For example, the Spirit rested on the head of Jesus at his baptism as also on the disciples on the Day of Pentecost to mark the beginning of the Church. In fact, Paul is the individual that has left us with the most comprehensive and sophisticated pneumatology, as Fee has aptly demonstrated in his magnum opus.[183]

At Antioch, Luke reports that the Holy Spirit chose Paul and Barnabas for missions and it was the Holy Spirit that sent them (Acts 13:2-4). The account also introduces the reader to a spiritual battle that involves Paul and a magician in his earliest experience of missions. Paul, empowered and sent by the Spirit (Acts 13:9) confronted the false prophet/magician Elymas and cursed him to blindness. Luke "adduces the inherent connection between spreading God's Word and demonstrations of power (here in punitive miracle), and at the same time stresses the importance of Christian teaching and distinguishes it from magic."[184] Christian mission has a spiritual component first and foremost, before socio-anthropological concerns become issues for discussion. In Pauline missiology, messengers of God need vigilance and divine enabling to counteract activities of the forces of evil (cf. Eph. 6:12). For Paul the unreached are subject to the control of evil powers (Eph. 2:1-3) and the reached are sealed by the Spirit as a mark of God's ownership (Eph. 1:13-14). Consequently, they bear the "fruit of the Spirit" (Gal. 5:22-23) in good conduct and are given spiritual gifts to strengthen and edify the communities (Rom 12:6-8; 1 Cor. 12, 14; Eph. 4:9-12). Paul exorcised, healed diseases, and threatened to deliver erring believers to Satan. The Spirit was a guide to Paul's mission. On one occasion, the Holy Spirit prevented them from further ministry in Asia until it was revealed to Paul in a vision to go to Macedonia.

It is not the objective here to rehearse all spiritual encounters with Paul but to underline the Pauline concept of mission as a battle between God and evil spirits over the souls of mankind and the exigency to be empowered by the Spirit for such endeavor. The presence of the Spirit of God in ministry is crucial in Pauline missiology. Scholars have observed that the rapid spread of Christianity in the last half of the 20th century was evident mainly in areas where society believed in the existence of spiritual forces[185] and where Christians saw the presence of the power of God as a significant part of

---

[183] Gordon D. Fee, *God's Empowering Presence: The Holy Spirit in the Letters of Paul* (Peabody, MA: Hendrickson, 1994), 799-895. Fee examines all Pauline passages referring to the Spirit and provides insightful synthesis how Paul understood the Spirit as an empowering agent, fulfillment of eschatological promise and instrumentality in salvation, among other areas.

[184] Gerd Lüdemann, *The Acts of the Apostles* (Amherst, NY: Prometheus, 2005), 165.

[185] Kabiro wa Gatumu, *Pauline Concept of Supernatural Powers: A Reading from the African Worldview* (Eugene, OR: Wipf & Stock, 2008), 88.

evangelism. For most Africans, the gospel about a "Jesus" stripped of power to deal with evil spirits is an impotent gospel.

Most Africans still live in the world of the New Testament, where belief in demons and a host of invisible supernatural powers was potent and real. A Jesus who confronted evil spirits and demons in the Gospels will probably fit in the African thought world. A Jesus emptied of all the supernatural contained in the Gospels would be meaningless in the African context.[186]

## Paul's Legacy #4 – Mission as Service

The missionary par excellence describes himself as a servant/slave with the obligation to do his master's will (1 Cor. 3:5-11). This is not self-abasement but assertion of commitment to service in analogous terms with that of a slave to his master. The Apostle's primary loyalty lies in pleasing his master (*kyrios*). He did not lord it over his followers in the churches he founded but projected an image of a servant, the very least of all (Eph. 3:8), working in concert with others to propagate the gospel. He asserts, "For we do not proclaim ourselves, but Jesus Christ as Lord, and ourselves as your slaves for Jesus' sake." (2 Cor. 4:5, NET). "Churches that arise from missionary work are not the possession of Paul or of other teachers: the Church is and always remains 'God's field, God's building' (1 Cor. 3:9)."[187] The servant-missionary seeks not to vie for power based on status or superior knowledge of Christ but deems himself a fragile "jar of clay" bearing the treasures of the gospel to the unreached.

Paul had something to boast about: He was a resident of Tarsus with excellent Greek education, a Roman citizen, and a student of Rabbi Gamaliel.[188] Though a former member of the prestigious Jewish separatist movement (Pharisees), he surrendered his pride and prestige for humble service to the Lord. On the road to Damascus, his previous vision was blinded and replaced by a burden for the salvation of Gentiles: he gained a new self-understanding, worldview, and a new attitude towards those he had deemed unworthy of his care. In Paul's own words,

> Even though I, too, have reason for confidence in the flesh. If anyone else has reason to be confident in the flesh, I have more: circumcised on the eighth day, a member of the people of Israel, of the tribe of Benjamin, a Hebrew born of Hebrews; as to the law, a Pharisee; as to zeal, a persecutor of the Church; as to righteousness under the law, blameless. Yet whatever gains I had, these I have

---

[186] Gatumu, *Pauline Concept of Supernatural Powers,* 89. This also holds true for demythologization of Gospel accounts; and even the discussion on "Historical Jesus and the Christ Faith" has not attracted the interest of African theological students, most of whom are already ministers or being prepared for ministry in their immediate context.

[187] Eckhard J. Schnabel, *Early Christian Mission: Paul & the Early Church* (Downers Grove: InterVarsity, 2004), 2:981.

[188] Schnabel, *Early Christian Mission,* 926-27.

come to regard as loss because of Christ. More than that, I regard everything as loss because of the surpassing value of knowing Christ Jesus my Lord. For his sake I have suffered the loss of all things, and I regard them as rubbish, in order that I may gain Christ (Phil. 3:4-8 NRSV).

Such a perspective changes the emphasis from self to God, embraces others as *imago Dei* and missions as indeed *Missio Dei*. Introductions and concluding greetings of Paul's letters attest to his servitude and gratitude as a privileged servant of the Lord, an attitude worthy of emulation.

### Paul's Legacy #5 – Missions as Mediation of Faith and Culture

Paul was a Jew with cross-cultural experience. He had been a Jewish boy in Tarsus. Sensitive to the Jerusalem church and the concerns of Judaizers, the former Pharisee made deliberate efforts to seek clarification and conciliation in matters of dispute (Acts 15). The Jerusalem council made a landmark decision when it ruled that cross-cultural missionaries should not impose traditional Jewish customs on non-Jews. They rightly prohibited idolatry, as well as eating strangled animals and blood,[189] and they established that Gentiles could be part of the church without circumcision. Arguably, this set precedence for negotiations on matters of culture and doctrine between sending churches and host nations.[190] Paul did not seek to assimilate Gentiles into Jewish customs or dismiss reasonable cultural concerns of Gentiles as insignificant to Christian ethics. "His free association with Gentiles, his casual attitude towards the laws of purity and the role the Messiah plays in his thought."[191] In fact, his ethics usually builds on values that were shared by philosophers and moralists of his day to show how his readers' identity in Christ makes them imperative for

---

[189] See a textual variant in Chester Beatty papyrus that affects the listing of the key items.

[190] This is an important observation, as some Euro-American missionaries fail to appreciate the efforts of African leaders to discourage polygamy in churches without demonizing those in polygamous marriages. For example, one of my uncles assisted us in establishing a mission station in Borai II in the Krachi District of Ghana, but he would never accept Jesus as his Lord and Savior, as he shared, because his second wife was asked to divorce him when she became a Christian. She has since married another man who has a first wife while still attending the same church. My uncle resents this aspect of Christianity that has destroyed his family and ruined his children's lives. He would always find a way to bring the subject up whenever I was with him because he did not understand why I should continue to be minister and participate in hurting families. What would Paul do as the pioneer missionary?

[191] Calvin J. Roetzel, *The Letters of Paul: Conversations in Context* (Louisville: Westminster John Knox, 1998), 39.

cohesion in the early churches.[192] Paul departs from strict Pharisaic ethos and Jewish "particularism" to find in Jesus a means to social parity.

The grounds for the Apostle's response to the issue of head/hair covering in Corinthian pneumatic worship, for instance, was partially located in the custom of the people (1 Cor. 11:16). Cross-cultural dynamics and socio-economic disparities (ethno-racial, class, or gender) become prominent themes in Paul's quest for mutuality in the early churches (Gal. 3:26-29; Eph. 2:11-22, etc.). He therefore condemns Peter's unfriendly attitude towards Gentiles at the arrival of certain Jews as hypocritical and incompatible with the gospel (Gal. 2: 7-14). Paul was skillful in maneuvering and negotiating around different customs without compromising the essence of the gospel. He did not demonize other cultures but condemned immorality therein. It was not part of his *modus operandi* to immerse Gentile converts in Jewish customs—an attitude often neglected by Christians who like to go where CNN or FOX news sends.

### Paul's Legacy #6 – Missions as a Theater for Mutual Cooperation

Like Jesus, Paul perceived ministry as team work (Acts 11:26; 13:13) and often traveled with a few companions, Barnabas, Luke, Timothy, Mark, etc. His teamwork transcended gender distinction to include women and sometimes couples (Acts 18:1-4, 18-28; Rom. 16:3, 6-7). He constantly encouraged believers to live in unity and work together as many parts of one body (1 Cor. 12). Paul's concept of ministry partnership also transcends class (Philem.) and ethnicity (Gal. 3:26-28). The Lukan depiction of the ethnic composition of the leadership gathering at the "missions headquarters" in Antioch (Acts 13) is particularly instructive:

Barnabas was there, a Cypriot landowner and Levite. Beside him sat Simeon "who was called *niger*"—meaning "black," possibly from Africa. Next sat Lucius of Cyrene, also from Africa. Beside Lucius sat Manaen—an aristocrat of the court of the ruler, Herod. Saul, that fiery intellectual from Tarsus, completed the table fellowship.[193]

Christian mission is not a place for internal competition but cooperation, not even with those who preach out of selfish ambitions (Phil 1:15-18; 4:2-3). A survey of Paul's willingness to announce or commend his companions by name shows that up to 57 of his fellow workers are mentioned by name in the New Testament.[194] His trusted disciple and confidant, Timothy, was a Gentile. Paul

---

[192] Daniel K. Darko, *No Longer Living as the Gentiles: Differentiation and Shared Ethical Values in Ephesians 4:17–6:9* (London: T&T Clark, 2008), 68; and David D. G. Horrell, *Solidarity and Difference: A Contemporary Reading of Paul's Ethics* (London: T&T Clark, 2005), 164-65.

[193] Norman E. Thomas, "The Church at Antioch: Crossing Racial, Cultural, and Class Barriers," in *Mission in Acts: Ancient Narratives in Contemporary Context*, ed. Robert L. Gallagher and Paul Hertig (Maryknoll: Orbis, 2004), 152.

[194] See Lietaert Peerbolte, *Paul the Missionary*.

was only one of the servants the Lord was using to build his Church (1 Cor. 1–3). His colleagues were fellow workers (*synergos*). One does not find a quest for power to control others or egoistic tendency.[195] Paul refused to take credit for others' work and acknowledges, recommends, and commends his colleagues for their comradeship. "Paul the Apostle was essentially a team worker. His roving little community of apostles was at once a training school, a miniature church, and a mutual source of growth and support in every difficult vocation."[196] His sense of otherness is also reflected in the efforts to promote solidarity in the churches. Paul was not a maverick, and neither did he consider "rugged individualism" in Christian service a virtue.

Paul was accessible to all and open to receive from those he served. By being "all things to all people" (1 Cor. 9:19-23), he reached people at their level. In Corinthians 9:19-23, he mirrors the tradition of "condescension" in the claim to be "all things to all people," a custom in which a person of higher standing kowtows to meet those they want to reach at their level.[197] Paul was open about receiving financial support from churches (Phil. 4:15-16 and 2 Cor. 11:7-11) and bemoans the fact that no church supported him prior to that of the Macedonians (Phil. 4:15-16). He was supported by wealthy individuals and gathered support from Gentile churches to meet the needs of the mother church in Jerusalem. His concept of generosity is not conditioned upon terms of power and control, but on the sheer notion of brothers and sisters in Christ supporting one another (2 Cor. 8–9). Luke seems to suggest that Lydia and a couple (Priscilla and Aquila) were instrumental in this regard (Acts 16:14-15 and 18:1-3), though elsewhere he writes about earning his own living (1 Cor. 4:11-12) as a tentmaker (Acts 18:1-3).

## Paul's Legacy #7 – Missions as a Long-term Commitment and Communication

In light of both short and long term mission endeavors, I deem it necessary to highlight the legacy of Paul as a minister who maintained contact and found mutual interdependence between himself and the people he served. This legacy has left us with what is now over half of the New Testament (including disputed letters) that continue to shape our understanding of church doctrine

---

[195] Rom. 16:3, 9, 21; 1 Cor. 3:9; 2 Cor. 1:24; 8:23; Phil. 2:25; 4:3; 1 Thess. 3:2.

[196] Joseph A. Grassi, *The Secret of Paul the Apostle* (Maryknoll: Orbis, 1978), 63.

[197] Margaret M. Mitchell, "Pauline Accommodation and 'Condescension' (*sugkata, basij*) 1 Cor. 9:19-23 and the Influence of History" in *Paul Beyond the Judaism/Hellenism Divide,* ed. Troels Engberg-Pedersen (Louisville: Westminster John Knox, 2001), 197-214. Mitchell reviews the history of interpretation of this text and places the text, among others, in the Philonic tradition, where it is impossible to separate Jewish or Greek adaptations in the works of Paul, whose cosmopolitan and poly-cultural experiences are reflected in his writings.

and praxis in early Christianity. The Kingdom mission did not end when Paul left one group of people for another. He counted himself a member of a larger body of believers in the household of God, even to the extent of using kinship metaphors (brother and sister) to express the nature of relationships. Bridges were not burned nor relationships simply cut on account of mere disagreements, though he would not tolerate those who sought to impede the progress of the work of God (Gal. 2). Paul's framework is what God was doing, and he found the need to resolve conflicts as part of his ambassadorial commission in the Kingdom of God.

### Paul's Legacy #8 – Missions as a Place of Conflict and Conflict Resolution

Ministry involves conflict and conflict resolution; so is every work that involves people. It may take the form of conflict with a fellow worker like Paul and Barnabas (Acts 15:36-41) or others trying to undermine leadership. Sometimes Paul depicts tensions with other believers as a spiritual battle in which arguments need to be won (2 Cor. 10:3-6). A common area of tension in Paul's ministry occurred with false teachers, moral laxity, and Jew-Gentile relations (ethno-racial). There were times when he had to concede and move on, and often when he had to confront the issues at stake. Paul's obvious occasional letters dealing with conflicts are 1 Corinthians and Galatians. He consistently establishes the framework of resolution in his readers' identity in Christ and in the nature of the gospel as the starting point. He chastised, disciplined, and encouraged members to conduct themselves and their meetings within the framework of their new identity in Christ and their new sense of community.

Conflict is part of working with people, and Paul understood the need to listen, address them, and even compromise his own rights if necessary. "The basic rule of missionary existence requires the missionary to take the listener seriously in a fully consistent manner (1 Cor. 9:19) … Paul is prepared to relinquish his freedom if he can win people for faith in Jesus Christ."[198] This is not relativist Christianity, nor does it contradict his commitment to the Lord. It is an adaptation of relevant posture and suitable emotional intelligence to gain a hearing for his apostolic prescriptions or proclamation.

### Paul's Legacy #9 – Missions as Intercession

This legacy permeates the writings of Paul so much so that it does not require lengthy rehearsal. Along the lines of Jesus' own ministry that began with prayer and fasting (Matt. 4) and the birth of the Church in prayer (Acts 1–2), Paul's early experience was marked by the prayer of Ananias. Subsequently, the mission to Gentiles began when Paul and Barnabas were set apart during prayer

---

[198] Schnabel, *Early Christian Mission*, 953-54.

and fasting, and commissioned at Antioch by the laying on of hands to take the gospel to Gentiles (Acts 13:1-2). It later became Paul's custom to inform his readers about his prayers for them, and he constantly asked for their prayers for effective ministry. The Apostle also informs his readers about their shared need for God in all that they do. Perhaps Paul would even pray for Pauline scholars today if he saw what we are making out of his writings. This pastoral quality of Paul is often overlooked in the quest to understand his complex theological framework. The Christian missionary cannot afford to set prayer aside if he/she genuinely desires to share the gospel with lasting effect.

**Paul's Legacy #10 – Missions as a Call to Suffering**

Lastly, Paul understood suffering as something to embrace in the service of the Lord. He recounts his own suffering as a privilege and expresses a great wish "to know Christ" in both his victory over death and in "the fellowship of his sufferings" (Phil. 3:10 KJV).[199] Paul accepts suffering as part of the challenges of a missionary, notwithstanding the "thorn in his own flesh" that is brought up 2 Corinthians 12.

> Five times I have received from the Jews the forty lashes minus one. Three times I was beaten with rods. Once I received a stoning. Three times I was shipwrecked; for a night and a day I was adrift at sea; on frequent journeys, in danger from rivers, danger from bandits, danger from my own people, danger from Gentiles, danger in the city, danger in the wilderness, danger at sea, danger from false brothers and sisters; in toil and hardship, through many a sleepless night, hungry and thirsty, often without food, cold, and naked. And, besides other things, I am under daily pressure because of my anxiety for all the churches (2 Cor. 11:24-28 NRSV).

At the very onset, he faced persecution in Damascus and had to escape by the aid of believers in the city (Acts 9). For Paul, suffering that is associated with the work of God identifies the missionary with Christ and ushers him/her into an eschatological hope of triumph with Christ. The missionary who quits because of challenges to personal comfort may be letting God down. Sometimes God uses suffering to build character. It is not pleasant, but he expects unwavering trust from those he calls to missions (Rom. 5).

---

[199] David Wenham, *Paul: Follower of Jesus or Founder of Christianity?* (Grand Rapids: Eerdmans, 1995), 326-27. Wenham explores the question of whether Paul was influenced by Jesus' teaching on suffering and concludes this is possible. It is, however, important to note that the lack of evidence regarding direct contact with the historical Jesus does not necessarily mean disconnection with the theology of the Lord he met on the Damascus road. Paul's writings about suffering for the Kingdom of God are evidence to that effect.

## Conclusion

There is "a charge to keep and a God to glorify" among those who teach missions and those who respond to the call of missions. Missions begins by asking what makes a missionary: the role of the transcendent and attitude towards God and others. Understanding that this is a call to participate in God's service, regardless of status, race, or gender, brings about suitable demeanor for missions. It is in this vein that social anthropology in missiology becomes meaningless unless it is intrinsically linked to the concept of *Missio Dei*. A true servant of God would see the Gypsy, Black, Hispanic, Caucasian, low caste, homeless, fatherless, etc., as people made also in the image and likeness of God, deserving to be reached by the love of God.

### *The Missionary and the Transcendent*

The Pauline legacy clearly shows that a personal encounter and relationship with God is essential for mission initiatives. Instead of pride or prejudice, the missionary may respond in gratitude, a sense of unworthiness, and yield to divine enabling. What is monetary power, status, or national pride compared to what we have in Christ? As Paul puts it, "what do we have that we did not receive?" Moreover, the arrogance of host leaders that is often rooted in nationalism, jealousy, and insecurity is tantamount to protectionism and territorialism that have no place in the work of God. It is true that so many missionaries have taken advantage of their hosts and distorted data for selfish ends. But should we give up the privilege of working together because of such problems? Paul argues that we are in partnership even with those who preach out of selfish ambitions. It must be said that the ignorance clothed in arrogance among some host leaders (in Africa, Eastern Europe, South America) calls for the urgency to reflect a great deal on Pauline legacy for cooperation in order to rectify some of the misplaced notions. Admittedly, the West and South are often lost in "the sin of prejudice"; this will not go away until we are ready to do some deep and honest soul-searching.

The missionary must surrender to Christ and pant for more of the power of the Holy Spirit to exercise pneumatic gifts in the service of the Lord—an issue that can no longer be taken for granted. The fruit and gifts of the Spirit must go together. As Peter Kuzmič likes to put it, "charisma without character is catastrophe." The missionary should be prepared to confront the Kingdom of darkness as a natural part of sharing the gospel. Prayer and devotion to the Word of God is crucial in this regard. As an early 20th-century revivalist put it:

> For the sake of the bruised and dying, and the lost in darkness lying, we must get the flame. For the sake of Christ in glory, and the spreading of the story, we must get the flame. Oh my soul, for thy refining, and thy clearer, brighter s "Curriculum for Economic Transformation" by David Lim.hining, do not miss the flame. On the Holy Ghost relying, simply trusting and not trying, you will get the

flame. Brothers, let us cease our dreaming, and while flood-tide is screaming, we will have the flame.[200]

## The Missionary and the Context

Christianity did not begin in the West, and Western culture is not akin to Christian culture. This was the mistake of the "colonial missionaries" who demonized every cultural difference and confused their home culture with Christian culture. For example, Jesus grew up in a permissive polygamous tradition, yet we find no overt condemnation of polygamy in his teachings. We need to promote monogamy among believers, but the missionary enterprise may revisit how it engages patriarchal and polygamous societies without compromising the gospel. It is important to draw from early missionaries like Paul, be conscious of our own biases, and seek to expand the work of Christ in the spirit of Christ. Cultural sensitivity is imperative. The missionary must be ready to negotiate and be open to compromise where it does not conflict with the core of the gospel.

Gender stereotypes and feminism are areas where I find so many missionaries clueless and insensitive both to biblical teachings and to the cultures they serve. To promote egalitarianism in patriarchal cultures with texts that are born out of patriarchal contexts requires skillful maneuvering and acute hermeneutical prowess to succeed. The demonization of non-Western cultures has been counterproductive. Perhaps it will be helpful to seek counsel with the local leaders running those vibrant churches in matters of this kind. Those who invoke "21st-century global culture" as a criterion for a Western assimilation agenda fail to accept the third-world critique that the 21st-century Western Church is rather one that is plagued with family breakdowns, sexual scandals, and countless moral failings.

The missionary needs to be ready to accept the cultures and the people to whom God sends them to ensure effective undertakings. Like the prophet Jonah, the one who responds to the call of God must be prepared to work on God's terms. Elsewhere I have shown that the "sin of prejudice" is still rampant among Western and indigenous mission endeavors.[201] We need to confront racial and ethnic prejudices among Christians in Africa, Asia, and Latin America. It is not only Western attitudes towards non-Western cultures, it is also discrimination based on color complexion, social classifications, and tribalism that are hampering Christian cooperation in Africa and Latin America. Let us confront the "sin of prejudice" as Paul did with Peter and seek to pursue a Kingdom mission that is genuinely global in nature.

---

[200] Frank Bartlemen, *Azusa Street* (South Plainfield, NJ: Bridge, 1980), 65.

[201] Daniel K. Darko, "Divine Commission and Human Conviction: A Missiological Reading of the Jonah Narrative," *Trinity Journal of Church and Theology* 16, no. 2 (2008): 26-38.

The Pauline legacy of cooperation challenges us to broaden our horizon and adapt to the emerging changes in global missions. We may need to be creative, compromise our personal whims, and count on others more in order to maximize our effectiveness. I found it ironic to visit places where indigenous Christians who are illiterate, do not speak English, and have a completely different culture were being made to learn how to worship with translated hymns. What is wrong with composing local songs and enjoying the singing, dancing, and drumming associated with their culture in the church service? No! Apparently that would not be an appropriate form of worship. To sum it all up, Christian workers in the West and South need each other, so let us build on Pauline legacy to explore better ways to serve God together.

## Bibliography

Bartleman, Frank. *Azusa Street.* South Plainfield, NJ: Bridge, 1980.

Conzelmann, Hans. *An Outline of His Theology of the New Testament.* London: SCM, 1969.

Darko, Daniel K. "Divine Commission and Human Conviction: A Missiological Reading of the Jonah Narrative." *Trinity Journal of Church and Theology* 16, no. 2 (2008): 26-38.

Darko, Daniel K. *No Longer Living as the Gentiles: Differentiation and Shared Ethical Values in Ephesians 4:17–6:9.* London: T&T Clark, 2008.

Dunn, James D. G. *The Theology of Paul the Apostle.* Grand Rapids: Eerdmans, 1998.

Fee, Gordon D. *God's Empowering Presence: The Holy Spirit in the Letters of Paul.* Peabody, MA: Hendrickson, 1994..

Horrell, David D. G. *Solidarity and Difference: A Contemporary Reading of Paul's Ethics.* London: T&T Clark, 2005.

Gatumu, Kabiro wa. *Pauline Concept of Supernatural Powers: A Reading from the African Worldview.* Eugene, OR: Wipf & Stock, 2008.

Gonzalez, Justo L. *Acts: The Gospel of the Spirit.* Maryknoll: Orbis, 2001.

Grassi, Joseph A. *The Secret of Paul the Apostle.* Maryknoll: Orbis, 1978.

Lietaert Peerbolte, L. J. *Paul the Missionary.* Leuven: Peeters, 2003.

Little, Christopher R. *Mission in the Way of Paul: Biblical Mission for the Church in the Twenty-First Century.* New York: Peter Lang, 2005.

Lüdemann, Gerd. *The Acts of the Apostles.* Amherst, NY: Prometheus, 2005.

_____. *Paul: The Founder of Christianity.* Amherst, NY: Prometheus, 2002.

Martin, Ralph P. "New Testament Theology: A Proposal—The Theme of Reconciliation." *Expository Times* 9, no. 12 (1980): 367.

Mitchell, Margaret M. "Pauline Accommodation and 'Condescension' (*sugkata, basij*): 1 Cor. 9:19-23 and the Influence of History." In *Paul Beyond the Judaism/Hellenism Divide,* edited by Troels Engberg-Pedersen. Louisville: Westminster John Knox, 2001.

Munck, Johannes. *Paul and the Salvation of Mankind.* Richmond, VA: John Knox, 1959.

Robert, Dana L. "Shifting Southward: Global Christianity Since 1945." *International Bulletin of Missionary Research* 24, no. 2 (2000): 56.

Roetzel, Calvin J. *The Letters of Paul: Conversations in Context.* Louisville: Westminster John Knox, 1998.

Schnabel, Eckhard J. *Early Christian Mission: Paul and the Early Church.* 2vols. Downers Grove: InterVarsity, 2004.

Thomas, Norman E. "The Church at Antioch: Crossing Racial, Cultural, and Class Barriers." In *Mission in Acts: Ancient Narratives in Contemporary Context,* edited by Robert L. Gallagher and Paul Hertig. Maryknoll: Orbis, 2004.

Wenham, David. *Paul: Follower of Jesus or Founder of Christianity?* Grand Rapids: Eerdmans, 1995.

Wright, N. T. *Paul: In Fresh Perspective.* Minneapolis: Fortress, 2005.

# "Unlikely" Contributions Toward a Global Social Ethic: Can Anything Good Come from There?
Ruth Padilla DeBorst

"Im-poss-ible!" they mutter under heavy breath as they plod up the steep hill, hardly able to keep up with her. The old woman, skin and bones under wrinkled skin, races ahead with bare feet. Balancing on her head is the tree the two of them have been unable even to lift from the ground. Who would expect this poor, frail, and undernourished, Central American woman to be more capable at that tough job than two well-built, well-fed, well-to-do, well-trained American house framers? Astounding!

Three more stories complete this collage of "unlikeliness." But before, a couple of words about this chapter. An essential consideration regarding the possibility of a global social ethic concerns the "builders," i.e., who is actively involved in the construction of that ethic. It is the author's thesis that women and men from "unlikely" "underdeveloped" places have meaningful contributions to make to the global Church and its mission in the world. Underlying this thesis is the assumption that a Christian contribution toward a global social ethic necessarily depends on the existence of a global Church in which Christians from North and South encounter one another as equal partners in Christ and constitute a just community of mutual respect and care that transcends borders of nationality, race, ethnicity, gender, language, and even economic and political ideology. In keeping with this assumption, the present chapter humbly proposes to raise questions and suggest some possible first steps so that those "unlikely" contributions can be made.

I sat down after addressing the students gathered for chapel. The college president shook my hand effusively: "Thanks! That was great! You've surely read a lot of Kuyper!" Now I must confess, to the horror of my Reformed sisters and brothers, that to that date I had never read a word by the Dutch statesman and theologian. I did believe wholeheartedly, as Kuyper did, that Christ is sovereign over "every square inch" of human existence; and I had studied and reflected theologically for years in Latin America. I had even been a Christian Reformed missionary for some time. But how on earth could someone from Latin America have something worthwhile to say without ever having read Kuyper!

She's short. She's young. She's cute and bubbly, yet shy and unassuming. She is—obviously, yet worth emphasizing—a woman. And she's heading up the Center for Interdisciplinary Theological Studies in El Salvador. Not your "typical" dean, she's had to learn to use a skirt because most of the students are male pastors from a—broadly speaking—Pentecostal mega-church, which ten years ago most people would have qualified as a sect. The facilitators of the group-study program are Baptist, Nazarene, Reformed, Mennonite, and Pentecostal young people, leaders of the *Movimiento Universitario Cristiano*, an interdenominational student ministry affiliated to the International Fellowship of Evangelical Students. None of them are professional theologians or ordained ministers; but most of them are members of the local chapter of the Latin American Theological Fellowship. The study material, created by the Kairos Foundation, from Buenos Aires, Argentina, is organized around the topics Church, Work, Family, and Society, not divided into classic seminary classes like New Testament, Hermeneutics, Life and Teaching of Paul, and so on, as in "proper" seminaries. The program has no facility of its own: it goes where the students are and meets in their churches and offices. Although there is plenty of reading, acute social analysis, and serious Bible study, no formal academic papers are produced. The impact of this theological education, instead, includes community, family, and church projects like micro-credit for women, literacy for street children, an anti-violence campaign in a rough neighborhood, vows for increased respect to their wives, and a recycling project, among others. The Church itself is being radically transformed as it engages in mission inside and beyond its walls. And this is occurring in the same small "underdeveloped" country that is blasting off the world charts on account of its murder rate. Amazing!

"Nazareth! Can anything good come from there?" Nathanael's incredulity, recorded in John's Gospel account (1:43-51), is absolutely logical. After all, the long-awaited Messiah was naturally expected to come from Jerusalem, the local seat of imperial power, the center of the religious activity surrounding the Temple. But Nazareth, that lost, insignificant, underdeveloped spot! Nothing worthwhile would ever come from there!

Nathanael's bewilderment—his disbelief that something good could possibly come from a place other than the one officially recognized as powerful, prestigious, particularly blessed—is not unique. His is the voice of bias and presumption that has echoed even throughout the history of the church: from the Rome of the first Christendom to the secluded monasteries of the Middle Ages; from the Enlightened and reformed first nation-states to the "civilizing" British Empire; from the cross-and-sword brandishing Conquistadores to the current Crusaders against the "axis of evil." The assumption has been that those centers own the pure gospel, the inspired theology, the appropriate ecclesiology, and the right ethical answers to the questions of Christian life in the world. But Nazareth! Can anything good come from there? Highly unlikely.

## Come and See

According to the Gospel account, Philip will not take skepticism for an answer. So he challenges Nathanael to get up from his comfortable shady spot under the fig tree and to see for himself.

A man ahead of his time, Rolland Allen almost a century ago issued a similar challenge to his fellow Christians. He mourned the religious and racial pride that stunted their own growth: "We have not understood that the members of the body of Christ are scattered in all lands, and that we, without them, are not made perfect."[202] And he decried the Western self-sufficiency that bred paternalism and denied the new churches an equal standing in Christian fellowship and mission: "We have been anxious to do something for them. And we have done much… We have done everything for them except acknowledge any equality. We have done everything for them but very little with them. We have done everything for them except give place to them. We have treated them as 'dear children,' but not as 'brethren.'" And for Allen it all boils down to a lack of faith, not merely in the churches of the rest of the world but in the very Holy Spirit who has birthed, sustained and enlisted them for God's mission.

In recent years, thousands and thousands of well-meaning North American short-term mission teams have boarded planes, donning their distinctive T-shirts and destined to do much for the people of the developing world. Schools, churches, orphanages, and houses have been built. Wells have been dug and fields have been cleared. Mime and theatre groups have performed on street corners. Meals have been cooked and sermons have been preached. Many valuable things have been done. And in some cases, meaningful relationships have been built that outlast the "mission" trip. But Allen's challenge must still be faced: The "missionaries" are doing many things, but how much of this work has been done with the people? And to what extent are those people being acknowledged as Christians with equal value in God's Kingdom? Today, missionaries are going, but what—or rather who—do they see? Do they see simply "the poor," "the underdeveloped," "the victims"? Or do they open up enough to encounter Jesus in the life of their brothers and sisters in the rest of the world? Are their eyes too accustomed to their way of "doing church" for them to recognize other ways as valid and to learn from others? And are their own lives, churches, and communities significantly affected by those encounters, are new insights gained that modify the way they look at the world, their privilege, the inequities of world economy, and their responsibility in light of them? Are lasting partnerships established? Or does it all become a faded memory bound in a filed-away scrapbook?

Nathanael's face-to-face encounter with Jesus ripped off the blinders of prejudice that had made him so skeptical. No doubt now remained. Something,

---

[202] Roland Allen, *Missionary Methods: St. Paul's or Ours?* (Grand Rapids: Eerdmans, 1962; first published 1912), 143.

or rather somebody, good surely could come from Nazareth! Nathanael would need a lifetime to figure out the implications of his confession: "Rabbi, you are the Son of God; you are the King of Israel" (John 1:49). But he had got the picture: Not Herod in his guilty wealth, not Pilate, the Emperor's representative, not Caiaphas with his religious power, none of them but this man from that unlikely place was the sovereign ruler, the King of Israel. All he could now do was follow this King, along with other men and women of "unlikely" backgrounds.

## Where Is Jesus Recognized as King?

### *Where Christ Is Confessed as King, Women and Men Identify their "Accents"*
I grew up in Buenos Aires; and we used to think people from other areas of Argentina had peculiar accents, more musical, more staccato, and so on. In our conceit, we believed ours was the only neutral pronunciation of the Spanish language. In a similar fashion, missionaries, teachers, preachers, and development workers from the wealthy North have often been quick to identify the "accents" of the people they have gone to serve, and the evidences of syncretism in other contexts; but they have been slow to recognize that they too have cultural biases, paradigms, values, and traits that are just as accented. The North American Church, for all its powerful mega-churches, theological and academic institutions, publishing houses, conferences, and so on, is still not free of syncretism. All too often the gospel is shrouded in affluence, branded by consumerism, and packaged with power to such a degree that its transformative impact is drowned both at home and abroad. Valuable as are global partnership and Northern contributions in the South, US evangelicals need to scrutinize their own churches and explore to what extent they are being an alternative and prophetic community in the midst of the pulls of autonomy, individualism, racism, competition, activism, consumerism, and aimlessness which so characterize this society. Faithful action and word proceed from faithful being.

Could engaged response to the cries of lives broken by poverty, injustice, and oppression in its many forms—at the hand of unscrupulous employers, of sexual aggressors, of corrupt landowners, of immigration officials, of invading armies, of drugs and alcohol—be directly related to the layers of comfort, satiation, and excess insulating us from those in need, whether we live in the North or the South? Might there be lessons to be learned from those Majority World churches that not only serve the poor "out there" but *are* the poor, and wrestle daily with the need to see God in the midst of their plight?

### *Where Christ is Confessed as King, Men and Women Realign their Loyalties*
Christians are primarily called to remain faithful to the one and only Lord, the One whose lordship was exercised by giving himself away, in life and in death. In God's social ordering, Number One is someone other than self. Might it not

be true, then, that when individual rights are erected as the baseline for all ethical decisions, personal boundaries are staked out over and against those of others, and personal and national security become the main goals of life, the radical call of the King who gave himself away to others in life and death gets muffled and tucked away?

If Christ's lordship precludes primary loyalty to self, neither does it grant space to hegemonic claims of the nation or ruler of the day. As Rasmussen points out, "the social ethics [of the church] are... formulated from the nature of the new order under the lordship of Jesus, and not from the requirements of culture and its maintenance by whoever happens to possess access to power in the moment."[203]

Christians from places as diverse as Iraq and El Salvador, Palestine and Colombia would concur: An enormous contribution of North American Christians to the rest of the world would be the realignment of their loyalties, a discerning separation of the claims of God and those of American national interests, and an adamant unwillingness to legitimize imperial crusades.

*Where Christ Is Confessed as King, Every Person Has "Full Citizenship"*

The Reformation rearticulated the biblical portrayal of the priesthood of all believers: No one is excluded from full, active, and responsible citizenship in God's Kingdom. Now, in business one chooses partners with care and background checks. In marriage, possibly, also. (I must confess my guilt in that regard. In my youth, I vociferously declared I would never marry an American. And here I am, widowed to one American and married to another American!) Under Christ's reign, however, the Church is called to never say never, to overcome prejudices and fears, and to receive strangers as family members. We all need God to remove our cultural blinders. We all need his Spirit to move us away from positions of "us" and "them," of "either/or" and into sacrificial, covenantal, "unlikely" partnerships across geographic, racial, denominational, economic, and ethnic borders. Only when we take that prayerful step will all the resources God has given us, including but not reduced to the financial ones, be freed up for God's just purposes in the world.

Yet further, active citizenship enrolls all Christians into ethical discernment and action:

> It is my hunch that the most effective public theology will be carried forward by laity who are more expert in their fields than theologians and ethicists will ever be. These laypeople will be informed by theologians but will filter their religious

---

[203] Larry Rasmussen, "The Meaning of the Cross for Social Ethics in the World Today," in *From Christ to the World: Introductory Readings in Christian Ethics*, ed. Wayne G. Boulton, Thomas D. Kennedy and Allen Verhey (Grand Rapids: Eerdmans, 1994), 311-13 (313).

notions through the conceptual apparatus of their own fields. The laity have come of age; they are on the front lines of public theology.[204]

In light of this, we may ask: Could not the North American Church, so reliant on its professional, formally educated, officially ordained, and fully paid clergy, pastors, youth ministers, and worship directors, possibly learn from Majority World churches with much smaller budgets but with visible lay initiative, involvement, and responsibility in the life and ministry of the church?

*Where Christ is King, Women and Men Take Responsibility for the Impact of their Actions on Others.*

The map of Christianity has been re-drawn. The church in the Majority World has also become by far the majority church in the world. But the economic map shows not the slightest change. Wealth is ever more concentrated in fewer hands; and, with the exception of the ruling elites of many nations, those hands are mostly in North America and Europe. In addition, the natural goods of the earth continue to be exploited mostly by the wealthy minority, who is also responsible for its degradation. "As Americans," Novey confesses, "we each generate an average of 22 tons of carbon per year, more than three times the average for those in the rest of the world."[205] Those emissions accelerate global warming and are already affecting people at the bottom of the world-economy totem pole, like nomadic herders in northern Kenya. Yet worse: "By 2025, 480 million people in Africa could be encountering the desperate water shortages that Kenyan pastoral peoples are facing now."[206] Meanwhile, US investment to curb world poverty is dwarfed by its military expenditure, leading economist Jeffrey Sachs to state in 2005, in relation to the US war on Iraq, that "the costs continue to mount, at roughly $5 billion a month, compared with just $1 billion for the Millennium Challenge Account for all of 2005."[207]

These are but some evidences of an unjust world order. How long can Christians in the North simply go about their business, untouched by the plight of fellow human beings—including millions of brothers and sisters in Christ—when that plight is avoidable and depends at least partially on their lifestyle choices? How willing are North American Chris137, tians to listen to the voices from "unlikely" downtrodden places?

---

[204] Robert Benne and Preston N. Williams, "Responses to 'A Postcommunist Manifesto': Ethics, Economics, and the Corporate Life," in *From Christ to the World: Introductory Readings in Christian Ethics,* ed. Boulton, et al. (Grand Rapids: Eerdmans, 1994) 489-92 (490).

[205] Joelle Novey, "The Climate Crisis: Impacts on Africa," *Co-op America Quarterly* 71 (Winter 2007): 18.

[206] Novey, "The Climate Crisis," 18.

[207] Jeffrey D. Sachs, "The Millennium, 9/11, and the United Nations," in *The End of Poverty* (New York: Penguin, 2005), 221.

## Some Ways to Open the Door for "Unlikely" Contributions

Can Christians in the East and the West, the South and the North engage as partners in God's reconciling mission, in spite of all the differences and distances between them? I am convinced that it is possible by God's grace. As Paul reminds the Church in Corinth, "in Christ, the new creation has come: The old has gone, the new is here! All this is from God, who reconciled us to himself through Christ and gave us the ministry of reconciliation" (2 Cor. 5:17). We no longer need to cling to labels as "missionary" and "national," "home" and "field," "old" and "young" churches. We can celebrate signs of God's reconciling love among us all here and now.

And what would this reconciliation look like inside the borders of this country [the US]? Jesus' reconciling reign will be made visible when theological institutions, mission agencies, and local churches seriously consider the space they are granting to voices from outside their traditional establishments. To what extent are doors open to Majority World Christians on boards, in leadership positions, in strategic planning for mission activity in their own regions of the world? And how willing are local North American churches to include among their pastors and leaders persons originally from the Third World? Might they support multi-national, multi-ethnic ministry teams in major cities as part of their church development efforts? What steps must be taken so that Third World theological and ethical articulations are explored with as much respect as those formulated in this country or inherited from Europe? What self-sufficiencies and guild standards need to be broken in theological institutions so people from unlikely places can contribute?

Summing up, what ethnocentric pride and imperial pretensions need to be put at the foot of cross to allow Christ—in the shape of our Christian sisters and brothers—to make his home among us? Far from marginal, these considerations lie at the core of any attempt to renew the North American church and to involve it in a world-transformative mission that is faithful to the gospel of Christ, the Servant King from "unlikely" Nazareth.

# Bibliography

Allen, Roland. *Missionary Methods: St. Paul's or Ours?* Grand Rapids: Eerdmans, 1962; first published 1912.

Benne, Robert and Preston N. Williams, "Responses to 'A Postcommunist Manifesto': Ethics, Economics, and the Corporate Life." In *From Christ to the World: Introductory Readings in Christian Ethics*, edited by Wayne G. Boulton, Thomas D. Kennedy, and Allen Verhey, 489-92. Grand Rapids: Eerdmans, 1994.

Novey, Joelle. "The Climate Crisis: Impacts on Africa." *Co-op America Quarterly* 71 (Winter 2007): 18.

Rasmussen, Larry. "The Meaning of the Cross for Social Ethics in the World Today." In *From Christ to the World: Introductory Readings in Christian Ethics,* edited by Wayne G. Boulton, Thomas D. Kennedy, and Allen Verhey, 311-13. Grand Rapids: Eerdmans, 1994.

Sachs, Jeffrey D. "The Millennium, 9/11, and the United Nations." In *The End of Poverty,* 221. New York: Penguin, 2005.

# John Sung Revisited

Hwa Yung

John Sung (Song Shangjie; 1901–1944) was one of the three best-known Chinese evangelist-pastor figures of the 20th century, the other two being Watchman Nee (Ni Tuosheng) and Wang Mingdao. John Sung came from the home of a godly Methodist pastor. Even as a young teenager, he was known as the "Little Pastor," because he would assist his father in preaching. At 19, God wonderfully provided for him to study in America. A brilliant student, he sailed through his studies all the way to a Ph.D. in chemistry in less than six years. Although the world lay at his feet, his heart was restless until he yielded to God's call to return to China to preach the gospel. After another eventful year he sailed home in 1927. As the boat neared China, he took all the gold medals and diplomas he had won at university, with the exception of his doctoral certificate, and threw them into the ocean. For the next 14 years he burnt his life out for Christ!

His preaching ministry took him all over China and Southeast Asia. His ministry hit the Chinese churches like an earthquake. Tens of thousands found Christ, hundreds of churches revived, and many were healed. Talking to older folks who witnessed his ministry in 1930s, you invariably see a glint in their eyes. His active ministry ended only when his health finally broke. An operational wound from his student days never healed. But his sense of urgency prevented him from taking time off to undergo the treatment required. When he finally entered hospital in December 1940, it was too late. Despite the best medical attention given under wartime conditions in Beijing, he finally died more than three years later.

Writing some 30 years after his death, one of his closest friends and a one-time missionary in China, William Schubert, asserted that

> Dr. John Sung was probably the greatest preacher of this century. I have heard almost all the great preachers from 1910 until now, including R.A. Torrey, Billy

---

[208] *Editors' Note: This article was first written for the republication of Leslie Lyall,* John Sung—Flame of God for the Far East, *in 2004, and needs to be read in that context. For the Asian Church to move forward effectively in mission, the author acknowledges the need to have a clear sense of their own indigenous Christian identity.*

Sunday, Henry Jowett, the great holiness preachers, the Methodist bishops, including Bishop Quayle, even Harry Emerson Fosdick ... and finally Billy Graham. Yet John Sung surpassed them all in pulpit power, attested by amazing and enduring results.[209]

Schubert's judgment would of course be contested by others. But to dwell on this would be to miss the point, which is that China produced one of the most outstanding evangelists and revivalists in the world in the 20th century, and certainly the most outstanding in the Chinese Church before the Second World War.

Yet it is strange that many in the church in Asia have never heard of him, let alone knowing anything about the impact of his ministry. In part this is because the Asian church remains very Western in its orientation. Our theologies and ways of thinking, modes of mission and ministry, music and hymns, worship patterns and architecture, and even our heroes and self-identities are often rooted in the history and life of the Western Church. I remember speaking at a certain theological college in this part of the world, to a majority Chinese audience, and asked how many knew about John Sung. At most, about one-third of the hands went up. The same students would have had no difficulty rattling off the names of Billy Graham, Cho Yong-Gi, and John Stott, as well as the big-time American preachers who have been frequenting the charismatic circuit in Southeast Asia in recent years. Much of the Church in Asia remains a Church in Western captivity in heart and soul! This unfortunate fact was reason enough for Leslie Lyall's biography on John Sung to be reissued in 2004.[210]

I first read his biography in my university years. Like John Sung, coming from a poor family, the opportunity for me to study overseas was an impossible dream come true. Yet apart from personal ambitions concerning my own future, I also had strong parental expectations to meet. And then it happened—the call to the ministry came, gently and yet incessantly. A long battle over obedience to God's will ensued. As the turmoil intensified in my soul, one of the things that helped me most was the sterling example of John Sung's obedience and sacrifice. That was a long time ago. Over the years I have found out more about the man, and my admiration for him has steadily grown.

A new biography on him is very much needed. Of those available in English, Leslie Lyall's easily stands out.[211] But that was written some 50 years ago. Since then much new information has surfaced. Some of his own writings are

---

[209] William E. Schubert, *I Remember John Sung* (Singapore: Far Eastern Bible College Press, 1976), 14.

[210] Leslie T. Lyall, *John Sung: Flame of God for the Far East*, 4th ed. (London: OMF, 1961); reissued as *A Biography of John Sung* (Singapore: Armour Publishing, 2004).

[211] Apart from those by Lyall and Schubert, there is only one other, by Timothy Tow, *John Sung: My Teacher* (Singapore: Christian Life Publishers, 1985). There are also biographies in Chinese, but none particularly outstanding.

now in print, both in Chinese and English, as well as those by others. His family has also released an edited version of his personal diaries.[212] These have shed more light on him and his ministry.[213] But a good critical study and definitive biography of John Sung is still being awaited. It is hoped that some thoughtful scholar or a younger Ph.D. student will take up the challenge to produce such a work. That would be a real blessing to the Church.

When I was first tasked with writing a new introduction for the reissue of Lyall's biography, I had to ask myself: "Is there anything fresh that I can say?" Much can be learned from Lyall's story itself, as well as from John Stott's "Foreword" in Lyall's book.[214] To avoid repeating Lyall and Stott unnecessarily, I have therefore restricted myself to doing two things. First, I will seek to draw attention to the relevance that John Sung's story still has for us in 21st-century Asia. Although the world has changed much since his time, there are still things in his life that have a challenging relevance today. Second, to do this effectively, I will also include some other details not found in Lyall's biography. I suggest that there are still at least four lessons that we can learn.

## Sung's Significance in the Context of the Present-day Pentecostal-Charismatic Renewal

The first lesson relates to the Pentecostal-charismatic movement that has hit us in recent years. All over Asia, wherever the churches have been or are growing rapidly, they almost invariably take on characteristics that are described as Pentecostal or charismatic in Western theological terminology. "Signs and wonders" such as healing, deliverance from demonic powers, prophetic utterances, and other demonstrations of the power of the Holy Spirit are often found. This is true of the Indonesian revival in the late 1960s, the growth of the Korean Church from the 1960s to the 1980s, and the rapid expansion of house churches in China today and elsewhere. It is also true of the charismatic renewal that has swept across many churches in Southeast Asia in the last three decades.

Because of the Western captivity of Asian churches, there is a strong tendency in many circles to interpret what is happening largely in terms of the

---

[212] Compiled by Levi Sung, *The Journal Once Lost—Extracts from the Diary of John Sung*, trans. Thng Pheng Soon (Singapore: Armour Publishing, 2008). An earlier shorter translation appeared under the title, *The Diaries of John Sung—An Autobiography*, trans. Stephen L. Sheng (Brighton; MI: Luke H. Sheng & Stephen L. Sheng, 1995). It should also be noted that his complete diary is now digitalised and kept in a secure place, and available for serious research.

[213] The following of his writings are available in English. *My Testimony: The Autobiography of Dr. John Sung* (Kowloon, HK: Living Books for All, 1977); and *Forty John Sung Revival Sermons*, vol. 1 & 2, trans. Timothy Tow (Singapore: Alice Doo & Christian Life Distributors, 1978 & 1983).

[214] Lyall, *John Sung*, vii-xii.

Pentecostal-charismatic renewal that came from the West. This is perceived to have begun with the Pentecostal revival in Azusa Street in 1906 in America, spilt over into the charismatic renewal that hit traditional denominations there from the 1960s onward and emerged as the Third Wave from the 1980s onward. This results in an understanding of the work of the Spirit in the Church and a theology and practice of signs and wonders that is largely borrowed from the Western Pentecostal tradition. But this understanding is now increasingly being recognized as a distorted Western reading of Church history.

What many may not know is that in many parts of the non-Western world, indigenous versions of Christianity have invariably tended to look like what in the West is called Pentecostalism or charismatic Christianity. Again and again, wherever Christians in the non-Western world have read the Bible from within their own contexts and through their own worldview lenses, they have taken the work of the Holy Spirit seriously. The result is a Christianity marked by signs and wonders. Often these manifestations predate Azusa Street or owe nothing to it whatsoever.[215]

John Sung was officially an evangelist-at-large of the Hinghwa Conference of the Methodist Church in China, and certainly not a Pentecostal. He first encountered some form of Pentecostalism in 1931, but the account indicates that he was largely unimpressed.[216] Yet he was clearly fully 'Pentecostal' in the New Testament sense. From the very beginning of his ministry, the Spirit's anointing was confirmed by revival in churches and numerous personal conversions. In particular, during the Nanchang revival, two weeks of preaching culminated one Sunday night in March 1931, when the Holy Spirit came powerfully upon some 300 people present, in true Pentecostal fashion as in Acts! The group burst aloud repeatedly into spontaneous confession and prayer, and many came to faith in Christ.[217] John Sung also had the gift of tongues, which was given to him unsolicited on March 25, 1934.[218] His healing ministry through prayer is well documented.[219] And there are countless

---

[215] See, for example, Gary B. McGee, "Pentecostalism," in *A Dictionary of Asian Christianity*, ed. Scott W. Sunquist, et. al; Grand Rapids: Eerdmans, 2001), 646-50 and Hwa Yung, "Pentecostalism and the Asian Church," in *Asian and Pentecostal: The Charismatic Face of Christianity in Asia*, ed. Allan Anderson and Edmond Tang (Oxford: Regnum, 2005), 37-57.

[216] Cf. Lyall, *John Sung*, 67.

[217] Cf. pp. 60-65 below; and Schubert, *I Remember John Sung*, 27-39. The loud spontaneous prayer and confession by the whole congregation persisted in spite of repeated efforts by John Sung to bring "order" to the meeting! When asked why he tried to stop the spontaneous praying aloud, he replied, "I didn't want the missionaries to say 'That crazy Sung made all the students crazy'." (Schubert, *I Remember John Sung*, 35). This event may well be the beginning of the tradition still practiced by Chinese churches in which whole congregations pray aloud together.

[218] Sung, *Journal Once Lost*, 265.

[219] Cf. Lyall, *John Sung*, 132-35.

accounts of his prophetic gifting, especially the ability to know and rebuke secret sins.

The point that needs to be made here is that Asian Christians, as well as all others who would desire to learn more about the work of the Spirit in revival, would do well to read John Sung's biographies and diaries. They should also look at the records of other Asian Christian leaders like Pastor Hsi, Sadhu Sundar Singh, and Bahkt Singh, whom God has used so marvellously in similar ways in earlier years. The tragedy is that many Asian Christians look only to the Western Pentecostal-charismatic tradition for inspiration, especially when some teachings that are coming from this direction are positively harmful to the Church. This brings us to our second lesson.

### Sung's Example of Sacrificial Living and Holiness

The Pentecostal-charismatic renewal that has impacted Asian churches in the past few decades has brought much renewal and vitality to both churches and individuals. At the same time, it is not an unmixed blessing, because some of the influences that have come from the Western, especially American, tradition have been far from wholesome. Among the problems is that of the "gospel of prosperity," or the "health and wealth gospel," taught by some leaders of the renewal. This distorted version of the gospel originated in the "Faith Movement" in American charismatic Christianity, under teachers like Kenneth Hagin, his son, Kenneth Hagin, Jr., Kenneth Copeland, and others. It stresses the power of faith in obtaining the twin blessings of physical health and financial prosperity. Sickness, in this view, is the result of sin or lack of faith, thus leaving no room for God's sovereignty in the Christian understanding of healing prayer. Similarly, the teaching on prosperity distorts the Bible's promises that God will bless and provide for all those who trust him, into something else that leaves little or no room for sacrificial living. Instead, intentionally or otherwise, it tends to encourage Christians to chase after material prosperity and financial success as the main goals of life.

Added to this is the problem which success brings. In many wealthier parts of Asia, the rapid growth of the Church in the last generation has given rise to an increasing spirit of competition and rivalry among churches and Christian leaders. Success in the eyes of the world, measured by congregation numbers, financial clout, and building size, appears to be taking priority over more basic issues. Thus biblical fundamentals such as prayer, the centrality of the Bible, holy living, community building, servanthood, humility of the leadership, concern for the needy, and so forth, often end up merely as means by which success can be achieved, rather than as important ends in themselves.

What many fail to realize is that such things inevitably lay the ground for the Church's eventual decline. For example, the Korean Protestant church, known for its 'wild-fire' church growth in an earlier period, is facing a serious crisis today. Available figures show that growth peaked in the early 1990s, and thereafter the Church entered a period of stagnation and then slow decline. Research and other anecdotal evidence indicate that this has much to do with the neglect of biblical fundamentals. We do not have to look very hard to find similar patterns in other parts of Asia. Spiritual pride is a deadly thing.

Against this background, John Sung's life forces us once again to return to the basics. Certainly he was thoroughly familiar with the temptations of success, having tasted it both in the academic world as well as in the church. Repeatedly he warned of the triple temptations of "fame, money, and sex."[220] Yet early in his life he had fought and won the crucial battle of learning to die to self. At his graduation, with job offers from all over, the world lay at his feet. But the words of Christ, "What will it profit a man if he gains the whole world and forfeits his soul?" (Matt. 16:26 ESV) came as a solemn warning.[221] Again, soon after his recovery from a supreme crisis of his faith while studying at Union, New York, God spoke to him again in a dream. He saw himself in an open coffin, all dressed in his academic regalia. And he heard an angel's voice crying, "John Sung is dead—dead to the world!"[222] That set the pattern for the rest of his life.

For example, his attitude towards money places him in sharp contrast to many, both then and now. By all accounts, he lived simply and had little time for luxuries. In the later phase of ministry when he was on his own, he handed all money received to a committee who oversaw its disposal to ensure complete transparency. And only the necessary portions were set aside for the family. At times he would use the same gifts to subsidize the cost of the revival and evangelistic campaigns when local funds fell low. Among his requirements for preachers of the gospel was that they must not exploit their positions for "personal gain."[223]

John Sung never sought to build his own organization, mega-church, or personal kingdom. He turned down repeated requests to pastor what must have been sizable churches. God had called him to an itinerant ministry, and there he stayed. He never sought popularity as a preacher. Everywhere he went, he proclaimed the centrality of the cross, rebuked sin fearlessly, and called for repentance without hesitation, regardless of high or low. For this, many, including pastors and missionaries, disliked him intensely. The sense of competition and one-upmanship so rampant today in the church does not appear to have bothered him. Instead, especially in his later years, he possessed a genuine meekness which allowed him to fully appreciate how God was using others, without himself retreating into a false humility. This is clearly seen in the comparison that he once made of himself with his contemporaries.[224]

---

[220] Sung, *Journal Once Lost*, 318; cf. also Lyall, *John Sung*, 176.
[221] Sung, *Journal Once Lost*, 37.
[222] Lyall, *John Sung*, 34.
[223] Sung, *Journal Once Lost*, 471f.
[224] Lyall, *John Sung*, 164.

His sacrificial and total disregard of himself is perhaps most clearly illustrated by his death. As indicated earlier, his active ministry ended only when his health finally broke. His sense of urgency prevented him from taking time off for the treatment required for the unhealed surgical wound from his student days. When he finally entered hospital in December 1940, the fistulas had developed interstices and eventually grew to almost one foot deep! He languished in that condition until his death.[225] Although his ministry ended too late to save his life, his sense of God's timing was perfect. War had already engulfed China by that time, and in another year, the rest of East Asia. Had he pressed his ministry with less urgency, much less would have been achieved because later war conditions would have prevented travel. So he completed his task.

### The Challenge of Revival and the Place of Prayer

The third lesson for us today concerns how God brings revival. In the Church today, many are seeking greater spiritual vitality and dynamism. However, there is a tendency to put the emphasis on numbers in church growth and methods which enhance it, rather than on a genuine revival that comes through radical repentance and persistent prayer. This, of course, is not true of all, but is rather an indication of the general direction in which many are moving. Part of the problem lies with some modern church growth theories. These tend to emphasize the search for better human methods of bringing in the harvest, including those such as "cell churches," "natural church growth," "evangelism explosion," "strategic level spiritual warfare," the use of "signs and wonders," and the like.

It is important to state emphatically that the search for better human methods is not wrong in itself. Many of us have seen too much traditionalism in our churches, and its associated rigidity in structures and outmoded methods, to want to glorify human inefficiency. Certainly we should by all means search for the best human methods possible as we seek to advance the cause of the Kingdom of Christ. At the same time, we must never forget that the criteria by which we make such judgments may well be faulty, because we are all too human and our values so often compromised by the world's standards.

But having said this, we are still left with a paradox. When we look at, for example, the growth of the church in China today and ask what human methods are driving it, we can never find a complete and satisfactory human answer. This is the same story with every revival throughout history. Historical and sociological analyses yield at best partial and incomplete answers. Because what cannot be explained by such analyses are the sovereign will of God in revival on the one hand and the humble prayers of his people on the other. This

---

[225] Sung, *Journal Once Lost*, 482ff, 522ff. Lyall incorrectly attributed John Sung's death in part to cancer.

is precisely why we need to look again at John Sung's practice of prayer, something which John Stott noted in his "Foreword" to Sung's biography by Lyall.

From childhood he had learned the importance of prayer. One day his father was struck down by a severe respiratory ailment when John Sung was just eight years old. As death threatened, he prayed, "O My God, please save my father so that he can raise me up into adulthood!" He described the almost instantaneous answer he received to his prayer as "the foundation for my faith in God."[226]

His prayer life throughout his ministry displayed certain distinct features. First, it was marked by constant and meticulous self-examination to ensure that his life was right with God. He wanted no barrier between God and himself. Second, it was marked by regularity. In the midst of his busy ministry, at least two to three hours were set aside daily for personal prayer. Thirdly, he was an intercessor par excellence. Whenever he traveled from place to place, he would carry suitcases full of letters, bearing prayer requests from church members and converts. Fourthly, he prayed with passion and intensity, pleading incessantly with God for revival. One eyewitness in Sitiawan, Malaysia, saw as a little girl how, at the end of his prayer sessions, his singlet was so drenched in sweat that her mother could actually wring it out like water. And how God answered his prayers!

But that is not all. From the time he entered Beijing Union Medical College Hospital for treatment in December 1940 till his death in August 1944, he was unable to engage in any public ministry. But during that period, much time was spent in little else but prayer. To his friend William Schubert he wrote, "In the past, I had viewed the work of the evangelistic bands as of paramount importance. Now, I think that praying is more important than anything else."[227] And in his last letter to the churches in Southeast Asia, he also said,

> For God to do a work of great revival, he must first give us a deep hunger and thirst ... If there were one hundred evangelistic teams in Southeast Asia that have tasted of the sweetness of prayer, the whole of Southeast Asia would turn to the Lord ... For 98 days now I have been praying with brothers and sisters here. Sometimes we pray for 5-6 hours nonstop, without feeling fatigued ... If every church could have one of these teams, it would receive revival.[228]

Does not this provide a necessary corrective today in our tendency to place too much emphasis on human methods?

---

[226] Sung, *Journal Once Lost*, 9; cf. Lyall, *John Sung*, 10f.
[227] Sung, *Journal Once Lost*, 502.
[228] Sung, *Journal Once Lost*, 498-502; quotation here taken from the earlier edition, *The Diaries of John Sung*, 202f.

## The Implications of His Concern for an Independent Chinese Church

The fourth lesson that we may draw from John Sung comes from his concern for the Chinese church to shake off its dependence on Western missions and become truly independent. To understand fully his concern, we need to remember the historical context of the 1920s and 30s. On the Chinese side, there were at least two issues. Some had become Christians or used their new faith as a means of self-advancement. This had given rise to the term "rice Christians." Further, the 1920s saw the emergence of the anti-Christian May 4th movement led by the intellectuals and Marxists. These rejected Christianity as being superstitious on the one hand and supposedly tied to Western imperialism against China on the other. Their feelings were summed up in the slogan, "One more Christian, one less Chinese!"

On the part of the missionaries, there were also related problems. Many missionaries, though certainly not all, were indeed guilty of imperialistic associations with Western powers. Then there were the modernists or liberals among the missionaries. Though their social gospel did much good through education, medicine, and the like, they had little or nothing to offer for the spiritual hunger of China. There was also a lot of ethnic insensitivity. For example, one missionary report on the evangelization of China was clumsily titled, "The Christian Occupation of China"! Finally, what irked John Sung most was perhaps what he saw of missionary domination over the church through control of the purse strings. It was something that he saw regularly and even experienced personally, especially in the forced dissolution of the Bethel Band by a missionary, at a time when it was being used greatly by God.[229]

In response, John Sung was at times fairly critical of missionaries. Repeatedly he urged the church to stop relying on missionary funds. He rightly perceived that Western control and dependency on Western funds often prevented the Chinese church from growing. Instead it should look "to the Lord of all things and realize that the time has come for the church to be self-propagating, self-governing, and self-supporting—truly independent!"[230] This vision found its outworking in the ministry of many, including especially Wang Mingdao, his contemporary and Beijing pastor of later fame.[231] Asked shortly before his death about the future of the Chinese church, John Sung revealed that God had showed him that a great revival was coming. But the Western missionaries would all have to leave first. The history of the last 60 years

---

[229] Lyall, *John Sung*, 119f; also see Sung, *Journal Once Lost*, 251-55.

[230] Lyall, *John Sung*, 77; also see Sung, *Journal Once Lost*, 271 and various other similar references.

[231] See Thomas A. Harvey, *Acquainted with Grief: Wang Mingdao's Stand for the Persecuted Church in China* (Grand Rapids: Brazos, 2002), esp. 27-46.

proves that this was the most profound prophecy uttered about the Chinese Church in the 20th century![232]

As a result, John Sung is sometimes seen as being anti-Western. But that would be an unfair description of the man. Among some of his closest friends were Westerners like Dr. Rollin H. Walker and William E. Schubert. What then was his underlying concern? He saw the problem of Western domination and how that prevented the church from growing. That simply could not be the way of the future. With characteristic clarity, he recognized that the Chinese church needed to learn true independence and to look to God alone, for both provision and direction—as it eventually did in the great revival that has swept over China and is still ongoing today. Only then could the Holy Spirit have the freedom to do his work! Throughout his ministry, we see him attempting to live this out in different ways.

For example, despite his American Ph.D., he was never in a Western suit but always in a Chinese coat! Further, his public exercise of spiritual gifts in ministry, especially the gifts of prophecy and healing, seems to fit into the same pattern. It was not something he learned from Western Pentecostals or some modern-day charismatic preachers. Neither was it commonly practiced in public by others, because very few in China at that time had such gifts.[233] It was thoroughly innovative, especially when much of the time he ministered in traditional mainline churches. Many of these were directly or indirectly under Western missionaries who would have frowned upon such practices, to say the least. Certainly these gifts were the result of the Spirit's anointing. Their public exercise developed naturally in the course of his ministry in response to the felt needs of his congregations. But it also appears to be another expression of the indigenous Christianity he was striving for, which was independent of the missionary practices of his time.

Again, we see a similar concern in the response he once gave when asked what he thought of Harry Emerson Fosdick's teachings. His reply was characteristically blunt. "China does not need the teaching of Fosdick …The teaching of Confucius is better … What the Chinese need is Jesus Christ and his Cross."[234] It is important to note that John Sung did not reject Fosdick simply for his liberal theology, but also because he deemed China to have a superior ethical teacher in Confucius! Not many Chinese Christians would have the confidence in his or her own culture to say the same. Here is another indication of his concern for an indigenous mode of thinking about Christianity.

---

[232] Schubert, *I Remember John Sung*, 65f. But see also Sung, *Journal Once Lost*, 271, 495, and various other similar references.

[233] He first began to pray for the sick publicly during the Bethel Band's visit to Hongkong in 1932; cf. Lyall, *John Sung*, 92.

[234] See Lyall, *John Sung*, 69. Fosdick was a professor of Union Theological Seminary in New York when John Sung studied there, and one of the most famous liberal scholars of his day.

Perhaps his concern for the independence of the Chinese Church is most clearly seen in that, in spite of the confusion of voices clamouring for attention, he grasped clearly God's agenda for the Chinese church at a particular moment in history. Without wavering, he stuck to the pursuit of national revival singlemindedly until his work was done. Yet to this day, some 60 years after his death, it may be questioned whether we have yet to fully understand his concern. Christianity in most parts of Asia is still viewed by many as a Western religion. Further, although we may be organizationally and financially independent, much of the church and its agenda remain in Western captivity, as earlier noted. One would have to say that truly indigenous forms of Christianity have yet to emerge in most parts of Asia.

Yet, there are two reasons at least why we must take seriously the concern for an indigenous Christian identity. The first is that everywhere in Asia people are seeking to recover their indigenous cultural roots. Witness the resurgence of the traditional religions all over Asia today. If a Western Christianity was a hindrance to the advance of the gospel in the early 20th century, it is no less so today. If you think otherwise, you might want to ask why Buddhism, for example, has been growing faster than Christianity in the 1990s in Singapore—possibly the most westernized city in Asia!

The second is this. One of the most notable things in world Christianity is that, after centuries of dominance, many parts of the Western Church are in serious decline. As some scholars like Andrew Walls have noted, sometime in the late 20th century, the center of gravity of world Christianity has moved out of the West into the Majority World. Why then are indigenous non-Western Christians still always looking to the West for guidance and inspiration? Of course we must never forget the debt of love that we owe to our Western brethren for bringing the gospel to us in the first place. Moreover, there is still much we can learn from them. But certainly we should not be constantly looking over our shoulders, even if unconsciously, to Western Christianity for leadership and direction. Instead, we should look to the Holy Spirit and the Bible. Only this will make possible the emergence of truly indigenous Christianity, without which churches in the non-Western world will never mature!

Sensitive Christians throughout the world are recognizing that, with the decline of the church in the West, the burden of world mission will increasingly fall on the younger churches in the non-Western world. But for us in Asia to respond effectively to such a high calling, we will need to appropriate wisely the lessons that John Sung still has for us. To begin with, given the magnitude of the challenge, Paul's words, "And who is equal to such a task?" (2 Cor. 2:16), come as a timely reminder. Without the Holy Spirit's power, both human strength and the Church will fail! Does our Christianity know Pentecostal power? Further, the Bible and Church history repeatedly show us too that, although God in his mercy brings revival, it is the holiness and sacrificial lives of his people, together with their faithful prayers, that sustain it. Already in some places, because these fundamentals have been neglected, there are clear indications of decline.

Finally, for the Asian Church to move forward effectively in mission, we need to have a clear sense of our own indigenous Christian identity. Such an identity would be firmly rooted in Christ on the one hand, and freed from a sense of bondage and subservience to Western Christians on the other. At the same time it will allow us to humbly take our place in equal partnership with them. Only with such an identity can Christians in Asia develop a clear vision of what God's distinctive agenda for the Asian church is, and possess the necessary confidence in Christ to bring it to pass!

## Bibliography

Harvey, Thomas A. *Acquainted with Grief: Wang Mingdao's Stand for the Persecuted Church in China.* Grand Rapids: Brazos, 2002.

Lyall, Leslie T. *John Sung: Flame of God for the Far East.* 4th ed. (London: OMF, 1961); reissued as *A Biography of John Sung.* Singapore: Armour Publishing, 2004.

Schubert, William E. *I Remember John Sung.* Singapore: Far Eastern Bible College Press, 1976.

Sung, Levi, compiler. *The Journal Once Lost—Extracts from the Diary of John Sung.* Translated by Thng Pheng Soon. Singapore: Armour Publishing, 2008.

McGee, Gary B. "Pentecostalism." In *A Dictionary of Asian Christianity*, edited by Scott W. Sunquist, et. al, 646-50. Grand Rapids: Eerdmans, 2001.

Yung, Hwa. "Pentecostalism and the Asian Church." In *Asian and Pentecostal: The Charismatic Face of Christianity in Asia*, edited by Allan Anderson and Edmond Tang. Oxford: Regnum, 2005.

# Hermeneutics:
# Christian-Muslim Perspectives

Bruce J. Nicholls

The goal of this essay on hermeneutics as biblical interpretation is to enable our Asian church leaders to be better expositors of God's Word in their preaching, teaching, and counseling ministries in their own cultural context and to understand how a Muslim interprets the Bible from the perspective of his own worldview and that of the *Qur'an*. This task acknowledges the diversity of Asian cultures in the context of rapid cultural change. I will focus on one context, Islam, which is the dominant religion in Indonesia, Malaysia, Bangladesh, Pakistan, and Kashmir, India. Islam is also a steadily growing minority in most other countries in Asia. In the Middle East, it dominates almost each country, from Iran to the Gulf States and south to Egypt. In Eastern Europe, Islam is the controlling factor in several nations.

Luther is reported to have said, "If you preach the gospel in all respects, except the issues that deal specifically with our time, you are not preaching the gospel at all." The tragedy is that some evangelicals continue to give theological answers to questions people are no longer asking. Some pastors focus on good exegesis but ignore the cultural contexts of their congregation, while others use Scripture as a proof-text peg on which to hang their own thoughts and prejudices. In both cases, they fail to accomplish their missiological calling. Our hermeneutical task is to expound God's Word and subjectively interpret it for the people and their community to whom it is being addressed. It is both a science and an art. Our challenge is to integrate both concerns.

In interpreting the biblical message for the Muslim community, this calls for an understanding as to how Muslims understand and interpret the *Qur'an* and secondly the Bible, using the methodology that they use in interpreting the *Qur'an*. It is a mistake to begin with the Christian understanding of how they think Muslims interpret the biblical story.

## Traditional Hermeneutics

Traditionally, hermeneutics has been limited to a study of the historico-grammatical rules and practices for interpreting the texts. In recent times, especially since Friedrich Schleiermacher (1768–1834), hermeneutics now includes understanding the process of communication, the meaning of language, and the cultural and religious contexts of the writer and his readers, as well as the interpreter, and the mindset of those who receive the message. In missiological terms, it is a three-way dialogue of question and answer between the final and unchanging text and the relative and ever-changing context of human thought and practice. The questioning may begin at either point, but the process of understanding must proceed from text to context. In the words of Chris Marantika of Yogyakarta, "The message is of primary significance. The method is secondary. To reverse this priority is unbiblical."[235]

Thus our theological task is both an ongoing dialogue between the academic and the spiritual, always moving to an eschatological goal of knowing God and his purpose and will for all creation, which will culminate in the coming of Christ and his Kingdom on earth. It is not an endless cycle of subjective uncertainties and relative truths. In the context of theological education, our hermeneutical task is "symbolized by holding together in partnership the chapel, the classroom, the local church, and the marketplace."[236] "Thus hermeneutics is an interpretive science with a clearly recognized objective."[237] However, pure objectivity is impossible, as every scientist knows. Richard Dawkins, the Oxford scientist, refuses to distinguish between evolution as a science and evolution as a philosophy intending to promote atheism. As an art, hermeneutics is subjectively based on human attitudes and experiences shaped by heritage, past events, education, economic status, and, above all, by religious beliefs and practices.

## Hermeneutical Authority

The precondition for a fruitful hermeneutic understanding is to begin with the issue of authority. To the question, on what authority can the Bible be claimed to be the unchanging infallible record of God's self disclosure? The answer is simply Jesus Christ. He gave authority to his Bible, the Old Testament, when he said, "these are the very Scriptures that testify about me" (John 5:39). He

---

[235] Chris Marantika, "Towards an Evangelical Theology in an Islamic Culture," in *The Bible and Theology in Asian Contexts,* ed. Bong Rin Ro and Ruth Eschenauer (Taichung: ATA, 1984), 309.

[236] Bruce Nicholls, "Our Theological Task," in *The Unique Christ in Our Pluralistic World,* ed. Bruce. J. Nicholls (Carlisle: Paternoster, 1994), 11.

[237] A. C. Thiselton, "Hermeneutics," in *The New Dictionary of Theology,* ed. Sinclair B. Ferguson, David F. Wright, and J. I. Packer (Leicester: InterVarsity, 1998), 293.

saw his mission in the world as the fulfillment of the mission of God in the Old Testament story. In his sermon in the synagogue at Nazareth recorded in Luke 4:16-21, he claimed to fulfill the prophecy of Isaiah 61:1-2. During his temptation in the wilderness, he rebuked Satan on the authority of texts from Deuteronomy. At his Last Supper, he actualized the promise of the new covenant prophesied by Jeremiah (31:31-34). Thus, the authority of the biblical text depends on the authority of Jesus Christ and is confirmed by the amazing unity and historical reliability of the text.

To accept Christ's authority is a "leap of faith" which is justified by the confidence in the text which follows from it. Anselm's dictum "*credo ut intelligam*"—I believe so that I may understand—is the distinctive Christian way forward. It is faith seeking understanding. Anselm stated, "I am not seeking to understand in order to believe, but I believe in order to understand. For this, too, I believe: unless I believe, I shall not understand."[238] The level of trust that we have put in the trustworthiness of Scripture will determine the direction of our understanding of the hermeneutical process. It is the watershed for evangelical interpretation.

## Inspiration by the Holy Spirit

Accepting the Bible as the trustworthy Word of God also depends on the auxiliary truth that it is wholly inspired by the Spirit of God. What the writers wrote was what God chose to reveal to them. As B.B. Warfield decisively showed, the *theopneustos* of 2 Timothy 3:16 points to all Scripture as being "outbreathed" by the Spirit of God. In the words of J.I. Packer, "The biblical idea of inspiration relates not to the literary quality of what is written but to its character as divine revelation."[239] The inspiration of Scripture is verbal, as in such phrases as "the Word of the Lord came to me" or "thus said the Lord."

However, Scripture has a double authorship. While God, through his Spirit, is the primary author, the human writers are secondary, but equally important. In the process of writing, the human authors "spoke from God as they were carried along by the Holy Spirit" (2 Pet. 1:20-21). It was not a case of mechanical dictation, as is found in the Talmud or Philo and some of the Fathers. The writers' personalities were not obliterated. Their freedom and creativity was heightened rather than controlled. They wrote from their own historical and cultural context. Each had a purpose in writing, so that each of the four Gospels had a specific readership in view. The four Gospels are portraits, rather than photographs, of the life and work of Jesus Christ. In a similar way, each of the prophets of the Old Testament reflects his own context

---

[238] Thiselton, "Hermeneutics," 26.

[239] J. I. Packer, "Inspiration," in *New Bible Dictionary*, ed. I.H. Marshall, A.R. Millard, J.I. Packer (Leicester: InterVarsity, 1999), 509.

and personality. One has only to compare the writings of Isaiah and Jeremiah, Amos and Hosea, to recognize the distinctive personalities of the writers.

This Christian understanding of the authority of the inspired Bible differs from the way the Muslim understands the authority of the *Qur'an* and how he understands the authority of the Bible. He also believes so that he might understand, but in his case it is on the authority of Muhammad, the messenger of God.[240] The majority of *Sunni* Muslims believe the *Qur'an* is the eternal, uncreated and inerrant Word of God, while the *Shia'ite* Muslims of Iran believe the *Qur'an* is created.[241] The *Qur'an* itself claims to be an exact copy of the original book *Umm-ul-Kitab* preserved in a tablet of stone in Paradise. Since it is eternal and was revealed in Arabic, it cannot be translated into other languages. All language versions of the *Qur'an* are therefore classified as paraphrases. The inerrancy of every word of the *Qur'an* is grounded in the belief that the angel Gabriel dictated every *surah* to Muhammad over a period of 23 years. Ninety of these *surahs* were given in Mecca and 24 in Medina. It is believed Muhammad was illiterate. As he received the revelations, he repeated them to his followers for memory or to write them down on whatever was available—pieces of leather, bone, palm leaves, or stones. Many of these followers were later killed in battle prompting the first Caliphate, Abu Bakr, to collect the entire writings. Later, in the year 653 CE, Caliphate Othman compiled the version as authoritative and had all other copies destroyed.[242] This version continues intact today in contrast to the many versions of the Bible in existence. Thus it is believed that every word of the *Qur'an* is the word of Allah, a belief that motivates literalist Muslims to ruthlessly punish or kill those whom the *Qur'an* condemns.

## Responses to the Muslim Acceptance of the Bible

The *Qur'an* asserts that all previous revelations were sent down to prophets direct from Allah (Q 10:37, 38). In this way the *Tawrat* (Torah) was sent to *Musa* (Moses), the *Zabur* (Psalms) to *Dawud* (David), and the *Injil* (Gospels) to *Isa* (Jesus) (*Surah* 3:113). The *Qur'an* confirms that all the earlier revelations in their original wording came direct from Allah as did the *Qur'an*, the final revelation from Allah. To explain the contradiction between these authentic Old Testament books and the Gospels which were directly revealed by Allah, and our present Bible, Islam assumes that the Jews corrupted the original text of the Old Testament and Christians corrupted the original text of the Gospels. These

---

[240] For a contemporary introduction to Islam history, belief, and practices, and guidance in approaching Muslims with love and understanding, see Patrick Sookhdeo, *A Christian Pocket Guide to Islam* (Fern, UK: Christian Focus, 2002).

[241] Joseph M. Mutei, "The Bible: Classical and Contemporary Muslim Attitudes and Exegesis," *The Evangelical Review of Theology* (October 2007): 207.

[242] I. D. Deshmukh, *The Gospel and Islam* (Bombay: GLS, 1982), 47.

original texts had been revealed to the *Ahl-al-kitab*, "the people of the Book" (Jews and Christians). Where the Bible differs from the *Qur'an* it is assumed it was corrupted by the "people of the Book" in order to conceal the true prophecies concerning the coming of Muhammad and Islam. Joseph Mutei quotes "Lazarus-Yafeh,"[243] who outlines three accusations against Christians, namely *Tahrif* (falsification) or distortion of the text, or willfully changing the Word of God. An oft-quoted example is the claim that Christians changed *perikleitos* (praised one) for *parakletos* (counselor) to hide the truth that Jesus foretold the coming of Ahmad (Muhammad). The second accusation is *Naskh* (abrogation), by which the *Qur'an* supersedes the Bible, revoking the earlier revelations where they conflict with the *Qur'an*. Islamic scholars claim to have found explicit confirmation in Daniel of the rise of Islam. The third accusation is *Tawatur* (lack of reliable transmission) of the Bible, compared to the miraculous, unbroken, and reliable transmission of the *Qur'an* since its revelation.

The interpretation of Jesus in the *Qur'an* deserves special reference, since he is referred to 93 times. Jesus is a prophet, or messenger, from God, no different from the other prophets, while Muhammad is the seal, or final prophet, of God's truth. The *Qur'an* claims Jesus was born of a virgin, performed miracles, and was a spirit from God. His deity is strongly denied (*Surah* 5:17; 6:101-102). The *Qur'an* denies Christ's death on the cross and claims he was replaced by a substitute (*Surah* 4:157, 158), the reason being that Allah would never allow one of his prophets to die such a shameful death. Other *surahs* claim that he did die. Theologically, it was unnecessary for Jesus to die as an atonement for sin, for the all-powerful God can forgive at will. Instead, Allah took him to heaven, from where he will return at the end of the world as a Muslim to lead people to the Truth.

The convincing response to the accusation that Jews and Christians corrupted the text is that the accepted text preceded the birth of Muhammad by several hundred years and it has not been changed in our Bible today. The Dead Sea Scrolls of no later than the first century CE confirm the current accuracy of the text of the *Tawrat* and the *Zabur*. In interpreting the Bible, Muslim scholars have resorted to the dangerous practice of proof-texting. (Alas, some Christians do the same).

A second response is that while Allah is great, the Creator of all things, he is beyond the reach of human desiring and beyond personal knowing. His unity is the absolute Oneness, and therefore, while he is just and merciful and compassionate, in his essence he is not loving, for love is always reciprocal and involves a dual relationship. Of the 99 names for God in the *Qur'an*, only in one is he called "the all-loving – the Affectionate." He is loving to those who follow him but not to those who have gone astray; in contrast, Christ's

---

[243] Lazarus-Yafeh, *Intertwining Worlds: Medieval Islam and Biblical Criticism* (Princeton: Princeton University Press, 1992), 19, cited by Mutei, "The Bible," 209.

unconditional love is for all people. The Christian understanding of God is trinitarian. God is love, because he is Father in relation to the Son.

A third response is that Islamic hermeneutics are selective in choosing the text on which they comment. Joseph Mutei illustrates this in the Muslim approach to prayer, one of the five pillars of Islam.[244] Correct forms of prayer become more important than the content of prayer. Preparatory ablution and posture in prayer are all important. Bowing in prayer is symbolic of submission to Allah. Thus selected texts are taken out of their context and given undue prominence.

A fourth response is that Muslim exegetes are strictly rational in their exegesis. For them, religion is not a relationship, but law. Allah can only be known through his revealed will in *Shariah*, Islamic law, which is the path of submission to Allah. Early in the development of Islam, rationalistic theology begun when *Mu'tazila* scholars introduced dogmatic theology into Islam. Other scholars have reacted to this, especially Ghazzali and the *Sufis*; but rationalism continues to dominate Islamic theology. In the later development of rationalism, the concern for the unity of God became so obsessive that his attributes become part of his essence.[245] Then rationalism gave way to legalism, applying *Shariah* law, as interpreted from the *Hadith*, to every detail of behavior in daily life. To the Muslim, the Christian Trinity is irrational and a major stumbling block to understanding and accepting the Christian faith. Thus Islam presents itself as rational truth, for the knowledge of God is not through acts of faith but is one of "conviction."[246] Anselm's dictum is reversed: "I understand, therefore I believe."

A fifth response is to the Islamic worldview that integrates all knowledge and all human behavior and in which religion and society are one.[247] There is no distinct separation of religion and politics. Muhammad was both a prophet and a politician, called by Allah to establish an Islamic society, not only in Medina but worldwide. The mosque and the state are one.[248] Christians respond by pointing to Christ's distinction, separating what belongs to God and what belongs to Caesar. This separation of church and state has been a blessing in

---

[244] Mutei, "The Bible," 218.

[245] Michael Mazir-Ali, *Islam, A Christian Perspective* (Exeter: Paternoster, 1983), 53-55.

[246] Isma'il al-Faruqi, "On the Nature of Islamic Da'wah," *International Review of Missions* (October 1976): 394-95.

[247] For an extensive exposition of the Islamic worldview, see Ayatallah Murtaza Mutahhari, *Fundamentals of Islamic Thought*, trans. R. Campbell (Berkeley, CA: Mizan, 1985), 67-131. Further, Ali Shariati, *Man and Islam*, trans. Fatollah Marjani (Houston: Free Islamic Literature), 10-28.

[248] Mahathir Mohamad, "The Role and Difference of Religions in Society," *Islam and Muslim Ummah* (Subang Jaya: Pelanduk, 2001), 227-35. This is a speech delivered at a seminar on "Muslim and Christian Minds," September 14, 1993, when Dr. Mohamad was Prime Minister of Malaysia.

modern democratic society, enabling Christians to freely proclaim the gospel. However, it has created a dichotomy between life on earth and life on heaven, and by inference the church should not become involved in political action. This has resulted in the belief that social justice is not part of the church's mission, a view that is being increasingly rejected in today's political world. Similarly, Christians have been slow to accept responsibility for the increasing destruction of nature and the need to sustain what God has so wonderfully created. It has also led to a truncated view of the Kingdom of God. It needs to be recognized that the increasing persecution of Christians and the destruction of their property in nations controlled by Islam is ultimately a political act, and not a religious one.

A sixth response is to the Islamic view that all humanity, beginning with Adam, are born as Muslims. Isma'il al-Faruqi, a former professor of Islamics at Temple University in Philadelphia, argues that Islam is *din al-fitrah*, man's natural religion. "Islam is *din al-fitrah* which is already present in its fullness in man by nature. It is innate, as it were, a natural constituent of humanity. The man who is not *homo religiosus*, and hence *homo Islamicus*, is not a man."[249] *Da'wah* is the *Qur'anic* commandment "to call man unto the path of Allah." Al-Faruqi then adds, "*Da'wah* is based on the Islamic assertion that primeval religion, or monotheism, is found in every man (*din al-fitrah*) and all he needs to do is to be reminded of it. The function of the prophets is to remind people of what is already in them."[250] This fundamental worldview is a clear denial of the biblical belief that all people, beginning with Adam, are sinners and in need of forgiveness. To be reminded of the true path is not enough. Obedience to the law is an inadequate motivation for social action. The Christian response is that true knowledge and obedience to truth is made possible by the indwelling power of Christ and by the empowering of the Holy Spirit. *Da'wah* is the Islamic equivalent of the Great Commission.

A seventh response is to the role of tradition in religious authority. The *Sunnah* and *Hadith* traditions of the deeds and sayings of the prophet Muhammad are given authority second only to that of the *Qur'an*. Muslims look to the *Hadith* for the interpretation of the *Qur'an*. Christians also have traditions. Every denomination has its own traditions. No church exists without traditions. In some churches, the Bible, tradition, and reason, like a three-legged stool, have equal authority. The evangelical response is that all tradition and rational thinking must be brought under the authority of the written Word of God.

---

[249] Isma'il al-Faruqi, 395.
[250] Isma'il al-Faruqi, 395.

## Response to *Da'wah*

Christians are challenged to take the grammatico-historical approach to hermeneutics more seriously as the starting point for biblical interpretation. Christians need to affirm the givenness of the content of their faith as recorded in the Bible. The history of the Church has an important role in developing theological understanding, but as with the reformers it must be constantly subjected to the test of Scripture. It is of some significance that most Protestant missionaries who have made an effective response to Islamic *Da'wah* have been those belonging to the Anglican and Presbyterian traditions, for they are better able to respond to Islam on rational grounds, having their own creeds and confessions of faith. The Christian challenge is to give priority to sound exegesis of the Bible and serious theological reflection on the history of the church throughout the centuries. Only then can we begin to interpret the gospel in terms of the culture, felt needs, and spiritual hunger of the people who belong to other faiths or no faith. Paul's comprehensive exegetical method in confronting orthodox Jews in the synagogue and then pagan philosophers in the marketplace of Athens is a model for our missiological calling in Asia and a hermeneutical method in responding to cross-cultural diversity. Liberal Christianity has no answer to Islamic dogmatics. The trustworthiness of the transmission of the biblical texts, especially in the light of the Muslims' respect for the Torah, the Psalms, and the Gospels, needs to be defended with good reason and with compassion and love for Muslims, for whom Christ died.

While this defense is necessary, it needs to be acknowledged that the comparison is not between the Bible and the *Qur'an*, but between Jesus Christ as the final Word of God and the *Qur'an* as the final Word of God. This comparison points to the primacy of our hermeneutical task is the expounding of Jesus Christ as the Creator, Savior, and Lord. From Jesus honored as a prophet in the *Qur'an*, we point to Jesus Christ in the Bible as the Savior of the world.

Since Islam is a rationalistic religion, little is gained by debating with Muslims on rationalistic grounds. An earlier generation of evangelical missionaries felt called to scholarly debate. The classic example is Dr. C.G. Pfander, *The Balance of Truth*, composed in Persian and published in 1835, and revised and republished in English by the Religious Tract Society in London, 1910. Muslim scholars have attempted to reply to this work with editions in Arabic, Persian, Urdu, and Turkish. While *The Balance of Truth* is a valuable resource in the confrontation of Christianity with Islam, it is possible "to win a battle but lose a war." It is better to attack the worldview of Islam without attacking the *Qur'an* or the prophet Muhammad. It is counterproductive to compare the Bible with the *Qur'an*. In most cases, we need to move from controversy to persuasion. The Bible as Word of God has its own power in pointing seekers of truth to Jesus Christ. Under the influence of the Holy Spirit, many Muslims have met Christ through reading the Bible, even without human intervention. Our task is to point all inquirers to the Christ of Scripture.

## Progressive Revelation

As with the *Qur'an*, the Bible recognizes the progression of revelation in the Word from God. While the content of biblical revelation and the methods of receiving it are distinct, they do overlap. They share many aspects of their cultural heritages. In his sovereignty, God chose a Semitic Hebrew culture through which to reveal himself and his law. The Arabic culture of Islam has many parallels with the Semitic culture of Jews and Christians in Palestine. Muslims share a common history with the people of the Old Testament. Hebrew and Arabic belong to the same Semitic language family, with classical/biblical Hebrew being established from the 12$^{th}$ century BCE, and classical Arabic from 300 CE It is important to recognize that God chose to reveal himself in a Father/Son relationship rather than in a mother/daughter relationship in order to counter the female fertility cults of the polytheistic religious culture of Mesopotamia. In his attributes God has no gender; he is Spirit.

In the providence of God, the emerging Hebrew Semitic language and culture became the vehicle for the divine-human relationship, a relationship which began with Abraham in his departure from Ur of the Chaldees and with whom he entered into a covenant relationship. Although the New Testament was written in Greek, the culture of the New Testament remained predominantly Hebrew. God's covenant with Abraham, renewed with Moses and David, was fulfilled in the new covenant in Jesus Christ, in which the new universalism of relationships becomes global, transcending the limitations of Semitic culture. In the progress of God's self-revelation, he transformed the Hebrew culture, rejecting all forms of idolatry and transforming customs including circumcision and agricultural festivals into celebrations of redemptive history. The story then of the patriarchs is one of both deculturalization, the purification of cultural practices, and the introduction of new cultural factors. Through the captivity of Egypt and through the wilderness journey, God prepared a people to be his people, dependent upon him and his law. Immoral practices were to be severely punished. The story of the Judges, the institutionalized Kingdom, the Exile, and the restoration of prosperity were the steps through which God prepared Israel for the coming of the promised Messiah. "In the fullness of time" Christ was born at a time when the dominance of the Roman Empire made possible the growth of the Church throughout the Mediterranean world and beyond.

This process of deculturalization and transformation of culture is a process that is needed universally and for every age.[251] One example of the progress of revelation is the progression from retributive justice of "an eye for an eye" as recorded in the Pentateuch to the restorative justice of "love your enemies" in the New Testament. Bernard Ramm comments that "progressive revelation" involves the enlargement of the idea of God, the purification of ethical ideals, the spiritualizing of worship, and progress in divine redemption. He adds, "The locus of the text in the corpus of revelation determines the mode of its exegesis and the theological weight that can be associated with it."[252] However, the latter revelations do not abrogate the earlier revelations, as in Islam; rather, as Jesus stated, "I came to fulfill them." The New Testament writers had also to interpret God's revelation for people who were part of the Greco-Roman culture. The New Testament is written in Greek, not Hebrew, and many of the Old Testament quotations were taken from the Greek Septuagint. Greek words were given a new meaning, for example *Kyrios* (Lord), *logos* (word), *soter* (Savior). Paul used *mysterion* (mystery) as an "open secret" of God's grace, contrary to the secret initiation rights in pagan religions.

## Scripture Interprets Scripture

During the medieval and reformation periods, the Roman Catholic Church insisted that it alone was gifted by God with the ability and grace to rightly interpret the Scriptures for the common people. The priest alone was the only mediator between the Scriptures and the congregation. The Reformers, Luther and Calvin, vigorously rejected this claim and insisted that Scripture interprets Scripture. By this they meant that the whole of Scripture interprets the parts of Scripture and the parts of Scripture are interpreted by the whole. No truth depends on one biblical reference. Luther called this understanding of the text of Scripture, the perspicuity of Scripture. The *sensus penior*, or the natural and literal sense of Scripture, was, Luther claimed, in the reach of all who are genuine seekers of truth. He emphasized this principle as the application of "the priesthood of all believers," so that understanding the plain text is sufficient for salvation and daily ethical living.

Today we make the same assumptions in our daily devotional life of Bible reading and prayer. We prayerfully read a passage, reflect on its message in the background as far as we know it and apply it to our own lives and to our own contexts. It is an intuitive approach known as pietism. By it, we assume that our own situation parallels the situation of the original writer. This inductive method is the common practice in our home Bible study groups. Pietism is an important element in worship. The Psalmist declares, "Oh, how I love your

---

[251] See Bruce. J. Nicholls, *Contextualisation: A Theology of Gospel and Culture* (Exeter: Paternoster, 1979).

[252] Bernard. L. Ramm, *Hermeneutics* (Grand Rapids: Baker, 1976), 21-23.

law! I meditate on it all day long" (Ps. 119:97). Meditating on the Scriptures is foundational to all prayer. The public reading of Scripture in worship is itself an act of worship. In cases of less plain passages of Scripture the use of commentaries may be necessary. Christian doctrine which appears to be illogical, such as the trinity or the deity of Christ or predestination, can only be understood in worship and in prayer from inside the Christian faith.

The rational mindset of Muslims finds these doctrines incomprehensible. We maintain their meaning and significance can be grasped only from within the Christian faith, not by critiquing it from the outside. Our Lord's self-understanding in relation to the Father is seen in his prayer life and not in his debate with the Pharisees and Sadducees. The nature of the Trinity was first articulated by Tertullian and only formally stated as doctrine at the council of Nicaea in 325 CE. Bernard Ramm maintains that the work of the Holy Spirit in illuminating the mind of the reader takes priority over appeal to human reason. The Holy Spirit who inspired the writers of the biblical text also illuminates the mind of the reader without which the spiritual truths of the text are hidden. A living relationship with Christ and dependence on the Spirit are the prerequisites for the true interpretation of Scripture. Ramm comments, "The intangibility of the work of the Spirit might be far more real than all the scientific procedures applied to the text."[253] Ramm further notes that the spirit-gifted Church Fathers and the Reformers, Luther and Calvin, are better guides to understanding the real substance of the New Testament than many scholars of today with all their aids to exegesis.

On the day of the Resurrection, Jesus, first on the road to Emmaus and then in the upper room, opened the minds of those with him so they could understand the Scriptures. However, while the work of the Spirit is an indispensable necessity for biblical understanding, this is no excuse for neglecting careful exegesis. The inner meaning of the text and its application to the complexity of modern life is revealed to those who hold together the objectivity of careful exegesis and the subjectivity of understanding the social contexts, and who rely on the Spirit for guidance. Heretical Christianity, as espoused, for example, by those who promote a prosperity doctrine, or who promote partial truths such as Zionism, extreme dispensationalism, or liberation or feminist theologies, suffers from the lack of careful exegesis. While we have all been blessed through individual verses of Scripture, their use to proof-text theology is dangerous and can be misleading.

In summary, "the basic problem of biblical hermeneutics is to transpose the biblical message from its original context into the context of the modern

---

[253] Ramm, *Hermeneutics*, 19.

readers or hearers so as to produce in them the same kind of impact that the message was meant to produce in the original readers or hearers."[254]

## From Exegesis to Interpretation

The Bible is the revelation of God's act in history and the interpretation of those acts. For example, the Exodus and the Cross are two central events in the biblical story that need to be understood in their own historical contexts. They are meaningless events unless Scripture interprets them for us. Understanding begins with language, the meaning and use of words to describe and interpret these events. Words, phrases, and sentences need to be understood in their historical setting and against the background of the local cultures at the time of writing. This background study will include worldviews, values, societal structures, and the customs of the people to whom the Word was first addressed and to which it needs to be applied today. A further complication is the context of later editors, if these are known. In the case of Paul, language used by his amanuensis in some of his letters differs from Paul's regular usage. This is evident in his pastoral epistles, especially 2 Timothy. The use of grammar books, lexicons, dictionaries, concordances, and commentaries are necessary tools for detailed exegesis, especially when the text is uncertain or obscure. Words have to be interpreted in the context of their literary genre, be it prose, poetry, proverbs, parables, etc. Understanding the literary genre is an essential part of exegesis. Good exegesis seeks to avoid *eisegesis* in which the interpreter reads into the text his own understanding. This has always been a common temptation of exegetes and continues today, especially in Asian contexts.[255] Likewise, the modern obsession with the subjectivity of the interpreter and receiver of the text is to be avoided. It is the weakness of Bultmann and of the exponents of the New Hermeneutic. Since we do not have the original autographs, we depend on the science of textual criticism to establish confidence in the reliable accuracy of the texts that we now have. The discovery of the Dead Sea Scrolls confirms this confidence.

A further complication for ordinary Christian leaders is in choosing the right translation for the Bible in English and in regional languages. Modern translations cover the spectrum from textual accuracy, as with the NRSV, to the more popular NIV, to paraphrases from J.B. Phillips and Eugene Peterson. Missionaries unskilled in the grammatico-historical method have often unconsciously, or even consciously, assumed that their Western understanding of the text was equivalent to that of the original writers. The disastrous results

---

[254] C. Rene Padilla, "Hermeneutics and Culture: A Theological Perspective," in *Gospel and Culture*, ed. John Stott and R.T. Cotte (South Pasadena, CA: William Carey Library, 1979).

[255] Ralph. P. Martin, "Approaches to New Testament Exegesis," in *New Testament Interpretation*, ed. I. Howard Marshall (Exeter: Paternoster, 1977), 222-23.

are seen in churches which have become alienated from their national cultures. Asian missionaries face the same challenge. The grammatico-historical method must be upheld as the foundation of our hermeneutical method. This method has often been extended to develop a theological exegesis, commonly called dogmatic theology. This development has put individual texts into the context of Scripture as a whole in order to develop coherent doctrinal beliefs such as the doctrine of Scripture, the Trinity, the uniqueness and finality of Jesus Christ, original sin, the atonement, grace, and the return of Christ, etc. Creative minds such as those of Augustine, Luther, and Calvin have produced dogmatic theologies with their distinctive but coherent foci. In our own time Karl Barth has produced his own dogmatic theology. He has attempted to put the entire Bible into the context of each passage in a fresh way. For example, he brings items from the history of Israel and the New Testament into his interpretation of Genesis 1.[256] While Barth's particular exegesis may be questioned, his attempt to bring the entire text of the Bible to bear on particular texts is commendable. Kenneth Cragg and Michael Nazir-Ali have attempted to do the same for Christian theology in response to Islamic dogmatic theology.

An amusing but sad abuse of dogmatics is when the young William Carey proposed missionary work in India, and the elders of his Calvinistic, Strict Baptist Congregation replied, "Sit down, young man. When God wants to convert the heathen, he will do it without your help."

## Allegory and Typology

As an oversimplification, typology is the correlation between ideas and principles while allegory correlates historical events. There is little evidence of allegory in Scripture, but there is frequent use of typology. Moses lifted up the bronze snake on a pole so that all who were bitten by snakes and looked up at it were healed (Num. 21:4-9). In John's Gospel, this event is correlated with salvation through Christ's death on the cross (3:14-15). Jesus frequently employed the symbols of the vine and branches, the good shepherd, and (of special significance) the bread and the wine at the Last Supper, symbols of his body broken and blood poured out for the forgiveness of sins. The use of allegory was common in Greek culture. The Stoics covered up the embarrassing absurdities of their mythology by allegorizing the acts of gods and goddesses in terms of ideals of human behavior. Hindus do the same in interpreting the immoral acts of their deities. The Jew Philo used allegory to reinterpret the early chapters of Genesis in order to commend the Jewish faith to educated Greeks and Romans. Origen and the Alexandria School made frequent use of allegory in interpreting the letter of the law by its spirit. In contrast, the Antioch Fathers, especially Theodore of Mopsuestia and John Chrysostom, while not rejecting the principle of allegorization, opposed the

---

[256] Ramm, *Hermeneutics*, 27-28.

excesses of Alexandria. The Medieval Church continued this practice by explaining earthly events in terms of spiritual and heavenly ones. Karl Barth did the same. On the other hand, Luther and Calvin emphasized the literal meaning of the text. Luther insisted on the grammatical meaning of the text, and Calvin on its unity. In today's hermeneutical debate, the advocates of the New Hermeneutic are prone to use allegory to explain away the supernatural and miraculous in Scripture and even the deity of Christ.

### From Meaning to Significance

The hermeneutical process begins with discovering the meaning of the text and then progressing to its significance. E. D. Hirsch (*Validity in Interpretation*, 1967) made a distinction between inherent meaning and significance for us, a distinction that began with Friedrich Schleiermacher, now recognized as the father of modern hermeneutics. Schleiermacher was the first to emphasize the role of the reader in the hermeneutical process. Schleiermacher, who had been influenced by the pietistic theology of the Moravian Seminary where he studied, sought to move the discussion from the objective and scientific approach to the subjective and psychological process of the mind of both the author and the interpreter. His goal was to understand the biblical authors better than they understood themselves. He sought to go behind the mind of the author and his motives in creating the text, and explain the meaning of the parts of the text in relation to its whole. He searched for the subjective meaning, rather than the objective truth, since we have the benefit of historical distance. He added that we need to take an intuitive leap of faith across the centuries to a person-to-person relationship with the author.[257] Schleiermacher would no doubt have identified with Phillip Brooks, who in 1870 defined preaching as "truth mediated through personality."

The interpreter as a teacher or preacher needs to radiate a Christ-like attitude and behavior when he/she interprets the meaning of Scripture as significant for contemporary living and witness. Many of us have been deeply influenced by the lives of our theological teachers, long after we have forgotten the content of their lectures. The former Bishop of Durham, New Testament scholar Tom Wright, calls for "a hermeneutic of love" in our relationship to the biblical authors, their texts, and our contemporary neighbors. This love for the Bible and its authors is paramount in every effort to interpret the Bible to Muslim inquirers. The Psalmist loved the Scriptures and praised God by singing, "I hate and abhor falsehood, but I love your law. Seven times a day I praise you for

---

[257] Steve Motyer, "Hermeneutics for Preachers," *The Evangelical Review of Theology* (July 1997): 215-24. Steve Motyer, of the London School of Theology (formerly known as the London Bible College), has a sensitive appreciation of Schleiermacher's contribution of the role of the preacher's life and experience in his preaching ministry, an identity much needed today.

your righteous law. Great peace have those who love your law" (Ps. 119:163-165).

The New Hermeneutic movement associated with the names of Ernest Fuchs of Marburg, Gerhard Ebeling of Zurich, and Hans-Georg Gadamer, drew its inspiration from Schleiermacher. These authors also emphasized the need for a "leap of faith" over the centuries if the meaning of the biblical text is going to transform the lives and preaching of today. They rightly emphasized that the text must translate us before we can translate it. Most Western theologians have devoted considerable space in their writings to the impact of the New Hermeneutic since they live under the shadow of Rudolf Bultmann, who in his scientific rationalism denied the supernatural, miracles, the deity of Christ, the saving wonders of the cross, and the resurrection in his attempt to make the gospel relevant to our secular age. In the context of Asian religions and spirituality where the supernatural is a daily experience, Bultmann and the theologians of the New Hermeneutic have little to contribute.[258] To a Muslim, with his belief of the transcendence of God and the *Qur'an* as the inerrant Word of God, Bultmann's denial of demons, angels, miracles, and the supernatural, is heresy and only confirms the bankruptcy of Christianity.

The goal of the New Hermeneutic is to bring to consciousness the interpreter's worldview and his life and experience in interpreting the Scriptures. Its advocates locate Jesus within the horizon of the interpreter's and the hearer's "common understandings." Fuchs and Ebeling, however, do not underestimate the power of the New Testament to interpret itself. Ebeling insists that hermeneutics "only consists in removing hindrances in order to let the Word perform its own hermeneutic function."[259] We agree that a literalistic repeating of the text is no guarantee that it will speak to the minds and hearts of the hearers. Every translator of Scripture into a modern language knows this difficulty, while the preacher faces it in expounding the Scriptures every Sunday. The interpreter, the preacher, and the listener are all influenced in their understanding by their own cultural worldview and by their psychological processes. This universal experience, now called our "pre-understanding," is a reality that was recognized by the Reformers and then articulated first by Schleiermacher and now by all biblical scholars. The different schools of Islamic jurists owe more to the experience of the prophet in the traditions of the *Sunnah* and the *Hadith* than they may be willing to admit. We must let the text address us before we interpret it to others. Fuchs is right to see empathy, or common understanding, *einverständnis*, as crucial to our understanding of the text. As noted, Tom Wright calls it a "hermeneutic of love."

---

[258] A. C. Thiselton, "The New Hermeneutic," in *New Testament Interpretation*, ed. I. Howard Marshall (Grand Rapids: Eerdmans, 1977), 308-33. In this chapter, Thiselton gives a detailed but balanced analysis and critique of the new hermeneutic.

[259] Thiselton, "The New Hermeneutic," 309.

During my student days in London I remember meeting a Muslim studying for his London B.D. with the view of refuting its message. Because he was not motivated by love, there is no way he could have rightly understood the text of the Bible. Sadly, this is also true of fundamentalist, liberal, and even conservative Christians. Zionist Christians, who have little love for Muslims, have the same difficulty.

In our response, we need to argue that our own experience of life must cohere with our objective knowledge of the text. Bultmann was right when he stated that "there is no such thing as a presuppositional exegesis," but he was wrong in denying that we can know the truth revealed by God.

The perspective of this essay is that we can, in confidence, know the mind of Christ. The process of gaining this assurance is best understood by a "hermeneutical spiral," eschatalogically understood as an alternative to the endless relativity of a closed circle.[260] Communication takes place in the dialogical relationship between the text and the one receiving it. On the assumption that there is progress in revelation, the process of sustained dialogue enables us to enlarge our own horizons, culturally understood, and to "merge or fuse" them with the horizon of the text.[261]

## Implications for Theological Education

From this dialogue with Islam, we recognize that in theological education the curriculum must be biblically centered and Christ-centered as the two foci of the Christian faith. At the same time, the pedagogical method needs to be sensitive to the plurality of Asian cultures in which the inductive method takes precedence over the deductive, the community over the individual, and shame over guilt. Theological education needs to respond to the Islamic policy of the Islamization of the whole society by including economics, politics, and social justice in its curriculum. Alongside the traditional educational subjects, Dr. Chris Marantika, the well-known evangelical scholar and leader in Indonesia, has outlined the curriculum for teaching theology in the Islamic context. He suggests the curriculum ought to begin with the doctrine of God as Father, his name, nature, transcendence, and immanent presence; then God as Holy Spirit, his name, work, and nature; God as Son, his name, work, and nature; the doctrine of angels; the doctrine of the messengers of God, prophets, and apostles; eschatological hopes for Christ, humanity, and nature; man in the image of God; sin and salvation; practical ethics of life in the world.[262] In summary, theological education in the Muslim context needs to correct the Muslim misunderstanding of the Bible, critique the proof-texting method, and

---

[260] Grant R. Osborne, *The Hermeneutical Spiral* (Downers Grove: InterVarsity, 1991).
[261] Thiselton, "The New Hermeneutic," 317.
[262] Marantika, "Towards an Evangelical Theology, 365-82.

outline a coherent Christian worldview. It needs to expound the true doctrines of God in Christ and in the Holy Spirit, and of his angels, and respond to misunderstandings of Christ and his nature and saving work. It must offer hope in this life and in the eternal future.

## The Response that Communicates

The weakness of the New Hermeneutic is that it is one-sided in emphasizing the subjective experience of the receiver while ignoring the objective knowledge of the message of the revealed text. In terms of preaching, teaching, and pastoral care, the communicator must focus both on the content of the message, and on his skill in communicating it. We can learn from politicians who have learnt this skill. It is said of Prime Minister Winston Churchill that in preparing an address to the nation he would spend as much time before a mirror practicing his speech as he did in preparing it. When Hitler was about to invade Britain in 1939, Churchill addressed the nation with a memorable, well-rehearsed speech in which he declared, "Never in the course of the history of the human race has so much been owed by so many to so few." That one sentence galvanized the nation to prepare to resist the threatening invaders. Scripture holds in harmony the "thus said the Lord" of God's propositional Word and the explanation of it in his saving acts in history.[263] The historic events of the Cross and the Resurrection would have little significance if God did not interpret them for us. Therefore, all hermeneutical questions become missiological questions.[264]

A major concern of biblical hermeneutics is reductionism, the giving of greater authority to one part of Scripture over another, what Carson calls "the canon within the canon." Particular ecclesiastical traditions may overemphasize one biblical practice at the expense of others, such as baptism, the Eucharist, or speaking in tongues. Or they may narrow Scripture into a theological mould, as in covenant theology, dispensational theology, or Zionist prophetic theology. Or Scripture may be reduced to a particular sociological mould, such as the primacy of the poor, feminist rights, or climate change. In each case, we must respond with what Carson calls "a self-conscious dependency upon the Word of God and an equally self-conscious brokenness and contrition that hungers for the illumination of the Holy Spirit as that Word is studied."[265]

A second much needed response is to learn from the history of the Church over the centuries and to recognize the strength and weaknesses of the Church's

---

[263] D. A. Carson, "A Sketch of the Factors Determining Current Hermeneutical Debate in Cross-cultural contexts," in *Biblical Interpretation and Church: Text and Context*, ed. D. A. Carson (Exeter: World Evangelical Fellowship, 1984), 18.

[264] See Bruce. J. Nicholls, *Contextualisation: A Theology of Gospel and Culture* (Exeter: WEF, 1979).

[265] Carson, "A Sketch of the Factors," 15.

response in times of crisis. This includes learning from our contemporary ecumenical history, both liberal and evangelical, at global and national levels. Every church has traditions which reflect its history. It is true of the New Testament church which modeled its worship on the worship in the synagogue, a pattern that many denominations seek to emulate today. Liturgical churches look back to the priesthood in temple worship, while the Old Testament canon is the product of its own history. We acknowledge that the Bible Jesus used is the same 39 books that we continue to recognize as the Old Testament. The religious rulers of Israel did not create the canon but recognized these writings as uniquely revealed by God. Similarly, the New Testament canon of 27 books was authenticated by their direct or indirect apostolic authorship and by their coherent message. It was not until Athanasius's *Festal Letter* of 367 CE that the Church officially acknowledged the limits of the New Testament canon. The 16th-century Reformers rejected the accretions that the Roman Catholic Church had added to Scripture. In reply, Rome called the Reformers heretics for rejecting the teaching and authority of the Church. In some churches today it is common to speak of authority as a three-legged stool of Scripture, tradition, and reason. Evangelical churches respect these three sources of authority but insist that the traditions of the church and reason must always be tested by the Scriptures. When we speak of "the historic evangelical church" we are acknowledging that evangelicals have their roots in history.

The Bible cannot be interpreted in a cultural vacuum. In the past, some Western missionaries have failed to recognize that the gospel they brought to the non-Christian world was clothed in the cultural values of their own sending mission or church. Now some Asian missionaries serving cross-culturally are making the same mistake. In 1955 the door opened for Christian missions to enter Nepal. Many dreamed of establishing a pure New Testament church. Today, 50 years later, the Nepal church is divided into Anglican, Presbyterian, Baptist, and Pentecostal churches, to name a few of the many church traditions that fragment the body of Christ in that land.

## From Contextualization to Globalization

Mission is the defining goal of both the Old Testament and the New Testament.[266] The focal point of all biblical mission is Jesus Christ, the Creator and Redeemer of all things (Col. 1:15-20). He is the promised Messiah of the Old Testament, the Servant King of the New Testament, the returning Judge of the nations, and Redeemer of all creation at the Last Day. He is the Alpha and Omega, the one who is, and who was, and who is to come (Rev. 1:8). When on the resurrection night Jesus said to his followers, "as the Father has sent me, I am sending you" (John 20:21), he was commissioning them as his chosen

---

[266] See Christopher Wright, *The Mission of God: Unlocking the Bible's Grand Narrative* (Nottingham: InterVarsity, 2006).

community to take the whole gospel to the whole world. "The Church," states the Lausanne Covenant, "is at the very center of God's cosmic purpose and is his appointed means of spreading the gospel" (#6). The gospel is universal and unchanging, but its significance for our time and in the plurality of our Asian cultures must be contextualized if the communication of it is to lead to changed lives and the transformation of society. Contextualization is the translation of the message from one culture to another. Its goal is not just to inform, but to evoke a response, be it to pray, or to repent, or to believe, or to act. Hence, the purpose of contextualizing our understanding of the biblical message is to reproduce the same effect in the receivers' lives and behaviors that the original text produced in the lives and hearers of its readers. Charles Kraft and others have called this "the dynamic equivalence principle" in contrast to the "formal equivalence principle" of seeking literal and verbal accuracy. Modern translations of the Bible into English can be plotted on a continuum from formal to dynamic equivalence. This is illustrated in the progression from the King James Version to the RV, to the RSV and NIV, to the TEV and the CEV. The NRSV and the NIV are examples of translations of the generic use of "man" into non-sexist language. The increasingly common use of the benediction "Creator, Redeemer, and Giver of life" is a truncated version of the trinitarian "Father, Son, and Holy Spirit," since all three persons of the Trinity are involved in God's act of creation and redemption.

The translation of the term for God in some modern Asian languages is creating difficulties for Christian believers. The Hindi term for God, *"Parameshwar,"* or Great Spirit, captures only one element of the Godhead. Christians in Indonesia, Malaysia, and the Middle East use "Allah" for God but ascribe different attributes to Allah from those understood by Islam. Allah is the pre-Islamic term for deity chosen by Muhammad with a view to denying the use of names of lesser deities.[267] Islamic leaders in Malaysia are now demanding that Christians stop using the name "Allah" for God and that all Bibles and Christian literature using the name Allah be destroyed. Christians are vigorously defending in the courts their right to keep this long-held tradition of using Allah in their churches and literature.

The Incarnation is the ultimate paradigm of contextualization. Christ's every command was, *de facto*, a command to contextualization.[268] It goes beyond the concept of indigenization, which was traditionally limited to forms of worship, social customs, and methods of evangelism. Contextualization now includes understanding cultural distinctives and social ethics. That contextualization took place in the New Testament Church itself is seen in the decisions of the Jerusalem Council of Acts 15. From the time of Origen and the School of

---

[267] Kenneth Cragg, *The Call of the Minaret*, 2nd ed. (Maryknoll: Orbis, 1992), 29-33.

[268] Bruce. J. Nicholls, "Contextualisation," in *New Dictionary of Theology*, ed. Sinclair B. Ferguson, David F. Wright and J. I. Packer (Leicester: InterVarsity, 1998).

Alexandria, contextualization has been integral to the Church's mission. Now it has become global. The globalization of religious ideologies and social practices is a post-World War II phenomenon. Secularism is invading every local community, and youth culture is universal. The World Council of Churches calls for mission as "humanization," the Lausanne movement calls for "world evangelization," and the World Evangelical Alliance calls for "evangelical unity and comprehensive mission."

Forty years ago the Asia Theological Association began as a movement for the contextualizing of theology and theological education by developing research centers and establishing accreditation standards for theological education. The competition between globalization and contextualization can be either creative or destructive. With Islam there is no tension. Islamic culture is only global as it enforces *Shariah* law on every culture. Its goal is nothing less than the Islamization of the whole world, so that from one universal culture peace and prosperity will come to all. It needs to be remembered, however, that Marxism had the same agenda.

The Christian challenge to Islam is to reaffirm the global values of unconditional love and social justice for all peoples. The Christian response to Islam is first to help Muslims recognize their own diversity and the internal conflict between *surahs* revealed in Mecca and those in Medina; between worship in the mosque and worship at the shrines of the *pirs*; between the warring communities of *Shia'ites, Sunnis,* and *Sufis*; between moderates and extremists fighting for power, between Muslim women striving for freedom and dignity; between the *Shariah* law of the *Qur'an* and the common expediencies of *Taqiyya*—the concealing of truth and the telling of lies to preserve one's own life and religion.[269] Global secularism is making inroads into Islam as it has done into Christianity. When Islam comes to recognize its inherent weaknesses, Christians must be ready to show a better way to life and happiness. Above all, Christians need a life-centered motivation to unconditionally serve and love their Muslim neighbors. If we fail at this point, we have failed in our hermeneutical calling as the Christians of Asia to witness to the living Christ who rose from the dead and offers forgiveness and renewal of life to all who will bow in his presence and call on the Holy Spirit, the Giver of life eternal.

A determining characteristic of postmodern globalization is "connectedness."[270] The effectiveness of biblical hermeneutics in the 21st century will be determined by our success or failure in achieving "connectedness," while the future peace and prosperity of the globe will be determined by the future of Christian-Muslim connectedness.

---

[269] See Patrick Sookhdeo, *Islam and Truth* (Barnabas Fund, 2007).

[270] See Joseph Shao, "The Changing Mission of the Church in Changing Asia," in *The Church in a Changing World* (Manila: ATA, 2010) for ATA's consultation on Globalization in Malang, 2009.

# Bibliography

al-Faruqi, Isma'il. "On the Nature of Islamic Da'wah." *International Review of Missions* (October 1976): 394-95.

Carson, D. A. "A Sketch of the Factors Determining Current Hermeneutical Debate in Cross-cultural contexts." In *Biblical Interpretation and Church: Text and Context*, edited by D. A. Carson, 18. Exeter: World Evangelical Fellowship, 1984.

Cragg, Kenneth. *The Call of the Minaret*. 2nd ed. Maryknoll: Orbis, 1992.

Deshmukh, I. D. *The Gospel and Islam*. Bombay: GLS, 1982.

Lazarus-Yafeh, *Intertwining Worlds: Medieval Islam and Biblical Criticism*. Princeton: Princeton University Press, 1992.

Marantika, Chris. "Towards an Evangelical Theology in an Islamic Culture." In *The Bible and Theology in Asian Contexts*, edited by Bong Rin Ro and Ruth Eschenauer, 309. Taichung: ATA, 1984.

Martin, Ralph. P. "Approaches to New Testament Exegesis." In *New Testament Interpretation*, edited by I. Howard Marshall, 222-23. Exeter: Paternoster, 1977.

Mohamad, Mahathir. "The Role and Difference of Religions in Society." *Islam and Muslim Ummah*, 227-35. Subang Jaya: Pelanduk, 2001.

Motyer, Steve. "Hermeneutics for Preachers." *The Evangelical Review of Theology* (July 1997): 215-24.

Mutahhari, Ayatallah Murtaza. *Fundamentals of Islamic Thought*. Translated by R. Campbell. Berkeley, CA: Mizan, 1985.

Mutei, Joseph M. "The Bible: Classical and Contemporary Muslim Attitudes and Exegesis." *The Evangelical Review of Theology* (October 2007): 207.

Nazir-Ali, Michael. *Islam. A Christian Perspective*. Exeter: Paternoster, 1983.

Nicholls, Bruce. J. *Contextualisation: A Theology of Gospel and Culture*. Exeter: Paternoster, 1979.

_____. "Contextualisation." In *New Dictionary of Theology*, edited by Sinclair B. Ferguson, David F. Wright, and J. I. Packer. Leicester: InterVarsity, 1998.

_____. "Our Theological Task." In *The Unique Christ in Our Pluralistic World*, edited by Bruce. J. Nicholls, 11. Carlisle: Paternoster, 1994.

Osborne, Grant R. *The Hermeneutical Spiral*. Downers Grove: InterVarsity, 1991.

Padilla, C. Rene. "Hermeneutics and Culture: A Theological Perspective." In *Gospel and Culture*, edited by John Stott and R.T. Cotte. South Pasadena, CA: William Carey Library, 1979.

Ramm, Bernard L. *Hermeneutics*. Grand Rapids: Baker, 1976.

Shao, Joseph. "The Changing Mission of the Church in Changing Asia." In *The Church in a Changing World*. Manila: ATA, 2010.

Sookhdeo, Patrick. *A Christian Pocket Guide to Islam*. Fern, UK: Christian Focus, 2002.

Sookhdeo, Patrick. *Islam and Truth*. Barnabas Fund, 2007.

Thiselton, A. C. "Hermeneutics." In *The New Dictionary of Theology*, edited by Sinclair B. Ferguson, David F. Wright, and J. I. Packer, 293. Leicester: InterVarsity, 1998.

Thiselton, A. C. "The New Hermeneutic." In *New Testament Interpretation*, edited by I. Howard Marshall, 308-33. Grand Rapids: Eerdmans, 1977.

Wright, Christopher. *The Mission of God: Unlocking the Bible's Grand Narrative*. Nottingham: InterVarsity, 2006.

# Christendom, Christianity, and Islam—Does Europe Need to Hear the Gospel? A Brief Reflection from a Pentecostal Perspective

Gregory M. Mundis

### Thesis

Europeans, as well as many Muslim immigrants living in Europe, have not had an adequate witness of the gospel of Jesus Christ. The Western Church (including the evangelical stream of the Church and European state churches) has been deceived into believing that because of Europe's history of Christendom, Europeans are not in need of a gospel witness. The deception extends, apparently, to believing Muslim immigrants either do not need to hear the gospel or they are not in a position to believe the gospel because of their belief system. The fact is that Muslims in Europe have not had an adequate witness of the gospel. It is my assertion that the Pentecostal wing of the evangelical church (specifically in this case the Assemblies of God) is with renewed deliberation reaching the inhabitants of the continent. They are reaching out through the leadership and power of the Spirit, partnering with like-minded European Pentecostals such as Peter Kuzmič, and intentionally planning and working to share the gospel with Europeans and Muslim immigrants.

### Christendom, Christianity, and Islam

For the purpose of this article, the gospel is "that God has provided a way of salvation for men through the gift of his Son to the world. He suffered as a sacrifice for sin, overcame death, and now offers a share in his triumph to all who will accept it. The gospel is good news because it is a gift of God, not something that must be earned by penance or by self-improvement (John 3:16; Rom. 5:8-11; 2 Cor. 5:14-19; Titus 2:11-14)."[271]

In contrast to this definition of "to all who will accept it,"

---

[271] Merrill C. Tenney, "Gospel," in *Wycliffe Bible Encyclopedia,* ed. Charles F. Pfeiffer, Howard F. Vos, and John Rea (Chicago: Moody, 1975).

Europeans are typically considered Christian in their religious faith, primarily because of the heritage of the Catholic Church and the Protestant Reformation. Consequently, Europe is not considered a priority as a mission field compared to other areas in the 10-40 window [sic] where there are a higher percentage of unreached people groups.[272]

Add to this perception that, "for generations, 'you didn't become a member when you were baptized. You became a member when you were born,' says Carl Johan Lidén, a priest for the church in Stockholm."[273]

This view has prevailed through the decades of the 19th and 20th centuries and now in the 21st century in regard to Europe. This perception also dominated the worldview of the European Church in the Middle Ages. For all practical purposes in the mind of Western historians, Europe was *Corpus Christianum*. Others viewed Europe in geographical terms as a picture of Mary, the mother of Jesus. The 20th-century manifestation of this perception began with the Edinburgh Conference in 1910. The assumption by the organizing bodies was that the world outside of North America and Europe needed to hear the gospel and be the focus of the conference. Unfortunately, the organizers, caught in their perception, failed to realize the great spiritual need in Europe that was manifesting itself at that time. We should, however, note that,

> When judging the population of 'Christian Europe,' we should also recall that large parts of Europe did not even nominally accept Christianity until well into the Middle Ages. ... In the 13th century, the height of medieval Christian civilization in Europe, there may have been more Christian believers on the continent of Asia than in Europe, while Africa still had populous Christian communities.[274]

Throughout this long period Christendom remained an unchallenged reality, but the moment of truth had arrived. By the beginning of the 20th century two observations seemed incontestable: (1) Western civilization was entering a twilight zone—a long historical period was ending and something new was emerging, and (2) historical Christendom effectively had collapsed. ... Europe was becoming the showcase for a decaying Christendom, on the one hand, and a dynamic secularization on the other.[275]

---

[272] Greater Europe Mission, "European Christian Demographics," accessed March 20, 2006, http://www.joshuaproject.net/assets/Unreached Europe.pdf.

[273] Noelle Knox, "Religion Takes a Back Seat in Western Europe," *USA Today*, August 8, 2005, accessed September 27, 2011, http://www.usatoday.com/news/world/2005-08-10-europe-religion-cover_x.htm.

[274] Philip Jenkins, *The Next Christendom: The Coming of Global Christianity* (New York: Oxford University Press, 2002), 23.

[275] Wilbur R. Shenk, "Contemporary Europe in Missiological Perspective," *Missiology: An International Review* 35, no. 2 (April 2007): 126.

This decay and secularization contributed to what we term a nominal Christianity. The workshop "Nominalism Today" at the 1989 Lausanne Congress on World Evangelization in Manila estimated that at least one billion, or 75 to 80 percent, of professing Christians are nominal. The conclusion was that this is the largest religious group in need of evangelization today.[276] The workshop divided the nominal Christians into four categories: "ethnic-religious identity" nominal, the second-generation nominal, the ritualistic nominal, and the syncretistic nominal. The Catholic, Protestant, and Orthodox churches in Europe are in themselves a complex mission field in which all four types of nominals exist and should become priority concern for intentional programs of evangelization. ... These realities are descriptive not only of the more secularized Protestant West European countries but also of their Catholic counterparts, as evident from the recent Vatican encyclicals and repeated calls of Pope John Paul II for the "re-evangelization" of Europe.[277]

I contend that the nominalism afore cited was a by-product of centuries of Europe being under the sway of Christendom. Christendom "usually refers to Christianity as a territorial phenomenon. It can also refer to the part of the world in which Christianity prevails. The term Christendom has been used to refer to the medieval and renaissance notion of the Christian world as a sort of social and political polity."[278]

The history of the development of Christendom (East and West) is quite fascinating. It gives us insight into the fact that,

> The Reformation and the ensuing decline and breakup of the Holy Roman Empire into independent states caused the term 'Christendom' to take on a more informal meaning in Western Europe signifying countries which were predominantly Christian as opposed to Islamic or pagan countries.[279]

For further clarification purposes, the term *Corpus Christianum* "can be seen as a Christian equivalent of the Muslim *Ummah*."[280] This Christian body was incorporated under the umbrella of the Catholic Church and had common endeavors like the Crusades against the Moors and Ottomans, as well as the Inquisition and the anti-Jewish pogroms.

Stuart McAlister says, "The Parish system, with its territorial approach to identifying the people of an area as a part of the national church, is entrenched

---

[276] J. D. Douglas, ed., *Proclaim Christ Until He Comes* (Minneapolis: World Wide Publications, 1990), 446.

[277] Peter Kuzmič, "Europe," in *Toward the 21st Century in Christian Mission,* ed. James M. Philips and Robert T. Coote (Grand Rapids: Eerdmans, 1993), 148-63 (153-4); cited in Douglas, *Proclaim Christ*, 446.

[278] "Christendom," Dictionary.com, accessed June 12, 2010, http://dictionary.reference.com/browse/christendom.

[279] "Christendom."

[280] "Christendom."

in European minds. To be Polish is to be Catholic, to be Greek or Russian is to be Orthodox, to be German or Danish is to be Lutheran, and so on, even though people are rapidly departing from their heritage or never desired it in the first place. Christendom's apparent mission was to pastor the faithful, not reach the lost. A deep nominalism often resulted amongst those reared in the approach which is quite resistant to evangelism."[281]

Christianity, on the other hand, is defined as a:

> religion founded in Palestine by the followers of Jesus. One of the world's major religions, it predominates in Europe and the Americas, where it has been a powerful historical force and cultural influence, but it also claims adherents in virtually every country of the world ...The central teachings of traditional Christianity are that Jesus is the Son of God, the second person of the Trinity of God the Father, the Son, and the Holy Spirit; that his life on earth, his crucifixion, resurrection, and ascension into heaven are proof of God's love for humanity and God's forgiveness of human sins; and that by faith in Jesus one may attain salvation and eternal life (see "creed"). This teaching is embodied in the Bible, specifically in the New Testament, but Christians accept also the Old Testament as sacred and authoritative Scripture.[282]

A Christian, particularly of the evangelical persuasion, is referred to by the *World Christian Encyclopedia* (*WCE*) "as one who believes in, professes or confesses Jesus Christ as Lord and Savior, or is assumed to believe in Jesus Christ." Furthermore, *WCE* amplifies the definition of Christians as followers of Jesus Christ as Lord, of all kinds, all traditions and confessions, and all degrees of commitment. Evangelical Christians are a subset of the general definition of Christians, primarily as a result of their higher level of commitment. Evangelical Christians are centered on the person of Jesus and obedient to his Great Commission, are committed to the gospel by means of their day-to-day personal witness to Christ, their organized evangelism and their involvement in his mission to the world, and are looking and working toward his second and final Advent.[283]

For the purpose of this article, the definition of an evangelical Christian as stated will serve as an essential element of definition for Pentecostals, a subset of evangelicals. However, a further and very important element is that Pentecostals are "relating to, or constituting any of various Christian religious bodies that emphasize individual experiences of grace, spiritual gifts (as

---

[281] Stuart McAlister, "Younger Generations and the Gospel in Western Culture," in *Global Missiology for the 21st Century: The Iguassu Dialogue*, ed. William D. Taylor (Grand Rapids: Baker Academic, 2000), 367-68.

[282] "Christendom," Dictionary.com, accessed June 12, 2010, http://dictionary.reference.com/browse/christianity.

[283] David B. Barrett, George T. Kurian, and Todd M. Johnson, eds., *World Christian Encyclopedia: A Comparative Survey of Churches and Religions in the Modern World*, 2nd ed. (New York: Oxford University Press, 2001), 1: 2.

glossolalia and faith healing), expressive worship, and evangelism."[284] Evangelism was at the heart of the first Pentecostal outpouring as recorded in Acts 2, and according to Grant McClung's article in *The Globalization of Pentecostalism*, it was the heart of the 20th-century outpouring of the Holy Spirit at Azusa Street and beyond. He quotes Peter Kuzmič who says:

> When we speak about the Great Commission, we speak about the Divinely ordained globalization because the gospel of Jesus Christ is a universally valid, globally relevant message of hope and salvation. We as Pentecostals know that through the power of the Holy Spirit this Word is not only preached but confirmed by signs and wonders and by millions of changed lives who have found the true, internal liberation in Christ and who have been drinking at the well of the living water and who are the *avant garde* of the new creation.[285]

I would note that classical Pentecostals (movements that started at the turn of the 20th century), such as the Assemblies of God, put heavy emphasis on the baptism of the Holy Spirit for the purpose of witnessing and missions. The distinctive of the initial physical evidence of speaking in other tongues (glossolalia) when one is baptized in the Holy Spirit is held as well by the Assemblies of God.

Gary B. McGee also speaks to the results of this outpouring:

> When the Pentecostal movement emerged at the beginning of this century (twentieth), many participants felt called to overseas evangelism. The early records of the revival speak of a close and abiding association between the baptism in the Holy Spirit as evidenced by speaking in tongues for an enduement of power in Christian witness, a fervent belief in the premillennial return of Christ, and his command to evangelize the uttermost parts of the world. This Baptism, viewed as the fulfillment of Joel's prophecy for the "last days," seemed to heighten the imperative for world evangelism. The history of Pentecostalism cannot be properly understood apart from its missionary vision.[286]

There is an interconnectedness of Islam, Christendom, and Christianity, and it finds its roots in Judaism. The father of the Jews (from which Christendom

---

[284] *Merriam-Webster's Collegiate Dictionary*, 10th ed. (Springfield, MA: Merriam-Webster, 1994), s.v. "Pentecostal," accessed June 13, 2010, http://www.merriam-webster.com/ dictionary/pentecostal.

[285] Peter Kuzmič, "Globalism and the Post-Communist World" (paper presented at the ICI World Missions Conference, October 1992), as cited in L. Grant McClung Jr., "Try to Get People Saved," in *Globalization of Pentecostalism—A Religion Made to Travel*, ed. Murray W. Dempster, Byron Klaus, and Douglas Peterson (Oxford: Regnum, 1999), 48.

[286] Gary B. McGee, "Early Pentecostal Missionaries—They Went Everywhere Preaching the Gospel," in *Azusa Street and Beyond: Pentecostal Missions and Church Growth in the Twentieth Century*, ed. L. Grant McClung (South Plainfield, NJ: Bridge, 1986), 33.

and Christianity springs) is also the father of Arabs (from which Islam springs). Abraham's son of his maidservant Hagar is the father of the Arab nations, and the son of his wife Sarah is the father of the Jewish nation. The book of Genesis records this Old Testament "soap opera" in Genesis chapters 16-25.

> Islam (īsläm`, ĭs`läm), [Arab.,=submission to God], world religion founded by the Prophet Muhammad. Founded in the 7th cent., Islam is the youngest of the three monotheistic world religions (with Judaism and Christianity). An adherent to Islam is a Muslim [Arab.,=one who submits]. ... At the core of Islam is the *Qur'an*, believed to be the final revelation by a transcendent Allah [Arab.,=the God] to Muhammad, the Prophet of Islam; since the Divine Word was revealed in Arabic, this language is used in Islamic religious practice worldwide. Muslims believe in final reward and punishment, and the unity of the *umma*, the "nation" of Islam. Muslims submit to Allah through *arkan ad-din*, the five basic requirements or "pillars": *shahadah*, the affirmation that "there is no god but God, and Muhammad is the Messenger of God"; *salah*, the five daily ritual prayers (see liturgy, Islamic); *zakat*, the giving of alms, also known as a religious tax; *Sawm*, the dawn-to-sunset fast during the lunar month of Ramadan; and *hajj*, the pilgrimage to Mecca. The importance of the *hajj* can hardly be overestimated: this great annual pilgrimage unites Islam and its believers from around the world.[287]

Throughout the centuries the intersecting of Islam, Christendom, and Christianity has ranged from peaceful coexistence to brutal wars, including the Crusades of the 11th, 12th, and 13th centuries. Other wars between the two major religions took place on the Iberian Peninsula and in Eastern Europe. The atrocities committed by "Christians" (in my opinion, people in Christendom) certainly have not demonstrated the principles and commands of the Bible as practiced by evangelical/Pentecostal Christianity. I denounce the lack of harmony between biblical truth and the behavior of our forefathers and pray that the present and future generations of evangelicals and Pentecostals will demonstrate biblical Christianity not only to Muslims but also to everyone of another faith or of no faith.

### The Need for the Gospel

Europeans and Muslim immigrants share this common bond: Without an understanding of the gospel there is not enough data and testimony to make a present-day and an eternal-life decision about the gospel of Jesus Christ. They both need to have an adequate witness of the gospel to make such a decision. Consider the following chart.

---

[287] *The Free Dictionary*, s.v. "Islam," accessed August 1, 2010, http://encyclopedia2.thefreedictionary.com/Islam.

## Number of Christians and Evangelical Christians in Major Regions of the World:[288]

| Continent | Population, 2000 (WCD) 6 | % Christian (WCD) | % evangelical (WCD) | % evangelical Christian 2000 (OW) 7 | % evangelical (JP) 8 |
|---|---|---|---|---|---|
| Asia | 3.7 Billion | 8.58% | 4.41% | 3.6 | 2.29% |
| Africa | 784 Million | 48.4% | 18.73% | 14.8 | 4.75% |
| Europe | 729 Million | 71.13% | 4.64% | 2.4 | 1.85% |
| North America | 309 Million | 81.57% | 26.95% | 30.3 | 26.36% |
| Latin America | 519 Million | 91.65% | 30.22% | 10.59 | 8.59% |
| Pacific | 31 Million | 73.34% | 14.89% | 15.2 | 0.97% |

Legend: WCD—World Christian Database; OW—Operation World; JP—Joshua Project

Europe's data indicates a great contrast between Christian (as understood in the term Christendom) and evangelical Christian (as defined in this chapter). Evangelical Europeans and evangelical immigrants living in Europe do not have the numbers of believers, churches, means, and media means necessary to fully evangelize the continent. I have not yet used the term, "unreached people," in this article, but we can certainly bring it into the conversation at this point. The term has pregnant meaning in the evangelical world. I quote Edward Dayton and David Fraser and share their understanding of "unreached people" in relation to Europeans and Muslim immigrants in Europe. For clarification purposes here, unreached people "refers to a group among whom there is no indigenous community of believing Christians with adequate numbers and resources to evangelize the group to its margins."[289] In this context Christians would be of the evangelical variety. I would contend, based upon the table presented, that since only one out of every 40 Europeans is an evangelical Christian (2.4%) and in more than 20 European nations less than 1 percent claim to be evangelical Christians (including the nations of Albania, Austria, Croatia, France, Greece, Italy, Poland, and Spain),[290] Europe is in need of an adequate witness of the gospel. In addition, Muslim immigrants, according to

---

[288] Greater Europe Mission, "European Christian Demographics."
[289] Edward R. Dayton and David A. Fraser, *Planning Strategies for World Evangelization*, rev. ed. (Grand Rapids: Eerdmans, 1990), 29.
[290] "Why Europe? Isn't It a Christian Continent?", accessed August 6, 2010, http://www.ecmi-usa.org/latest/why-europe-isnt-it-a-christian-continent.

common knowledge and the data available from the Joshua Project and *Operation World*, have not had an adequate witness of the gospel.

Considering the direction and flow of this article, the comment of Franz Cumont seems to fit appropriately into this context. Written in 1911, his insight bears repeating in light of the present spiritual state of Europe:

> Let us for a moment suppose that modern Europe were to witness the believers abandoning the Christian churches in order to venerate Allah or Brahma, to observe the commandments of Confucius or Buddha, to accept the fundamental principles of Shintoism; let us imagine a great congeries of all the races of the world, with Arabic *mullahs*, Chinese literary scholars, Japanese *bonzes*, Tibetan *lamas*, Hindu *pandits* preaching at one and the same time fatalism and predestination, the cult of ancestors and the adoration of the divinized ruler, pessimism and redemption through self-annihilation, while all these priests built temples in foreign styles in our cities and celebrated their various rites in them—this dream (which the future may perhaps one day see realized) would give us a rather accurate picture of the religious confusion which characterized the ancient world of Constantine.[291]

Europeans and Muslim immigrants need to hear the gospel because the spiritual confusion that reigns throughout the continent is like a loud noise that prevents Europeans from hearing the clarion call of the message of Christ. They need to hear the gospel because an anemic, disenfranchised, and nominal church of the Christendom era is ringing its bells to come to church, but this has worked in reverse because of the lack of life in the church, because Europeans are hardened to the gospel, and because the gospel is not spiritually attractive to Muslims. In fact, some would say that the present generation of Europeans is not "post Christian" but rather pre-Constantine Christian. In other words, they need to hear the gospel for the first time.

Muslim immigrants need to hear the gospel because they have come from countries and societies that have limited what they can hear and know about the gospel. They have not had a body of evangelical Christians in large enough proportions to bring the gospel to them. They have not had an adequate opportunity to understand the claims of the gospel in their fullness.

## Summary

Christendom has run its course in history and has left in its wake an anemic and nominal church. Its influence in European society has radically diminished in contrast to the centuries of power and authority that it exercised in the past.

Europe, devoid of the "light and salt" of a biblically relevant witnessing church in society, has languished in a spiritual vacuum for over a century. This

---

[291] Frank Cumont, *The Oriental Religions in Roman Paganism* (Chicago: Open Court, 1911), 197.

void has been filled with secularism and a potpourri of religions and spiritualities.

Islam has left a historic footprint in Europe, particularly on the Iberian Peninsula and in the Balkans, because of its territorial conquests. It is now leaving a legacy of Islam because of immigration and a birthrate among Muslims that dwarfs the meager European birth rate. Both Europeans and Muslims need to hear the gospel.

## Assemblies of God World Missions Response to the European Situation

The historical response of the Assemblies of God to the need in Europe has been characterized in the past by Don Mallough in an article titled "The Stepchild of Missions." He said:

> While the mother heart of American missions has been concerned for Africa, India, and China, it has largely overlooked the cry of Europe ... Have we fallen into a belief that civilization and culture are enough to save a nation? ... The gospel is not preached to countries, cities, and provinces, but to the men in those geographical areas. ... The descendents of the reformers in European countries stand in need of the simple message of salvation ... There are 400 million unevangelized white people on the European continent![292]

This historical response began to change in the 1970s and 1980s and made a radical leap forward in 1998, when Assemblies of God World Missions (AGWM) bifurcated Europe out of the region of Eurasia and made it an autonomous region of its own. The decision was motivated in part by a prompting of the Holy Spirit and in observation of the evident need of gospel proclamation to Europeans and Muslim immigrants that was seen by the leadership of AGWM.

The mission statement of AGWM is "reaching, planting, training, and touching."[293] These four verbs are folded into a missiology that embraces the principle of the indigenous church and partnership.[294] The purpose statement of the Europe Region provides a fleshing out of the mission statement and the two principles mentioned. It states, as missionaries "we accelerate the spread of the gospel, model biblical integrity, minister in the power of the Spirit, and partner with those of like vision to build the Church of Jesus Christ."

The Assemblies of God is making a positive spiritual difference in Europe. This is because of a combination of supernatural intervention of the Holy Spirit and his manifesting himself in power, partnership with European Pentecostal

---

[292] Don Mallough, "The Stepchild of Missions," *Missionary Challenge* (December 1954): 6.

[293] Gregory M. Mundis, *Eye on Europe: Charting the Course for Our Mission in Europe* (Springfield, MO: Assemblies of God World Missions, 2000), 36.

[294] "Core Values of Assemblies of God World Missions" (Springfield, MO).

churches and movements, and the formulation and implementation of a Europe-wide AGWM plan.

The leadership of the Holy Spirit is deeply entrenched in the life of the Assemblies of God World Missions. I would say it is a part of their spiritual DNA. Although individuals have abused this leading in some instances, it nevertheless is counted upon by the corporate and individual leadership in the mission. Consider what J. Philip Hogan (former executive director of AGWM) says about the leadership of the Holy Spirit:

> Make no mistake, the missionary venture of the Church, no matter how well planned, how finely administered, or how fully supported, would fail like every other vast human enterprise were it not that where human instrumentality leaves off, a blessed ally takes over. It is the Holy Spirit who calls, it is the Holy Spirit who inspires, it is the Holy Spirit who reveals, and it is the Holy Spirit who administers.[295]

Melvin Hodges (former regional director for Latin America and author of *The Indigenous Church*) adds, "None of us is wise enough to chart the future course of missions. We don't have to be! The Holy Spirit will lead us on a better course than we could possibly plan. He is already doing so!"[296] The role of the leadership of the Spirit is coupled with the manifestation of his power. After all, Pentecostals are people not only of the Spirit but of the Word as well. The Word states that signs will accompany them who believe (Mark 16:17-19). Some would question the authenticity of this passage, but throughout the book of Acts signs such as mentioned in this passage followed them who believed. Pentecostal history is full of people believing that the God of the Old and New Testament is the same today as ever. This brings us, indeed, to the power of the Spirit confirming his Word.

Wilbur Shenk, in a response to the challenge of the post-Christendom or post-Christian European society, which seems to be inoculated against Christianity, observes:

> This culture will not readily grant to religion the kind of defining role it had in the past. Instead religion has been pushed to the margins of society. However, throughout history mission and renewal have always started on the periphery and moved toward the center. The clues as to the future of faith in Europe will in all

---

[295] Quoted by Peter Kuzmič in his foreword to Gary B. McGee, *This Gospel Shall Be Preached: A History and Theology of Assemblies of God Foreign Missions Since 1959*, vol. 2 (Springfield, MO: Gospel Publishing House, 1989), 10.

[296] McGee, *This Gospel*, vol. 2, 106, as cited in Everett A. Wilson, *Strategy of the Spirit: J. Philip Hogan and the Growth of the Assemblies of God Worldwide 1960–1990* (Irvine, CA: Regnum, 1997), 73.

likelihood be found on the margins, not by looking to the historic centers of religion.[297]

I would suggest that the Spirit's manifestation of power is being evidenced on the periphery of society in the plethora of Pentecostal and charismatic groups springing up around Europe and in the Gypsy Pentecostal communities, as well as a renewed passion of classic European Pentecostals to reach their continent with the gospel.

In regard to the Pentecostals on the continent, consider the following observation:

> In comparison with other continents, the Pentecostal movement in Europe has not shown the same spectacular growth. In 2000 D.B. Barrett and T.M. Johnson estimated a total of 37,568,700 Pentecostals/ Charismatics/ Neocharismatics in Europe. About 8 percent (= 3 million) refers to the classical Pentecostals, 56 percent to the Charismatics and 36 percent to the Neocharismatics. While these high numbers of Charismatics and Neocharismatics are questionable, the 3 million belonging to Pentecostal denominations correspond well with the figures established by Patrick Johnstone and Jason Mandryk (2001) and by Paul Schmidgall (2003)."[298]

Testimonies of the moving of the Spirit among the periphery of European society abound in Europe. I share from personal encounters and experience the following examples. Vienna Christian Center (VCC) in Vienna, Austria, is one example. Three families of AGWM missionaries started the Center in the late 1980s. It began as an English-speaking service, and English still is the *lingua franca* of the Center, but VCC now embraces over 50 nationalities. It has fellowship groups that include Iranians, Turks, Filipinos, a multitude of African nations, and an Austrian church. The Center embraces all these and more nationalities and is located on two campuses in the third district of Vienna. It houses upwards of 1,500 attendees.

Another example would be the Hispanic fellowship in Brussels, Belgium. Although the majority of Hispanics are from Ecuador, it embraces many Hispanics from all over Latin America and the Caribbean. On a typical Sunday morning there will be around 450 attendees. It has developed children's programs and fellowship groups. They have instituted a church Bible school with a missionary director from the Assemblies of God of Argentina and reach about 100 students.

Yet another example would be the myriad of African fellowships across Europe. Pentecostal African immigrants have found their homes in Paris,

---

[297] Shenk, "Contemporary Europe," 135-36.
[298] Mark Cartledge, "Europe," GloPent: European Research on Global Pentecostalism, accessed October 11, 2010, http://www.glopent.net/global-pentecostalism/europe.

London, Hamburg, and other major cities of Europe. They spring up on the edges of society and in many cases on the edge of the established Pentecostal church movements. However, there seems to be an indication that several of the established Pentecostal movements are embracing these immigrant congregations, as indicated by a partner of AGWM, the German Pentecostal Movement (*Bund Freikirchlicher Pfingstgemeinden* [BFP]). They have appointed an African minister trained in Germany (who is a member of the BFP) as their liaison to the many dozens of African congregations scattered across Germany and have given him a place on their executive council. They are intentional about fellowshipping with immigrant groups.

The last illustration is the Roma or Gypsy communities located in various European countries. Two groups come to mind with which the AGWM works. The first example is in Leskovac, Serbia. A Roma congregation of over a thousand gathers weekly to worship the Lord and reach out to their community. It is a vibrant fellowship with a choir and ministries for the congregation and the community. After preaching in one of their services the author learned that a drug-addicted Roma Muslim young man found Christ, was freed from his drug addiction, and healed of a tracheal condition brought about by sniffing glue.[299]

The second example is the Roma community in France. Roma evangelical/Pentecostal leaders believe that there are around 300,000 Roma in France, and roughly 130,000 of these are believers, with many of them being Pentecostal believers. Large groups of Pentecostals that congregate annually have over 10,000 in attendance.[300] The author participated in a commissioning service that sent out over 100 evangelists around the world to preach the gospel.

As one can see, there is a sampling of anecdotal evidence to illustrate that there is substance to the observation of Shenk and to the author's contention that the Spirit is leading the work of sharing the gospel in Europe. These examples illustrate the point that the Spirit is at work.

I would also suggest that European evangelicals and Pentecostals, as well as neo-Pentecostals, would be considered by a majority of mainline churches and society in general as the periphery of society. The Lord through the Spirit will bring about renewal in God's way, and there seems to be evidence that elements of this way include the Pentecostal immigrants and the Pentecostal Europeans who are open to the moving of the Spirit to reach their continent and the world with the gospel. Presently the Pentecostal European Fellowship (PEF) sends out over 1,700 missionaries around the world.

---

[299] Ken Horn, "Gypsy Breakthrough in Serbia," *Pentecostal Evangel* (May 2, 1999): 17.

[300] John W. Kennedy, "Life Light Among the Gypsies in France," *Pentecostal Evangel* (July 1, 2001): 6.

Much has been written about partnership in missions over the preceding decades, and this article will not make any startling contribution to the plethora of literature on the subject. However, my objective is to illustrate partnership in the AGWM and European Pentecostal church context.

One of the values of AGWM is that they are "committed to the principles of the indigenous church and partnership."[301] One must understand that partnership in this context is working with national church organizations for several reasons.

> Because of our [AGWM] history, philosophy, and structure, we relate much easier to a family of indigenous churches who have come together in a cooperative spirit to form an organization. ... We relate to organizations that have a similar doctrinal stance as we have. We relate to organizations with which we have historic roots and contacts. We relate to organizations that have a mission similar to ours—Reaching, Planting, Training, and Touching.[302]

Naturally, there are various stages of partnership that need to be taken into account when speaking to this subject. AGWM is in various stages of development with its partners in Europe. I would describe the stages in the following way: initial, developing, maturing, and mature. The length of time in a partnership is not the only factor that determines the stage of the partnership. Other contributing factors would include the measure of trust between AGWM and the movements, the relationship of the missionaries, and the European movement pastors, and the relationship between the leaders of the mission and the movement's leadership. The contribution of the mission to the goals of the European movement and vice versa is also an important element in the stages of the partnership. It should be noted that the stages of partnership involve progression as well as regression, depending upon the factors described above. A mature partnership could regress to an initial stage of partnership or be broken because of a breach of trust or change in leadership of the mission or movement. Likewise, an initial stage of partnership could progress to a developing stage relatively quickly if a leadership relationship blossoms or a bridge of trust in a mutually important matter is established. It is a given that time in relationship is a very important factor and perhaps the most important factor in determining the level of partnership, but as stated, there are other contributing factors as well.

Several examples can serve to illustrate this point. AGWM's partnership with the Spain Assemblies of God at one point in history resulted in what was termed as a divorce. However, there was a "changing of the guard" on AGWM and the Spanish AG's leadership level within the missionary family. The result, over a period of more than a decade, has been a stage of partnership that could

---

[301] "Core Values of Assemblies of God World Missions" (Springfield, MO).
[302] Mundis, *Eye on Europe*, 36.

be determined mature. Both entities are in constant dialog and communication with one another, and common projects and consultation on important matters such as church planting, missions, ministerial training, and church development are discussed, and agreed-upon strategies are implemented. An example of a developing relationship is with the Assemblies of God of the United Kingdom. Dating back to the turn of the 20th century there was an unspoken agreement that the AGWM would not send missionary personnel to the UK. However, after a number of spiritual revelations, including prophetic visions, the district of Scotland invited AGWM to partner with them in Scotland, planting churches and working with youth and children. The leadership of the UK was called upon to bless this partnership, which they did. Shortly thereafter a delegation from the UK AG leadership traveled to Springfield, Missouri (the National Resource Center for the US Assemblies of God), and a partnership was agreed upon between the two movements. There are now AGWM personnel in Scotland, Northern Ireland, Wales, and England. The partnership is developing.

I am sure one can understand the hesitancy in mentioning a partnership that has regressed. However, I am prepared to say there a couple of situations that the AGWM faces in Europe that can be categorized in this manner. Without disclosing the details, it can be said that the partnership regression is not one-sided. In my opinion, both parties have contributed to the regression. Speaking from the AGWM perspective, this regression may have been exacerbated by a growing lack of trust when relational issues with local pastoral leadership escalated to include national leadership. Other contributing factors to this regression could be the perception that AGWM is only valued as a "money partner" or "Uncle Sam." This perception accelerates the distrust and contributes to a breakdown in relationships. Overcoming the negative factors is definitely an uphill climb. Memories are "long" in Europe, and trust is normally built slowly. Intentional bridge-building in relationships is necessary to change present circumstances toward a more positive change and a progressive stage in the partnership.

Intentional planning involving a Pentecostal almost sounds like an oxymoron. Pentecostals are more known for their spontaneity and impulsiveness. However, this has been changing over the past several decades. AGWM history is filled with strategic plans and the implementation of those plans. There is a concerted effort to marry the moving of the Spirit and the strategic plans of man. One outstanding example of this would be Everett Wilson's book which records the life of J. Philip Hogan, entitled, *Strategy of the Spirit*.

The Europe Region of AGWM has, since its inception, made conscious efforts to marry the moving of the Spirit with the strategy of man. After its inception, the effort to discover the mind of the Spirit and the strategy of man resulted in surveying the missionary family as well as European partner leadership. The result was the 4C focus: Campuses, Cities, Children, and Culturally Diverse Communities. The key words were the emphasis of Europe

AGWM and their ministry on the university campus (Students for Christ), which increased from three countries to fifteen countries. Churches were planted in major cities in Portugal, Romania, Spain, Germany, Albania, Scotland, Czech Republic, and Kosovo. Children's ministry increased from a minor role in just a few countries to a ministry called Europe's Children in the majority of European countries. Seizing the opportunity to challenge non-Christian background immigrants (including Muslims) with the gospel, AGWM is now working in partnership with European churches and movements with these immigrants to share the love of Jesus in tangible and intangible ways in Spain, Belgium, the UK, Albania, Bosnia and Herzegovina, Macedonia, Bulgaria, France, Austria, and Italy.

Recognizing that the Holy Spirit moves in different ways in different seasons and that strategies have a limited effective life, AGWM Europe began a process of addressing the future of its ministry in the fall of 2008. From the beginning the emphasis was placed on the internal ministry structure and not on the outward relationship with European churches and movements. (The European leadership was informed about the internal process and change in the middle of the process.) A think tank was created involving 35 missionaries, including the leadership, and through a process of brainstorming a plan was born for the next season. The implementation of the plan involved asking the missionary body to dedicate the first hundred days of 2009 to seeking the mind of the Spirit for the future and praying for the 100 missionaries involved in small groups brainstorming and recording their observations about the ministry infrastructure leading us into the future. Subsequently, the leadership (seven leaders accompanied by their wives) sifted through the vast amount of material and began to implement immediate changes from the suggestions made. In addition, a meeting was called with representatives from each work group, and the plan was discussed and developed further. The changes are noted in the title "Europe Region Network." Leadership again met to sift through the material derived from the previous meetings and called for a second hundred days of prayer in 2010. The emphasis during these days for the whole missionary family was on the results of the previous meetings. The Europe Region Network now involves geographical areas with an area director in each area, a regional leader for each of the five geographical areas, and, because of the new plan, specialized networks consisting of Church Planting, International Churches, Church Transformation, Evangelism, Youth/Student, Children, Compassion, Ministerial Training, Culturally Diverse Communities, Media, and a Missionary Resource Team have been integrated into the ministry structure.

The "sea change" is affecting AGWM's role in ministry in Europe. With the power of networking each ministry network can utilize the strength, experience, and resources from within their network and can also work in harmony and synergy with other networks and our European Pentecostal and evangelical partners to fulfill the Great Commission, our mission, and our Europe purpose statement, which is to "accelerate the spread of the gospel, model biblical integrity, minister in the Spirit, and partner with those of like vision to build the Church of Jesus Christ." The effectiveness of this plan is yet to be seen and measured, as it is still in the early implementation stage. However, the intentionality and focus on the ten areas of outward ministry address the concern of taking the gospel in the power of the Spirit and with the strategy of man to Europeans and Muslims on the continent in a concrete way. It also unleashes the creativity of the individuals in each network, along with an increased opportunity to hear from the Spirit for the boots on the ground. A large majority of the missionary family has embraced this sea change and signed up to be involved in networks. Of the 440 missionaries and missionary associates in Europe, 312 are committed to the plan. The future will reveal if it, indeed, is a good marriage of Spirit and strategy.

## Concluding Summary

Europeans as well as Muslim immigrants need to hear the gospel. Scripture says, "The Lord is ... not willing that any should perish, but that all should come to repentance" (2 Pet. 3:9 KJV). The Assemblies of God is, with renewed deliberation, following the leading of the Spirit in his power, partnering with European evangelicals/Pentecostals and implementing a plan to share the gospel across the length and breadth of the continent. The results of this renewed deliberation are illustrated in part in this chapter, yet this renewal will only truly be measurable after a season of time. There is a spiritually optimistic anticipation among missionaries and European Pentecostal church leaders of an outpouring of the Holy Spirit and a growth in the Church of Jesus Christ on the continent. There is a sense of spiritual momentum as European Pentecostal leaders meet, pray, strategize, and plan for the future work of the church. The Assemblies of God shares this sense and recognizes that since 1998, when Europe became its own region in the AGWM structure, the missionary body has grown from 289 to over 450. In addition, nine countries have for the first time received AGWM personnel. The Lord of the harvest is calling workers and pointing out harvest fields to reap that harvest. As the missionaries strategize and plan, they also humble themselves under the sovereignty of an almighty God and move forward, believing God to direct their steps and see Europeans and Muslim immigrants find a place in the Kingdom of God and in his Church.

# Bibliography

Barrett, David B., George T. Kurian, and Todd M. Johnson, eds. *World Christian Encyclopedia: A Comparative Survey of Churches and Religions in the Modern World.* 2nd ed. 2 vols. New York: Oxford University Press, USA, 2001.

Cumont, Frank. *The Oriental Religions in Roman Paganism.* Chicago: Open Court, 1911.

Dayton, Edward R. and David A. Fraser. *Planning Strategies for World Evangelization.* Rev. ed. Grand Rapids: Eerdmans, 1990.

Douglas, J. D., ed. *Proclaim Christ Until He Comes.* Minneapolis: World Wide Publications, 1990.

Horn, Ken. "Gypsy Breakthrough in Serbia." *Pentecostal Evangel* (May 2, 1999): 17.

Jenkins, Philip. *The Next Christendom: The Coming of Global Christianity.* New York: Oxford University Press, 2002.

Kennedy, John W. "Life Light Among the Gypsies in France." *Pentecostal Evangel* (July 1, 2001): 6.

Kuzmič, Peter "Europe." In *Toward the 21$^{st}$ Century in Christian Mission,* edited by James M. Philips and Robert T. Coote, 148-63. Grand Rapids: Eerdmans, 1993.

Kuzmič, Peter. "Globalism and the Post-Communist World." In *Globalization of Pentecostalism—A Religion Made to Travel,* edited by Murray W. Dempster, Byron Klaus, and Douglas Peterson, 48. Oxford: Regnum, 1999.

McAlister, Stuart. "Younger Generations and the Gospel in Western Culture." In *Global Missiology for the 21$^{st}$ Century: The Iguassu Dialogue,* edited by William D. Taylor, 367-68. Grand Rapids: Baker Academic, 2000.

McGee, Gary B. "Core Values of Assemblies of God World Missions." In *This Gospel Shall Be Preached: A History and Theology of Assemblies of God Foreign Missions Since 1959,* vol. 2, 10. Springfield, MO: Gospel Publishing House, 1989.

_____. "Early Pentecostal Missionaries—They Went Everywhere Preaching the Gospel." In *Azusa Street and Beyond: Pentecostal Missions and Church Growth in the Twentieth Century,* edited by L. Grant McClung, 33. South Plainfield, NJ: Bridge, 1986.

_____. *This Gospel.* vol. 2 as cited in Everett A. Wilson, *Strategy of the Spirit: J. Philip Hogan and the Growth of the Assemblies of God Worldwide 1960–1990.* Irvine, CA: Regnum, 1997.

Mallough, Don. "The Stepchild of Missions." *Missionary Challenge* (December 1954): 6.

Mundis, Gregory M. *Eye on Europe: Charting the Course for Our Mission in Europe.* Springfield, MO: Assemblies of God World Missions, 2000.

Shenk, Wilbur R. "Contemporary Europe in Missiological Perspective." *Missiology: An International Review* 35, no. 2 (April 2007): 126.

Tenney, Merrill C. "Gospel." In *Wycliffe Bible Encyclopedia,* edited by Charles F. Pfeiffer, Howard F. Vos, and John Rea. Chicago: Moody, 1975.

**The Integration of All of Life under Christ's Reign**

# Faith and Life: A Pauline Perspective on the Integration of Faith and Everyday Life

Corneliu Constantineanu

In today's pluralistic context, Christian leaders must find appropriate ways not simply to cope with "otherness" and "difference," but to engage, with their congregations, in the public square in order to promote a culture of dialogue, respect, and love. There is thus an urgent need in the contemporary world, felt more dramatically among the younger generation of Christians, to find ways to relate faith and everyday life, gospel and culture, church and society.

In this chapter I would like to reflect on a holistic understanding of Christian life and mission, an integrative understanding of the gospel as public truth—concerned with and addressing the entire reality. In the first part of the chapter I will present in more personal terms a vision for theological education and Christian life grounded in the lordship of Christ over every aspect of life. In the second part of the chapter I will offer an argument for a holistic understanding of Christian life from the apostle Paul and the way in which he maintains this unity between theology and ethics, between indicative and imperative, between faith and life. According to Paul, the gospel is not divorced but fully integrated into the realities of life, and there is an effective and transforming power of the gospel that operates in the believer. When a person responds to the gospel one is bound to follow the logic of that gospel and live accordingly. In a world in which there is a sharp dichotomy between doctrine and life, between theology and ethics, it is essential that we recover a biblical view of the "obedience of faith." I am convinced that a fresh reading of Paul will represent an important resource for churches in their mission to follow Christ faithfully in a fallen world.

## "Take Every Thought Captive to Obey Christ"
## (2 Corinthians 10:4-5 ESV): A Vision for Theological Education

There is nowadays a great cry for integration, for a meaningful way that makes sense and integrates faith within everyday realities of life in society. Young people especially, but not only they, raise serious and urgent questions: is faith just for private life or has it also to do with the public domain? Is there a place for Christian witness in a secular environment, and if so, how is that witness to be displayed with integrity in such a context? What does it mean to be an authentic Christian in a secular and pluralist context? Fundamental for any attempt to answer these crucial questions is the double truth of the lordship of Christ over all of reality and, consequently, the gospel being a public truth.

The continuous drive for integration of many Christians today has its starting point in a perception of reality in which the lordship of Christ over all creation, in all matters private and public, is a given. This is excellently illustrated in the life and writings of Abraham Kuyper (1837–1920), a Dutch theologian, journalist, university founder, and statesman, one of the most remarkable Reformed Christians. In his inaugural speech ("Sphere Sovereignty") at the opening of Free University, which he founded in 1880, Kuyper expresses this in remarkable and unforgettable words: "Oh, no single piece of our mental world is to be hermetically sealed off from the rest, and there is not a square inch in the whole domain of our human existence over which Christ, who is Sovereign over all, does not cry: "Mine!"[303]

Such a holistic perspective is vital also for theological education, and we have to emphasize the complex dynamic and intrinsic relationship between mind and heart, between the academic/intellectual and spiritual dimension of life. For too long evangelicals in this part of the world [Eastern Europe] have worked with a false dichotomy between the academic and spiritual aspects of theology. This is the old but ever present misunderstanding of the place of scholarship in Christian life and the confusion about the so-called "pretense" of those seriously engaged in academic pursuits. In that old misunderstanding and confusion, it is often pointed out that "advance" in scholarship leads inevitably to "pride" and self-confidence. This observation is not to be ruled out immediately as false or untrue because it is validated by many who pretend that they are "scholars" of sorts, and who display just such kinds of attitudes described above. The perception of the common people is thus many times justified and is then attributed invariably to all scholarship. Having said this, however, I should immediately point out that the so-called "scholars" are not true scholars at all, because they have not yet come to understand the inescapable and immutable law that governs every truthful academic inquiry: the more one learns, the more one discovers how much there is yet to learn, and how tentative all the "assured" results must remain. The realization/ understanding of this truth represents the only possible "pretense" of advanced scholarship! True scholarship is, inevitably, a very humbling enterprise! I believe it is mandatory that in our efforts to emphasize the importance of the spiritual dimension in the life of students of theology, we should always be careful to do it in a way that will enhance, not undermine, the intellectual,

---

[303] Abraham Kuyper, *A Centennial Reader* (Grand Rapids: Eerdmans, 1998), 461.

academic aspect. In fact, the rejection of any such false dichotomies is, ironically, the sign of a true, biblical spirituality!

### The Lordship of Christ and Theological Education

Not only is a healthy and true spirituality not in contradiction with the highest academic pursuits but, in fact, it is required by it! To "take every thought captive to obey Christ" (2 Cor. 10:5 ESV) is, for Paul, both the strongest statement of true spirituality and a lifelong academic pursuit—because what else is Paul advocating here if not his constant preoccupation to make the lordship of Christ bear on every single aspect of life. However, discerning and being able to answer the question, "what does the lordship of Christ means in this and that situation?" takes years and years of prayerful and extremely hard work. Our effort in theological education is nothing more than an effort to equip and discipline young men and women to be able to "make every thought captive to Christ," that is, to bring the lordship of Christ to bear on every aspect of reality: their own personal life, the surrounding environment, culture, society, politics, economics, religion (!). But we will only be able to succeed in our efforts if we preserve the same balance as Paul on both spirituality and academic work. It is our task in theological education to inspire students to pursue with all the intellectual seriousness the love of God and God's dealing with the world. Our efforts in theological education should always be directed to finding new ways in which we can transmit to the students "habits that sustain a lifelong intellectual exploration of love of God and knowledge of God in service of God's world" (as remarkably put by Professor Miroslav Volf).[304] Our passion for God cannot be separated from God's reality and his passion for the world, but must encompass it.

### A Radical Shift in Christian Leadership

One of the fundamental strengths of a theological school should be the fact that it communicates and shapes such a profound understanding of the lordship of Christ over every single aspect of reality. This is the only and true basis for a holistic, integrative understanding of the Kingdom of God in which the gospel is not only a private and spiritual thing but also a public truth, concerned with and addressing the whole of reality. It is only such a holistic vision that can represent the solid foundation for a much-needed radical shift in our understanding of Christian leadership. In our complex, pluralistic, global world, the churches around the world need leaders who are trained to cope with living among the existing deep differences in all levels of our societies. Unfortunately, we have to admit with profound sadness, that many evangelical schools around the world do not provide even this minimum minimorum. In addition, and more

---

[304] "The Lordship of Christ over Entire Reality," http://www.evtos.hr/~tecee/index.html.

significantly, we need leaders who have a holistic understanding of reality, who are trained to engage deeply with God's world, with all aspects of cultures and societies; leaders who are able to offer Christian, biblically based alternatives to the many puzzles of this world; leaders who instead of denying the painful realities of this world with an escapist mentality, agonize over these realities and struggle to contribute and give appropriate solutions both in the light of the fallen state of creation and subsequent social evil, and in the light of the present reality of the presence and power of the Kingdom of God among the kingdoms of this world. The churches around the world need leaders who are caught by an irresistible vision of "making every thought captive to Christ."

### Believing and Practicing Scholars!

Such leaders, however, cannot be formed or modeled just anywhere. We need schools with the ability, resources, and the environment to shape what I call "believing and practicing scholars." The future belongs to those leaders who maintain a strong faith in God as the only one who can ultimately bring the Kingdom of God; leaders who will have a passion for God, for the world and for people, and who will embody the gospel in concrete manifestations of love, truth, justice, and reconciliation; and leaders who are able to articulate the gospel in contemporary relevant language and categories. It will only be such leaders who are able to integrate their beliefs, their praxis, and their scholarship into a holistic vision of the Kingdom of God, leaders capable of proclaiming the gospel for what it was, is, and shall ever remain: a public statement. The gospel was never a matter of private interest; it is not, and should never be, reduced to a means of getting souls to heaven, or restricted to the individual inner soul! The gospel was always, and it should remain, a public statement about the whole of reality, about God, about the world, about truth, about meaning, about life.

As Bible teachers, educators, and Christian leaders, we take it as our task to inspire a new generation of believers and Christian professionals, to pursue with all intellectual seriousness a holistic vision of the Kingdom of God, a vision in which faith determines a particular way of being in and for the world. In the contemporary context in which the Christian heritage is disappearing and the place and significance of the Bible is fading away, it is crucially important to attempt to bring back the centrality of the Bible and of biblical thinking as a solid and significant basis, not simply for living as Christians in the world, but also for the life of contemporary culture and society. There is, thus, a great need to rediscover, to reinterpret, to read afresh the Bible in such a way that it speaks to all aspects of life, as, in fact, it does! We now turn to the apostle Paul for a closer look at the way in which he maintained this fine balance between theology and ethics, between faith and life. I believe that a new understanding and explication of the social meaning of beliefs in Paul will represent an important resource for churches in their efforts to find a solid biblical basis and a model for their social engagement and responsibility in the world and ultimately to enable churches to act as reconciling agents in carrying out their transformational mission in the world.

## The Integration of Faith and Life in Paul

It was often believed that Paul was not concerned with the social, political realities of the world, but rather with solely preaching the gospel of salvation. Further, the claim goes, Paul expected the imminent end of the world and so he did not care much about what happened with the wider world. Research in this area has shown, however, that this is not an accurate view of Paul, as the following remarks will indicate.[305]

Paul's writings have not been generally used as a resource for dealing with contemporary social and political issues. It is often assumed that although the earthly life and ministry of Jesus was dominated by his concern for the poor and the oppressed, Paul, on the contrary, transformed Jesus' original message and intention into a purely spiritual religion—a message of eternal salvation for sinners. Paul, it is argued, had little, if any, interest for the affairs of "this world." There are many reasons for this individualistic, narrowly religious, and spiritual reading of Paul. But certainly one important reason for this (mis)reading of Paul is due rather to his interpreters than to his own writings. Interpreters were unable to see any concern for the "secular" matters in the letters of Paul because they operated with a modern presupposition of a dichotomy between "sacred" and "profane" aspects of reality. However, for Paul and for all first-century Christians, there was one realm of reality in which body and soul, religion and politics, private and public, individual and social aspects of reality were intermingled in a complex, unified vision of life. It was primarily because of our own presuppositional "assignment" of Paul to the "sacred" or "spiritual/religious" realm that we were unable to perceive him as being interested in social and political issues as well. Once we become aware of the unified worldview of Paul and attempt to read him on his own terms, we may discover a new facet of Paul.

Conventional interpretations of Paul have generally either evaded political and social issues in Paul's theology, or understood him as simply endorsing the existing political powers in a conservative attitude of maintaining the social and political status quo. Several recent trends in Pauline studies, however, seem to challenge this view and to argue instead that Paul was more profoundly political than is usually perceived and that the gospel he preached had

---

[305] For a fuller and more comprehensive discussion of what follows, see my chapter, "From Creation to New Creation: The Underlying Framework of Paul's Understanding of Reconciliation," in *The Social Significance of Reconciliation in Paul's Theology. Narrative Readings in Romans*, ed. Corneliu Constantineanu (London/New York: T&T Clark, 2010), 43-61.

significant social and political dimensions.[306] It is true, the extent of such concerns and the basic orientation of Paul's political thought is a matter of debate in recent scholarship, and there is a wide spectrum of views among scholars regarding Paul's attitude to and reflection on social and political issues.[307] What is becoming clearer, however, is the fact that the gospel Paul proclaimed was not in any way detached from everyday reality and that it had also a political message at its heart. Further still, some studies show that the political dimension of the gospel was not secondary or accidental to Paul's writings but rather an integral and fundamental element of it. The gospel of the crucified and resurrected Christ, it is claimed, not only has a few "social and political implications," but rather is political at its core.[308]

Far from having an escapist mentality, Paul's creational theology, i.e., his understanding of God's relation to and sovereignty over creation, over nations, and over history, and the way this reality was irreversibly affected by God's intervention in Christ, gave him a positive view of the world and of the place and role of the larger structures of society. Furthermore, the way he formulated his gospel shows that Paul was well acquainted with the religious, cultural, social, and political matrix of the Greco-Roman world with which he thoroughly engaged. So within this larger framework of reference it is plausible, indeed necessary, to enquire about the social meaning of his theological statements, since his theology, like much of the theological discourse of the New Testament, was meant not simply to offer salvation in a

---

[306] The most recent and significant studies include two excellent books edited by Richard Horsley, *Paul and Politics: Ekklesia, Israel, Imperium, Interpretation* (Harrisburg, PA: Trinity Press International, 2000), and *Paul and Empire: Religion and Power in Roman Imperial Society* (Harrisburg, PA: Trinity Press International, 1997). There are also a few very significant monographs: Bruno Blumenfeld, *The Political Paul: Justice, Democracy, and Kingship in a Hellenistic Framework* (London: Sheffield Academic, 2001); Neil Elliott, *Liberating Paul: The Justice of God and the Politics of the Apostle* (Sheffield: Sheffield Academic, 1995); Mark Strom, *Reframing Paul: Conversation in Grace and Community* (Downers Grove: InterVarsity, 2000); R.A. Horsley and M.A. Silberman, *The Message and the Kingdom: How Jesus and Paul Ignited a Revolution and Transformed the Ancient World* (Minneapolis: Fortress, 1997); Elsa Tamez, *The Amnesty of Grace: Justification by Faith from a Latin American Perspective* (Nashville: Abingdon, 1993); Robert Grant, *Paul in the Roman World: the Conflict at Corinth* (Louisville, KY: Westminster John Knox, 2001).

[307] On the one hand, there are those who interpret Paul as having a basic conservative attitude (among which R. Grant, E. E. Ellis, D. Tidball, B. Blumenfeld). On the other hand, there are those who argue that Paul had a more profound political thought reflected in his letters (T. Gorringe, W. Wink, D. Georgi, N. Elliott, M. Strom, R. Horsley, N. T. Wright, and others).

[308] These are the initial findings of two research groups, one in the USA, "Paul and Political Group" led by Richard Horsley (published in the two volumes *Paul and Politics* and *Paul and Empire*), and the other in the UK, "Scripture and Hermeneutics Group" led by Craig Bartholomew, particularly the third volume, *A Royal Priesthood? The Use of the Bible Ethically and Politically*.

narrow spiritual sense, but also to affect moral dispositions, to shape particular communities, to determine specific behavior and a particular way of being in the world.

Paul's Jewish matrix provided him with a worldview that shaped fundamentally his thought and praxis. Particularly, his strong belief in a creational monotheism gave him an understanding of the world as God's good creation in which God is present and active and in which God's people should be actively engaged towards its eschatological transformation. Based on insights from the various social-scientific approaches to Paul, interpreters have concluded that the message of the New Testament is intrinsically related to the complex social realities of everyday life, and that the social dimension is an integral part of the meaning of the text. Therefore we need to resist the temptation of understanding the New Testament and Christianity as limited to an "inner-spiritual dimension" or to "an objective-cognitive system," and see it within the complex of social, cultural, political, economic, and religious contexts in which it initially developed. Equally significant, regarding the relation to the outside world Paul encourages a positive engagement. While Christians should maintain their different and specific identity, this should not cause them to separate or be indifferent towards the outside world, but rather to be engaged in its renewal and transformation.

## Theology and Ethics in Paul

One reason why many Pauline doctrines have been treated exclusively in their vertical, theological, and spiritual dimension is that theology and ethics in Paul have been studied separately, as two distinct bodies of teaching. As such, as long as one paid exclusive attention to theology, the ethical dimension of that particular doctrine and its social significance were neglected. Therefore, for a proper treatment of Paul's understanding of any doctrine, especially in its social dimension, one has to pay considerable attention to the close relationship between theology and ethics in Paul's thought.

In his significant study, *Theology and Ethics in Paul*,[309] Victor Paul Furnish puts forward the thesis that "ethical concerns are not secondary but radically integral to his [Paul's] basic theological convictions."[310] He argues persuasively that for Paul, theology, and ethics are intrinsically related, and that we cannot understand properly one without the other:

> ...the relationship between proclamation and exhortation is not just formal, or only accidental, but thoroughly integral and vital to the apostle's whole understanding of the gospel. Just as his ethical teaching has significant theological

---

[309] Victor P. Furnish, *Theology and Ethics in Paul* (Nashville: Abingdon, 1968).
[310] Furnish, *Theology*, 13.

dimensions, so do the major themes of his preaching have significant ethical dimensions.[311]

Thus, according to Furnish, in order to understand Paul's ethics one must see its theological presuppositions; and vice versa, for an understanding of his theology one must see its ethical implications. In his words, "the relation of indicative and imperative, the relation of 'theological' proclamation and 'moral' exhortation, is the crucial problem in interpreting the Pauline ethic."[312] This implies that for an adequate treatment of any concept in Paul, one should pay considerable attention not only to the explicit theological statements but also to their ethical implications within the teaching of Paul. And yet, these two aspects should not be considered separately, as one resulting from the other. If the indicative and imperative are indeed in such a close connection, we should keep them somehow together. Again Furnish is to the point:

> Paul understands these two dimensions of the gospel in such a way that, though they are not absolutely identified, they are closely and necessarily associated. God's claim is regarded by the apostle as a constitutive part of God's gift. The Pauline concept of grace is inclusive of the Pauline concept of obedience. For this reason it is not quite right to say that, for Paul, the imperative is "based upon" or "proceeds out of" the indicative. This suggests that the imperative is designed somehow to "realize" or "actualize" what God has given only as a "possibility."
> ... The Pauline imperative is not just the result of the indicative but fully integral to it.[313]

Paul's ultimate concern in his writing was not simply with "doctrine" or theology for its own sake, but with the life of people in concrete historical situations. To be sure, for Paul theology is essential, but it is never detached from life, from a specific way of life appropriate to its theological foundation. Theology and ethics belong together, faith and conduct are inseparable. We find this complex dynamic in Paul whereby one's beliefs determine a specific way of life and one's practices in the world have a strong theological basis. Paul is not simply telling Christians that they should behave in a reconciling way towards the other but he also tells them why, thus offering the strongest possible ground for their practice of reconciliation—God's reconciling his enemies through Christ. Furthermore, and equally significant, Paul also shows Christians how to live in a reconciling way towards the other, thus offering

---

[311] Furnish, *Theology*, 112.

[312] Furnish, *Theology*, 9. This was also the conclusion he reached after his survey of the 19th- and 20th-century interpretation of Paul's ethics.

[313] Furnish, *Theology*, 224-25. In a subsequent book, *The Love Command in the New Testament* (London: SCM, 1973), Furnish summarizes the issue in this way: "No better title for Paul's 'theology' can be devised than his own formulation in Gal. 5.6: 'faith active in love.' Love is both the context and the content of faith; *God's* love makes faith possible and *man's* love gives it visibility and effect in the world." (94)

them the model for their practice of reconciliation—Jesus Christ's self-giving love in his obedient life, death on a cross, and resurrection.

Paul's life, mission, and writings, indeed his theology, were informed and supported by a narrative framework, a unifying worldview and redemptive vision of reality which determined a particular way of being and living in the world. His gospel was fundamentally related to his vision of final cosmic reconciliation and peace. The precise and complex nature of the relationship between indicative and imperative in Paul's theology[314] needs thus to be carefully considered. A narrative reading of Paul's letters offers an excellent way to understand this dynamic and intrinsic relationship between indicative and imperative, between theology and ethics in Paul. This is, indeed, one of the most relevant features that emerges from a survey of the literature on narrative approaches to Pauline studies. For the proponents of a narrative reading of Paul, the major consequence of such a reading is an enhanced account of Pauline ethics.[315] After Wayne Meeks, who has stressed this issue very much, more recently David Horrell concludes his essay "Paul's Narrative or Narrative Substructure?" with this statement: "in a world conscious of the power of stories to form identity, values, and practice, the rediscovery of Paul's gospel as story is of critical value."[316] And indeed, it seems that the importance of narrative for moral formation is not a recent invention. Paul's contemporary, the Jewish theologian Philo of Alexandria, considered Moses to have been a superior legislator exactly because he established the laws in a narrative framework.[317] It is thus very plausible to consider that Paul shared Philo's view

---

[314] Beginning with Bultmann's "The Problem of Ethics in Paul," many other New Testament scholars came to understand the relationship between indicative and imperative as being essential not only for Paul's ethic but for the understanding of his thought in general. We mention only a few here: W. Schrage, *The Ethics of the New Testament;* A. Verhey, *The Great Reversal*; W. Dennison, "Indicative and Imperative: The Basic Structure of Pauline Ethics"; and Michael Parsons, "Being Precedes Act: Indicative and Imperative in Paul's Writings."

[315] See Alexandra Brown, "Response to Sylvia Keesmaat and Richard Hays," *Horizons in Biblical Theology* 26, no. 2 (December 2004): 115. Among theologians and ethicists, Stanley Hauerwas and Alistair MacIntyre have emphasized the formative place of narrative in the shaping of moral identity, and even more, the indispensable role of narrative in moral instruction and developments. For them, it is narrative that shapes identity and community, forms character and informs conduct. Especially relevant are Hauerwas, *A Community of Character: Toward a Constructive Christian Social Ethic* (Notre Dame: University of Notre Dame Press, 1981), *Vision and Virtue* (Notre Dame: Fides, 1974), and *Character and Christian Life* (San Antonio: Trinity University Press, 1975); MacIntyre, *After Virtue* (Notre Dame: University of Notre Name Press, 1984).

[316] David Horrell, "Paul's Narrative or Narrative Substructure? The Significance of 'Paul's Story,'" 170 (italics in original).

[317] Philo of Alexandria, *On the Creation of the World,* 3 and *Life of Moses,* 2.47-51. See Wayne A. Meeks, *The Origin of Christian Morality* (New Haven: Yale University Press, 1993), 189.

not simply with regard to Moses but also of the importance of narrative. In his latest study on Pauline ethics, Horrell pursues the issues further and offers a more nuanced and complex dynamic between narrative, theology, and ethics as a conceptual framework for reading Paul's texts. He writes:

> Paul's letters are to be seen as reflecting, and contributing to, a narrative myth which constructs a particular symbolic universe, giving meaning and order to the lives of those who inhabit it. This myth, enacted in ritual, is an identity and community-forming narrative which shapes both the world-view (the "is") and the ethos (the "ought") of its adherents. ... This broad framework of interpretation suggests that, at least at a general level, everything in Paul's letters is potentially relevant to a consideration of his "ethics." If the myth itself—the central story and its symbols and ideas—shapes the ethos and social practice of the community, then our inquiry cannot be limited only to certain explicitly paraenetic sections of the texts.[318]

As Paul himself made clear, the ultimate goal of the gospel, was "to bring about the obedience of faith" (Rom. 1:5; 16:26 ESV). This thesis has been well established by James Miller in his study, *The Obedience of Faith*. There the author shows that the theme of "obedience" plays a significant role in Paul's argument in Romans, as he uses it in connection with other key themes in the letter, and that by "the obedience of faith" Paul meant "specifically the obedience of welcoming one another after the model of Christ to the glory of God (15:7)."[319] He also finds that the term "obedience" indicated the proper response to the hearing of the gospel of Christ and that the obedience Christ showed plays a crucial role within the argument of Romans as ground and model for the believers' obedient life as they embody their true identity "in Christ."[320] This is indeed significant. It shows the intrinsic relationship between theology and ethics in Paul and that we simply cannot study one without the other without the risk of misreading Paul. Theology and ethics are so intertwined in Paul's argumentations that we have to keep them together. In what follows, based on the theoretical/methodological framework for a narrative reading of Paul's letters, I will offer a brief analysis of Romans 5–6 with special reference to the function of the story of Jesus Christ and reconciliation for community formation, for the shaping of identity, values, and practices of the community.

---

[318] David G. Horrell, *Solidarity and Difference: A Contemporary Reading of Paul's Ethics* (London: T&T Clark, 2005), 97-98.

[319] James C. Miller, *The Obedience of Faith, the Eschatological People of God, and the Purpose of Romans*, Society of Biblical Literature Dissertation Series 177 (Atlanta: SBL, 2000), 21.

[320] Miller, *Obedience*, 51-54.

## Participants in the Redemptive Story of Christ in Romans 5–6

One of the major problems confronting the Christians in Rome had to do with their differences, dissensions, and even divisions among various groups vis-à-vis such issues as ethnicity, religious practice (observance of dietary rules, of days, and of Jewish laws), and relationships with others within and outside the Christian community. This background explains Paul's interest in reconciliation, peace, love, unity, welcome—as he attempts not simply to put an end to any conflict and reconcile different groups[321] but, especially, to articulate so forcefully the inner logic of the gospel as being incompatible with such behavior. For Paul, these misunderstandings and the inappropriate conduct were not only a sign of the failure of the Christian community but a departure from, and a denial of, the very essence of the gospel. Paul makes a sustained argument for the seriousness of the ethical implications that are intrinsic to the gospel and their life "in Christ." In order to hold together these different aspects of theology and ethics, of indicative and imperative, of faith and Christian life, Paul uses a threefold strategy in his argumentation in Romans 5–6: interchange of metaphors, a change in personal pronouns, and the incorporation of the believers in the story of Christ.

### *The Interchange in Metaphors and Personal Pronouns*

It is significant that beginning with chapter 5 Paul shifts his emphasis from *dikaiōsis* "justification" terminology, which is predominant in Romans 1–4, to terms that are more personal-relational such as *eirene* ("peace," 5:1), *agapē* ("love," 5:5, 8) and *katallassō*, ("reconciliation," 5:10, 11).[322] Similarly, there is a significant shift in the use of personal pronouns in these chapters, from a clearly rhetorical "you" (chs. 1–4), to "we" and "us" not only in 5:1-11 but throughout chapters 5–8,[323] as Paul addresses the family of those "in Christ."

The unavoidable question is: why did Paul consider it necessary to make such changes at this point in his argument? Why does he bring in terms that are more social, horizontal in character, and metaphors rooted in the everyday realities of life? And why does he switch from an argumentative to a more confessional tone in this section? Is it simply a matter of linguistic preferences, whereby Paul decides to make use of his rich vocabulary but not necessarily with a particular purpose in mind? This is unlikely, given the carefully

---

[321] A.J.M. Wedderburn, *The Reasons for Romans* (Edinburgh: T&T Clark, 1988), 64-65 and 140-42.

[322] Much of this section is adapted from my book, *Social Significance of Reconciliation*, 120.

[323] Douglas Moo points out that Paul uses the first plural verbs only 13 times in Romans 1-4, "mainly editorially or as a stylistic device," but in chapters 5-8 he uses 48 such verbs. See Douglas J. Moo, *The Epistle to the Romans* (Grand Rapids: Eerdmans, 1996), 592.

structured grammatical and conceptual parallels between *eirene* and *katellage*, (vv.1, 10a) and between *dikaiosune* and *katellage*, (vv.1, 9, 10). Is then reconciliation simply a consequence of justification, or is it a larger, more comprehensive concept? Or, perhaps, Paul is using different metaphors interchangeably to express different dimensions of the same, multifaceted reality?

Several answers have been suggested. Thus, Porter argues that the different metaphors Paul is using in Romans 5 overlap semantically, but each individual metaphor highlights a different aspect of the same work of God.[324] Paul does that, he maintains, first by using synonymously *eirenen echomen*[325] *pros ton theon* (we have peace toward God) (v.1a) and *katellagemen to theo* (we were reconciled to God) (v.10a), both having God as the common object. Secondly the structure of vv. 9-10 reveals an overlapping meaning for *dikaio* (justified) and *katallasso (reconciled)*.

*Pollo ... mallon dikiothentes ... sothesometha* (much more, having been justified ... we will be saved) (v. 9)

and

*Pollo mallon katallagentes sothesometha* (much more, having been reconciled, we will be saved) (v.10)

Porter's point is significant because it explains the use of two different metaphors, one from the courtroom sphere (*dikaiosune*) and the other from the personal relational sphere (*eirene* and *katellage*). When used together they

---

[324] He states: "justification and reconciliation or enjoying peace are to be seen as overlapping metaphors, even verging on equation, each suggesting a different perspective on God's one work." Stanley E. Porter, *Katallasso* in Ancient Greek Literature, with Reference to the Pauline Writings, in *Estudios de Filologia Neo Testamentaria*, ed. Juan Mateos, vol. 5 (Cordoba, Spain: Ediciones el Almendro, 1994), 155. Other scholars who hold similar positions are Charles Kingsley Barrett, *The Epistle to the Romans: Black's New Testament Commentaries Series* (London: A & C Black, 1962), 108; *Word Biblical Commentary: Volumes 38a & 38b, Romans 1-8; Romans 9-16, 1988] (author)* James D. G. Dunn (Nashville: Thomas Nelson, 1988); Martin L. Smith, *Reconciliation: Preparing for Confession in the Episcopal Church* (Cambridge, MA: Cowley Publications, 1985), 134; and Victor Furnish, "Ministry of Reconciliation," *Currents in Theology and Mission* 4, no. 4 (1977): 212.

[325] Against this common reading, Porter prefers the variant reading, *echomen*, and argues for the hortatory subjective reading: "let us enjoy peace." He makes a very helpful clarification: "In this context the exhortation to enjoy peace (v.1), using the hortatory subjunctive, is not to be seen as exhorting movement to a subsequent stage, but as exhorting appropriation of circumstances attendant with justification. Therefore, the juridical and the personal categories of the two metaphors are linked inseparably, making an obvious and immediate association between justification and peace." *Katallasso*, 155.

express a multifaceted reality[326] and also show the inseparable link between the two metaphors in Paul. He concludes:

> *Katallasso* used to denote the same event which is described by Paul on the one hand as an initiatory juridical event, justification, treated at some length in chaps. 3 and 4… and on the other hand as the appropriation of attendant peaceful status, developed further in subsequent chapters in the letter.[327]

Porter makes an important contribution to the relationship between justification, peace, and reconciliation in Romans. However, it is somewhat regrettable that he does not carry through the implications of his observations for the concept of reconciliation at the horizontal level in Romans, a concept that Paul introduces in chapter 5 and then develops in the remaining chapters of Romans. This is indeed a classical example of an interpretation of reconciliation in Paul that suffers from the limited association of the concept solely with the word-group *katallasso / katēllagē*. Thus, the difficult question still remains: why does Paul consider it necessary to make such an interplay in his metaphors at this place in his argument? Does this make any difference to the way in which we used to interpret Paul's presentation of reconciliation in Romans?

Another attempt to answer Paul's important shift to reconciliation has been made by Gregory Allen, who offers a cogent and, at least in part, satisfactory answer to the issue.[328] Building on the work of Mitchell, he argues that Paul uses reconciliation language in Romans 5:1-11 as a strategic attempt to bring about unity and mutual acceptance in a fractured community in Rome. He further shows that the rhetoric of reconciliation in 5:1-11 functions in three ways: 1) to create common ground between Jewish and Gentile Christians; 2) to strengthen the new communal identity among the believers; and 3) to create the premise or the "preparatory grammar" for the later exhortation of 15:7-13 for mutual acceptance among believers.[329]

Allen's reading of 5:1-11 is very helpful and advances the discussion of reconciliation in Romans. The significance of his study consists in the fact that he reads reconciliation in the light of the contingent circumstances of Christians

---

[326] C. K. Barrett captures well this interplay: "Justification and reconciliation are different metaphors describing the same fact. The meaning of the verb 'to reconcile' is determined by the noun 'enemies'; it puts an end to enmity, just as 'to justify' puts an end to legal contention. 'Reconciliation' evokes the picture of men acting as rebels against God their king, and making war upon him; 'justification' that of men who have offended against the law and are therefore arraigned before God their judge." *Romans*, 108.

[327] Porter, *Katallasso*, 156.

[328] Gregory Allen, *Reconciliation in the Pauline Tradition: Its Occasions, Meanings, and Functions* (Boston: Boston University, 1995), 52-69.

[329] Allen, *Reconciliation*, 55-69.

in Rome and emphasizes correctly the believers' reconciliation with God as the basis for their mutual acceptance. It also points to the importance of reconciliation rhetoric in the whole argument of Romans and highlights Paul's effort to effect reconciliation in Rome. However, he seems to present a rather limited understanding of the complex and dynamic interplay of the metaphors that Paul is using (justification, peace, and reconciliation). He writes:

> Reconciliation and peace are equivalent expressions for Paul that describe the believers' new relationship with God. Reconciliation and justification are different metaphors used by Paul to describe the same fact. Reconciliation is a relational metaphor while justification is a forensic and covenantal metaphor, yet both point to the believers' new standing before God.[330]

Not only is Allen unable to allow the various metaphors to express different aspects of the reality Paul is referring to, but he also limits their meaning to the vertical dimension of reconciliation with God. Thus, he does not answer adequately why Paul uses different metaphors. Furthermore, by limiting himself to the text of 5:1-11, he does not seem to take into account Paul's larger and richer symbolism of reconciliation which is found in other places of Romans as well, as we saw in chapter 4.[331]

If, in the light of our previous discussion, the two metaphors "righteousness" and "reconciliation" denote different aspects of the same, multifaceted reality of salvation, and if Paul uses them synonymously, I propose that by changing the emphasis towards metaphors of social interaction, Paul shows 1) that reconciliation is an essential aspect of salvation, and that it contains an intrinsic social, horizontal dimension; and 2) that the vertical reconciliation with God is inseparable from the horizontal aspect, as two dimensions of the same reality. Paul is thus trying to communicate that unity, reconciliation, harmony, and acceptance among the believers in Rome are an intrinsic part of the very gospel of reconciliation they profess. Through chapters 5–8 and particularly 12–15, Paul highlights the implications of such an understanding of reconciliation for their everyday life, in the concrete circumstances at Rome. Beginning with Romans 5:1-11 Paul presents the reality of the believers being reconciled with God and implicitly with one another through the death of Christ. Indeed, as McDonald observes, the "dynamics of this pericope require that the readers admit that we believers (including Paul) are united with one another."[332] If Paul's overall goal was "to bring about the obedience of faith," he wanted to show that the gospel they have received has clear and concrete implications for

---

[330] Allen, *Reconciliation*, 69.

[331] Patricia McDonald also notices the shift in Romans 5, particularly of the personal pronouns, and argues that Paul's purpose in his change was to emphasize his own unity with the believers in Rome. See her "Romans 5:1-11 as a Rhetorical Bridge," *JSNT* 40 (1990): 81-96.

[332] McDonald, "Romans 5:1-11," 90.

the believer's everyday life. To be justified and reconciled with God is to be reconciled and at peace with your sister and brother, to be at peace with "the other." The believers in Rome seem to have "forgotten" these aspects and so Paul sends them a "reminder," as he himself puts it in 15:15: "I have written you quite boldly on some points to remind you of them again, because of the grace God gave me." From the variety of dissensions, mutual criticisms, and contempt among the various groups of believers in Rome, Paul seems to have sensed a profound misunderstanding on their part regarding the implications of the gospel of reconciliation for their life. He writes to correct that. But, as we will see, Paul's understanding of the social dimension of reconciliation includes peace between Jews and Gentiles, between Christians and the surrounding world, and peace within different Christian groups.[333]

Furthermore, if we consider the intentional changes in Paul's argumentation in the light of the abundance of references to Jesus Christ throughout Romans 5–8 and of the importance of the ethical dimension permeating this section, I suggest that Paul intended his readers to understand his argument in these chapters in close connection with the story of Christ and with their new status and responsibilities resulting from their being "in Christ." Indeed, Paul's shift in the personal pronouns seems to support this proposal. By using the "we" and "us" pronouns in a context in which he is retelling the story of Jesus, Paul includes himself and the believers in Rome in the same story of Christ, and prompts them to live out the "story of Christ" as active participants in the ongoing story of God's reconciliation of the world in Christ.[334] As we will see, the story of Christ functions not only as the ground of their reconciliation with God, but also as the model for their reconciliation with the other.

### Righteousness, Reconciliation, and the Social Ethical Aspect

The theme of *dikaiosune* ("righteousness"/ "justification") is, beyond any doubt, a central theme of the entire letter to the Romans. The concept of "righteousness" (*dik-* words) is very much present in chapters 1–4 (31 times) and in 5–8 (21 times). However, there is a thematic shift in the use of the word in the second section. If in the first four chapters the emphasis is on the status

---

[333] These points are excellently developed by Klaus Haacker, *The Theology of Paul's Letter to the Romans* (New York: Cambridge University Press, 2003), 45-53, in his chapter "Romans as the Proclamation of Peace with God and on Earth."

[334] This proposal goes beyond several other proposals which suggest that the shift in the personal pronouns signifies Paul's continuation of the dialogue with Judaism in 5–8 (see Thomas R. Schreiner, *Romans* [Grand Rapids, Mich.: Baker Academic, 1998], 247), or the continuation of the diatribe style in Romans 5 (so S. Porter, "The Argument of Romans 5," *Journal of Biblical Literature* 110, no. 4 [1991]: 655-77), or even a celebration of Paul's unity with the Roman believers (so Patricia McDonald, "Romans 5: 1-11 as a Rhetorical Bridge," *Journal for the Study of the New Testament* 13 (1990): 87.

of justification attained by faith in Jesus Christ, i.e., how God has fulfilled his Old Testament promises in Christ and that they are now available by faith to all, in the next chapters (5–8) there is a shift towards an ethical, transformational aspect of "righteousness" for the life of the believers. Several authors point to this aspect.[335]

The beginning of the paragraph in 5:1, *dikaiothentes oun ek pisteos* ("Therefore, since we have been justified through faith..."), shows that Paul presupposes the discussion on "justification by faith" previously established in 3:21–4:25, and that now he builds on it and describes the consequences and implications of that justification.[336] This is clearly and immediately seen in 5:9 where the reality of past justification represents the assurance of future salvation. The same aspect is found in the subsequent uses of *dik-* words, particularly in 5:12-19 and 8:10, 31, 33. But equally important with this future dimension of righteousness are the present implications of righteousness described by such words as *eirene* ("peace"), *kauchaomai* ("rejoicing") *thlipsis* ("suffering"), *elpis* ('hope'), *agape* ("love") and *katallage* ("reconciliation") throughout chapters 5–8. There is now a new dynamic of relationships in the life of those "justified": there is love and acceptance instead of enmity and rejection (5:5, 10). One has to be cautious again and state that this very intense and personal relationship of love between the "justified" and God as well as between all those "in Christ" is not simply a "consequence" of justification but, as Wright correctly remarks, a "necessary further dimension of the doctrine of justification by faith."[337] The argument in Romans 6:1–8:17 (particularly 6:15–23) is a clear illustration that by "righteousness" Paul does not understand simply a vertical, legal transaction between God and people, but

---

[335] See particularly Schreiner, *Romans*, 246-69; Moo, *Romans*, 292; Thomas H. Tobin, *Paul's Rhetoric in Its Contexts: The Argument of Romans* (Peabody: Baker Academic, 2005), 11, 155-60.

[336] Schreiner is thus partially correct to note that "[t]he primary function of the *dik-* words in Rom. 5-8 is not to explicate righteousness by faith, but to build on that justification and show what flows from it" (*Romans*, 249). But while it is true that Paul's emphasis in these chapters is on the ethical aspect of righteousness, one has to be very careful how one states it so as to avoid the danger of a too rigid, two-step sequential explanation of Paul's understanding of "righteousness," as if one could have first "justification" and then think about the consequences of that justification. I would argue that for Paul the ethical aspect of the believers life is in itself an "explication" of the same "justification by faith," i.e., the present transformation of the believer's life is an essential and intrinsic part of the "justification by faith."

[337] N. T. Wright, "Romans," in *The New Interpreter's Bible Acts – First Corinthians: A Commentary*, ed. Robert W. Wall, J. Paul Sampley, and N. T. Wright (Nashville: Abingdon, 2002), 10: 514.

rather a process which necessarily involves a moral transformation in the lives of the believers.[338]

If it is true that with regard to "justification" Paul maintains both aspects together, i.e., the juridical and relational, then we argue that he does the same with regard to "reconciliation," i.e., holding together the vertical and the horizontal dimensions of reconciliation. In fact, to put it the other way around, the very careful, parallel structuring of verses 5:1, 9, 10—with *dikaiosune*, *eirene*, and *katellage* inseparably linked—point to the fact that this is exactly what Paul intended to argue: that the juridical and the personal, the vertical and the horizontal dimensions of salvation belong together, inseparably.[339] Thus, one can say that Paul uses justification/reconciliation in the following chapters to highlight not only the legal, vertical aspect of these concepts but also their communal, horizontal dimension. The language of reconciliation introduced in chapter 5 and continued for the rest of the letter is thus not simply to point out the stance of the individual with God (as it has traditionally been understood), but also to indicate the believers' responsibility to extend this reconciliation to the others in their own community and outside of it.

### Incorporation "in Christ"

In Romans 6 Paul describes explicitly the dynamic by which the believers are incorporated "in Christ," through baptism,[340] and the implications of this new reality. Before their baptism the believers were under the power of sin and so

---

[338] Moo (*Romans*, 292) shows also that the ethical dimension of righteousness is emphasized in chapters 5–8.

[339] Analyzing this complex dynamic between justification and reconciliation in Romans 5, Cranfield argues for the inseparability of the two concepts. He writes: "What did Paul understand to be the relation between reconciliation and justification? The correct answer would seem to be neither that reconciliation is a consequence of justification, nor that 'Justification and reconciliation are different metaphors describing the same fact' [C. K. Barrett], but that God's *justification involves reconciliation* because God is what He is. Where God's justification is concerned, justification and reconciliation though distinguishable, are inseparable. ... Thus *dikaiothentes ... eirenen echomen* is not a mere collocation of two metaphors describing the same fact, nor does it mean that, having been justified, we were subsequently reconciled and now have peace with God; but its force is that the fact that we have been justified means that we have also been reconciled and have peace with God." C.E.B. Cranfield, *(International Critical Commentary), vol. 1 of A Critical and Exegetical Commentary on the Epistle to the Romans* (New York: T&T Clark, 2004), 258 (emphasis added).

[340] A brief history of the interpretation of this chapter, particularly of the first 14 verses, reveals the multifaceted and complex issues being raised vis-à-vis the theme of baptism as it relates to other important themes in Paul's theology. For an excellent presentation of the issues involved, see Hendrikus Boers, "The Structure and Meaning of Romans 6:1-14," *CBQ* 63 (2001): 664-82; and A. Petersen, "Shedding New Light on Paul's Understanding of Baptism: A Ritual-Theoretical Approach to Romans 6," *Studia Theologica* 52 (1998): 3-28.

unable to break out of its domain and influence. However, their baptism into Christ's death meant a "death" to sin and, as a consequence, a breaking out from its power and jurisdiction (6:2). As a result of their being buried with Christ they share in the effects of his death to sin. They are now free to belong to another, to Jesus Christ.

It is interesting to note that for Paul, since the death of Christ on the cross and the subsequent resurrection, death itself receives a new meaning: it is a gateway to life. By being baptized into Christ's death, the believers share in it and also in its liberating effects from the reign of sin and unto life—symbolized by their raising from the water. The resurrection was always a sign of the eschatological age to come. Christ's resurrection thus inaugurated this age to come and so Christ, as the new Adam, has displaced the old Adam. By their dying-and-rising with Christ, the believers have been transferred from the realm of sin ("in Adam") to the realm of the power of the eschatological new age. They are now "in Christ." It is here, in its clearest expression, that Paul explains the fact of being "in Christ" as a transmutation from the dominion of sin to the reign of life under the power and lordship of Christ. To be "in Christ" is to have been transferred into a new mode of existence, from sin to righteousness, from death to life—a life within the sphere of the power and lordship of Christ.[341] Paul describes the event of baptism—with immersion into water and rising from it—as signifying a death "with Christ" and a rising "with Christ." But, as Nygren pointed out, for Paul the significance of baptism cannot be limited to its symbolical representation.[342] It also points to something that really happens: "we have been united" with Christ "in a death like his ... [and] a resurrection like his" (6:5). Being united with Christ, in his body, whatever is true of him is true of those "in Christ."

In 6:1-11 Paul presents both in a negative and positive way, two inherent implications of baptism into Christ's death, of this new reality of being "in Christ." First, because they are united with Christ in a death "like his" and because through his death Jesus has conquered and has broken the power of sin, the believers have been taken out of the power of sin and have entered another dominion, that of Jesus Christ. Second, being buried with Christ in his death, their rising means a radically new way of life, a "walk in newness of life" (6:4 KJV): the mode and nature of life in the new age inaugurated by Jesus' resurrection has been radically changed. Paul showed in the previous chapter that as humanity shared "in Adam," so now it shares or participates "in Christ" in a real sense. And further, as God has made Christ the head of a new, true

---

[341] Commenting on the meaning of the expression "in Christ" in Romans 6 and in Paul in general, John Ziesler equates this expression with "in Spirit" and so "being in the Spirit is in effect being in Christ, and *vice versa.*" John Ziesler, *Paul's Letter to the Romans* (London: SMC Press, 1989), 163.

[342] Anders Nygren, *Commentary on Romans* (Philadelphia: Augsburg Fortress Pub, 1949), 233-34.

humanity, to participate "in Christ" means to share in this new humanity, to live a life appropriate for the new age inaugurated by Christ's death and resurrection. Not being enslaved to sin any longer (6:6) they are free to act in accordance with their new master. Paul is resolute: *houtos kai humeis logiesthe heautous einai nekrous men te hamartia ontas de to theo en Christo Iesou*: "So you also must consider yourselves dead to sin and alive to God in Christ Jesus" (6:11 ESV). It is here that we can see most clearly that by retelling the story of Christ, Paul intends to show that those "in Christ" share in the same story by the virtue of their union with Christ. The story of Christ is their own story in which they participate as *hupekousate de ek kardias*, "obedient from the heart" (6:17) and *edoulothete te dikaiosune*, "slaves of righteousness" (6:18). Christ is not only the basis for their new life but also the model.

The discussion on baptism in chapter 6 seems to play a crucial role in Paul's larger argument of the ethical seriousness of the Christian life under grace. Paul starts from the significance of baptism: it represents the dynamic of incorporation into Christ. For Paul, it is precisely the believer's participation "in Christ" that represents the basis for Christian ethics—as both its possibility and its necessity.[343] And, as Paul showed in Romans 5, this is all based on the continuing power of the grace of God, operating through Christ and the Spirit— grace which acts both to rescue people from their totally alienated situation of sin (5:1, 6-10) and also to guide and empower them to "reign in life" (5:10, 17, 20-21). But it was this very abundance of grace, without the detailed specifications of the law for ethical living, which might have been troublesome to at least some of the members of the Roman Christian community. This we understand from Paul's rhetorical question at the beginning of chapter 6: "What shall we say then? Shall we continue in sin, that grace may abound?" (6:1 KJV). So, Paul's argument in 6–chapters 8 is also responding to this possible "ethical objection"[344] while building his case for the seriousness of ethical life

---

[343] Such a thesis is put forward by Brendan Byrne who shows that there is an intrinsic link between righteousness and obtaining eternal life. Byrne states: "The saving righteousness of God proclaimed in the letter (1:16-17) operates precisely in and through this link: through association with Christ by faith and baptism the Christian is drawn into the sphere of the righteousness of God; it is through living out or, rather, allowing Christ to live out this righteousness within oneself that eternal life is gained." Even though this position is very close to an "ethical" view of righteousness, by pointing clearly to its Christological substance and foundation Byrne is careful to avoid a sense of righteousness as a human accomplishment. But he is right to emphasize the crucial point Paul is making in Romans 6-8 concerning the living out of the righteousness of God, a dynamic participation of the believer in the life of faith "in Christ." (B. Byrne: "Living Out the Righteousness of God: The Contribution of Rom. 6:1–8:13 to an Understanding of Paul's Ethical Presuppositions," *Catholic Biblical Quarterly* 43, no. 4 [1981]: 557-81.)

[344] Byrne, "Living Out": 562. However, I believe Byrne is mistaken to see the entire section (6:1–8:13) as simply a "long excursus" in which Paul addresses this

for the believers and a complete break with a life of sin: "How can we who died to sin still live in it?" (6:2 ESV).

In a very important sense Paul's argument in chapter 6 is crucial not only for this section but also for the entire letter, because it is here that he describes in detail the very dynamic of the believer's incorporation "in Christ"—which is at the heart of Paul's understanding of salvation and the new life. It is here that Paul shows how Christ's story is not his story alone but it is also their story by virtue of their being "in Christ." Their union and participation with Christ is expressed by Paul's characteristic use of *"sun-"* ("with") references in 6:4, 5, 6, 8. It is through baptism "into Christ" that the believers were baptized "into his death," were "buried ... with him" (6:3, 4a), "united with him in a death like his" (6:5 ESV), and the "old self was crucified with him" (6:6 ESV). But also, through their participation in Christ's death, the believers share in the risen life of Christ (though it is not yet a total sharing, since there is still a future aspect to be played out, as verses 5, 7, and 8 show). So now, through their union with Christ, they are able to live out their new existence "in Christ": *en kainoteti zoes peripatesomen* "walk in newness of life" (6:4c ESV), *meketi douleuein hemas te hamartia*, no longer be enslaved to sin" (6:6 ESV), *suzesomen auto*, "live with him" (6:8 ESV). And this living with him is climactically described in vv. 10 and 11: as Christ "lives to God" so the believers, who live "in Christ," are to consider themselves "dead to sin" and "alive to God." It is clear now that those who are "in Christ" are becoming part of Christ's continuing life for God and so they are, in a sense, active participants in the same story of Christ, by their continuation into a similar life for God. It will be now also more clearly understood what this "life for God" means for the believers, since Paul's point about Christ's life to God in chapter 5 is fresh in their minds: it is a life of total submission and obedience to God, a life of self-giving for the other, a life of righteousness and reconciliation. A key feature of the life of Christ that Paul described in chapter 5 is his voluntary self-giving, in love, for others—a life that led to death on the cross, but was followed by resurrection, i.e., a new life given by God, totally transforming the old existence into a new dimension. Through baptism, the believers are incorporated "in Christ" and so in their new

---

question. Byrne is unable to see any other function of this section in the structure of chapters 5–8, because he places everything within his designated theme for these chapters, namely "the hope of salvation (eternal life)." While the theme of hope is indeed vital for Paul's argument, it does not stand apart from other important themes that Paul deals with here, such as "peace," "reconciliation" and "love". A much better view which accommodates all these important topics, is that Paul addresses here the complex dynamic of salvation with its past, present and future dimensions, and the clear implications of the gospel for the new life "in Christ" that the believers are now living. Rather than being an excursus, this is a key passage within the larger argument in which Paul is offering the dynamics of the believers incorporation "in Christ"—without which his whole argument is groundless.

life they are animated by the same life of obedience to God manifested through a renunciation of their own desires and a concern for the needs of others.

And this is exactly what Paul is saying next: *parastesate heautous to theo hosei ek nekron zontas kai to mele humon hopia dikaiosunes to theo*, "present yourselves to God as those who have been brought from death to life, and your members to God as instruments for righteousness" (6:13b ESV); *charis de to theo hoti ete ... hupekousate de ek kardias ... edoulothete te dikaiosune*, "But thanks be to God, that you ...have become obedient from the heart ... and ... slaves of righteousness" (6:17, 18 ESV). So, while the grace of God is the foundation for the new ethical life of the Christian (6:14), this does not mean a life devoid of ethical specifications. On the contrary, it is a life of obedience and righteousness—life that is totally defined and shaped by their union with Christ, in the power of the Spirit. Indeed, Paul concludes his argument, as one might expect, with the strong affirmation of the necessity and possibility of a new life of righteousness: *hamartia gar humon ou kurieusei ou gar este hupo nomon alla hupo charin*, "For sin will have no dominion over you, since you are not under law but under grace" (6:14 ESV).

Another relevant point for our discussion is Paul's reference to the "pattern of teaching" in verse 17: *charis de to theo hoti ete douloi tes hamartias hupekousate de ek kardias eis hon paredothete tupon didaches*, "Once you were slaves of sin, but thank God you have given whole-hearted obedience to the pattern of teaching to which you were introduced" (NJB). We remember that Paul sets the entire discussion of chapter 6, with its solid argument about baptism, in the context of the death and resurrection of Christ (with his consequent enthronement in God's glory, as Lord). So the believer enters the new life in a pattern of dying and rising with Christ. Thus, it is very possible that the *tupon didaches*, "pattern of teaching" here refers to this pattern of dying and rising into which they were introduced and in which they live. Their life is now a life in accordance with this pattern of Christ and under his lordship: a dying to self, to sin, and a rising for life to God as "slaves of righteousness" (6:18).

By thoroughly anchoring his argument in the work of Christ and the initiative of God, Paul is avoiding the danger of a "self-righteous" human "contribution" to the saving act of God. However, arguing from the perspective of the life "in Christ" that the believers share in, Paul is able to show what this new life entails. Their "obedience which leads to righteousness" (6:16) is a voluntary submission to Christ who, recalling 5:19, is defined by his obedience to God. As Christ's obedience made many righteous (5:19), so their obedience leads to righteousness (6:16). Not only are they freed from the necessity of sinning, but also it is the empowering presence of the Spirit who makes this new life possible and actual, as Paul begins and ends the larger section of chapters 5–8 with strong references to the indwelling of the Spirit—especially 8:9-11. Their "walk in the newness of life" is simply a manifestation of their intimate union with Christ and of their participation "in Christ"—a participation in the logical sequence of the same story of Christ, whereby the resurrected and living Christ has "drawn" the believers into his own story which they enact now for God, in the world.

## Conclusion

I have tried to present an argument for a holistic understanding of Christian life and mission which will lead to an appropriate involvement of the Church in the world. I believe that building on Paul's teaching on the integration of theology and ethics, of faith and life, churches can become agents of change and social transformation. We have seen that in Romans 5–6 Paul shows that the inner logic of the gospel contains both the decisive intervention of God to redeem the world, through the death and resurrection of Christ, and a distinctive way of life, a "walk in the newness of life" for those who profess to be "in Christ."

Paul's concern was also with the implications of the lordship of Christ for the life of each individual believer and of the Christian community in the world: he wanted the believers to understand that it was only by their faithful and obedient life in total allegiance to the true Lord of the world, Jesus Christ, that the lordship of Christ would be extended. We have seen that Paul's discussion of the complex dynamic of the incorporation of the believer "in Christ," through baptism, signifies a real sharing and participation of the believers in the same story, as active participants. From this perspective, we concluded that Paul does not simply write about how God's reconciliation is achieved in Christ, as something done from afar, to which the believers are passive recipients. Rather, Paul includes the readers, their story, into the larger story of God's decisive reconciliation in Christ; they are themselves integral part of this ongoing story of reconciliation.

The examination of the interchange of metaphors and personal pronouns beginning with Romans 5 has led to the conclusion that by these intentional moves Paul shows two things: first, that reconciliation is an essential aspect of salvation, and that it contains an intrinsic social, horizontal dimension; and second, the vertical reconciliation with God is inseparable from the horizontal aspect, as two dimensions of the same reality. Paul's intention was to show that the gospel they have received has clear and concrete implications for the believer's everyday life. To be justified and reconciled with God is to be reconciled and at peace with one's sister and brother, to be at peace with "the other." We have shown that Paul's shift in the personal pronouns supported that conclusion. By using the "we" and "us" pronouns in a context in which he is retelling the story of Jesus, Paul included himself and the believers in Rome in the same story of Christ, and prompted them to live out the "story of Christ" as active actors in an ongoing story of God's reconciliation of the world in Christ.

The mechanism of this incorporation "in Christ" with all its implications was explicitly described by Paul in chapter 6 under the rubric of baptism. By their dying-and-rising with Christ, believers have been transferred into a new eschatological reality "in Christ" which is a real transfer into a new mode of existence, from sin to righteousness, from death to life—a life within the sphere of the power and lordship of Christ. Being buried with Christ into his death, their rising means that the mode and nature of their present life in the new age inaugurated by Jesus' resurrection has been radically changed. To participate "in Christ" means to share in his new and true humanity, to live a life appropriate for the new age inaugurated by the resurrection of Christ. We concluded that Paul retold the story of Christ with the purpose of showing that those "in Christ" share in his story, their new life being a manifestation of their intimate union with Christ. In the light of Paul's argument for the complex dynamic of the incorporation of the believers "in Christ," we have seen that Paul included his readers in the larger story of God's decisive reconciliation in Christ whereby they become themselves an integral part of the ongoing story of God's reconciliation of the world. The reality of believers' reconciliation with God, and their new identity and status "in Christ," carry with them the responsibility of engaging in reconciling practices grounded in, and modeled by, Christ's work of reconciliation. Finally, it highlights how Paul's ultimate vision of the reconciliation of all things in Christ gives assurance and hope, and an irresistible impetus to the believer's ministry of reconciliation in all its forms and manifestations.

If there is any truth in the affirmation that our conduct is shaped by the condition of our vision, it follows that to transform this world we need a particular vision of life. Not just any vision but a vision similar to that presented by the apostle Paul: a vision of righteousness, reconciliation, and hope for this world; a vision for a culture of love and acceptance, of forgiveness and grace, of justice and mercy, a vision of the Kingdom of God; a vision of the lordship of Christ over every aspect of reality. While we are always painfully aware that we ourselves will never bring the Kingdom of God on earth, and so we will always bear with us, on this earth, at each little progress toward the final Kingdom of God, the condition of provisionality, this will not hinder us from struggling and pouring our lives to spread the Kingdom of God until God finally brings everything to a perfect completion.

It is out of our passion for God, for his people, and his world, and out of this vision for the transformation of the world and the anticipation of the Kingdom of God, that we continue to devote our life to theological training. And it is this vision that we hope to inspire in the younger generation of leaders. What greater dream can there be than to help our students to find themselves caught up in this vision! It is to that end that, together, guided by this powerful vision and full of hope in the final triumph of God in history, we earnestly pray, study, live, work, and rejoice.

# Bibliography

Allen, Gregory. *Reconciliation in the Pauline Tradition: Its Occasions, Meanings, and Functions*. Boston: Boston University, 1995.

Barrett, Charles Kingsley. *The Epistle to the Romans: Black's New Testament Commentaries Series*. London: A & C Black, 1962.

Blumenfeld, Bruno. *The Political Paul: Justice, Democracy, and Kingship in a Hellenistic Framework*. London: Sheffield Academic, 2001.

Boers, Hendrikus. "The Structure and Meaning of Romans 6:1-14." *CBQ* 63 (2001): 664-82.

Constantineanu, Corneliu. *The Social Significance of Reconciliation in Paul's Theology. Narrative Readings in Romans*. London: T&T Clark, 2010.

Cranfield, C.E.B. *The Epistle to the Romans*. New York: T&T Clark, 2004.

Elliott, Neil. *Liberating Paul: The Justice of God and the Politics of the Apostle*. Sheffield: Sheffield Academic, 1995.

Furnish, Victor P. *Theology and Ethics in Paul*. Nashville: Abingdon Press, 1968.

Grant, Robert. *Paul in the Roman World: The Conflict at Corinth*. Louisville: Westminster John Knox, 2001.

Haacker, Klaus. *The Theology of Paul's Letter to the Romans*. New York: Cambridge University Press, 2003.

Hauerwas. *A Community of Character: Toward a Constructive Christian Social Ethic*. Notre Dame: University of Notre Dame Press, 1981.

Horrell, David. "Paul's Narrative or Narrative Substructure? The Significance of 'Paul's Story'." Louisville: Westminster John Knox, 2002.

_____. *Solidarity and Difference: A Contemporary Reading of Paul's Ethics*. London: T&T Clark, 2005.

Horsley, Richard. *Paul and Empire: Religion and Power in Roman Imperial Society*. Harrisburg, PA: Trinity Press International, 1997.

_____. *Paul and Politics: Ekklesia, Israel, Imperium, Interpretation*. Harrisburg, PA: Trinity Press International, 2000.

Horsley, R. A. and M.A. Silberman. *The Message and the Kingdom: How Jesus and Paul Ignited a Revolution and Transformed the Ancient World*. Minneapolis: Fortress, 1997.

Kuper, Abraham. *A Centennial Reader.* Grand Rapids: Eerdmans, 1998.

McDonald, Patricia. "Romans 5:1-11 as a Rhetorical Bridge." *JSNT* 40 (1990): 81-96.

Miller, James C. *The Obedience of Faith, the Eschatological People of God, and the Purpose of Romans.* Atlanta: SBL, 2000.

Moo, Douglas J. *The Epistle to the Romans.* Grand Rapids: Eerdmans, 1996.

Nygren, Anders. *Commentary on Romans.* Philadelphia: Augsburg Fortress, 1949.

Peterson, A. Petersen. "Shedding New Light on Paul's Understanding of Baptism: A Ritual-Theoretical Approach to Romans 6." *Studia Theologica* 52 (1998): 3-28.

Porter, Stanley E. "*Katallasso* in Ancient Greek Literature, with Reference to the Pauline Writings." In *Estudios de Filologia Neo Testamentaria*, edited by Juan Mateos, vol. 5. Cordoba, Spain: Ediciones el Almendro, 1994.

———. "The Argument of Romans 5." *Journal of Biblical Literature* 110, no. 4 (1991): 655-77.

Schreiner, Thomas R. *Romans.* Grand Rapids: Baker Academic, 1998.

Smith, Martin L. *Reconciliation: Preparing for Confession in the Episcopal Church.* Cambridge, MA: Cowley Publications, 1985.

Strom, Mark. *Reframing Paul: Conversation in Grace and Community.* Downers Grove: InterVarsity, 2000.

Tamez, Elsa. *The Amnesty of Grace: Justification by Faith from a Latin American Perspective.* Nashville: Abingdon Press, 1993.

Tobin, Thomas H. *Paul's Rhetoric in Its Contexts: The Argument of Romans.* Peabody: Hendrickson, 2004.

Wedderburn, A. J. M. *The Reasons for Romans.* Edinburgh: T&T Clark, 1988.

Wright, N. T. "Romans." In *The New Interpreter's Bible Acts – First Corinthians (Volume 10): A Commentary*, edited by Robert W. Wall, J. Paul Sampley, and N. T. Wright, 514. Nashville: Abingdon Press, 2002.

Ziesler, John. *Paul's Letter to the Romans.* London: SMC Press, 1989.

# Pentecostalism and the Collegiate Institution: A History and Analysis of This Strained Alliance[345]

Barry H. Corey

Place this society in the world, demanding that it be not of the world, and strenuous as may be its efforts to transcend or to sublimate the mundane life, it will yet be unable to escape all taint of conspiracy and connivance with the worldly interests it despises. (H. Richard Niebuhr) [346]

## Introduction

In 1955, a liberal arts college was created from within the relatively young Pentecostal religious movement. Such a decision is not uncommon among organizations, both sectarian and nonsectarian, which graft collegiate institutions into their organizational structures. The decisions' processes, however, may vary greatly. To understand why a particular course of decisions was made necessitates an inquiry into a complex web of variables.

The characteristics of the decision process become more understandable when placed in the context of the social movement occurring within the church between 1914 and 1955. Specifically, the church's early charisma evolved into a need for routinization. The routinization process resulted in a type of ecclesiastical structure which began to encase the church. The ambiguity that accompanied institutionalization led certain actors to survey and imitate what they perceived to be successful forms of organizational structure in the external environment. Out of this ambiguity, a collegiate institution was formed.

Though the precise pattern of decisions is complex rather than discrete, what surfaces through the story's events and actors makes it apparent that the decision to establish Evangel College was rooted in the belief that a rationalized form of education is a socially legitimate means of survivability.

---

[345] Editors' Note: *This chapter is an edited excerpt from the author's dissertation, included here both to demonstrate the wide interests of Peter Kuzmič, for whom this volume was originally compiled, and to illustrate the wideness of God's rule and reign—extending to the realm of higher education and a denominational administration's efforts to hear the voice of God.*

[346] H. Richard Niebuhr, *The Social Sources of Denominationalism* (Cleveland: World Publishing, 1967), 4-5.

## The History

The announcement went out a few days before Christmas in 1913. A group of Pentecostals sensed that the time had come to organize their grass-roots movement into a loosely structured cooperative. This cooperative would become the General Council of the Assemblies of God. The group circulated news of the forthcoming April 1914 meeting via word of mouth and through the tabloids of various Pentecostal publications. The printed notice listed five reasons for the "united meeting of Pentecostals." The fifth reason concerned education. It stated that one of the purposes for the assembly of Pentecostal believers would be to act on a proposition "for a general Bible Training School with a literary department for our young people."[347] E. N. Bell and the other founding fathers of the Assemblies of God made it clear that at least Bible training and possibly a college of general education would be intrinsic to the educational structure of the new denomination.[348] Precisely what was meant by "literary department," however, would remain a source of debate.

The debut General Council of the Assemblies of God held that April in Hot Springs, Arkansas, came and went with scarcely anything mentioned about establishing a Bible training school with or without a literary department. Founding participants in Hot Springs, nonetheless, were encouraged "to attend faithfully to a diligent search of the Scriptures, and if possible to attend some properly and scripturally accredited Bible Training School."[349]

With the Pentecostal movement growing as it was, T. K. Leonard's Pentecostal school in Ohio and a few others scattered across the country were not enough to train pastors, missionaries and evangelists. Leaders of the new church understood that this deficiency demanded prompt attention if the church was going to indoctrinate believers in the ways of the faith. To solve this problem, they encouraged the creation of "Ten Day Bible Conferences" or "Itinerary Bible Schools" to be held in different sections of the country. The content of these courses would be to give "due attention to evangelistic work for the unsaved, and solid scriptural teaching for the saints."[350]

Clearly a concern existed to indoctrinate believers in sound Pentecostal teaching, but organizing this effort was not an initial priority. During the denomination's first five years, 1914–1919, no formal efforts were made to address educational needs. Instead, church leaders were engaged in defining doctrine, building an organizational base, and creating a publishing center, Gospel Publishing House.

The earliest years of the Assemblies of God denomination were known more for their evangelistic initiatives than their educational initiatives. Yet, as

---

[347] *Word and Witness*, December 20, 1913, 1.

[348] Betty Chase, "Evangel College Buildings and the Pioneers for Whom They Were Named," *Evangel College Archives* (1990): 8-9.

[349] General Council of the Assemblies of God Minutes, 1914–1917, 23-24.

[350] General Council of the Assemblies of God Minutes, 1914–1917, 23-24.

evident in some of the church's proceedings, there were those who envisioned a college with a general education program in the Assemblies of God's future. Denomination-wide appeals for such an institution in 1914 in Hot Springs, in 1929 in Wichita, and in 1935 in Dallas remained without a clear definition or strategy. As a result, the church passed through its first three decades without any substantive progress toward a liberal arts college. During these formative years it was not so much hostility as priority that kept the church from adopting a more aggressive platform for such a college. More important was the creation of Bible schools such as Central Bible Institute (CBI) and others across the country. Also of importance, in word if not in deed, was the standardization and centralization of the church's educational programs. In 1925, 1937, and 1939 the General Council passed motions that rooted the Springfield, Missouri, headquarters as the consummate authority of all educational institutions affiliated with the Assemblies of God.

The years 1943 to 1948 marked the emergence of Assistant General Superintendent Ralph Riggs as the principal educational advocate in the Assemblies of God. His self-sanctioned crusade was concerned primarily with reforming Bible schools, standardizing and centralizing church educational programs, and, of most importance, establishing a denominational liberal arts college. Diplomatically, he presented his agenda before self-appointed educational committees as well as the Executive and General Presbyteries. Each forum sanctioned his work. The one legislative obstacle he could not clear was approval from the General Council, the church's largest policy-making body. In 1945, the delegates of the General Council in Springfield forbade Riggs from taking further steps toward the establishment of a liberal arts college without their approval. When at the 1947 Grand Rapids General Council the college issue first came to a vote, the delegates—stirred by a message in tongues and a word of prophecy— overwhelmingly defeated the motion.

After the jolting rebuff by the delegates of the 1947 General Council in Grand Rapids, Riggs had to retreat from his ardent campaign for a denominational liberal arts college. During the few years that the liberal arts college issue was dormant, Riggs worked toward revising and enforcing the church's educational criteria for its Bible schools. It was also during this time that Riggs and several other Assemblies of God educators participated in the founding of the American Association of Bible Institutes and Bible Colleges (AABIBC) as an interdenominational accreditation body. When presenting the 1949 General Council in Seattle with a motion to approve accreditation steps for CBI, the latent ardor of many in the constituency was unleashed. It has since been remembered as the Great Educational Debate, when pastors and evangelists retaliated against the reform measures of the church. The emotional harangues, however, failed to convince the majority of the delegates that secular accreditation was ungodly. The sentiment of the church was clearly shifting from its anti-education stance of only two years earlier. By the early

1950s, petitions for an Assemblies of God liberal arts college began to come from across the country, reflecting a broad-based support of the idea. At the Milwaukee General Council in 1953, delegates overwhelmingly approved the establishment of a liberal arts college. Riggs' forbearance and determination had finally been rewarded.

In the wake of the 1953 victory in Milwaukee came a new cast of players to assist Riggs in preparations for the liberal arts college. J. Robert Ashcroft was selected as the church's Education Secretary and Thomas Zimmerman elected to the post of Assistant General Superintendent. By December of that year, the first planning committee had been assembled to flesh out the strategy for creating the college. What church officials expected to be a congenial meeting instead turned into a fiasco. The Bible school representatives, many of whom where hostile to the idea of a church-supported liberal arts college, throttled the agenda by insisting that the new college not contain any academic programs which would compete with theirs. Unable to convince this contingent otherwise, Riggs and his associates concluded that a different planning body would serve the church better. Within four months a Board of Directors was created. Though all the components seemed to miraculously fall into place, the college was still plagued by a dearth of financial resources. This plague would continue through the early years of the college.

During these early years of Evangel College, those commissioned with fiduciary responsibilities began groping for ways to salvage the college from its financial straits. Though enrollment continued to increase and strides to secure proper accreditation gained momentum, church leaders could not maintain control of the runaway fiscal crises. These monetary needs were so stark that they eclipsed the encouraging indicators of progress in other areas of the college. Aimlessly, the church and college leaders implemented a litany of programs to regain control of Evangel College's finances. None of these methods, however, proved to be successful. By 1958 Ralph Riggs was forced to retract his promise that no General Council funding would be used to support the new liberal arts college. A continued looming financial forecast forced the General Presbytery to be assembled for an unprecedented special meeting in 1959, and later that year the administrations of Evangel College and CBI were merged to cut down on duplicity and inefficient spending. That same year Riggs, bearing the weight of the financial burden, was voted out of office as the church's general superintendent, and Thomas F. Zimmerman was elected as his successor.

## The Analysis

The story of the founding of Evangel College is about the process of change in a religious or social movement. It is about the passage traveled by the infant Assemblies of God church from its charismatic origins to its emergence as an organized ecclesiastical structure, a structure that accommodated a collegiate institutional form.[351] An understanding of this process of change helps explain the reason why the church made certain decisions, specifically the choice to graft into its structure Evangel College.

A single collegiate liberal arts model was certainly not the only viable option in which these leaders could invest years of the church's time and resources. Various alternatives were argued by the gainsayers, but the church leaders leveraged their authority in favor of the creation of a liberal arts college. One might wonder why the decision to adopt this model prevailed. The answer is by every means complex and lies in an indiscrete sociological web of external influences and internal choices, both inextricable from the process of institutionalization.

Given the historical data in the decision to found Evangel College, it is argued that the formation of the college was a result of an institutionalization process at work within the church. In making sense of the decision, it is necessary to begin with the charismatic origins of the church and the sense of crisis and isolation out of which the church was born. As the church matured, it began to routinize its functions into bureaucratic forms, and this led to an ambiguity among leaders of the fledgling church. At the core of this ambiguity was the question as to what form of organized, ecclesiastical structure would be necessary for the church's survival. This gave rise to certain actors, specifically Ralph Riggs, who were profoundly affected by the notion of routinization and the need for the containment of charisma. These actors, who surveyed and copied what they understood to be successful means of containment in other religious movements, convinced the church that a collegiate structure was a legitimate means of survivability. Convincing the church's constituencies necessitated a calculated use of symbols and norms in the distribution of information.

During the early years of the church, when the formation of charisma was the principal concern of Assemblies of God decision makers, choices were made without regard to outside social elements. As the church evolved into a stage characterized by a form of routinization, its decisions had more complex ramifications than the decisions of its first generation. Permanent regional Bible schools were established, affiliations were made with interdenominational organizations such as the National Association of Evangelicals (NAE) and AABIBC, and the church created a separate department to centralize and control its growing educational initiatives. With routinization came increased ambiguity and the tendency to survey and copy the structures of other churches.

---

[351] Among Pentecostal circles, the term "charismatic" is popularly associated with the charismatic renewal movement of the mid-1960s, when liturgical churches such as the Catholics and Episcopalians infused the personal activity of the Holy Spirit into their ecumenistic traditions. Though this renewal movement encompassed many characteristics of charisma, or the charismatic, what is sociologically meant by the term is significantly broader and will be defined further in this chapter.

Decisions were made during this period to move toward adopting educational functions popular among other denominations, e.g., regional accreditation, a theological seminary, baccalaureate degrees, and a four-year liberal arts college. As routinization continued, an increasingly complex organizational structure emerged in the church. A liberal arts college was founded, a full-time Secretary of Education position created, lay boards formulated, and formal fund-raising mechanisms installed.

It follows that the decision to establish Evangel College corresponded to the church's institutionalization process and was rooted in the belief that a rationalized form of education was a socially legitimate means of survivability. The following sections extract from the historical narrative and from a broader field of scholarship the nuances of decision making that led the Assemblies of God church to create Evangel College.

### *The Institutionalization of Religious Movements*

The origins of the Assemblies of God were rooted in what some sociologists call "the charismatic," and the church's history followed a discrete pattern known among scholars in the same field as "the routinization of charisma."[352] A basic understanding of the phenomena of the charismatic as the entry point in the process toward the church's institutionalization is fundamental to discussions of decision-making theory as it relates to the establishment of Evangel College.

As a rule, religious movements begin as charismatic experiences. Shils describes charisma as a quality imputed to a person movement because of its connection with ultimate powers, i.e., transcendent powers.[353] The charismatic has something to do with what Emile Durkheim, who espoused purely social origins of religion, calls the sacred, something other than this "utilitarian sphere."[354] Rudolf Otto identifies these universal elements of the religious experience as the "the holy" or "the numinous," which he implies is a guiding force or spirit beyond rational and ethical conceptions.[355] Max Weber, a pioneer in the sociology of religion, treats charisma as the breaking point in the world of everydayness. In other words, it is extraordinary as opposed to mundane. Weber's definition applies the qualities of charisma to individuals, but he also acknowledges the existence of these same charismatic qualities in organizations or movements.

---

[352] Parts of this discussion of the institutionalization of religion have been supplemented by the text of Thomas F. O'Dea and Janet O'Dea Aviad, *The Sociology of Religion*, 2nd ed (Englewood Cliffs, NJ: Prentice-Hall, 1983), 38-64.

[353] Edward Shils, "Charisma," *International Encyclopedia of the Social Sciences* (New York: Free Press), 117

[354] Emile Durkheim, *The Elementary Forms of Religious Life*, trans. Joseph Ward (Swain Glencoe, IL: Free Press, 1954), 72ff.

[355] Rudolf Otto, *The Idea of the Holy*, 2nd ed, trans. J. W. Harvey (London: Oxford University Press, 1950).

From its inception a charismatic movement, by virtue of its rituals, beliefs, and type of organization, is fundamentally at odds with the established society and with other religious groups. It could be said that charisma is born out of a crisis. Within ecclesiastical systems religious controversies or ideological fissions over such matters as doctrine or governance are prone to occur. If unreconciled, the result is a schism. The new religious movement displays a break with the past and reflects a new spirit of coherence and unity.[356] How the new group grapples with its relationship to the established social order is often its foremost dilemma. The movement's leaders might ask themselves, "What is our relationship to the established society? Interaction or isolation?"

The answer usually unfolds through a gradual evolution of choices, in which leaders move toward a more rationalized form of organizational structure. Sociologically, charismatic movements tend to gravitate toward the functional and, consequently, the routinized. This is defined by Weber as the "routinization of charisma." By this he means that charismatic movements evolve or are transformed from their grass-roots beginnings into more stable forms of thought and practice legitimized by society. He argues that the motivation for such changes lies in the leaders' desire to contain the community created by its founders. Naturally, new offices develop as new functions arise, and precedents established in action lead to a transformation of existing offices.[357]

The institutionalization of religion grows out of the need for stability and continuity, out of the need to preserve the content of religious beliefs, and out of the concern for safeguarding doctrines and teachings from distortion. When routinization of charisma has begun to take hold within a religious movement, the ecclesiastical organization emerges. Sociologically, the institutionalization of religious movements happens. It is necessary in transmitting the church's beliefs to others and, ultimately, necessary in the church's very survivability. It provides continuity and identity, stability and social legitimacy.[358] Few dispute the reality of the institutionalization phenomena evolving from within a charismatic movement. It is inherent to virtually all religious movements. In varying degrees, it has occurred in Catholicism, Methodism, and Pentecostalism.

The routinization of charisma is therefore a process which also involves the containment of charisma, e.g., doctrine defined in terms, authorization of a cooperating fellowship, a constitution and bylaws, required ordination for ministers, and religious catechism programs. In the story of the Assemblies of

---

[356] Joachim Wach, *The Sociology of Religion* (Chicago: University of Chicago Press, 1944), 110.

[357] Max Weber, *The Theory of Social and Economic Organizations*, ed. Talcott Parsons; trans. A. M. Henderson and Talcott Parsons (New York: Oxford University Press, 1947), 363-92.

[358] O'Dea and Aviad, *The Sociology of Religion*, 49-53.

God, this process resulted in, among other formal establishments, a church hierarchy of governing bodies, a denominational headquarters office, accredited Bible schools, a publishing house, and a liberal arts collegiate institution.

## The Church, Crisis, and Charisma

Charisma has its roots in crisis. A charismatic movement, because it begins as a counter-movement to the establishment, is fundamentally at odds with society. This certainly characterized the young Assemblies of God church in the 1920s and 1930s. Routinization was stalled in the church's early years because there existed no need to interact with its larger religious and social environments. The church was content to be self-contained. As the church matured in years and created more and more bureaucracies to support its actions, interaction with the environment resulted and routinization ensued.

The Assemblies of God church emerged out of a crisis of religious order. During the last quarter of the nineteenth century there was a growing dissatisfaction with the traditional church among holiness believers. They saw the church increase its affinity with an industrial society they believed to be corrupt and uninterested in spiritual matters. Theologically, the 19th-century church experimented with liberal ideologies which made room for a relativistic framework, allowing doctrines of Social Darwinism and individualism to undermine the literal-minded biblicism of holiness followers. This evolutionary theory, claimed holiness believers, detracted from the supernatural and personal attributes of the Deity.[359]

With the increasingly complex nature of the 19th-century Protestant church came the need to institutionalize. Here again those of the devout holiness persuasion accused the church of allowing bureaucracy, education, wealth, and a growing power and prestige to displace personal piety and social service. For them, the assumed role of the church was "friendship with the world" and thus "enmity with God." At the same time leaders of the established Protestant churches were leveling criticisms at the holiness movement for its disregard for authority, organization, and "established usages" within the church.[360]

Early Pentecostalism harbored an enmity toward ecclesiasticism, and as a result it considered religious organizations dubious. Mainline denominations had failed because they had allowed structure and a neo-orthodoxy to obscure the zeal and passion for Christ evident in these churches' founders. Pentecostals were convinced these denominations' proclivity toward secularism had detracted such faiths as the Methodists and Presbyterians from an absolute trust in God for all things. The 19th-century secular drift of the mainline churches instilled a distrust of organized religion among Pentecostals.

---

[359] Robert M. Anderson, *Vision of the Disinherited: The Making of American Pentecostalism* (New York: Oxford University Press, 1979), 31-32, 84, 214-15, 236.
[360] Anderson, *Vision of the Disinherited*, 31.

From its earliest days, the Assemblies of God adherents believed that the world was a dangerous environment for the believer, that it was under Satan's domain, and therefore Christians, while in the world, were to be withdrawn and aloof from it. Further, the church's four dominant ideological norms alienated it from pursuing interactions with external environments. Specifically, an enmity toward ecclesiasticism, belief in the imminent rapture of the church, personal asceticism, and an emphasis on the supernatural as an everyday phenomenon placed the church at odds with the American religious mainstream as well as the larger society.

The decision makers within the church during the period beginning in 1914 were engrossed in last-days evangelism to the extent that adopting permanent auxiliary institutions seemed superfluous. Because the coming of the Lord was at hand, the urgency to spread the gospel as quickly as possible demanded the attention of these actors. To accomplish this mission, the church's leaders devoted their attention to establishing Bible training schools, formalizing doctrinal positions, commissioning missionaries to evangelize overseas, planting new churches, and building a publishing house. The church was not ready at this time to establish a liberal arts collegiate structure. In his discussion of why timing plays a dominant role in organizational decision making, James G. March explains that it is because individuals who are attending to some things are not attending to others.[361] Although at its General Council sessions in 1914, 1929, and 1935 the church had expressed itself favorably on the idea of creating a liberal arts college, those actors who were in the position to initiate the process did not do so because of the more immediate claims on their attention. The erratic character of decision making during the 1910s, 1920s, and 1930s is more explicable by placing it in the context of the church's multiple and changing claims of attention.

"Problems, solutions, and decision makers come together," March explains, "because they are available at the same time and the same place."[362] As the decades passed and the Lord did not return, those in leadership positions began to sense the need to construct support systems within the structure of the church. Clearly articulated by the top levels of the church's leadership, these support systems were constructed to strengthen the denomination for the upcoming generations. With this came some of the earliest tangible signs that the church was undergoing a process of institutionalization. A new cast of leaders emerged beginning in the 1940s and, led by Ralph Riggs, became the progenitors of the idea to create a liberal arts college. Their ardent campaigning for the college was rooted in their profound sense of the need for the church's routinization and survival.

---

[361] James G. March, "Emerging Developments in the Study of Organizations," in *ASHE Reader on Organization and Governance in Higher Education*, ed. Marvin W. Peterson (Needham Heights, MA: Ginn Press, 1989), 141-42.

[362] March, "Emerging Developments," 142.

### Routinization and Increased Ambiguity

As time passed, the supernatural characteristics of the church needed to be grounded in the very natural framework of organizational structure. If the first phase of the church's development can be characterized in terms of the charismatic, the second can be characterized in terms of routinization. During this period, which is difficult to isolate in specific chronological dimensions, the church leaders began to explore and implement new formal functions. As they did, the church became increasingly institutionalized. The essence of Pentecostalism, they argued in justifying their decisions, had to be contained and preserved for upcoming generations. The way in which the charisma happened to be contained was manifested in rational forms of institutionalization. As the church matured and began to routinize its functions into bureaucracies, uncertainties among the leadership resulted. Ambiguity centered on the issue of what form of organized, ecclesiastical structure would be necessary to ensure the church's survival.

In its earliest stages of growth, the church was bound by a doctrinaire position that kept it secluded from other denominations or elements of society. The first generation of leadership emphasized the imminent return of Christ and the urgent need for evangelism. Consequently, itinerant ministerial training schools and regional Bible institutes were the first practical means of containing charisma. These educational institutions boasted a succinct mission and curriculum designed to prepare church members in an expedient manner to evangelize the lost. Additionally, Assemblies of God leaders began a publishing house to print gospel tracts and training literature to supplement the church's mission of spreading the "good news" as quickly and as widely as possible. The principal emphasis of the church during these initial years was to save the lost, not to educate the saved. Because of this system of prioritizing, the occasional mention of creating a liberal arts college for the church's young people was disregarded.

Institutionalization of the Assemblies of God included changes in response to conditions internal to the religious movement, while at the same time it included adjustments precipitated by external environments. Aldrich and Pfeffer, who have undertaken studies on the relationship between organizations and their environments, argue that organizations aggressively seek to manage or strategically adapt to their environment.[363] Whereas this was not true early in the life of the Assemblies of God church, by examining the movement longitudinally it becomes clearer that adaptation did occur. Because the early Assemblies of God church did not sense a need for acceptance by its environment or environments and because it did not respond to environmental demands, it bore no substantive adaptations in its formal structure. When in later years it began to prospect its environment for acceptance, environmental

---

[363] H. E. Aldrich and Jeffrey Pfeffer, "Environments of Organizations," *Annual Review of Sociology* (1976): 79.

demands were inevitably heeded. Also, the specific characteristics of form to which the church adapted depended on the demands of the environment in relation to the proximity of the organization to its environment.

The environments of the Assemblies of God church became increasingly important over time, and they began assuming a dominant role in its organizational structures and decisions. This was due in part to the conscious decisions of the church leadership to extend the denomination beyond its early ideologically imposed boundaries. Nearly one generation old in 1942, the Assemblies of God church ventured outside its denominational security and became a founding member of the National Association of Evangelicals. In order to broaden the affiliations of the church's higher educational institutions, five years later administrators of Assemblies of God Bible schools allied their institutions with the new American Association of Bible Institutes and Bible Colleges. Because the progressive decisions of the church leadership outpaced the orthodox position of most local churches, the result was a string of mild insurrections from the rank and file pastors. Zald explains that this conflict might occur when a denomination's leadership, due to interests or value preferences, justifies involvement in an environment as part of its moral or ideological beliefs.[364] Riggs and his associates in Springfield, as a result, went to extremes to make it clear that the primary reason they were leading the church in a direction that seemed to many to mirror the institutionalization process of other denominations was to guarantee the survivability of the Assemblies of God.

At the same time the church leaders were aggressively affiliating with associations such as the NAE and the AABIBC, the church was also being affected by trends of societal change. After World War II, more and more ministers wanted to serve as chaplains in the armed forces, and the church responded by abridging its Bible school standards and beginning programs to accommodate government requirements. Additionally, negotiations for O'Reilly General Hospital and the decision to create Evangel College forced the church's leadership into daily interactions with federal bureaucracies, state agencies, and municipal boards. The result was a more cosmopolitan breed of leadership.

The advent of Evangel College compounded the demands on the Assemblies of God church. With its first Bible colleges and earliest educational programs, the church was not obligated to abide by formal criteria in order to maintain operation. As demographic changes took place in the larger societal environment, e.g., the GI Bill's educational assistance, military chaplaincy requirements, and a growing need nationwide for higher education, the church answered with motions for accreditation of Bible schools, for a theological seminary, and for the establishment of a liberal arts college. Suddenly, the

---

[364] Mayer N. Zald, "Theological Crucibles: Social Movements In and Of Religion," *Review of Religious Research* 32 no. 4 (June 1982): 328.

church had to rely on academic credentials for faculty and administrators, strict adherence to accreditation standards, and accountability to state and federal educational bureaus. As the church relied on these secondary controlling agencies in the creation and early years of Evangel College, the college began to adopt a form similar to other organizations in its field.

When planning the college, the church leaders were incapable of generating all the internal resources or functions necessary to maintain themselves. In this new venture, which demanded support from outside agencies, the church could not continue to be entirely self-sustaining. Consequently, it engaged in relations and transactions with elements in its environment in order to acquire the needed resources and services. The result was a stabilization of relationships within the environment and a mechanism to aid in the survival of the organization itself.[365]

Not only did the college adapt to external forces, its planners adapted to external standards of organizational structure modeled by other denominations. The inexperience of the men who accepted the responsibility of designing the college resulted in their imitating similar organizations outside of the Assemblies of God denomination. In the stages of planning during the 1940s, none of the college planning committee members had the advantage of prior experience in higher education administration in the secular sphere. None had ever before been involved in discussions concerning the creation of a liberal arts college. Most, in fact, had never attended a college other than one of the many Pentecostal Bible institutes. There were some like J. Roswell Flower, Irving J. Harrison, Klaude Kendrick, and J. Robert Ashcroft, who had completed or nearly completed their graduate studies, but the large majority had attained an education of only a high school diploma and three years of Bible school. Consequently, most of these men approached the planning table with few skills and no background in designing a liberal arts collegiate institution. The greater their uncertainty between the means of designing a college and the end product of the college itself, the greater the inclination to model the proposed college after other organizations they perceived to be successful.[366]

### *The Rise of New Actors*

Given the natural ambiguity among leaders of the young church and the precipitous growth of the Assemblies of God during the 1940s and 1950s, certain actors emerged who were profoundly affected by the notion of routinization. Most prominent among these actors were Ralph Riggs, J. Robert Ashcroft, Thomas Zimmerman, and Klaude Kendrick. The patterns of behavior evident among Riggs and his colleagues in their quest for ways to contain charisma make it apparent that collective rationality was preferred over ingenuity. Collective rationality is the notion that uncertain organizations

---

[365] Aldrich and Pfeffer, "Environments of Organizations," 84.
[366] Aldrich and Pfeffer, "Environments of Organizations," 154.

imitate stable organizations. These actors, who surveyed and copied what they perceived to be successful means of containment in other religious movements, argued that a collegiate structure would be a legitimate mechanism for the church's survivability.

After the charismatic movement passed through its early stages of formation and identity, there was a process of differentiation that occurred. This was caused by those who realized first that charismatic authority was inherently unstable and that its transformation into institutionalized leadership was necessary for the survival of the group. As the first few decades passed, a new cadre of church leadership emerged which was more concerned with preserving the Pentecostal faith for future generations than its predecessors had been. The 1930s and 1940s had come, but Christ had not. If Christ did not return and the church was to survive beyond its first generation of believers, it would have to implement a strategy of reproduction. About this time, Ralph Riggs emerged as an Assemblies of God leader who was deeply concerned about the survivability of the church. Not long after, others who shared with Riggs the vision for perpetuating the Pentecostal tradition were positioned in similar leadership roles. Through discussions as to various strategies for routinizing charisma within the church, these leaders concentrated their efforts on one option: the creation of a liberal arts college. The end result was Evangel College.

Stated by Riggs and his colleagues in a variety of ways and through a score of mediums, this contingent college would be the bastion of orthodoxy for the church's children bound for non-ministerial careers. The retention and transmission of knowledge from one generation to the next became the goal of this second wave of leadership. To the church leadership, successful retention mechanisms—which are instinctive to organizations—transmit knowledge from one generation to the next. As the denomination matured, it followed a trend toward rationalization, that is, more widely accepted means of transmitting information or doctrine. This rationalized process of retention manifested itself in the Assemblies of God church in terms of fraternal affiliations with other evangelical denominations, a stepped-up involvement in the local community, and the pursuit of financial and accreditation backing for Evangel College.

If at that time a different cast of actors had been placed in leadership roles, the decision might have been made to maintain the insular nature of the church. Its leadership might have shunned overtures to affiliate with interdenominational bodies and might have not proposed legislation to seek accreditation for Bible schools. This was not the case. In the 1940s and 1950s, the church's leaders, bound by incentives and commitments, expressed openness to pressures from the environment which forever altered the direction of the church. Once it had committed itself to these relationships, for whatever reason, the church had no choice but to adapt.

During these two decades, the Assemblies of God church was in the throes of an educational debate. At the stem of this debate was neither the issue of the liberal arts college nor the issue of formal accreditation. Rather, the educational debate became for the church the ideological forum in which it struggled for its own direction. On the one hand were men like Ralph Riggs and J. Robert Ashcroft, who believed that the church had to become routinized into practices of denominational reproduction sociologically common to other institutionalized religions. They conceded, therefore, that the rightful responsibility of the church was, like other denominations, to implement a collegiate system for the preservation of its tradition. On the other hand were the many less-dominant figures whose orthodoxy held that the organization of the church should preserve Pentecostalism by remaining isolated from mainstream society. Those of this belief counter-argued that adaptability, regardless of environmental demands, was antagonistic to the separationist origins of the Pentecostal and holiness movements.

At its core the debate was ideological. Within the church's structure was a complex of ideologies that gave the Assemblies of God form and meaning. The maturation process of the church, however, began to polarize its organizational structure and its ideology, and the church was forced to alter one of the two. When decision makers during that time were convinced that the church's organizational structure and its ideological history were not aligned, a transformation began to occur. To legitimize this transformation and to assure that change would be accepted demanded thoughtful negotiations with the church's important constituency audiences.[367] In the establishment of Evangel College, the transformation demanded that church leaders develop a rationale to legitimate the quality of the church's services.

In the process of lobbying for the college and subsequently planning the college, the decisions seemed based on a surveillance strategy; decisions were not embraced by a systematic in-depth strategy. What is meant by surveillance is that the information gathered was not necessarily characteristic of what would be most economically or ideologically prudent for the college.[368] Though a considerable amount of data and documents was amassed by men like Riggs and Ashcroft and circulated among the members of the planning committees, no systemic relationship followed between the information gathered and the choices made. As Assemblies of God leaders began to make decisions regarding the feasibility of a denominational liberal arts college, for them feasibility was already a foregone conclusion. In the minds of these leaders, the church needed a college. Other religious movements had come to similar crossroads in their development, most of whom had responded to the crisis of survival by creating collegiate structures.

---

[367] David H. Kamens, "Legitimating Myths and Educational Organization: The Relationship Between Organizational Ideology and Formal Structure," *American Sociological Review* 42 (April 1977): 209.

[368] Martha S. Feldman and James G. March, "Information in Organizations as Signal and Symbol," *Administrative Science Quarterly* 26 (1981): 173.

The 1940s and 1950s marked a period of development when the young church was facing uncertainties about its future. These uncertainties were the result of the tension between the denomination's founding ideologies and its instinctive drift toward a more complex organizational structure. The rapid routinization process occurring within the Assemblies of God placed its leadership in a type of crisis. At the crux of the crisis was the question of how to respond to the growing need to routinize. To confront these uncertainties, the decision makers within the Assemblies of God church looked to those religious organizations within the American religious mainstream they perceived as being legitimate and successful. Affiliation with the NAE and AABIBC provided the church leadership an alliance with other organizations within its own field. In addition, when the college was at its earliest stages of discussion, its planners faced many uncertainties about effective methods of establishing the college.

In response to this crisis of routinization, the church leaders began to mimic structures of other denominations. The notion of mimicking is not uncommon among researchers of organizational studies. March and J. P. Olsen argue that when organizational technologies are poorly understood, when goals are ambiguous, or when the environment creates symbolic uncertainty, organizations model themselves after other organizations.[369] Richard M. Cyert and March link mimicking within organizational fields to uncertainty. When an organization faces a situation with ambiguous causes or unclear solutions, it may respond by modeling itself after those who have faced similar problems.[370] According to R. R. Nelson and S. G. Winter, organizations which are weaker, younger, and more vulnerable are compelled to imitate those organizations within their field they perceive to be more successful and legitimate. Weaker organizations, therefore, select the most appropriate routine from the apparently successful organizations.[371]

This process of imitating organizational developmental mechanisms might have made the Assemblies of God more similar to other denominations, but in retrospect it did not necessarily result in optimum efficiency. In the absence of evidence that mimicking other colleges within its field would increase

---

[369] James March and J. P. Olsen, "The Uncertainty of the Past: Organizational Learning Under Ambiguity," *European Journal of Political Research* 3 (1975): 167-71, as quoted in Feldman and March, "Information in Organizations," 150.

[370] Richard M. Cyert and James March, *A Behavioral Theory of the Firm* (Englewood Cliffs, NJ: Prentice-Hall, 1963) as quoted in Paul J. DiMaggio and Walter W. Powell, "The Iron Cage Revisited: Institutional Isomorphism and Collective Rationality in Organizational Fields," *American Sociological Review* 48 (April 1983): 147-50 (150).

[371] R. R. Nelson and S. G. Winter, as quoted in Ted. I. K. Youn and Karyn Loscocco, "Institutional History, Ideology, and Organizational Decision Making: A Comparison of Two Women's Colleges," *History of Higher Education Annual* 11 (1991): 2.

organizational efficiency, the church leaders nevertheless modeled the proposed college after other colleges within the denomination's religious niche.[372] Instead of undertaking financial analyses and feasibility studies, it seemed most prudent to the leaders of the church to deal with their uncertainty by adapting the form of other evangelical denominations' liberal arts colleges that they perceived as being more successful. In the mid-1940s Riggs gathered information from other colleges—colleges that were decried by Riggs for their anti-Pentecostal philosophies—to use in modeling the contingent Assemblies of God liberal arts college. During the earliest stages of his planning, Ralph Riggs cursorily gathered information from the catalogs and bulletins of conservative evangelical colleges such as Wheaton (Illinois), Gordon, Anderson, Taylor, Houghton, Asbury, and Westmont to use as models for the proposed liberal arts college. In-depth discussion and analysis of any of this information, however, never materialized. He also frequently noted such religious movements as the Catholics, Mormons, and Seventh Day Adventists, who established colleges as a means of preserving their respective religious traditions.

### Information to Legitimize Routinization

The arbitrary ways in which information was gathered substantiates the notion that the decision to create Evangel College was based on actors responding to an evolutionary routinization within the church. Had information been collected which was vital to a particular decision, then it may be argued that the founding of the college was legitimized by a proven need. This, however, was not the case. The insubstantial amount of information collected by the decision makers had no correlation to the decisions made. Instead, planners gathered information to legitimize what they perceived to be successful methods of survivability implemented by other denominations.

A classical understanding of decision-making theory indicates that information is collected and utilized because it assists the decision makers in their choices. Information has value, therefore, if it can be expected to affect choice, that is, if it is relevant to the decision to be made. Essentially, decisions are derived from an estimate of uncertain consequences of possible actions and an assumption of future preferences for those consequences. Understanding this rational approach to decision making presupposes certain expectations. Feldman and March list five:

• relevant information will be gathered and will be utilized before the decision is made;

• information which is gathered for use in a decision will be used in making that decision;

---

[372] Paul J. DiMaggio and Walter W. Powell, "The Iron Cage Revisited: Institutional Isomorphism and Collective Rationality in Organizational Fields," *American Sociological Review* 48 (April 1983): 147-50.

- available information will be first examined before more information is collected;
- information irrelevant to a decision will not be gathered, and
- if irrelevant information is gathered, it will not be utilized.[373]

Some research affirms, however, that these presuppositions are not necessarily followed. Rather, many organizations seem to utilize information in a different way. Feldman and March, Youn and Loscocco, Allison, and Kamens hypothesize that the uses of information are embedded in social norms that make information highly symbolic and not based on rational principles.[374] In the establishment of Evangel College, there appears to be an absence of a logical relation between the collection of exploratory information and the decisions made. Arbitrary information was sought and considered, but the final decisions invariably disregarded the data in favor of the original opinion of the decision makers. It can be concluded, therefore, that the link between information and decisions was weak.

Though the collection of information by the college planners proved to have little value in the final decisions, the fact that information was collected engendered a belief among the planners and constituency that establishing the college was a necessity. In part, the decision makers established their legitimacy by a ceremonial accumulation of information. For them, it was better to have information and not use it than not to have information at all. In their studies, Feldman and March conclude that using information, asking for information, and justifying decisions in terms of information all come to be significant ways in which individuals and organizations symbolize that the process is legitimate, that they are good decision makers, and that the organization is well-managed.[375]

---

[373] Feldman and March, "Information in Organizations," 172.

[374] See Feldman and March, "Information in Organizations," 171-74; Youn and Loscocco, "Institutional History," 5; Graham T. Allison, *Essence of Decision: Explaining the Cuban Missile Crisis* (Boston: Little, Brown, 1971), 246ff; and Kamens, "Legitimating Myths," 208-09.

[375] Feldman and March, "Information in Organizations," 177–78. Zald explains through his research that the ways in which an organization's information is transmitted are directly related to the forms and rates of its social movements. In other words, those who control such resources as time, money, facilities, access to the media and data collection are more powerful than those who do not. Within the Assemblies of God, the college's most ardent proponents were not the rank and file members but were those situated in the church's executive offices. From their positions of status, these college proponents accessed church publications, established committees, channeled funding and adjusted agenda in hope of bettering the chances of an expeditious ratification by the General Council. By the time the motion came to the floor for the 1953 election, the church's several thousand voting delegates had been saturated by many forms of information detailing the church leadership's unequivocal position in favor of the college. Had the movement for the college been mobilized by those who did not enjoy access to Springfield's leverage, the college most likely would not have been authorized

The historical narrative of the founding of Evangel College exposes ways in which information was manipulated so as to make the decision appear to be made within the bounds of careful planning. Regardless of the rationale underlying the decision, the college planners had little choice but to offer incentives in order to placate those skeptics who believed secular education would have a detrimental effect on the young church. Those who were most involved in the college's planning were those associated with the church's senior leadership. The incentives they offered accentuated attributes of the decision, which were rooted in the purpose of the church. Zald refers to these as purposive incentives.[376] When the proposed liberal arts college was being considered, its supporters communicated to the local churches that the college would be an institution to preserve the morally and socially redemptive rudiments of the Assemblies of God. Parents who enrolled students in Evangel College could expect their children to achieve right living and to preserve the Pentecostal tradition.

It follows that church leaders were interested in a rational form of the collegiate institution as a mechanism for the containment of charisma. Given their uncertainty as to successful ways of continuing the institutionalization process, these leaders looked to other organizations for bureaucratic models. These actors undertook no in-depth analysis on their data, and the data they did collect were negligible. Data was collected by the planners merely to legitimate their already-made decision, a method common among organizations uncertain about successful planning strategies. The leading men of the church were ambiguous as to what direction the denomination should take. Since the idea of the need for a college certainly did not originate out of a feasibility study, it stands to reason that the idea originated in what the leaders perceived to be successful in other organizations. The outcome was a liberal arts college founded as a means of perpetuating Pentecostalism.

## Summary

Facing crisis and ambiguity, institutionalization made sense. The leaders made the choice—by copying what they deemed as successful structures in other

---

in 1953. See Zald, "Theological Crucibles," 321.

In understanding the nature of decision making in the establishment of Evangel College, it is necessary to analyze the powers and actions of the proponents *vis-à-vis* the opposition. As noted above, the men who were principal players in advocating a liberal arts college for the Assemblies of God were also those with ready access to the church's powerful control mechanisms, such as the Executive and General Presbyteries, church literature and influential pastors. These individuals realized their advantageous posture while at the same time understanding the negative implications many in the trenches believed the college might have on a large segment of the church's population. As a result, they worked tenuously to defuse the opposition's cynicism.

[376] Zald "Theological Crucibles," 326-27.

organizations—that charisma could be contained in part through a rational form of a collegiate structure. This led to the founding of Evangel College. The formation of Evangel College was the result of an institutionalization process occurring within the church. It was a method, Riggs argued, of preserving the Pentecostal tradition. Sociologists would understand this as a form of the routinization of charisma. In other words, the containment of the charismatic in a rational form led to the creation of a collegiate institution.

The church's early charisma evolved into a need for routinization. As a result of this routinization process, communicated through a process of symbols and rituals, the church developed a type of ecclesiastical structure.[377] The uncertainty that resulted from within this newly formed ecclesiastical structure created an increased ambiguity among the decision makers. Central to this

---

[377] When the choice was made in Springfield to move toward the establishment of a denominationally sponsored liberal arts college, the decision makers wanted their choice to be accepted by the organization's constituencies. This resulted in the decision makers constructing a two-fold message to the organization: first, that the choice was made intelligently, and second, that the choice was sensitive to the concerns of relevant people. To church leaders this meant that initiatory decisions to create the college reflected thoughtful planning, analysis and a systematic use of information. It also meant that when Riggs and his associates wanted to create a liberal arts college, they did so within the church's conventional channels of rules, symbol and rituals.

Because the college was a byproduct of the institutionalization process occurring at that time within the church, its planners chose to emphasize the ritual and symbolic activities of the process over and above the goal-related strategies. Symbols, rituals and norms inherent to the Assemblies of God accompanied each stage in the routinization of charisma. These symbols served to legitimize that the decision to found Evangel College was principally a decision to preserve Pentecostalism. The ritual or symbolic acts of gathering information that enhanced the culture of the church, therefore, became to the college planners most important. Information did not necessarily serve as the principal ingredient for action, but as a source of reaffirming the organization's values and norms.

Specifically, the college planners emphasized throughout their committee meetings, correspondence and reports that the contingent college would preserve the church's young people by educating them in a Pentecostal environment. In other words, the college would be an agent of the church created to contain the charisma of Pentecostalism. The planners pointed to programs, daily chapel services, admission criteria, non-academic faculty requirements and rules of behavior which would reassure the church's population that Evangel College was thoroughly a Pentecostal, value-laden institution. These symbolic mechanisms were intended to be evidence of the college's ability to transmit values and beliefs, and proof to the constituency that the students would acquire these values and beliefs. Created to be a moral agent of the Assemblies of God, as a symbol the college transmitted to church members that Evangel College students would undergo an intense socialization experience and be personally transformed into effective value carriers and agents of the church. Kamens refers to this as value socialization. Translated to the study of Evangel College, value socialization meant that the college was defined as an agent of the church to socialize its students to become increasingly committed to the church's values and traditions. See March, "Emerging Developments," 143; and Youn and Loscocco, "Institutional History," 19, 22.

ambiguity was the question as to what form of institution the church would take. Actors responded to this increased ambiguity through a form of collective rationality, that is, they imitated what they perceived to be successful in other denominations. Out of this collective rationality, a collegiate structure was formed.

The Assemblies of God church began in 1914 as a religious movement detached from virtually all interaction with elements of the larger social environment. As the denomination grew in numbers and years, however, so did its involvement in the affairs of its external environments. This is often explained in sociological terms in that religious movements, in order to survive, follow discrete patterns of institutionalization. In many ways, the case of the Assemblies of God and its decision to create Evangel College confirms the principles of institutionalization hypothesized by Weber, Durkheim, Niebuhr, et al. Specifically why and how the Assemblies of God has been patterned after Weber's routinization of charisma is unclear. The answer, as discussed above, lies in a complex web of external influences and internal choices, both interrelated with the issue of institutionalization and survivability.

As the church matured, it became increasingly routinized. Although its spokesmen at every level still lashed out against the suffocating effects of structure and bureaucracy, the creation of new offices increased precipitously within the church from 1920 to 1950. The church chose to, or was obligated to, form relationships with external elements which forced it even more to adopt to a more routinized structure. These relationships resulted from such environmental forces as the nationwide increase in the number of college matriculants, the GI Bill of Rights and the new market of students it created, and the educational requirements for chaplaincy in the armed forces. Evangel College was also the result of choices made within the ranks of the church's leadership which were based on surveillance of other denominations. The Assemblies of God leaders identified and imitated what they considered to be successful models of survivability within other sectarian organizations. Churches that had adopted collegiate programs as a method of indoctrinating the rising generations became the paradigms for the Assemblies of God leaders. Consequently, these men chose to do likewise.

The result of this routinization and ambiguity was the decision to establish a market-driven collegiate institution. This decision could be classified as rational because the college's academic programs were not principally based on philosophical models but rather on the reproductive strategies of similar institutions within the church's organizational field. The popular and economically profitable academic majors in education, nursing, and business were included in Evangel college's first-year curriculum, making the college appear at first to be as much a professional school as a classical liberal arts college. Essentially, its planners were packaging a product to sell to consumers that promised an institution where students could prepare for a profession, protected from the hazards of society, with others of similar ilk.

Given the historical data in the decision to found Evangel College, it is clear that the formation of the college was a result of an institutionalization process at work within the church. The charismatic origins of the church and the sense of crisis and isolation out of which the church was born gave way to routinization as the need for new functions and the need for legitimacy grew. As the church matured and it began to routinize its functions into bureaucratic forms, an ambiguity arose among leaders of the fledgling church. At the core of this ambiguity was the question as to what form of organized, ecclesiastical structure would be necessary for the church's survival. This gave rise to Ralph Riggs and other actors profoundly affected by the notion of routinization and the need for the containment of the charisma. These actors, imitating what they understood to be successful means of containment in other religious movements, convinced the church that a collegiate structure was a legitimate means of survivability.

In conclusion, certain patterns of choice were linked to the church's position in the institutionalization process at a given time. Likewise, the decision to establish Evangel College corresponded to the church's institutionalization process and was rooted in the belief that a rationalized form of education was a socially legitimate means of survivability.

## Bibliography

Aldrich, H. E. and Jeffrey Pfeffer. "Environments of Organizations." *Annual Review of Sociology* (1976): 79.

Allison, Graham T. *Essence of Decision: Explaining the Cuban Missile Crisis.* Boston: Little, Brown, 1971.

Anderson, Robert M. *Vision of the Disinherited: The Making of American Pentecostalism.* New York: Oxford University Press, 1979.

Chase, Betty. "Evangel College Buildings and the Pioneers for Whom They Were Named." *Evangel College Archives* (1990): 8-9.

Cyert, Richard M. and James March. *A Behavioral Theory of the Firm.* Englewood Cliffs, NJ: Prentice-Hall, 1963.

DiMaggio, Paul J. and Walter W. Powell. "The Iron Cage Revisited: Institutional Isomorphism and Collective Rationality in Organizational Fields." *American Sociological Review* 48 (April 1983): 147-50.

Durkheim, Emile. *The Elementary Forms of Religious Life.* Translated by Joseph Ward. Swain Glencoe: Free Press, 1954.

Feldman, Martha S. and James G. March. "Information in Organizations as Signal and Symbol." *Administrative Science Quarterly* 26 (1981): 173.

Kamens, David H. "Legitimating Myths and Educational Organization: The Relationship Between Organizational Ideology and Formal Structure." *American Sociological Review* 42 (April 1977): 209.

March, James G. "Emerging Developments in the Study of Organizations." In *ASHE Reader on Organization and Governance in Higher Education*, edited by Marvin W. Peterson, 141-42. Needham Heights: Ginn Press, 1989.

March, James G. and J. P. Olsen. "The Uncertainty of the Past: Organizational Learning Under Ambiguity." *European Journal of Political Research* 3 (1975): 167-71.

O'Dea, Thomas F. and Janet O'Dea Aviad. *The Sociology of Religion*. 2nd ed. Englewood Cliffs: Prentice-Hall, 1983.

Otto, Rudolf. *The Idea of the Holy*. 2nd ed. Translated by J. W. Harvey. London: Oxford University Press, 1950.

Wach, Joachim. *The Sociology of Religion.* Chicago: University of Chicago Press, 1944.

Weber, Max. *The Theory of Social and Economic Organizations,* edited by Talcott Parsons. Translated by A. M. Henderson and Talcott Parsons. New York: Oxford University Press, 1947.

Zald, Mayer N. "Theological Crucibles: Social Movements In and Of Religion." *Review of Religious Research* 32, no. 4 (June 1982): 328.

# Contextual Scripture Engagement and Transcultural Mission

C. René Padilla

Andrew Walls, an incisive observer of the massive southward shift of the center of gravity of Christianity that has taken place within the last century, has called our attention to the fact that in the past only a few Western missionaries "wrote significantly in biblical studies, in dogmatics, or even in the field of philosophy of religion; and few of those who did show any radical influence from their missionary service and knowledge. Theology was a *datum* to be explained and demonstrated in the new cultural setting, not something which would develop in it."[378]

The main reason behind this phenomenon was that Western theology was commonly regarded as having universal validity. Consequently, all that needed to be done was to translate it and to export it to the "mission fields" of the world for the benefit of the younger churches. This view of theology fails to take into account that faith is, by its very nature, conditioned by historical factors and that consequently all theology, including the one framed in the West, is contextual.

Once the contextual character of theology is recognized, the door is open for a Scripture engagement leading to contextualization—the incarnation of the gospel in a specific historical context—and to the construction of a variety of contextual theologies that spell out the meaning of the gospel and Christian discipleship in different local situations around the world.

## Scripture Engagement and Contextualization

In one of the most challenging books I have ever read, *Reading the Bible with the Damned*,[379] Bob Ekblad describes his theological pilgrimage. He shows how a Christian, spiritually blindfolded by wealth and socially domesticated by an evangelical subculture, is transformed into a facilitator of

---

[378] Andrew Walls, *The Missionary Movement in Christian History: Studies in the Transmission of Faith* (Maryknoll: Orbis, 2000), 197.

[379] Bob Ekblad, *Reading the Bible with the Damned* (Louisville, KY: Westminster John Knox, 2005).

Scripture engagement among people on the margins. His experience is a living illustration of contextualization of the biblical message for the sake of Christian obedience—a contextualization that gives birth to a theology that seeks to be faithful to the gospel and relevant to a specific life and mission context.

Justo L. González, in a masterpiece that only a Church historian of his caliber could write, has explained and compared three types of Western theology throughout the history of Christian thought.[380] Without denying that the three types share certain common elements, he claims that each one has emphases and perspectives that make it distinct.

Type A, centered in Carthage, is represented by Tertullian (born ca. 193 CE). He was probably a lawyer and has been regarded as the father of Latin theology. Strongly influenced by Stoicism, he conceived Christianity as "superior to any human philosophy, since in it one receives the revelation of the ultimate law of the universe, the law of God."[381]

Type B, developed in Alexandria, had Origen (born ca. 185 CE) as its main exponent. Living in an environment permeated by Platonism, he dedicated himself to the search for "immutable truths, realities that would not be dependent upon sensory perception, and scriptural interpretations to show that the Bible sets forth a series of unalterable metaphysical and moral principles."[382]

Type C had as its center the geographical area roughly comprising Asia Minor and Syria, with Antioch as the main city. The most outstanding exponent of it was Irenaeus (born ca. 130 CE). In contrast with Tertullian and Origen, he was not a prolific writer, but he was a pastor and had closer links with the sub-apostolic tradition. His interest was not in immutable truths but in the New Testament historical events that had taken place in Palestine, Antioch, and Asia Minor. Taking salvation history as his starting point, he sought to equip the believers with an ethical basis for a life worthy of the gospel. In *Faith and Wealth: A History of Early Christian Ideas on the Origin, Significance, and Use of Money*,[383] Justo González gives plenty of evidence to demonstrate that in this type of theology the issues of economics and social justice were a central concern.

González's typology shows how the most prominent feature of each type of theology—Law in type A, Truth in type B, and History in type C—colors the understanding of every theological theme, from creation to consummation, in patristic and medieval theology, in the Reformation and beyond. He claims

---

[380] Justo L. González, *Christian Thought Revisited: Three Types of Theology*, rev. ed. (Maryknoll: Orbis, 1999). González's focus is on theology, but the three types of theology that he analyzes are closely related to three types of approaches to Scripture.

[381] González, *Christian Thought Revisited*, 6-7.

[382] González, *Christian Thought Revisited*, 11.

[383] Justo L. González, *Faith and Wealth: A History of Early Christian Ideas on the Origin, Significance, and Use of Money* (San Francisco: Harper & Row, 1990).

that, although type A and type B are better known to Western Christians, type C is the oldest of the three. Originally, the three types were regarded as orthodox. After the conversion of Constantine in the fourth century, however, type A, revised with elements of type B, became the standard theology, especially in the West, while type C was generally set aside and ignored in theological creeds.

The relevance of this historical analysis to our subject lies in the fact that today, with the demise of modernity, there is, especially in the Majority World, a rediscovery of type C theology, and with it a return of social concerns as an essential aspect of Scripture engagement and theological reflection. The "new way of doing theology" which is being explored by most theologians in the Majority World is not, after all, so *new*! It is rather the unearthing of a pre-Constantine approach to Scripture as well as to theology—an approach that gives proper weight to the historical nature of biblical revelation, including the Incarnation, and understands the Church and its mission in light of God's action in history to manifest his Kingdom, his power, and his glory in the midst of the kingdoms of this world.

From this point of view, a genuine concern for the present-day cultural, socioeconomic, and political issues in the context in which people live is neither an optional concern nor a mere appendix to theology. What is theology good for, if it is not an effort to discern, in light of Scripture and under the guidance of the Spirit, the signs of the times and concrete ways in which the Church can incarnate the values of the Kingdom of God in the cultural, socioeconomic, and political realm?

Using González's typology, we would say that in Ekblad's theological pilgrimage (noted in his book, *Reading the Bible with the Damned*), Ekblad moves from the kind of concern for orthodoxy *per se,* which oftentimes characterizes adherents to Type A and Type B theologies, to the kind of concern for orthopraxis inherent to Type C theology.[384] The move that takes place in Ekblad, however, is not merely on an intellectual level; it is rather a process of transformation of an American assailed by "social and national guilt" into a Christian who is learning to accept himself as Jesus did and is thus freed to help "the damned" to believe Jesus loves them in all their entrapments."

Quite clearly, in that process of transformation, which is both theological and spiritual, contextualization has a prominent place. In fact, Ekblad's experience illustrates the role that contextual Scripture engagement plays in the

---

[384] This statement should not be interpreted as minimizing the importance of orthodoxy. As Anthony Thiselton has argued in *The Hermeneutics of Doctrine* (Grand Rapids: Eerdmans, 2007), properly understood, doctrine includes the *disposition* of belief, which always involves *formation* and leads on to *transformation*. From this perspective, true orthodoxy is inseparable from orthopraxis.

fulfillment of Jesus' purpose "to purify for himself a people that are his very own, eager to do what is good" (Titus 2:14). Let me explain.

Among the many international conferences I have attended throughout many years, one of the most important ones was the Consultation on Gospel and Culture held in Willowbank, Bermuda Islands, in January of 1978. It was sponsored by the Theology and Education Group and the Work Group on Strategy of the Lausanne Committee, led by John Stott, with the participation of 33 theologians, anthropologists, linguists, missionaries, and pastors from the six continents. As far as I know, no other conference has ever been held since then, at least in evangelical circles, surpassing the range and depth that the treatment of the proposed subject attained at that conference.

In the first of the nine sections that are included in the "Willowbank Report on Gospel and Culture,"[385] the following statement from paragraph 10 of the Lausanne Covenant is quoted: "Culture must always be tested and judged by Scripture. Because man is God's creature, some of his culture is rich in beauty and goodness. Because he is fallen, all of it is tainted with sin and some of it is demonic." This statement points to the ambiguity of all cultures—an ambiguity derived from the nature of the author of culture: humankind created in the image of God, yet at the same time affected by sin. As the Willowbank Report affirms, because we are fallen creatures, "All our work is accompanied by sweat and struggle (Gen. 3:17-19), and it is disfigured by selfishness. So none of our cultures is perfect in truth, beauty, or goodness. At the heart of every culture—whether we identify this heart as religion or worldview—is an element of self-centeredness, of man's worship of himself."[386]

The conclusion to which the Willowbank Report's acknowledgment of the ambiguity of culture leads is that we Christians are called to submit every aspect of our cultural life to the lordship of Jesus Christ, which presupposes a radical change of loyalty. Further on, the Willowbank Report explains the meaning of this change in terms of conversion to Jesus involving a process of transformation that affects the whole of life and has social and public consequences. On the basis of the New Testament, it views conversion as "the outward expression of a regeneration or new birth by God's Spirit, a recreation, a resurrection from spiritual death." It states that "the resurrection of Jesus Christ from the dead was the beginning of the new creation of God" and that we participate in it "by God's grace through union with Christ."[387] It adds that

---

[385] "The Willowbank Report" is included in John Stott, ed., *Making Christ Known: Historic Mission Documents from the Lausanne Movement 1974–1989* (Carlisle: Paternoster, 1996), 73-113. The nine sections of this Report are the following: 1) The Biblical Basis of Culture 2) A Definition of Culture 3) Culture in the Biblical Revelation 4) Understanding God's Word Today 5) The Content and Communication of the Gospel 6) Wanted: Humble Messengers of the Gospel 7) Conversion and Culture 8) Church and Culture 9) Culture, Christian Ethics and Lifestyle.

[386] Stott, ed., "Willowbank Report," 78.

[387] Stott, ed., "Willowbank Report," 93.

from this perspective we have already entered the new age and tasted its powers and joys. "This is the eschatological dimension of Christian conversion. Conversion is an integral part of the great renewal which God has begun, and which will be brought to a triumphant climax when Christ comes in his glory."[388]

According to Ekblad's description of his theological pilgrimage, his starting point was as a member of a faith community that had very little or no meaningful interaction with "outsiders." It is not surprising that in that context the values of the surrounding culture were taken for granted and Scripture was not allowed to fulfill its prophetic role. For Ekblad, when Scripture is read too long in limited circles or in a faith community marked by sameness and low expectations of God, the outcome is the *domestication* of Scripture. Christian religious groups like the one he describes tend to view the Bible as essentially a book of doctrines regarding the individual's relationship to God, with no bearing on cultural, socioeconomic, or political issues. The individualistic reading of Scripture, common in such groups, precludes contextual Scripture engagement. As a result, conversion is understood in terms of an intellectual assent to doctrines rather than in terms of a commitment to Jesus involving a process of transformation that affects the whole of life and has social and public consequences.

What made the difference in Ekblad's case? Quite clearly, it was his living interaction and Scripture engagement with people outside his cocoon, including atheists. His eyes were opened up to the world in new ways through relationships with people whose upbringings and experiences were quite different from his. Through interaction with those "outside" he came to a conviction that in time would color his ministry—that reading Scripture with the not-yet believing and also with believers from many different denominations and nations, will free us from the sterility of domestication. Other factors, such as the reading of Latin American liberation theologians, opened his eyes to see reality from another perspective and led him to examine his theological assumptions. He saw that if his "good news" didn't appear "good" to oppressed people, then a serious overhaul was necessary. The way was thus open for a Scripture engagement far more faithful to the gospel and far more relevant to transcultural mission.

## Contextualization and Transcultural Mission

The Willowbank Report points out that "the biblical writers made critical use of whatever cultural material was available to them for the expression of their message," and adds that "the process by which the biblical authors borrowed words and images from their cultural milieu and used them creatively was

---

[388] Stott, ed., "Willowbank Report," 93–94.

controlled by the Holy Spirit so that they purged them of false or evil implications and thus transformed them into vehicles or truth and goodness."[389]

This biblical precedent provides the basis for transcultural mission, with the contextualization of the gospel in the multiple cultures of the world as a basic premise. The same good news that was originally communicated in a Jewish and Greco-Roman context in the first century CE must be communicated today. If its communication is, under God, going to make the same kind of impact that it made in that context, however, the communicators need to be fully aware that, as Lamin Sanneh has rightly emphasized, because Christianity is a translated religion, all cultures are "equal bearers in their status as historical bearers of Scripture."[390]

Unfortunately, not always have Christians properly taken into account the critical role that culture plays in the communication of the gospel. As a result, much of the transcultural work done in the Majority World by Western missionaries has been marked by a serious lack of cultural sensitivity. The Willowbank Report makes reference to this problem when it states that sometimes "messengers of the gospel are guilty of a cultural imperialism which both undermines the local culture unnecessarily and seeks to impose an alien culture instead."[391] An inadequate appreciation of the positive values of the local culture, or a deficient view of the distortions of the alien culture, or these two factors combined, prevent an effective communication of the gospel.

In the absence of a contextualized gospel, the only kind of churches that transcultural mission can originate are Western-looking churches, unable to portray the practical meaning of the Incarnation in their own context, conditioned by a Christianity that, as Lamin Sanneh has put it, "in terms of intercultural engagement ... has remained in a state of splendid isolation."[392] Sad to say, many churches in the Majority world, as the Willowbank Report states, "are still almost completely inhibited from developing their own identity and programmes by policies laid down from afar, by the introduction and continuation of foreign traditions, by the use of expatriate leadership, by alien decision-making processes, and especially by the manipulative use of money."[393]

Without a contextualized gospel there cannot be a contextualized church. In a number of cases the reason for this problem may be the assumption that Western missionaries, because of their (supposedly) superior culture and education, must always be not on the receiving end as learners but on the giving end as teachers. There is a place for this acknowledgment included in the

---

[389] Stott, ed., "Willowbank Report," 80.
[390] Unpublished paper, "Mission, Translation, and the Incarnate Word," 8.
[391] Stott, ed., "Willowbank Report," 87.
[392] Stott, ed., "Willowbank Report," 15.
[393] Stott, ed., "Willowbank Report," 101.

Willowbank Report: "We repent of the ignorance which assumes that we have all the answers and that our only role is to teach."[394]

One of the most useful lessons my wife and I learned working among the poor is the importance of empowering them to read Scripture together, not by adopting the role of teachers but merely as facilitators. We have found that when simple people are given the opportunity to interact with the text, to relate it to their own situation and to dialogue among themselves about their findings, they can come out with amazing insights that are quite relevant to their own lives. It is my considered opinion that this is the sort of Scripture engagement that Christians should be fostering everywhere for the making of disciples who learn to obey everything that the Lord Jesus Christ commanded his disciples, according to the Great Commission (Matt. 28:18-20). Lamin Sanneh has shown the connection between interest in the laity and the effort to make Scripture accessible to common people. The same connection should lead Bible teachers and agencies to give priority to the training of grassroots Bible-study facilitators who are able to ask the right questions, to encourage people to dialogue and to relate text and context in search for faithfulness to the Word of God and relevance to practical life.

The contextualization of the gospel is inseparable from the contextualization of the Church. As a matter of fact, the contextualization of the gospel in a specific culture can only take place in the extent to which the Church embodies the gospel as "good news to the poor" and the values of the Kingdom of God such as love, justice, and the stewardship of creation as expressions of the will of God for human life. From this perspective, the truly indigenous church is the one that through death and resurrection with Christ embodies the gospel within its own culture. It adopts a way of thinking and acting in which its own cultural patterns are transformed and fulfilled by the gospel. In a sense, it is the cultural embodiment of Christ, the means through which Christ is formed within a given culture.[395]

## Bibliography

Ekblad, Bob. *Reading the Bible with the Damned.* Louisville: Westminster John Knox, 2005.

Gonzalez, Justo L. *Christian Thought Revisited: Three Types of Theology.* Rev. ed. Maryknoll: Orbis, 1999.

---

[394] Stott, ed., "Willowbank Report," 90.
[395] C. René Padilla, *Mission Between the Times: Essays on the Kingdom* (Grand Rapids: Eerdmans, 1985), 108. A second edition of this book is forthcoming this year as a Langham monograph.

_____. *Faith and Wealth: A History of Early Christian Ideas on the Origin, Significance, and Use of Money.* San Francisco: Harper & Row, 1990.

Padilla, C. René. *Mission Between the Times: Essays on the Kingdom.* Grand Rapids: Eerdmans, 1985.

Thiselton, Anthony. *The Hermeneutics of Doctrine.* Grand Rapids: Eerdmans, 2007.

Stott, John ed. "The Willowbank Report." In *Making Christ Known: Historic Mission Documents from the Lausanne Movement 1974–1989,* 73-113. Carlisle: Paternoster, 1996.

Walls, Andrew. *The Missionary Movement in Christian History: Studies in the Transmission of Faith.* Maryknoll: Orbis, 2000.

# The Kingdom of God in Conflict
with the Kingdoms of the World

# Divine Judgment and the Completion of the Missionary Task: Paul's Motivation for Ministry in 1–2 Thessalonians—A Response to Thor Strandenæs

Scott Hafemann

Professor Dr. Peter Kuzmič has encountered the evil of our world in the tangled web of ecclesial and political realities more than most Christian leaders of our generation. Rather than shrinking back in understandable horror or giving in to debilitating discouragement, he has worked tirelessly to match these realities with the reality of the Christian gospel, serving both church and state to bring about reconciliation with justice, to strengthen hope in the midst of suffering, and to pass on a vision for God's righteousness to his students. As a former colleague, it is an honor to honor him for his relentless mission work, in the very best sense of that calling, with some reflections on another missionary-theologian, the apostle Paul. For Paul too faced head-on the relentless evil of his day. This essay thus looks at Paul's early, programmatic letters to the Thessalonians in order to ask what motivated Paul in his mission-ministry in the midst of adversity, and in so doing to place Peter Kuzmič's own life of faithful perseverance in its biblical context. To that end, this essay offers a modest response to the insightful work on Paul's missionary motivation by the Norwegian missiologist, Thor Strandenæs.[396]

## Thor Strandenæs' Thesis

Strandenæs' thesis takes its starting point from the question first posed by Nils Dahl in response to Paul's use of the verb *enorkizo* ("to cause a person to say under oath") in 1 Thessalonians 5:27: "Why is it ... that Paul, in a letter so full of praise and commendations to the Thessalonian Christians, urged them to swear by oath [in the name of the Lord!] that they would read the letter to 'all

---

[396] This essay is based on my response to Thor Strandenæs' paper at the August, 2009, congress of the *Societas Novi Testamenti Studiorum* in Vienna, now published as "Completing the Mission: Paul's Application of the Gospel to the Faith and Life of the Thessalonian Converts in 1 and 2 Thessalonians," *Swedish Missiological Themes* 98 (2010): 69–98. Citations to his article will be given within the body of this chapter.

the brethren'?" (69). In other words, why would Paul make such a binding, divinely sanctioned demand?

The answer: Paul compels his readers to share his letter with all the believers in Thessalonica because of the 1) function and 2) purpose of Paul's letters themselves. As to their function, reading the letter to the churches "was a necessary ingredient in Paul's enterprise of completing his mission to the inhabitants of Thessalonike in that both 1 and 2 Thessalonians were needed to further confirm and develop Christian belief and behavior among all the Thessalonian Christians ..." (69). As to their purpose, the goal of the letters was to move their recipients "toward a modified or transformed worldview" (70; restated on 77). All Thessalonian Christians must hear these letters because of the "*role* of [Paul's] message in preparing common standards for Christian belief and behaviour when negotiating new core values in the Christian community in Thessalonike" (70, emphasis mine). Hence, "the likely reason for Paul's demand ... is that he wanted all the converts to be reminded and informed about common standards for belief and behaviour, and to abide by these." In other words, "all this is done with a view to confirm and further develop Christian faith and practices in harmony with the gospel and ethos which Paul serves as a missionary" (77). Paul's letters were therefore part of his missionary enterprise of sharing his life and gospel with them (cf. 1 Thess. 2:8), and in so doing of "contributing to their continuous conversion, by developing their Christian knowledge (1 Thess. 4:13-18) and behaviour (1 Thess. 4:1ff., 9ff.; 5:6-11, 12-22; cf. 2 Thess. 1:11; 3:5). This he did in order that the Thessalonians might *remain* sanctified (1 Thess. 3:13; 5:23-24; cf. 2 Thess. 2:13) and with the Lord until his *parousia* (1 Thess. 4:17; 5:10; 2 Thess. 2:14)" (86; emphasis mine). Paul's writing to the Thessalonians, like his visiting the newly converted, is part of the *process* of transforming their worldview begun at their conversion (70; emphasis mine).

Strandenæs' main point is well taken. The role of Paul's letters in confirming and developing the Christian worldview in order to continue the believers' life of faith was an important missiological point then, as it is now. It reminds us that the use of the epistle-genre as an extension of the apostolic mission and ministry was a crucial Christian "invention."[397] The equation in 2 Thessalonians 2:14-15 and 3:14 of the apostolic preaching of the "gospel" (*euangeliou*) or "word" (*logo*) with the apostolic epistle (*epistole*) reflected the authority of the apostolic ministry embodied in the letter as well as providing the beginning of the canon-consciousness that led to the eventual use of the epistles as Scripture in the life of the Church.

---

[397] For the unique role and key question concerning the function of Paul's epistles in regard to the apostolic ministry, see already Peter Stuhlmacher, "Theologische Probleme des Römerbriefpräskripts," *EvTh* 27 (1967): 374–89.

## The Ongoing Conversion of the Thessalonians

Against the background of the pagan polytheistic worldview from which the majority of the Thessalonians came, coming to trust in the gospel of the "God of history" entailed a radical conversion of worldview and cultural dislocation (74). In contrast to the remote, arbitrary, unpredictable, and mixed moral character of the pagan deities, Paul's writings detail what it means that God is the "living and true God," to whom they had turned from "idols" (1 Thess. 1:9). He does so "by focusing on the saving and sanctifying activities of God, Jesus Christ, and the Holy Spirit in the recent historical events of salvation – *including also the lives of the Thessalonians, and the expected parousia*" (72, emphasis mine; cf. 92).

Strandenæs rightfully stresses from the content of the letters to the Thessalonians themselves that for Paul their "conversion" is something that has both taken place in the past (1 Thess. 1:9-10) and is an ongoing process which is not yet complete (2 Thess. 1:11-12; 2:2-3; 2:15-17) (75). He points to the fact that the Thessalonian letters "contain further instructions in Christian faith (e.g., 1 Thess. 4:13-18; 2 Thess. 2:1-12), implications which these (and formerly preached) cognitive facts had for upholding Christian faith and living (2 Thess. 2:5-6, 14-17; 3:4), and for maintaining and further developing Christian practices in daily life, also in a time of persecution (1 Thess. 2:13-16; 3:1-13; 2 Thess. 1:4ff.)" (75). In short, Paul "spells out the standards which must continually guide their transformation. And, since conversion cannot be separated from their sanctification, he asks God in prayer to bring this process to a good conclusion (1 Thess. 5:23-24; 2 Thess. 1:11-12; 2:13-17; 3:4-5)" (75).

In addition to the ethical standards Paul spells out, which were of particular relevance to the recent Gentile converts (76), central to the worldview Paul wanted to communicate was the nature of the second coming of Christ and its preceding signs (1 Thess. 4:13–5:1; 2 Thess. 2:3–3:5). In particular, in 2 Thessalonians Paul combats a "'millenarian fever'" in the church, which, according to Jewett, is based on "'the belief that the *parousia* could be present while this evil age is still so clearly in evidence'" (quoted, 76). I.e., central to Paul's teaching is his desire to "demolish" this "millenarian worldview" (76), since it is not in harmony with the received Christian tradition he had taught them or they had received (2 Thess. 2:2, 15; 3:6-7).

Here too, Strandenæs' perspective is exceedingly helpful. Clearly, both the conversion-sanctification of the Thessalonians and the *parousia* of Christ must be included together in the "salvation historical events" that form essential aspects of God's salvific work in history. Doing so breaks down the faith/obedience dichotomy that has plagued our reading of Paul, in which obedience must be added to faith as a second step in the Christian life rather than being conceived of as the organic expression of faith itself (cf. the "work of faith" in 1 Thess. 1:3; 2 Thess. 1:11 KJV).[398] It also retains the integral, future aspect of the gospel that is so often lost in current readings of Paul that focus almost exclusively on the first coming of Christ as the "fulfillment" of redemptive history. Indeed, Strandenæs rightly emphasizes the eschatological focus of 2 Thessalonians 1:5. And in discussing Paul's references to Jesus, Strandenæs points out that the title "Son of God" is "particularly referring to his being sent on a divine mission into the world to die and resurrect, *a mission which will only be completed by his return from heaven* (1 Thess. 1:10)" (91, emphasis mine). As the Son of God, Jesus "delivers us from the wrath to come" (1:10) (91).

## Eschatology and the Epistle

Strandenæs sees clearly that the focus of Paul's gospel is on the future. He also highlights the centrality of ethics within the gospel itself. But why is there this dual focus in Paul's writings, and how is this eschatological emphasis to be integrated into the framework of Paul's gospel as a whole, with its corresponding stress on the necessity of conforming to the ethical standards of the life of faith? Surely the content of the good news contains the assurance to a bewildered church that the Thessalonians "will 'obtain salvation through our Lord Jesus Christ' (1 Thess. 5:9 ESV) and 'live with him' whether they are 'awake or asleep' (v.10)" (89).[399] Yet why then does Paul also stress being delivered from the wrath to come (1:10)? What is the relationship between the current realities of the life of faith and the coming *parousia* as the present and future consequences of God's past saving acts in Christ? Is it the case that the

---

[398] For a development of this point canonically, see my essay, "The Covenant Relationship," in *Central Themes in Biblical Theology: Mapping Unity in Diversity*, ed. Scott J. Hafemann and Paul R. House (Nottingham, UK: InterVarsity Press and Grand Rapids: Baker, 2007), 20–65.

[399] Cf. now Colin Nicholl, *From Hope to Despair in Thessalonica* (SNTSMS 126; Cambridge: Cambridge University Press, 2004), who argues that the young Thessalonian church had moved from their initial hope to a hopeless grieving and dread in view of the unexpected deaths of members of their community, which they took to be an omen of God's wrath toward them, since they did not yet know or clearly understand the Christian doctrine of the resurrection of the dead saints in relationship to the *parousia*. This despair was accentuated by their later belief that "the Day of the Lord had come" (2 Thess. 2:2), so that they had missed salvation. Paul writes 1 Thessalonians "to reassure the Thessalonians regarding the salvific eschatological destiny of their deceased and the whole community" (111). Paul writes 2 Thessalonians to "assure them that God's judgment will indeed be just, consisting of a reversal of fortunes for them and their persecutors ... [and to] make it clear that when that just judgment will come, who will be its victims and what it will look like ... there was a lack of hope and insecurity among 'the Thessalonians' regarding their status before God and 'Paul'" (185). The question before us is the means by which this reassurance is obtained personally as well as doctrinally.

power for a continuing change in worldview lies in the inextricable relationship between their current lives as believers, as determined by the life, death, and resurrection of the Messiah, and the future return of Christ as judge?

We may answer these questions raised by Strandenæs' observations on the function and purpose of Paul's letters to the Thessalonians more precisely by examining Paul's statements regarding his motivation in writing. As we will see, the structure of Paul's argument makes clear that the central consequence of knowing the "God of history" is to know that the history of this age ends in divine judgment. The second coming of Christ, with its sure and just judgment, is the event that demonstrates that the living God is not remote, arbitrary, unpredictable, or of mixed character. As such, it is also the foundation and motivation for Paul's call to a transformed worldview and for his insistence on its corresponding ethical transformation. For Paul, eschatology drives ethics, since the *parousia*, as the consummation of inaugurated eschatology, forms the core of the new distinctively Christian, salvation-history worldview. Therefore, it is the centrality of eschatology that integrates the various aspects of Paul's continuing missionary mandate rightly highlighted by Strandenæs, while also providing a clear rationale both for Paul's insistence on the importance of his letters and for his own perseverance in ministry.

### The Eschatological Focus of Paul's Ministry in Writing

In 1 Thessalonians 1:5, Paul is assured that the Thessalonians are among the elect because (*hoti*) the gospel did not come to them in word only, but in power and in the Holy Spirit, and (therefore) in much conviction. The reality of the power of the Spirit in their lives is evidenced by the fact that, as 1:6 puts it, the Thessalonians became imitators of [the faith of?] Paul (and his cohort?)[400] and of the [faith of the?] Lord. In particular, they received the gospel with joy in the midst of (and despite) much affliction, a response which can only be attributed to the power of the Spirit.

The Thessalonians' exemplary lives, characterized by their "work of faith and labor of love and steadfastness of hope" (1 Thess. 1:3 ESV), consisted in their having turned back from idols in order to serve the living and true God and to wait for his resurrected Son to return from heaven (cf. the two purpose infinitives of vv. 9–10: *douleuein* [to serve], *anamenein* [to await]), since Jesus is the one who will rescue them from the coming wrath" (1:10c, taking the appositional participle, *Iesoun ton rhuomenon* [Jesus who delivers], to function causally). For Paul these are not two distinct purposes. The Thessalonians serve the living God precisely because they are waiting for Christ to return. In other words, the Spirit-determined acceptance of Paul's gospel, testified to by its joy in the midst of adversity (1 Thess. 1:6; cf. 2:14-16), only makes sense when the gospel-produced life of serving the living and true God is inextricably linked to

---

[400] Cf. the call to "imitate us" in 2 Thessalonians 3:7-13.

the certain return of Jesus to rescue his people from eschatological wrath. One's hope for future deliverance motivates perseverance through the suffering of the present—even with joy!

Paul's statements concerning the Thessalonians reflect the fact that the gospel receives its life-transforming power from its future orientation toward final judgment, since the certainty of "the wrath to come" (1 Thess. 1:10c) creates the present life of "serving God" (1:9) in preparation for it (cf. 2 Thess. 1:5-10). For this reason, Paul defines Jesus first and foremost eschatologically as the one who, by transforming their lives now (1 Thess. 1:3, 9; 2:13-14; 3:7, 9; 4:1, 10), rescues his people from the wrath to come (1:10). Jesus does this by being not only the object of faith and hope (1:3), since Jesus is also defined in 5:10 as "the one who died on our behalf" (cf. the appositional participle [*Iesou christou tou apothanontos*), but also the model of what it means to live by faith and hope (1 Thess. 1:6; cf. 2 Thess. 3:5: *ten hupomonen tou christou*). In the same way, in 1 Thessalonians 2:12a Paul exhorts the Thessalonians to walk worthy of God, who, like Jesus in 1:10, is also defined first and foremost eschatologically in 2:12b (ESV) as the one "who calls you into his own kingdom and glory" (note the use again of the appositional participle, *tou theou tou kalountos*, God who calls you). This definition of who God is in terms of what he does is unpacked in 2 Thessalonians 2:16 as the one "who loved us and by his grace gave us eternal encouragement and good hope" (again using an appositional phrase). As with Christ, here too, God's identity grounds who the Thessalonians are to be. Moreover, their life of faith is made possible by the fact that the God who calls his people into his Kingdom eschatologically is also the God who already gives his Holy Spirit to them (1 Thess. 4:8; yet again expressed in an appositional participle, *ton theon ton didonta*, God who gives).

Because of his conviction concerning Jesus and God as eschatological Savior and Judge, the "negative" side of Paul's hope is equally clear: the deliverance of those who believe also entails the judgment "on that day" of those who do not know God (cf. the simultaneous occurrence of the eschatological revelation of the glory of God and of judgment in 2 Thess. 1:9-10). In 1 Thessalonians 2:16 (eschatological) wrath (*he orge*) is therefore said to have come upon those Jews who killed Jesus and continue to persecute believers "until the [eschatological] end" (*eis telos*).[401] And in 2 Thessalonians 1:7-9, when Christ is revealed from heaven "in flaming fire" he will give "vengeance" and "punishment"/"justice" (*ekdikesin, diken*; both from the *dik-* stem) to those who do not know God and hence do not obey the gospel. At that time, those who afflict the faithful will be "recompensed" (*antapodounai*) with affliction as the expression of what is "righteous" (*dikaion*) before God (2 Thess. 1:6).

---

[401] This meaning is confirmed by the other New Testament uses of *eis telos*; cf. Matt. 10:22; 24:13-14; Mark 13:13 for the use of *eis telos* as a time reference to the end of age and Luke 18:5 and John 13:1 for its use to refer to a completed period of time.

On the "positive" side, like the other churches of God whom they imitate by their endurance of such persecution (1 Thess. 2:14), the Thessalonians are Paul's eschatological hope, joy, crown of boasting and glory "before our Lord Jesus at his coming" (2:19-20 ESV; cf. 2 Thess. 1:4; cf. Rom. 15:17; 2 Cor. 1:14; Phil. 4:1). Inasmuch as the Thessalonians' faith and love are increasing, even as they endure in the midst of adversity, Paul is bound to give thanks to God for bringing it about and to boast of their endurance of faith among the other churches (2 Thess. 1:3-4). Their faithful endurance in the midst of adversity is "evidence" or "proof" (*endeigma*) of God's righteous (eschatological) judgment, since he has delivered them from unbelief so that they may be made worthy of the Kingdom of God, for which they are also suffering (2 Thess. 1:5). As a result, God will grant them (eschatological) "rest" at the revelation of the Lord Jesus in judgment (2 Thess. 1:7). Those who are "awake" during the "day" of a redeemed life therefore live sober lives of faith and love in expectation of Christ's return, since salvation (*soterias*) is their "hope" (*elpida*), albeit a sure one, since God has not appointed them for eschatological wrath (*orgen*) but for the attaining of salvation through Christ the Lord (1 Thess. 5:8-10).

This is true, however, only if they are "standing fast in the Lord," in which case Paul "lives" (1 Thess. 3:8 ESV). If they were to give up, Paul's work would be in vain (3:5). For this reason, Paul's present joy over the Thessalonians' current life of faith does not satisfy Paul (cf. 4:1 and 10); rather, he begs God more than ever to be able to see them again face to face in order to strengthen (*katartisai*) what is still lacking in their faith (3:10). In the meantime and to this same end, Paul writes his epistles and sends Timothy in his place as the ongoing extension of his own missionary efforts in his absence (cf. *sterixai*, 3:2). At the same time, he also prays for this same strengthening (*sterixai*) in holiness "before our God and Father (as judge), at the coming (*parousia*) of our Lord Jesus with all his saints" (3:13 ESV; cf. 5:23; 2 Thess. 2:16-17; 3:3). The goal of his prayers is that on this "day," Christ will be glorified in them and they in him through their ongoing, grace-created "work of faith" (2 Thess. 1:11-12 ESV). For God called them to salvation through Paul's gospel for the purpose of possessing the glory of the Lord Jesus Christ (2 Thess. 2:14).

The reason for the seriousness of Paul's ethical admonitions is thus clear: the Lord is an avenger (*ekdikos*) against all immorality, as Paul has already solemnly testified (1 Thess. 4:6). Paul's warning, even to the believing Thessalonians, must therefore be taken seriously. Not to persevere or increase in their work of faith would mean not that they were saved but had failed to respond sufficiently to the gospel, but that the gospel had in fact not taken root in their lives (cf. 1 Thess. 3:12-13; 2 Thess. 2:15). The Lord's work is to cause his people to increase in their love for one another in order to establish them before his own righteous judgment (1 Thess. 3:12-13); God has destined his people for salvation (5:9); the God who calls his people to sanctification and promises to keep them blameless at the coming of the Lord Jesus is faithful to do so (5:23-24). So there is no conversion that is not a "continuing conversion" (4:1, 10; 2 Thess. 1:3; 2:11-12; see above). God's life-changing grace is expressed not only in the believers' calling and election, but also in their ongoing and increasing obedience to God's ensuing commands (cf., e.g., the "work of faith" to be accomplished "in the power" of God in 2 Thess. 1:11).[402] Paul's commands and warnings simply reflect what God's calling and election look like in everyday life.

The return of Christ as Savior and vindicating judge thus plays a foundational role both in Paul's own motivation for ministry and in the Thessalonians' life of faith. This is why Paul is concerned to deal with any misunderstandings surrounding its universal applicability or its certain, but still future, reality (cf. 4:13–5:11; 2 Thess. 2:1-12). Paul's letters are consequently an essential continuing means of his missionary activity since, as Strandenæs points out so well, the goal of the gospel Paul preaches and the content of his prayer, like the sending of Timothy, is not a one-time act of conversion in the past, but the continuing strengthening of the church's faith in the present in anticipation of the future (1 Thess. 3:2). In support of this point, Paul's theological motivation for his writing is not to underscore their acceptance of the gospel in the past, but to continue to minister this gospel in the present in order to prepare his churches for the judgment to come. It is because of the gospel's future focus on God's judgment that Paul sees the value of his own ministry at stake in the perseverance of his churches (1 Thess. 2:19-20; 3:5; 2 Thess. 1:4).

## Conclusion

Strandenæs mentions the future judgment of God as an important part of the message Paul preached. I would make it central to that message, and hence to Paul's motivation for ministry as well. Eschatology drives not only Paul's ethics, but also Paul's missionary activity. Although the Kingdom has been inaugurated (cf. the preaching of the "gospel of God," which is equated with "the gospel of Christ," in 1 Thess. 2:8, 9; 3:2), the missionary period of repentance and of the corresponding necessary endurance of the "work of faith" has been extended until Christ returns. In response, both Paul's spoken "word" (*logoi*) and his "letter" (*epistole*) serve the same end: to pass on the traditions of the gospel that will prepare them for the coming day of the Lord (2 Thess. 2:15). Moreover, in 2 Thessalonians 3:14 Paul can speak of being obedient to "our word through this letter," thereby equating obedience to the gospel (2 Thess. 1:8) with obedience to Paul's preaching (2 Thess. 2:15), with obedience

---

[402] This same point is at the heart of the argument of 2 Peter; see now my "The (Un)Conditionality of Salvation: The Theological Logic of 2 Peter 1:8a-10a, in *Staying In*, ed. Charles H. Talbert and Jason A. Whitlark (Grand Rapids: Eerdmans, 2011), 240-62 (248, 260).

to Paul's letter (2 Thess. 3:14)—without which there will be no inheritance of God's glory in Christ on judgment day. It is no wonder, then, that Paul made them swear an oath to read his epistles (1 Thess. 5:27 ESV), authenticating them with his own hand (2 Thess. 3:17).

Strandenæs rightly concludes that "Paul's mission task toward the Thessalonians was not completed after his visit in Thessalonike;" rather, it continued on through the subsequent visits of Timothy and of Paul himself, and through Paul's letters, in order that the Thessalonians might "abide by the implicit and explicit values of the Christian faith to which they had converted and of which they were now taught to see more clearly the consequences" (94). For "the Thessalonians needed a more comprehensive understanding of the contents of faith as well as the ethos it required" (94). The reason for this need, however, is not only inherent (95); it is eschatological. The mission task is not complete until the judgment day of the *parousia*, from which it receives its impetus and for which it prepares. Eschatology was such a priority to Paul and so problematic in Thessalonica precisely because eschatology, inaugurated but not yet consummated, stands at the heart of the gospel and of the life of faith it creates. As Strandenæs puts it, "this Son, Jesus Christ, would certainly return— but not yet … Since not all the Thessalonian converts seem to have grasped this truth fully, nor its implications, Paul's mission was incomplete until all the brethren had come to believe and behave according to the standards of the new faith …" (95).

At the center of the Christian worldview is the reality that salvation history, indeed, all of history, climaxes at the day of judgment, when Christ returns to establish God's righteous rule over his creation. This is the "deep" counter-cultural lens through which believers are to evaluate and live in this world and from which their life of faith derives. As 1 and 2 Thessalonians demonstrate, the common Christian, ethical tradition that Paul passes on (2 Thess. 3:6!), like the focus of faith itself, both reflects and is driven by this eschatology. In turn, this future focus of the gospel is the integrating center of Paul's missionary task. As such, the necessity of persevering in faith, both for himself and for his churches, is also the motivation for his missionary endeavors.

# Bibliography

Hafemann, Scott. "The Covenant Relationship." In *Central Themes in Biblical Theology: Mapping Unity in Diversity,* edited by Scott J. Hafemann and Paul R. House, 20-65. Grand Rapids: Baker, 2007.

———. "The (Un)Conditionality of Salvation: The Theological Logic of 2 Peter 1:8a-10a. In *Staying In*, edited by Charles H. Talbert and Jason A. Whitlark, 240-62. Grand Rapids: Eerdmans, 2011.

Nicholl, Colin. *From Hope to Despair in Thessalonica.* SNTSMS 126. Cambridge: Cambridge University Press, 2004.

Strandenæs, Thor. "Completing the Mission: Paul's Application of the Gospel to the Faith and Life of the Thessalonian Converts in 1 and 2 Thessalonians." *Swedish Missiological Themes* 98 (2010): 69–98.

Stuhlmacher, Peter. "Theologische Probleme des Römerbriefpräskripts." *EvTh* 27 (1967): 374–89.

# "The Obedience of Faith among the Nations": Old Testament Ethics in Covenantal and Missional Perspective

Christopher J.H. Wright

## Introduction

Paul's phrase "the obedience of faith ... among all the nations," with which he begins and ends his greatest theological exposition (Rom. 1:5 and 16:26 ESV), is covenantal (specifically Abrahamic) in origin, ethical in substance, and missional in direction. It is thus eminently suitable as a key text for the journey ahead of us.

Faith and obedience were the quintessential marks of Abraham in the scriptural tradition. Abraham was the recipient of the foundational canonical covenant. Obedience points to a fundamentally ethical dimension in the relationship established through that covenant which remains valid through both Testaments.

And the nations are the goal of God's mission from the day he promised that all nations would be blessed through Abraham to the day the redeemed humanity from all nations will gather before his throne (Rev. 7:9).

Covenant, ethics, and mission, then, combine in the text in which Paul expresses the whole purpose of his apostolic ministry.

Our somewhat more limited purpose in this chapter is to show how Old Testament ethics is integral to the major biblical covenants in such a way that the ethical element of those covenants is shaped by the same missional purpose, or universalizing thrust, inherent in them. In the process I trust we shall also see two things. First, that the ethical demand on those who are God's people is an integral part of their mission. That is, we are to live by God's standards for the sake of God's mission to the nations. And second, that this perspective also facilitates significant hermeneutical release of the potential of Old Testament ethics for application in the contemporary church and society.

To keep the topic manageable, I have chosen not to extend the discussion to include God's covenants with Noah and David, or the prophetic promises of a new covenant, but rather to concentrate on the Abrahamic and Mosaic covenants, and even then to limit myself to certain key texts within those traditions.[403]

## Abraham: Ethics and Mission in Relation to Covenantal Election

The initial and best-known form of God's covenant of election with Abraham is Genesis 12:1-3, in which God summons Abraham to "go" and to "be a blessing," and promises that through Abraham "shall all families of the earth be blessed" (KJV). With these words God launched the history of redemptive blessing in the world. I have offered some exegetical analysis of aspects of God's promise to Abraham elsewhere.[404] Our focus here is on how Genesis also stresses the response of Abraham—in faith and obedience. Abraham's faith is highlighted in Genesis 15:6 as the reason God counts him righteous. Abraham's obedience is highlighted in Genesis 22:16-18 as the reason why God will fulfill his promise to bless all nations.

However, the text I want to focus on in this section is Genesis 18:18-19. Here Abraham is presented by God as the model for the continuing education of his descendants from generation to generation. They too must walk in the way of the Lord in righteousness and justice, so that God can accomplish the missional purpose of Abraham's election. The Abrahamic covenant is thus an ethical agenda for God's people as well as a mission statement by God. And in this text both are given as part of the divine purpose in the election of Abraham in the first place.

"Abraham will indeed become a great and mighty nation, and all nations on earth will find blessing through him. For I have known (chosen) him for the purpose that he will teach his sons and his household after him so they will keep the way of YHWH by doing righteousness and justice, for the purpose that YHWH will bring about for Abraham what he has promised to him" (Gen. 18:18-19, my translation).

This little divine soliloquy comes in the middle of the narrative of God's judgment on Sodom and Gomorrah found in Genesis 18 and 19. So this self-reminder of God's universal promise of blessing is actually nested within the

---

[403] A survey of all the Old Testament covenantal formulations from the perspective of ethics and mission is found in my chapter, "Covenant: God's Mission through God's People," in *The God of Covenant: Biblical, Theological, and Contemporary Perspectives*, ed. Jamie A. Grant and Alistair I. Wilson (Leicester: Apollos, 2005), 54-78. It is also important to acknowledge that the essential content both of that chapter, and indeed of the present paper, can be found embedded in the larger arguments of my book, *The Mission of God: Unlocking the Bible's Grand Narrative* (Downers Grove and Nottingham: InterVarsity, 2006). A much broader exposition of my understanding of Old Testament ethics as a whole is to be found in Christopher J. H. Wright, *Old Testament Ethics for the People of God* (Leicester and Downers Grove: InterVarsity, 2004).

[404] Wright, *Mission of God*, ch. 6.

story of one particularly notorious instance of God's historical judgment. We need to pay attention first of all to that surrounding context, since, like the story of the tower of Babel, it both stands in stark contrast to God's words to Abraham, and also shows us the reason why those redemptive words were so necessary.

## Sodom: A Model of Our World

Sodom represents the way of the fallen world. It stands in Scripture as a proverbial prototype of human wickedness and of the judgment of God that ultimately falls upon evildoers. A survey of some texts that refer to Sodom will demonstrate this.

Starting in this chapter, we hear the "outcry" (*zaaqat*) that comes up to God from Sodom.

> Then the lord said, "The outcry against Sodom and Gomorrah is so great and their sin is so grievous that I will go down and see if what they have done is as bad as the outcry that has reached me" (Gen. 18:20-21).

*Zaaqat* is a technical word for the cry of pain, or the cry for help, from those who are being oppressed or violated.[405] It is the word used for the Israelites crying out under their slavery in Egypt. Psalmists use it when appealing to God to hear their cry against unjust treatment (e.g. Ps. 34:17). Most graphically of all, it is the scream for help by a woman being raped (Deut. 22:24, 27). As early as Genesis 13:13 we were told that the men of Sodom "were wicked and were sinning greatly against the Lord." Here that sin is identified as oppression, for that is what the word, "outcry," immediately indicates. Some people in or near Sodom were suffering to such an extent that they were crying out against its oppression and cruelty.

In Genesis 19 we read further of the hostile, perverted and violent sexual immorality that characterized "all the men from every part of the city of Sodom—both young and old" (19:4).

Isaiah portrays the Jerusalem of his own day in the colors of Sodom and Gomorrah, when condemning it for its bloodshed, corruption and injustice (Isa. 1:9-23). And he further portrays the future judgment of God against Babylon (another prototypical city) for its pride as a replay of God's destruction of Sodom and Gomorrah (Isa. 13:19-20).

Ezekiel even more caustically compares Judah unfavorably with Sodom, describing Sodom's sin as arrogance, affluence, and callousness to the needy.

---

[405] For a full and detailed discussion of this word, including its use in Psalms and prophets, see Richard Nelson Boyce, *The Cry to God in the Old Testament* (Atlanta: Scholars Press, 1988).

They were over-proud, over-fed, and under-concerned—a very modern-sounding list of accusations (Ezek. 16:48).

So, from the wider Old Testament witness, it is clear that Sodom was used as a paradigm—a model of human society at its worst, and of the inevitable and comprehensive judgment of God upon such wickedness. It was a place filled with oppression, cruelty, violence, perverted sexuality, idolatry, pride, and greedy consumption, while void of compassion or care for the needy.

Philip Esler suggests that this catalogue of the vice and evil that characterized Sodom shaped the Jewish mind in relation to sin and judgment and, as such, is reflected in Paul's portrayal of human wickedness in Romans 1:18-32. Though Paul does not name Sodom, his own list of human sin reflects all of the above items in the sin of Sodom.[406] When Paul spoke of his mission of apostleship to the nations, it was to nations that he saw typified in Sodom. To bring about "the obedience of faith" among a world of humanity that could be soberly described in those terms would have to be nothing short of the miraculous power of God's grace operating in the gospel. It still is.

## Abraham: A Model of God's Mission

Sodom, then, stands as a model of the world under judgment. Yet it was also part of the world that was the context of Abraham's calling and residence. Inasmuch as Sodom was in the land to which Abraham was commanded to go, it was, in a sense, the context of his mission. There is a certain irony in the biblical narrative that records Abraham being called out of the land of Babel, not into some heavenly paradise, but into the land of Sodom. Whatever else the story of redemption will be, it is not a story of escapism.

So it is in this context of the wickedness of Sodom, the investigation being conducted by God with his two angels, and the likelihood of divine judgment upon the cities of the plain, that the conversations of chapter 18 are set. God's soliloquy in verse 18 is a recapitulation of the original covenant promise. This is the missional goal that sheds light on God's renewed promise to Abraham and Sarah of a son in the first half of the chapter (vv. 10, 14). God, on his way to act in judgment on a particular evil society, stops to remind himself of his ultimate purpose of blessing to all nations. It is almost as if God cannot do the one (judgment) without setting it in the context of the other (redemption). The immediate particular necessity is investigation and judgment. The ultimate universal goal is (as it always was) blessing.

So then, God stops for a meal with Abraham and Sarah. He need not have done so, any more than, strictly speaking, he needed to "go down" to discover what was going on in Sodom (though the language is identical to his inspection of the tower of Babel). The reason was that God saw in this elderly couple

---

[406] Philip E. Esler, "The Sodom Tradition in Romans 1:18-32," *Biblical Theology Bulletin* 34 (2004): 4-16.

camped on the hills above the cities of the plain the key to his whole missional purpose for history and humanity. The story is a further reminder to us (just as it is presented as a reminder by God to himself, vv. 17-19), of the centrality of Abraham in the biblical theology of the mission of God.

## "The Way of the Lord": A Model for God's People

Returning to the key central verse, Genesis 18:19, we find its ethical agenda connected on the one side to Abraham's election and on the other side to God's mission. We need to examine first the specific ethical content of the phrases: "the way of the Lord," and "doing righteousness and justice" (ESV). Then we shall take note of the clear missional logic of the structure and theology of the verse.

### The Ethical Content.

Abraham was chosen to be a teacher, specifically a teacher of the way of the Lord, and a teacher of righteousness and justice. This ethical pedagogy will start with his children and then pass on to "his household after him," which presumes the transmission of the teaching down through the generations. Already Abraham is anticipating the role of Moses as teacher, which is another way of seeing the ethical continuity between the covenants. Two phrases summarize the content of the Abrahamic family curriculum.

"THE WAY OF THE LORD"

The expression "keeping the way of the Lord," or "walking in the way of the Lord," was a favorite metaphor used in the Old Testament to describe a particular aspect of Israel's ethics. A contrast is implied: that is, walking in YHWH's way, as distinct from the ways of other gods, or of other nations, or one's own way, or the way of sinners. Here, the contrast is clearly between the way of YHWH and the way of Sodom, which immediately follows. As a metaphor, "walking in the way of the Lord" seems to have two possible pictures in mind.

One is that of following someone else on a path, watching their footsteps, and following along carefully in the way they are going. In that sense, the metaphor suggests the imitation of God: you observe how God acts and try to follow suit. "O let me see thy footsteps and in them plant my own," as the hymn says about following Jesus. "By mirroring the divine activity the people would become a visible exemplar to the nations as to the nature and character of the God whom they worshipped (Deut. 4:5-8)." [407]

---

[407] Eryl W. Davies, "Walking in God's Ways: The Concept of *Imitatio Dei* in the Old Testament," in *In Search of True Wisdom: Essays in Old Testament Interpretation in Honour of Ronald E. Clements,* ed. Edward Ball, JSOTSup 300 (Sheffield: Sheffield Academic Press, 1999), 99-115 (103).

The other picture is of setting off on a path following the instructions that someone has given you to make sure you stay on the right path and do not wander off on wrong paths that may turn out to be dead-ends or dangerous. According to Cyril Rodd, it is this second image which fits much better with the use of the metaphor in the Old Testament, since the expression "walking in the way (or ways) of the Lord" is most commonly linked to obeying God's commands, not to imitating God himself. The way of the Lord, according to Rodd, is simply another expression signifying God's law or commands—his instruction kit for life's journey.[408] However, obedience to the law of God and reflection of the character of God are not mutually exclusive categories: the one is an expression of the other.

One of the clearest examples of this dynamic at work is Deuteronomy 10:12-19. It begins with a rhetorical flourish, rather like Micah 6:8, summarizing the whole law in a single chord of five notes: fear, walk, love, serve, and obey.

> And now, Israel, what does the Lord your God ask of you but to fear the Lord your God, to walk [in all his ways], to love him, to serve the Lord your God with all your heart and with all your soul, and to observe the Lord's commands and decrees that I am giving you this day for your own good?

And what are the ways of YHWH in which Israel is to walk? When the passage gets down to details, it specifies:

> [Yahweh] shows no partiality and accepts no bribes. He defends the cause of the fatherless and the widow, and loves the foreigner residing among you, giving them food and clothing. *And you are to love those who are aliens, for you yourselves were aliens in Egypt* (vv. 17-19, emphasis mine).

To walk in the way of the Lord, then, means doing for others what God wishes to have done for them, or more particularly, in Israel's case, doing for others what God had already done for Israel in delivering them and providing for them.

Returning, then, to our main text, Genesis 18:19, a first-time reader of this whole narrative will hear the phrase "the way of YHWH" as a strong contrast to the ways of Sodom and Gomorrah, whose wickedness is raising the outcry God plans to investigate. The more experienced reader familiar with the rest of the Old Testament Scriptures will hear the phrase as a summary of the whole rich panorama of Old Testament ethics modeled on the character and action of YHWH.

---

[408] Cyril Rodd provides a very helpful survey of the usage of the metaphor "walking with, after, or before" Yahweh or other gods, in *Glimpses of a Strange Land: Studies in Old Testament Ethics* (Edinburgh: T&T Clark, 2001), 330-33.

DOING RIGHTEOUSNESS AND JUSTICE

Here is pair of words that would also come very high on the list of Old Testament ethical vocabulary. Each of them individually, in various verbal, adjectival, and noun forms, occurs hundreds of times.[409] In the broadest terms (and recognizing that there is a great deal of overlap and interchangeability between the words), *mispat* is what needs to be done in a given situation if people and circumstances are to be restored to conformity with *sedaqah*. *Mispat* is a qualitative set of actions—something you do.[410] *Sedaqah* is a qualitative state of affairs—something you aim to achieve.

Here in Genesis 18:19 the two words are paired, as they frequently are, to form a comprehensive phrase. Found together like this as a couplet they form a hendiadys, that is, a single complex idea expressed through the use of two words.[411] Possibly the nearest English expression to the double-word phrase would be "social justice." Even that phrase, however, is somewhat too abstract for the dynamic nature of this pair of Hebrew words. For, as John Goldingay points out, the Hebrew words are concrete nouns, unlike the English abstract nouns used to translate them. That is, righteousness and justice are actions that you do, not merely concepts you reflect on or ideals you strive for.[412]

Abraham, then, was to set in motion a process of ethical instruction in the way of the Lord and the doing of righteousness and justice. According to this verse, this was part of the purpose of his election and of the covenant made with him. There was an ethical core to his role in God's mission.

And the ethical curriculum is clear about what comes top of the list. For the very first point that God draws to Abraham's attention is his concern about the suffering of the oppressed at the hands of these cities. In the careful account of the conversation, verses 17-19, are soliloquy, that is, God speaking to himself. At verse 20 God speaks again to Abraham, and the first word in what he says is *zaaqat*, cry for help. The trigger for God's investigation and subsequent action

---

[409] A very thorough study of both words is found in Hemchand Gossai, *Justice, Righteousness, and the Social Critique of the Eighth-Century Prophets*, American University Studies, Series VII Theology and Religion (New York: Peter Lang, 1993), 141: 55-56.

[410] "As it is frequently used in biblical texts justice is a call for action more than it is a principle of evaluation. Justice as an appeal for a response means *taking upon oneself the cause of those who are weak in their own defense* [cf. Isa. 58:6 Job.29:16; Jer. 21:12]." Stephen Charles Mott, *A Christian Perspective on Political Thought* (Oxford: Oxford University Press, 1993), 79 (italics his).

[411] Other examples of *hendiadys* in English include "law and order," "health and safety," "board and lodging." Each word in a *hendiadys* has its own distinct meaning, but when put together in a commonly used phrase, they express a single idea or set of circumstances.

[412] John Goldingay, "Justice and Salvation for Israel and Canaan," in *Reading the Hebrew Bible for a New Millennium: Form, Concept, and Theological Perspective*, ed. Wonil Kim et al (Harrisburg, PA: Trinity Press International, 2000), 169-87.

is not only the appalling sin of Sodom, but the protests and cries of their victims. This is an exact anticipation of what motivated God in the early chapters of Exodus. In fact, this incident in Genesis is highly programmatic in the way it defines God's character, actions, and requirements. The way of the Lord, which Abraham is about to witness and then to teach, is to do righteousness and justice for the oppressed and against the oppressor. In this too, Abraham is the forerunner of Moses, who learned the same lesson in the way of the Lord, turned it into intercession (again like Abraham), and taught it to Israel (Exod. 33:13, 19; 34:6-7), within a covenantal framework of faith and obedience.

### The Missional Logic

Returning again to our key text, we must also give attention to its grammatical structure and the logic expressed thereby. It is a compact statement in which syntax and theology are closely intertwined with powerful ethical and missional impact.

Genesis 18:19 falls into three clauses, joined by two expressions of purpose. It opens with God's affirmation of the election of Abraham:

"I have known him," which is frequently used for God choosing to bring a person or people into intimate relationship with himself. God then states the ethical purpose of his election: "for the purpose that[413] he will command/teach his children and household after him to keep the way of YHWH by doing righteousness and justice." This in turn is followed by another purpose clause referring to God's mission to bless the nations (which had just been mentioned in verse 18): "for the purpose that YHWH may bring about for Abraham what he has spoken/promised to him."

This one verse thus binds together election, ethics, and mission into a single syntactical and theological sequence located in the will, action, and desire of God. It is fundamentally a missional declaration, explaining election and incorporating ethics. It could plausibly be regarded as the key Old Testament text standing behind Paul's famous phrase.

What is most noteworthy, in relation to our topic, is the way ethics stands as the mid-term between election and mission, as the purpose of the former and the basis for the latter. That is to say, on the one hand, God's election of Abraham is intended to produce a community committed to ethical reflection of God's character. And on the other hand, God's mission of blessing the nations is predicated on such a community actually existing. The Abrahamic covenant, as we have said, is both ethical and missional, and Paul's phrase echoes this precisely. Paul's mission was to replicate among the nations communities of faith and obedience, elect in Abraham and committed to Abrahamic ethics.

---

[413] The expression of purpose is emphatic, since the clauses are not merely joined (as they might easily be in Hebrew) by the ubiquitous conjunction *wa*, but by the purposive conjunction, *lemaan*.

This further shows us how important it is to recognize the missional reason for the very existence of the Church as the people of God. We cannot speak biblically of the doctrine of election without insisting that it was never an end in itself, but a means to the greater end of the ingathering of the nations. Election must be seen as missiological, not merely soteriological. And in recognizing the missional nature of election, we must also include the ethical thrust of our verse. For the community God seeks for the sake of his mission is to be a community shaped by his own ethical character, with specific attention to righteousness and justice in a world filled with oppression and injustice. Only such a community can be a blessing to the nations.

According to Genesis 18:19, then, the ethical quality of life of the people of God is the vital link between their calling and their mission. God's intention to bless the nations is inseparable from God's ethical demand on the people he has created to be the agent of that blessing.

There is no biblical mission without biblical ethics.

Before leaving Abraham, we should also merely note how both Genesis 22:18 and 26:4-5 make this same link, connecting God's intention to bless the nations with Abraham's tested obedience—which the latter text articulates in primary ethical categories.

The profound and disturbing story of the testing of Abraham in Genesis 22 ends with a climactic and intensified confirmation of God's covenant with Abraham and his descendants, specifically endorsed on the basis of Abraham's obedience.

And he said,

By myself I have sworn, oracle of YHWH,
> *it is because of the fact that you have done this thing*
>> and have not kept back your son, your only one,
>>> that I will most surely bless you,
>>>> and I will most surely multiply your offspring [seed],
>>>>> like the stars in the heavens and like the sand on the seashore,
>>>>> and your offspring will possess the gate of your enemies.
>>>> And in your offspring all the nations of the world will find blessing,
> *on account of the fact that you obeyed me*
(Gen. 22:16-18, my translation and italics).

This makes quite explicit the relationship between God's promised intentions on the one hand and Abraham's faith and obedience on the other. It should hardly need to be said that this does not in any way mean that Abraham has merited God's covenant promises. We are not slipping into some caricature of "works righteousness" by making these observations on the biblical text itself. God had addressed Abraham "out of the blue," and prior to any action on Abraham's part. But Abraham's response of faith and obedience not only moves God to count him as righteous, but also enables God's promise to move forward towards its universal horizon.

Abraham by his obedience has not qualified to be the recipient of blessing, because the promise of blessing had been given to him already. Rather, the existing promise is reaffirmed but its terms of reference are altered. A promise which previously was grounded solely in the will and purpose of YHWH is transformed so that it is now grounded both in the will of YHWH and in the obedience of Abraham. It is not that the divine promise has become contingent upon Abraham's obedience, but that Abraham's obedience has been incorporated into the divine promise. Henceforth Israel owes its existence not just to YHWH but also to Abraham. Theologically this constitutes a profound understanding of the value of human obedience: It can be taken up by God and become a motivating factor in his purposes towards humanity.[414]

Paul and James between them capture both poles of Abraham's response to God. Paul focuses on the faith that led Abraham to believe in the promises of God, and that was thereby counted as righteousness (Rom. 4; Gal. 3:6-29). James focuses on the faith that led Abraham to obey the command of God, thus demonstrating in practice the genuineness of his faith (James 2:20-24). Hebrews captures both, by headlining Abraham's faith while substantiating it through his obedience (Heb. 11:8-19).

For ourselves, the important point to notice is the way God's intention to bless the nations is combined with human commitment to a quality of ethical obedience which enables us to be the agent of that blessing. The foundational good news of the Abrahamic covenant is that God's mission is ultimately to bless all the nations. The enduring challenge is that he planned to do that "through you and your descendants." The faith and obedience of Abraham therefore are not merely models for personal piety and ethics. They are also the essential credentials for effective participation in God's mission of bringing blessing to the nations. There is no blessing, for ourselves or for others, without faith and obedience. Those whom God calls to participate in his redemptive mission for the nations are those who both exercise saving faith like Abraham and demonstrate costly obedience like Abraham. So, on the one hand, the things God said to Abraham become the ultimate agenda for God's own mission (blessing the nations), and on the other hand, the things Abraham did in response become the proximate model for our mission (faith and obedience).

**Exodus: Ethics and Mission in Relation to Covenantal Redemption**

We turn from one major programmatic text to two others, Exodus 19:4-6 and Leviticus 19:

---

[414] R. W. L. Moberly, "Christ as the Key to Scripture: Genesis 22 Reconsidered," in *He Swore an Oath: Biblical Themes from Genesis 12–50*, ed. R. S. Hess et al (Carlisle: Paternoster; Grand Rapids: Baker, 1994), 161.

> You yourselves have seen what I have done to Egypt,
> and I carried you on wings of eagles and brought you to myself.
> Now then, if you really obey my voice and keep my covenant,
> you will be for me (*li*) a special personal possession
> among all the peoples;
> for to me (*li*) belongs the whole earth
> But you, you will be for me (*li*) a priestly kingdom and a holy nation
> (Exod. 19:4-6, my translation).

This text is like a hinge in the book of Exodus, in between the Exodus narrative and the giving of the Law and covenant and the making of the tabernacle. It defines Israel's identity and role in the historical context of God's past action on behalf of Israel on the one hand, and in the universal context of God's ownership of the whole earth on the other. It functions as a preamble to the promulgation of the Sinai covenant in the rest of Exodus and Leviticus, so that we must view all the specific details of that covenant from the perspective of this word of orientation. This is a crucial context-setting orientation to all that follows. And once again we find that ethics and mission are combined in a covenantal setting, but this time in the aftermath of God's great historical act of redemption.

### God's Redemptive Initiative

"You have seen what I have done..." This reminder points to the preceding 18 chapters of the book of Exodus, the great narrative of God's deliverance of the Israelites from slavery in Egypt. It was a matter of historical fact and recent memory. Only three months ago they had been suffering genocidal oppression. Now they were liberated. "And I did it," says God, "and carried you here to myself." Before anything is said about what Israel has to do, God points to what he has already done.

The initiative of God's redeeming grace is the prior reality on which all that follows will be founded—including the giving of the Law, the making of the covenant, the building of the tabernacle, and moving forward to the promised land. The life they now live, they live by the grace of God. The life they will be required to live must flow from the same starting point. Of course there is an ethical imperative in these verses: to obey God's voice and keep God's covenant. But it is expressed as a condition, not of gaining God's redemption (for that has already happened), but of fulfilling the mission in the world that their identity lays on them. Identity and obedience flow from grace.

Biblical ethics, then, must be seen as response to God's redeeming grace. Any other foundation leads to pride, legalism, or despair. This principle is as foundational to Old Testament ethics as to the New.

## God's Universal Ownership

"Out of all the nations..."; "The whole earth is mine." With these phrases at its core, our text avoids any narrow exclusivity in God's relationship with, or intentions for, Israel. On the contrary, it affirms the universality of God's ownership of the whole earth and interest in all nations. But in the same breath it affirms the particularity of Israel's unique identity as YHWH's treasured personal possession, as his priestly kingdom and holy nation.

The effect of this double affirmation is that Israel is going to live on a very open stage. There will be nothing cloistered or closeted about Israel's existence or history. For good or ill (as the narratives and prophets will show), Israel was visible to the nations, and in that posture they could be either a credit or a disgrace to YHWH their God. Here, however, at the start of that historical journey in the midst of the nations, God's desire is that they should live consistently with their status as his treasured possession, in priestly and holy conduct.

Biblical ethics, then, from this text, cannot be a matter of the cozy esoteric behavior of a cloistered in-group accountable only to itself. The life of God's people is always turned outwards to the watching nations, as priests are always turned towards their people as well as towards God. Part of the mission of God towards the world that universally belongs to him is the task of shaping the life of his own particular people in the midst of that world. Once again we observe the connection between ethics and mission. Israel's calling to be holy is not set over against the nations and the whole earth, but in the context of living among them for God's sake as God's representatives.

## Israel's Identity and Responsibility

"You will be for me a priestly kingdom and a holy nation."

PRIESTLY

To understand what it meant for Israel as a whole to be called God's priesthood in relation to the nations, we have to understand what Israel's priests were in relation to the rest of the people. Priests stood in the middle between God and the rest of the people. In that intermediate position, priests then had a twofold task:

1. Teaching the Law (Lev. 10:11; Deut. 33:10; Jer. 18:18; Mal. 2:6f.; Hosea 4:1-9). Through the priests, God would be known to the people. This was a major duty of Old Testament priests, the neglect of which led to moral and social decay and the prophetic anger reflected in the words of Hosea and Malachi above.

2. Handling the sacrifices (Lev. 1–7, etc.). Through the priests and their work of atonement, the people could come to God. The priests did the actions with the blood at the altar and made the declaration of atonement to the worshipper.

The priesthood was thus a two-directional representational, or mediatory, task between God and the rest of the Israelites, bringing the knowledge of God to the people and bringing the sacrifices of the people to God. In addition to these twin tasks, it was of course a prime privilege and responsibility of the priests to bless the people in the name of YHWH (Num. 6:22-27)

It is thus richly significant that God confers on Israel as a whole people the role of being his priesthood in the midst of the nations. As the people of YHWH they would constitute his historical vehicle of bringing the knowledge of God to the nations, and bringing the nations to the means of atonement with God. The Abrahamic task of being a means of blessing to the nations also put them in the role of priests in the midst of the nations. Just as it was the role of the priests to bless the Israelites, so it would be the role of Israel as a whole ultimately to be a blessing to the nations. The priesthood of the people of God is thus a missional function which stands in continuity with their Abrahamic election and impacts the nations. Just as Israel's priests were called and chosen to be the servants of God and his people, so Israel as a whole is called and chosen to be the servant of God and all peoples.

It seems that the apostle Paul was conscious of this priestly aspect of the mission of Israel when he appropriated it for himself, on the only occasion when any New Testament writer speaks of individual ministry in priestly terms (otherwise the New Testament uses priesthood language either of Jesus, or collectively of the whole Church, as in 1 Peter 2:9). Paul speaks of "the grace God gave me to be a minister of Christ Jesus to the Gentiles ... [with] the priestly duty of proclaiming the gospel of God, so that the Gentiles might become an offering acceptable to God, sanctified by the Holy Spirit" (Rom. 15:15-16).

Paul's evangelistic mission among the Gentiles had indeed been the priestly task of bringing God the nations and bringing the nations to God. And this missional self-awareness stands very close to the text that stands in our title. For such priestly duty would undoubtedly have also implied holiness, or as Paul put it, bringing the nations to "the obedience of faith." So we turn to that second word in the key phrases of Exodus 19:6.

HOLY

This priestly role required holiness of Israel in the midst of the nations, just as it required holiness of their own priests in the midst of the ordinary people of Israel. Holiness, however, is one of those words (like priesthood) that have connotations in the popular religious mind that are not always in tune with its biblical meaning.

Being holy did not mean that the Israelites were to be a specially religious nation. A fundamental part of the meaning of the word holy is "different or distinctive." Something or someone is holy when set apart for a distinct purpose and kept separate for that purpose. For Israel, it meant being different by reflecting the very different God that YHWH revealed himself to be, compared with other gods.

> "You must not do as they do in Egypt, where you used to live, and you must not do as they do in the land of Canaan, where I am bringing you. Do not follow their practices. You must obey my laws and be careful to follow my decrees. I am the Lord your God" (Lev. 18:3-4). "Be holy because I, the LORD your God, am holy" (Lev. 19:2).

Israel was to be as different from other nations as YHWH was different from other gods.[415] Israel was to be "YHWH-like," rather than like the nations. They were to do as YHWH did, not as the nations did. Holiness for Israel was a practical, down-to-earth reflection of the transcendent holiness of YHWH himself.

While there certainly were ritual and symbolic expressions of Israel's holiness, in practical terms holiness had a strongly ethical dimension. Being holy meant living lives of integrity, justice and compassion in every area, including personal, family, social, economic and national life—in other words, living as the covenant community, in covenant relationship with the holy One of Israel, with covenant standards of social and personal behavior.

The most comprehensive single text that articulates the ethical dimension of holiness in Israel is Leviticus 19. The bulk of the chapter shows us that the kind of holiness that reflects God's own holiness is thoroughly practical, social, and very down-to-earth. Simply listing its contents highlights this dominant note. Holiness in Leviticus 19 involves:

- Respect within the family and community (3a, 32)
- Exclusive loyalty to YHWH as God; proper treatment of sacrifices (4, 5-8)
- Economic generosity in agriculture (9-10)
- Observing the commandments regarding social relationships (11-12)
- Economic justice in employment rights (13)
- Social compassion to the disabled (14)
- Judicial integrity in the legal system (12, 15)
- Neighborly attitudes and behavior; loving one's neighbor as oneself (16-18)
- Preserving the symbolic tokens of religious distinctiveness (19)
- Sexual integrity (20-22, 29)
- Rejection of practices connected with idolatrous or occult religion (26-31)
- No ill treatment of ethnic minorities, but rather racial equality before the law and practical love for the alien as for oneself (33-34)
- Commercial honesty in all trading transactions (35-36)

---

[415] Cf. the extensive survey of this theme, Peter Machinist, "The Question of Distinctiveness in Ancient Israel," in *Essential Papers on Israel and the Ancient Near East*, ed. F. E. Greenspan (New York and London: New York University Press, 1991), 420-42.

A glance at any cross-reference Bible will further show that the laws of Leviticus 19 are rich in parallels in Exodus and Deuteronomy. The chapter stands at the ethical heart of the Sinai covenant, and multiple links could be made to almost every aspect of Old Testament ethics.

In all of these ways, then—that is to say, in all the ways of down-to-earth practical social ethics—Israel was to respond to their redemption by reflecting their Redeemer. In doing so they would not only prove their own distinctiveness from the nations, but also make visible YHWH's difference from the gods of the nations. And making God known and visible to the nations was part of their very reason for existence, their mission. If Israel were to be God's priesthood in the midst of the nations, then they had to be ethically different from the nations.

From God's covenant with Abraham we know that the chief agent of God's mission is the people of God.

From the covenant anticipated in Exodus 19 and given the ethical content in Leviticus 19, we know that the chief requirement on God's people if they are to fulfill that mission is that they should be what they are: the holy people of the holy God.

In short, Israel's identity (to be a priestly kingdom) declares a mission; and Israel's mission demands an ethic (to be a holy nation).

## Deuteronomy: Ethics and Mission in Relation to Covenantal Community

So far we have seen, from Genesis, that the ethical response God required of his people was a core element in the covenant of election with Abraham; indeed, it was integral to the very purpose of election. Furthermore, that ethical intentionality of election was also directed towards God's mission, through Abraham, to extend God's blessing to the nations. Then we saw in Exodus and Leviticus that when the covenant with Abraham was renewed in relation to the whole nation of his descendants, the children of Israel at Sinai, it was presented as the essential response of the people to God's grace in the great act of historical redemption—the Exodus. Once again we saw that the same ethical demand on Israel and universal perspective towards the nations are both in view, this time seen through the twin lenses of Israel as a priestly and holy people in the midst of the nations.

In Deuteronomy we are still very much within the orbit of the Sinai covenant, but the gaze of the reader (as of the addressed Israelites) is towards the next phase of Israel's canonical journey: settlement in the land. There Israel would be summoned to live as a covenantal community, demonstrating covenantal loyalty to their one true living God, YHWH, and living in ethical obedience to his covenant law.

In view of this primary concentration on the nature of Israel's society, Deuteronomy is commonly perceived as a rather exclusivist and nationalistic document, uninterested in the wider purposes of God for the nations. In my view this is an unfortunate misconception.[416] In this section of our chapter we look at just one text which binds ethics, mission, and covenant together, in a chapter that has programmatic significance.

## The Nations in Deuteronomy 4

Deuteronomy 4:1-40 is a microcosm of Deuteronomy as a whole. It is an urgent call to covenant loyalty through exclusive worship of YHWH alone. This exclusive loyalty is in turn based on the unique history of God's redeeming and revealing activity through the Exodus and at Sinai, and worked out in practical ethical obedience to his laws in the land of promise, with a view to the impact this will have on the nations. In this framework the substantive call in the central portion of the chapter is that Israel must avoid idolatry. But this religious exclusivism must be seen within the wider vision of the framework (especially vv. 6-8 and 32-40) where Israel's role in relation to the nations and as witnesses to the uniqueness and universality of YHWH are emphasized.

In this rhetorically exalted articulation of the nature and demands of the covenant, the nations make their appearance no less than five times, and in very different modes.

The nations will observe the wisdom and understanding of Israel, providing Israel preserves the presence of God and the practice of justice (6-8).

The nations have been assigned the heavenly bodies (for whatever purpose),[417] but Israel is not to engage in any worship of such created things, but to worship only YHWH who delivered them from bondage for that purpose (19-20). The point of the reference is not so much on what God has allowed the nations, as what he demands of Israel in distinction from the nations.

The nations will be the location for the scattering of Israel in judgment, if Israel abandons YHWH for other gods (27). There is some irony in the language here: In verse 38 God promises to drive the nations out before Israel. But Israel faces the threat, if they turn apostate, of having God drive them out among the nations.

The nations have never experienced what Israel had recently experienced as the foundation of their unique covenant knowledge of YHWH, namely his revelation at Sinai and his redemption from Egypt (32-34). Once again, the

---

[416] In *Mission of God* (particularly in ch. 7), I explore a number of texts in Deuteronomy and the Deuteronomic History which express the universality of YHWH and of the significance of Israel in relation to that wider purpose.

[417] It is worth noting that Deuteronomy 4:19 does not say that God assigned the heavenly bodies to the nations *for them to worship.* That is a (possibly incorrect) inference from the immediately following words telling Israel *not* to worship them. The text (which is admittedly difficult) could mean no more than that God created the heavenly bodies for the benefit of the whole human race (according to the account in Genesis 1), and if the other nations turn them into objects of worship, that is not something Israel is to imitate.

emphasis is on the uniqueness and distinctiveness of Israel—this time in their knowledge of God (vv. 35, 39).

The nations will be driven out before Israel in the giving of the land of Canaan, as promised to Abraham (38).

Within this framework of "Israel among the nations," we focus particularly on verses 6-8.

### The Visibility of Israel's Society (Deut. 4:6-8)

> Observe [these laws] carefully, for this will show your wisdom and understanding to the nations, who will hear about all these decrees and say, "Surely this great nation is a wise and understanding people." What other great nation has their gods near them the way the Lord our God is near us whenever we pray to him? And what other great nation has such righteous decrees and laws as this body of laws I am setting before you today? (Deut. 4:6-8 my translation).

Verses 6-8 set Israel's obedience to God's law in the land within the context of the nations. The nations would observe and comment on the "greatness" of Israel (a paradox, since they were actually a very small people, as Deuteronomy 7:7 more truthfully if less tactfully points out). Three points may be made from these verses relevant to our theme.[418]

#### VISIBILITY ASSUMED

Obedience to the law was not for Israel's benefit alone. It is a marked feature of the Old Testament that Israel lived on a very public stage. All that happened in her history was open to the comment and reaction of the nations at large. Apart from being in any case inevitable, given the fluid international scene of the Ancient Near East, this visibility of Israel was part of its theological identity and role as the priesthood of YHWH among the nations. It could be either positive, as here, when the nations are impressed with the wisdom of Israel's Law (cf. 28:10); or negative, as when the nations are shocked by the severity of Israel's judgment when they abandon the ways of their God (28:37, 29:22-28). Either way, faithful or unfaithful, the people of God are an open book to the world, and the world asks questions and draws conclusions.

The nations will notice and take an interest in the phenomenon of Israel as a society, with all the social, economic, legal, political, and religious dimensions of the Torah. And that social system will lead the nations to the conclusion that Israel as a people qualifies as a "great nation,"[419] to be applauded as "wise and understanding."

---

[418] In addition to my discussion of this text in *Mission of God*; see also Christopher J. H. Wright, *Deuteronomy, New International Biblical Commentary Old Testament* (Peabody, MA: Hendrickson; Carlisle: Paternoster, 1996).

[419] As my own translation of Deuteronomy 4:6-8 above shows, the claim of the text is not that there is no other nation *greater* than Israel, as is implied in the NIV

But with two rhetorical questions, Moses goes on to sharpen the point by emphasizing the foundation of Israel's national greatness as defined. First (4:7), it is based on the nearness of God to his people. Second (v. 8), it is based on the righteousness of the Torah. Israel would have an intimacy with God and a quality of social justice that no other nation could match. These would be the factors that would lie behind the external reputation. As far as the nations could see, the thing that was different about Israel was simply a matter of wisdom and understanding. The inner reality was the presence of God and the justice of God's Torah. And both of these, of course, were covenantal realities. The nations could not "see" the covenant in itself. But they could certainly be expected to see its embodiment in the worship and justice of Israel as a community.

COMPARISON INVITED

The force of the rhetorical questions was to invite comparison, but in the confident expectation that nothing would invalidate the claims being made. The claim for Israel's social uniqueness was being made on a crowded stage, with plenty of other claimants for admirable systems of law. Israel itself knew of the ancient and acclaimed legal traditions of Mesopotamia; as a matter of fact, Israel's own legal traditions intersect with them at many points. Yet this claim for Old Testament law is advanced, quite possibly with deliberate polemical intent, since the law code of Hammurabi, for example, also claimed a divine quality of social righteousness.[420]

Old Testament law explicitly invites—even welcomes—public inspection and comparison. But the expected result of such comparison is that Israel's law will be found superior in wisdom and justice. This is a monumental claim. It grants to the nations and to the readers of this text, including ourselves, the liberty to analyze Old Testament law in comparison with other social systems, ancient and modern, and to evaluate its claim. And indeed, the humaneness and justice of Israel's overall social and legal system have been favorably commented on by many scholars who have done the most meticulous studies of comparative ancient law, and its social relevance can still be profitably mined today.

---

translation ("what other nation is so great as to have…"). Rather, the text assumes that Israel *is* a great nation, but then *defines* that greatness in surprising terms: not military might, nor geographical or numerical size, but the nearness of the living God in prayer and the social justice of their constitution and laws.

[420] On the claims of other Ancient Near Eastern law codes, see, for example, Moshe Weinfeld, *Social Justice in Ancient Israel and in the Ancient Near East* (Jerusalem: Magnes; Minneapolis: Fortress, 1995).

## MOTIVATION APPLIED

From the point of view of our concern for mission and ethics, these verses articulate a motivation for obedience to the Law that is easily overlooked but highly significant. The point is that if Israel would live as God intended, then the nations would notice. But Israel existed in any case for the ultimate purpose of being the vehicle of God's blessing of the nations. That was the reason for their election. That was in their "genetic code" from the very loins of Abraham. Here we find that at least one aspect of that blessing of the nations would be by providing such a model of social justice that the nations would observe and ask questions. The missional challenge, therefore, as we have seen in other texts above, is that the ethical quality of life of the people of God (their obedience to the law, in this context) is a vital factor in the attraction of the nations to the living God—even if only at first out of curiosity.

The motivation for God's people to live by God's law is ultimately to bless the nations. After all, what would the nations actually see? The nearness of God is by definition invisible. What, then, would be visible? Only the practical evidence of the kind of society that was built on God's righteous laws.[421] There is a vital link between the invisible religious claims of the people of God (that God is near them when they pray) and their very visible practical social ethic. The world will be interested in the first only when it sees the second. Or, conversely, the world will see no reason to pay any attention to our claims about our invisible God, however much we boast of his alleged nearness to us in prayer, if it sees no difference between the lives of those who make such claims and those who don't.

A very strong echo of the thought of this passage is found in the record of Solomon's prayer of dedication of the temple in 1 Kings 8. The missional hope expressed in the prayer that God would respond even to the prayers of the foreigner, in order that "all the peoples of the earth may know your name and fear you" (v. 43), is turned into a missional challenge to the people that they must be as committed to God's law as God is committed to such a worldwide goal. The Deuteronomic historian clearly endorses the ethical and missional logic of his foundational text.

> May [the Lord] uphold the cause of his servant and the cause of his people Israel according to each day's need, so that all the peoples of the earth may know that the Lord is God and that there is no other. And may your hearts be fully committed to the Lord our God, to live by his decrees and obey his commands, as at this time (1 Kings. 8:59–61).

---

[421] For further reflection on the strongly social ethical aspects of the covenant and their relevance to contemporary issues that are strongly taken up within liberation theology, see Christopher J. Baker, *Covenant and Liberation: Giving New Heart to God's Endangered Family*, European University Studies, Series 23, Theology (Frankfurt: Peter Lang, 1991), 411: especially ch. 13.

Thinking of our title text from the apostle Paul, one might say that the Deuteronomic historian has Solomon envisaging the nations coming to faith, but only as Israel lives in obedience.

## Conclusion

We have reached the end of the trajectory of Old Testament texts that seemed fitting to our purpose. I trust it has been apparent that, within the Old Testament context itself, the ethical demand of God upon his people Israel was integral to the covenant relationship between them, and also that this ethical dimension of the covenant was also integral to the wider, universal purpose of God for ultimately blessing the nations. There is not enough space here to argue in detail for the hermeneutical assumption that I defend elsewhere, that comparable ethical and missional demands fall upon us, as Christian readers of these texts who are committed to accepting their authority as Scripture in the same way that the New Testament does, and as those who live within the new covenant of God's redeeming grace through Christ. Nor does space permit an outline of the hermeneutical principles through which I believe such ethical and missional relevance can be perceived and applied today. I hope at least to have laid some biblical foundations for such assumptions and principles.

However, I cannot finish without a brief glance at two other texts, in which I think we see reflections of Paul's great phrase: "the obedience of faith among the nations."

### *1 Peter 2:9-12*

There are obvious quotations of Exodus 19:6 in 1 Peter 2:9, but it would seem almost certain that Peter's phraseology in 1 Peter 2:12 is also a conscious echo of the teaching he once heard from the lips of Jesus. "You," Jesus had said to his rough band of doubtless astonished disciples, "you are the light of the world... Let your light shine before men, that they may see your good deeds and glorify your Father in heaven" (Matt. 5:14-16).

The imagery of light chosen by Jesus undoubtedly echoes the task given by YHWH to Israel that they were to be "a light to the nations." Just as Israel should have let its light shine as an attraction to the nations (whether the ethical light of Isa. 58:6-10, or the light of God's presence in their midst, Isa. 60:1-3), so the disciples of Jesus must let the light of good works shine in such a way that people will come to glorify the living God. The missional purpose of Jesus' ethical teaching is clear, and Peter obviously took it to heart.

### *Matthew 28:18-20*

The famous ending of Matthew's Gospel, the so-called Great Commission, is equally covenantal in flavor, since it echoes Deuteronomy so strongly. Jesus assumes the position of the Lord God himself—whose authority in heaven and on earth has now been given to him. On that foundation, he commissions his own disciples to go out and replicate themselves by creating communities of faith and obedience among the nations. They are to teach, and the nations are to learn, what it means to "observe all that I have commanded you"—a piece of pure Deuteronomy. Thus, mission is self-replicating discipleship, entered by faith and baptism, expressed in ethical obedience, and passed on through apostolic teaching.

## Bibliography

Boyce, Richard Nelson. *The Cry to God in the Old Testament.* Atlanta: Scholars Press, 1988.

Davies, Eryl W. "Walking in God's Ways: The Concept of *Imitatio Dei* in the Old Testament." In *In Search of True Wisdom: Essays in Old Testament Interpretation in Honour of Ronald E. Clements,* edited by Edward Ball, JSOTSup 300, 99-115. Sheffield: Sheffield Academic Press, 1999.

Esler, Philip E. "The Sodom Tradition in Romans 1:18-32." *Biblical Theology Bulletin* 34 (2004): 4-16.

Goldingay, John. "Justice and Salvation for Israel and Canaan." In *Reading the Hebrew Bible for a New Millennium: Form, Concept, and Theological Perspective,* edited by Wonil Kim, et al, 169-87. Harrisburg: Trinity Press International, 2000.

Gossai, Hemchand. *Justice, Righteousness, and the Social Critique of the Eighth-Century Prophets.* New York: Peter Lang, 1993.

Machinist, Peter. "The Question of Distinctiveness in Ancient Israel." In *Essential Papers on Israel and the Ancient Near East,* edited by F. E. Greenspan, 420-42. New York: New York University Press, 1991.

Mott, Stephen Charles. *A Christian Perspective on Political Thought.* Oxford: Oxford University Press, 1993.

Moberly, R. W. L. "Christ as the Key to Scripture: Genesis 22 Reconsidered." In *He Swore an Oath: Biblical Themes from Genesis 12–50,* edited by R. S. Hess, et al, 161. Carlisle: Paternoster; Grand Rapids: Baker, 1994.

Rodd, Cyril. *Glimpses of a Strange Land: Studies in Old Testament Ethics.* Edinburgh: T&T Clark, 2001.

Wright, Christopher J. H. *Old Testament Ethics for the People of God.* Downers Grove: InterVarsity, 2004.

_____. "Covenant: God's Mission through God's People." In *The God of Covenant: Biblical, Theological, and Contemporary Perspectives*, edited by Jamie A. Grant and Alistair I. Wilson. Leicester: Apollos, 2005.

_____. *The Mission of God: Unlocking the Bible's Grand Narrative*. Downers Grove: InterVarsity, 2006.

# Evangelicals and Structural Injustice: Why Don't They Understand It and What Can Be Done?

Ronald J. Sider

According to Chris Smith in his important book, *American Evangelicalism*,[422] white American evangelicals care about the poor; in fact, they give money to help the poor and volunteer for local community organizations at least as frequently if not more frequently than Catholics, mainline Protestants, and liberal Christians.[423] Furthermore, they vote in elections just as often as mainline Christians and more often than liberals and Catholics.[424]

At the same time, they have what Chris Smith calls a "personal influence strategy" for social change: "[White] American evangelicals are resolutely committed to a social-change strategy which maintains that the only truly effective way to change the world is one-individual-at-a-time."[425] White evangelicals see themselves "as uniquely possessing a distinctively effective means of social change: working through personal relationships to allow God to transform human hearts from the inside-out so that all ensuing social change will be thorough and long-lasting."[426]

In his research, Smith found that even the political engagement of evangelicals reflected this individualistic approach. "The primary evangelical strategy for political reform articulated [in their interviews] was to elect good Christians to political office,"[427] not promote structural change such as campaign finance reform or alternative electoral approaches such as proportional representation.

In *Divided by Faith*, published two years later by Oxford University Press, Smith and his colleagues found the same thing in evangelical understanding of racial inequality. They used data from the General Social Survey to compare the different explanations of evangelicals and others for the fact that "on

---

[422] Christian Smith, *American Evangelicalism: Embattled and Thriving* (Chicago: University of Chicago Press, 1998).
[423] Smith, *American Evangelicalism*, 38, 41.
[424] Smith, *American Evangelicalism*, 41.
[425] Smith, *American Evangelicalism*, 187.
[426] Smith, *American Evangelicalism*, 188.
[427] Smith, *American Evangelicalism*, 193.

average blacks have worse jobs, income, and housing than white people." Respondents had to choose between four possible explanations:

- Because most blacks have less inborn ability to learn?
- Because most blacks just don't have the motivation or will-power to pull themselves up out of poverty?
- Because most blacks don't have the chance for education …?
- Mainly due to discrimination?[428]

Clearly the first two explanations (inability and lack of motivation) are personal and the last two (lack of education and discrimination) are structural.

In their responses, white conservative Protestants (a combined group of self-identified evangelicals and fundamentalists) put substantially more weight on the personal than the structural explanations. Almost two-thirds of white conservative Protestants but only one-half of other white Americans say black Americans are poor because they lack motivation. On the other hand, white conservative Protestants were less likely to point to lack of access to quality education or discrimination than other white Americans: only one-third of white conservative Protestants pointed to lack of access to education vs. almost one-half of other white Protestants. And only one-fourth (vs. over one-third) pointed to discrimination as a cause.[429]

Obviously, we need a great deal more sophisticated sociological analysis before we will know with any precision the full extent of this individualistic, one-person-at-a-time approach to solving societal problems. But we already have enough evidence to say with considerable certainty that white evangelicals have a one-sided, individualistic approach to societal transformation that does not understand the importance of structures and the reality of systemic evil. As a result, among other things, evangelicals still are more likely in their response to global poverty to respond to immediate disasters and also to the need for community development than they are to engage in changing economic structures to reduce poverty.

Why is this the case? Again, we need a great deal of sophisticated study before we have solid answers to that question. But I want to venture some initial ideas—all with the clear understanding both that I offer only the most modest beginnings of an answer, and also that there are many overlapping causal factors.

First, it may be that the fact that evangelicals frequently witness or hear about dramatic conversions that truly change broken people into transformed persons contributing to society leads evangelicals to emphasize the importance of personal conversion in a one-sided way. (Please note: I think personal

---

[428] Michael O. Emerson and Christian Smith, *Divided by Faith: Evangelical Religion and the Problem of Race in America* (New York: Oxford University Press, 2000), 94-95.

[429] Emerson and Smith, *Divided by Faith*, 96.

conversion is one important factor in societal transformation, but it needs to be accompanied by structural change.) Smith borrows the phrase the "miracle-motif" from Woodbridge, Noll, and Hatch to talk about this one-sidedly individualistic emphasis on conversion.[430] In this view, social problems would disappear if everyone were converted to personal faith in Christ. The solution to great economic inequality is "not a more equitable restructuring of income distribution, but for rich people to come to Christ and then practice voluntary generosity."[431]

Second, there is a very long history of individualism in evangelical thought and practice. It runs through the Protestant Reformation, Puritanism, the Free Church tradition, revivalism, pietism, and fundamentalism. Lacking Catholicism's emphasis on the community and the common good, evangelicals historically have been highly individualistic in their understanding of the Church, conversion, indeed, almost every aspect of Christian faith.

Third, the pioneering spirit of the American frontier where the strong-willed, daring individual was the hero certainly shaped American evangelicalism as 19th-century Baptist, Methodist, and other churches swept west across the continent along with the settlers. If the individual has the proper courage and persistence, one can solve one's own problems without governmental help.

Fourth, we ought at least to ask whether a certain kind of dispensational theology may contribute to evangelicalism's hyper-individualism. For those dispensationalists who link the anti-Christ with a powerful one-world government, every form of structural analysis of societal problems that would lead to structural changes implemented by government may lead to a fear that any substantial governmental intervention to solve social problems is just one step down a slippery slope toward the anti-Christ and one-world government.

Fifth, there is some evidence that political conservatism is linked to and is a strong predictor of individualistic explanations of economic equality between blacks and whites. In an article in the *Journal of the Scientific Study of Religion*, Hinojosa and Park show that those who are politically conservative are more likely to explain this inequality in terms of lack of motivation rather than lack of access to education and discrimination.[432] The fact that a majority of white evangelicals for several decades have been closely linked to political conservatives probably has contributed to their failure to understand the structural causes of poverty.

Sixth, I suspect that the fact that a Platonic spiritualism that emphasizes the soul over the body has exerted a powerful influence in the evangelical world has also contributed to our problem. Historically, evangelicals have talked

---

[430] Smith, *American Evangelicalism*, 190.
[431] Smith, *American Evangelicalism*, 192.
[432] Victor J. Hinojosa and Jerry Z. Park, "Religion and the Paradox of Racial Inequality Attitudes," *Journal of the Scientific Study of Religion* 43, no. 2 (2004): 229-38.

about "saving souls," not saving the whole person the way Jesus did. If what really matters is the soul, then thinking about the way socioeconomic, material structures, and institutions shape people is hardly important.

Seventh, and closely related to the last point, evangelicals have largely defined the gospel as the forgiveness of sins. Salvation means primarily asking God for forgiveness so that one can go to heaven when we die. I often say: if that is all the gospel is, then it is a one-way ticket to heaven and we can live like hell until we get there. Defining the gospel primarily as forgiveness of sins rather than, with Jesus, the gospel of the Kingdom, greatly heightens both the individualistic emphasis and the preoccupation with the soul in a Platonic sense.[433]

Finally, the fact that evangelical theology has been weak at a number of points where a more fully biblical perspective would have corrected our hyper-individualism is also surely a significant factor. Many evangelicals have a dreadfully weak doctrine of creation; an almost non-existent understanding of either the prophets' or the New Testament's understanding of social sin;[434] and a weak grasp of the Church as community.[435]

As you can see, I have only hinted at a number of issues that need much more exploration. We need several doctoral dissertations in sociology, Christian ethics, and theology to explore this in depth.

Before moving to a discussion of how we can begin to correct the problem, I want to note two things about the attitude of evangelicals toward government. My first comment is that I do not think the failure of evangelicals to understand structural injustice and their widespread tendency to be suspicious of governmental intervention in society are identical issues. But they are clearly very closely linked. A clear grasp of structural injustice certainly strengthens the likelihood that one will favor some substantial governmental action to modify unjust systems. And a strong libertarian orientation will strengthen one's inclination to point to the individual rather than structural causes and solutions.

Second, I am not convinced that the widespread evangelical suspicion of governmental intervention is rooted in substantial theological convictions rather than more accidental historical factors. Certainly the insistence on limited government is rooted in crucial theological convictions (about the danger of unchecked power in a fallen world, for example) but that does not in any way lead to a near libertarian view of government.[436] We need a lot more careful

---

[433] See my *Good News and Good Works* (Grand Rapids: Baker, 1999), Chapters 3, 4, especially pp. 76-79.

[434] See my *Rich Christians in an Age of Hunger*, 5th ed (Nashville: Thomas Nelson, 2005), Chapter 6.

[435] See my *Scandal of the Evangelical Conscience* (Grand Rapids: Baker Books, 2005), Chapter 4.

[436] See my *Scandal of Evangelical Politics* (Grand Rapids: Baker, 2008), Chapter 4, especially pp. 88-91.

study (both historical and systematic), but I will, until proven wrong, continue to argue that fundamental evangelical theological convictions are not only fully compatible with, but even demand, a substantial albeit limited role for government in the search for economic and social justice.

So how can we correct the problem?

The most obvious place to start is to seek a more biblically balanced theological framework that would correct the excessive individualism that shapes and supports the failure to grasp structural injustice. Several items would be important.

The first would be a deeper understanding and wider embrace of the biblical teaching on social sin or structural injustice. Since the first edition of my *Rich Christians in an Age of Hunger*, I have been writing about this biblical theme. The last two editions devote a full chapter to this topic. I won't repeat that material here. But I think it is very important to see that the prophets clearly understand that sin is both personal and social and that they insist that unjust legal and economic structures displease God. In the New Testament, both the word *cosmos* (usually it means "the structures of the world organized against God's designs") and the category of the principalities and powers (which refers both to fallen angelic beings and the distorted socioeconomic-cultural structures of this world which they help to shape) contain a clear social ethic and an understanding of structural injustice.

Second, evangelicals need a much deeper doctrine of creation. Humanity's creation in the image of the triune God who is a community of persons, and our creation as male and female who need each other to be fulfilled, both underline the fact that persons are made for community. We are not, as John Locke seems to have imagined, primarily isolated individuals. Designed for community, we find fulfillment only in social relationships that require wholesome structures.

Third, the biblical vision of salvation is not that of isolated individuals enjoying a personal relationship with God, but rather of communities of persons worshiping God and embracing God's design for their common life. That is not to deny in any way that individuals must come to a personal faith in Christ. But it is to insist that at the heart of God's plan of salvation in both testaments is a new people living out a new set of redeemed socioeconomic relationships that reflect God's intention for persons in community. Those who come to faith in Christ become part of Christ's one body which is a new communal reality. It is impossible to embrace the New Testament understanding of salvation and have it only affect one's personal relationship with God; it must also transform one's socioeconomic relationships with other sisters and brothers in the body of Christ as one submits to the other brothers and sisters in mutual accountability. A more biblical understanding of salvation and the Church would go a long way to correcting the excessive individualism of typical American evangelicalism.

Here, I have only hinted at the kind of extensive biblical/theological inquiry that would make evangelical thinking both more biblical and less individualistic. Again, we need a number of sophisticated dissertations and books.

Finally, a comment on the social sciences in general and sociology in particular. I am certain that it was no accident that one of the earliest major pleas for evangelicals to return to their 19th-century embrace of social justice came from evangelical sociologist David Moberg with his important book, *Inasmuch: Christian Social Responsibility in Twentieth Century America* (1965).[437] I have not seen studies, and I do not know how strong the departments of sociology are in evangelical colleges and universities, but I suspect stronger departments of sociology would help nurture better understanding of structural injustice. Certainly some more careful study of the comparative strength of sociology departments in evangelical, mainline Protestant, and Catholic colleges and universities—and the impact these departments have on the larger life of their respective communities—would be valuable.

I hope that in the next ten years we see a great deal of study and writing—biblical, theological, and sociological—on the many topics that I have only most briefly and superficially flagged here. We need to know a lot more in detail about both the extent of the problem and the ways to correct it.

I end with one sign that perhaps we are making a bit of progress. I quote from *For the Health of the Nation*, the unanimously approved official public policy document of the National Association of Evangelicals, which, at least theoretically, represents 30 million evangelicals.

> From the Bible, experience, and social analysis, we learn that social problems arise and can be substantially corrected by both personal decisions and structural changes. On the one hand, personal sinful choices contribute significantly to destructive social problems (Prov. 6:9-11), and personal conversion through faith in Christ can transform broken persons into wholesome, productive citizens. On the other hand, unjust systems also help create social problems (Amos 5:10-15; Isa. 10:1-2) and wise structural change (for example legislation to strengthen marriage or increase economic opportunity for all) can improve society. Thus Christian civic engagement must seek to transform both individuals and institutions. While individuals transformed by the gospel change surrounding society, social institutions also shape individuals. While good laws encourage good behavior, bad laws and systems foster destructive action. Lasting social change requires both personal conversion and institutional renewal and reform.[438]

I hope and pray for the day when all evangelicals, indeed all Christians, understand and live out that affirmation.

---

[437] (Grand Rapids: Eerdmans, 1965).

[438] See Ronald J. Sider and Diane Knippers, ed., *Toward an Evangelical Public Policy: Political Strategies for the Health of the Nation* (Grand Rapids: Baker, 2005), 366.

## Bibliography

Emerson, Michael O. and Christian Smith. *Divided by Faith: Evangelical Religion and the Problem of Race in America.* New York: Oxford University Press, 2000.

Hinojosa, Victor J. and Jerry Z. Park. "Religion and the Paradox of Racial Inequality Attitudes." *Journal of the Scientific Study of Religion* 43, no. 2 (2004): 229-38.

Sider, Ronald J. *Good News and Good Works.* Grand Rapids: Baker, 1999.

_____. *Rich Christians in an Age of Hunger*, 5th ed. Nashville: Thomas Nelson, 2005.

_____. *Scandal of the Evangelical Conscience.* Grand Rapids: Baker Books, 2005.

_____. *Scandal of Evangelical Politics.* Grand Rapids: Baker, 2008.

Sider, Ronald J. and Diane Knippers, eds. *Toward an Evangelical Public Policy: Political Strategies for the Health of the Nation.* Grand Rapids: Baker, 2005.

Smith, Christian. *American Evangelicalism: Embattled and Thriving.* Chicago: University of Chicago Press, 1998.

# Conclusion: He Will Reign Forever and Ever

Beth Snodderly

*Jesus Christ, who is the faithful witness, the firstborn from the dead, and the ruler of the kings of the earth. To him who loves us and has freed us from our sins by his blood, and has made us to be a kingdom and priests to serve his God and Father—to him be glory and power for ever and ever! Amen (Rev. 1:5, 6).*

## The Kingdom of God Opposed by the Kingdom of Satan

*"The whole world lies in the* power *of the evil one" (1 John 5:19 ESV).*

Something is wrong in this world. "Nature, red in tooth and claw," is a pattern acted out at all levels of life, from macropredators (social diseases caused by humans such as the wars that tore apart the former Yugoslavia) to micropredators (disease caused by microbes). Intelligent evil is at work in this world, distorting God's original good purposes. Even the spread of the gospel, as outlined in Timothy Tennents's chapter, exhibits frequent shifts away from the Kingdom teachings of Jesus, often with tragic results. Gregory Mundis described in his chapter the shift away from faith within Europe, a former stronghold of the faith. And so-called "success" can easily lead to eventual spiritual decline, as Hwa Yung points out in a review of Chinese Church growth.

These realities illustrate what missiologist Ralph Winter often talked about, "the existence of a hideous and cruel counterforce to God."[439] Similarly, Bruce McLaughlin wrote in the journal of the American Scientific Affiliation,

> Of their own free will, Satan and other spiritual beings rebelled against God in the primordial past and now abuse their God-given authority over certain aspects of creation. Satan, who holds the power of death (Heb. 2:14), exercises a pervasive, structural, diabolic influence to the point that the entire creation is in bondage to decay.[440]

---

[439] Ralph D. Winter, *Frontiers in Mission*, 4th ed. (Pasadena: William Carey International University Press, 2008), 300.

[440] Bruce McLaughlin, "From Whence Evil," *Perspectives on Science and the Christian Faith* 56, no. 3 (1976): 237.

## Cosmic Battle

*"Creation itself will be liberated from its bondage to decay and brought into the freedom and glory of the children of God" (Rom. 8:21).*

"Humans are made in the image of God and placed on earth so that they might gradually vanquish this chaos."[441] This interpretation of Genesis 1 implies that God's plan to strike back at the enemy was to overcome the free choices of evil agents with the free choices of good agents. Under a burden of evil that God did not intend for it, creation groans as it waits for the children of God to use their gift of free will to fulfill their responsibility to pray, "Let your Kingdom come; let your will be done on earth as it is in heaven;" "let the reign of Christ come in our lives and through our influence!" And in praying this, God's people join the cosmic battle and become channels through whom God can work to defeat evil and its resulting distortions. "Every action for the Kingdom is a prayer for the coming of the Kingdom," Lesslie Newbigin quotes Albert Schweitzer as having said.[442] In his contribution to the book, *Understanding Spiritual Warfare*, Walter Wink wrote, "An aperture opens in the praying person, permitting God to act without violating human freedom. The change in even one person thus changes what God can thereby do in the world."[443] Recognizing that everything of lasting importance begins and continues with prayer, in earlier chapters of this book Daniel Darko highlighted the apostle Paul's legacy of "missions as intercession," and Hwa Yung described the intercessory prayer life of Chinese evangelist, John Sung.

God's plan to reverse the evil one's influence (Gen. 3:15) called for humans to freely choose to obey and serve him as their rightful ruler. This plan was delayed numerous times by humans making wrong choices and experiencing the consequences, such as the Flood, or when the Israelites asked for a human king and ended up in Exile. Each time judgment was followed by a fresh beginning.

## The Kingdom Strikes Back

*"Now is the time for judgment on this world; now the prince of this world will be driven out" (John 12:31). "The reason the Son of God appeared was to destroy the devil's work" (1 John 3:8).*

---

[441] Gregory A. Boyd, *God at War: The Bible and Spiritual Conflict* (Downers Grove: InterVarsity Academic, 1997), 107.

[442] Lesslie Newbigin, *Signs Amid the Rubble: The Purposes of God in Human History*, ed. Geoffrey Wainwright (Grand Rapids: Eerdmans, 2003), 38.

[443] Walter Wink, "The World Systems Model," in *Understanding Spiritual Warfare: Four Views*, ed. James Beilby and Paul Eddy (Grand Rapids: Baker Academic, 2012), 66.

Finally, at the right time, God made a radical new beginning: the Word became flesh (John 1:14). In his wisdom God knew that humans would not be able to resist the wiles of the evil one without supernatural help. As Daniel Darko pointed out in his review of Pauline missiology, "messengers of God need ... divine enabling to counteract activities of the forces of evil." From the foundation of the world, God knew he would need a ruler for this world who was willing to identify with humans, one who was willing to risk being betrayed and killed by those he came to help. Since no other heavenly being would take on the terms of ruling the earth so that creatures of free will could live there under God's and heaven's rule, God himself, in the person of the pre-incarnate Son, had to be willing to take on the risk of being slaughtered. In this sense, the Lamb was "slain from the foundation of the earth."

The slaughtered lamb, the victim of violence, is God's paradoxical way of defeating the enemy. "When Revelation says that 'no one in heaven or on earth or under the earth was able to open the scroll or to look into it' (5:3) it means that absolutely no one else would have solved the cosmic conflict in this way."[444]

## Jesus' Acts of War against Evil

*"God anointed Jesus of Nazareth with the Holy Spirit and power, and ... he went around doing good and healing all who were under the power of the devil" (Acts 10:38).*

From the very first, Jesus' acts of ministry made it clear that he had come to wage war against evil. As Greg Boyd stated in his blog on the Reknew.org website, "Each one of Jesus' many healings and deliverances were understood to diminish Satan's hold on the world and to liberate people, to whatever degree, from his stronghold." Even the evil influences on nature had to obey him when he rebuked the storm (Mark 4: 39) with the same authority he used in casting out evil spirits (Mark 5:8). Peter Kuzmič pointed out in his chapter that Jesus explicitly announced that his victory over demons was the evidence that "the Kingdom of God has come upon you" (Luke 11:20). As Satan's kingdom is diminished, the Kingdom of God advances and "the prince of this world now stands condemned" (John 16:11).

> This judgment and casting out of the ruler of this world follows from the simple fact that a Man has appeared who is not, like all other men, subject to the compulsive power of corporate evil, but is able to live a life of obedience to God. It is this obedience of Jesus which is, *ipso facto*, the dethronement of the devil.[445]

---

[444] Sigve Tonstad, "Video Lecture 8," Revelation, Vision of Healing, May, 2013, accessed August 15, 2013, http://www.youtube.com/watch?v=SfcggURm9YI.

[445] Trevor Ling, *The Significance of Satan* (London: S P C K, 1961), 35.

In his obedience to the Father's will, Jesus did what the first Adam and his descendants could not do. Jesus' sinless death was the climax of the cosmic battle:[446] "Now shall the ruler of this world be driven out" (John 12:31), Jesus said, in the context of discussing his death. In his resurrection, Jesus triumphed over the one who holds the power of death, that is the devil (Heb. 2:14), and brought his people through a new exodus: out of the kingdom of darkness into his marvelous light, the kingdom of the beloved Son (Col. 1:12, 13; 1 Pet. 2:9).

## Overthrowing the Kingdom of Darkness, Disease, and Death

*"Let your kingdom come, let your will be done, on earth as it is in heaven"*
*(Matt. 6:10).*

"Alive in Christ, dead to sin, we are active participants in the same story of Christ," Corneliu Constantineanu pointed out in his chapter. Jesus passed on to his followers his Kingdom mission of defeating the works of the devil, teaching them to pray that God's will would be done "on earth as it is in heaven," and telling them the gates of hell would not prevail against the Church's initiatives. Jesus did what he saw the Father doing (John 5:19). He even told his followers they would do greater things than he had been doing (John 14:12). Christopher Wright explained in his chapter that from the time of Abraham, God had intended for his people to be "a community shaped by his own ethical character, with specific attention to righteousness and justice in a world filled with oppression and injustice." Believers should be prepared to confront the kingdom of darkness as a natural part of sharing the gospel, Daniel Darko insists in his chapter.

> It is [Jesus' followers'] obedience which will, through the working of God, result in the extinguishing of the evil now present in their midst. The whole realm of Satan suffers a defeat as a result of the obedience of the Christian church in one particular place.[447]

Overthrowing the kingdom of darkness and death means believers must engage in Kingdom warfare in whatever form they find it. A medical missionary in Shillong, India from 1939–1969 wrote in his journal, "This kingdom of disease, death, ignorance, prejudice, fear, malnutrition, and abject poverty [is] most surely a kingdom which ought to be overthrown by the Kingdom of our God."[448] As Peter Kuzmič said in the first chapter of this book,

---

[446] Judith Kovacs, "'Now Shall the Ruler of This World Be Driven Out': Death as Cosmic Battle in John 12: 20-36," *Journal of Biblical Literature* 114, no. 233 (1995): 227-47.

[447] Ling, *Significance,* 42.

[448] D. Ben Rees, *Vehicles of Grace and Hope: Welsh Missionaries in India 1800–1970* (Pasadena: William Carey Library, 2002).

"the Christ-given commission to preach the good news of the Kingdom of God is linked with the equipping power of the Holy Spirit to overcome the forces of evil."

Fighting the evil of disease is an integral part of the warfare between the two kingdoms, demonstrating that God is not the author of suffering, disease, and death. Believers and unbelievers alike fall victim to the evil one's weapon of disease. Bruce Nicholls pointed out in his chapter that when Moses lifted up the bronze snake on a pole in the wilderness, then all the people of God who had been bitten by snakes and looked up at it were healed (Num. 21:4-9). Moses was demonstrating that the evil one had been conquered, and the captured snake on a stake has been the symbol for the healing arts and sciences throughout history. Jesus said in John 3 that even as Moses lifted up the serpent (in demonstration of a defeat of one of the devil's works) so the Son of Man would be lifted up (also in defeat of the works of the devil—see 1 John 3:8).

Disease is a work of the devil keeping whole groups of people in bondage to suffering and evil. Maps from MARC publications[449] show the non-coincidental overlap of areas of the world that have the least influence of the gospel with those areas where there is the most suffering, disease, war, and poverty. Disease is a work of Satan, which the Son of God came to destroy.[450] One way believers can fight in the war against disease, and demonstrate that it is not God's will, is by participating in attempts to eradicate specific diseases.

Our mission is to defeat evil wherever we can, to bring about the "obedience of faith among the nations" as Christopher Wright highlighted in his chapter. In another chapter, Rene Padilla described the Church's mission as the responsibility to manifest God's Kingdom, his power, and his glory in the midst of the kingdoms of this world. In Jesus, "the Kingdom of God has come near, and our families and churches are outposts for the Kingdom of God."[451]

The chapters in this book have given examples of what the reign of Christ looks like in these outposts. God has called us "into his kingdom and glory" (1 Thess. 2:12) and Scott Hafemann's chapter showed how the Thessalonian letters aim to move their recipients toward a transformed worldview that recognizes that we must live lives worthy of the King. God desires love and respect across cultural and religious boundaries, as Miroslav Volf, Bruce Nicholls, and Ruth Padilla DeBorst described in their chapters. All of life should be an integrated expression of the reign of Christ, as Corneliu Constantineanu, Barry Corey, and Rene Padilla have demonstrated in their chapters. Padilla explained, from the Willowbank Report, that "a commitment to Jesus involves a process of transformation that affects the whole of life and

---

[449] Bryant Myers, *The New Context of World Missions* (Monrovia: MARC, 1996).

[450] Winter, *Frontiers*, 323.

[451] Ed Stetzer, *Subversive Kingdom: Living as Agents of Gospel Transformation* (Nashville: B&H., 2012), 231.

has social and public consequences." Ronald Sider called attention to these consequences, citing cultural and structural injustices and systemic evils that must some day yield to the reign of Christ. Believers should serve as a showcase or display window for what God's Kingdom looks like, in order to restore God's glorious reputation, so that the works of the devil are not attributed to God. We pray by our actions, "Your Kingdom come; Your will be done on earth as it is in heaven" (Matt. 6:10).

### He Will Reign Forever and Ever

*"He will swallow up death forever. The Sovereign Lord will wipe away the tears from all faces" (Isa. 25:8).*

"The rule and reign of God [is] the great eschatological fact to which all history is moving," Timothy Tennent points out in his chapter. Scott Hafemann elaborated, "at the center of the Christian worldview is the reality that salvation history, indeed, all of history, climaxes ... when Christ returns to establish God's righteous rule over his creation." Through demonstrations of God's will on earth, that there should be no sickness, no death, no hatred, injustice, or pain, believers' actions "vote" for God's Kingdom to come, and hold evil back from engulfing the earth. But the final victory comes in an unexpected way. "The way the Messiah won his victory is explained by the image of the Lamb, while the significance of the image of the Lamb is now seen to lie in the fact that his sacrificial death was a victory over evil."[452] "The one who is strong enough to bear the weight of the cosmic conflict, to break the seals, is the Lamb that was slaughtered."[453]

> *Then I saw a Lamb, looking as if it had been slain, standing at the center of the throne, encircled by the four living creatures and the elders. ... And they sang a new song, saying:*
>
> *"You are worthy to take the scroll*
> *and to open its seals,*
> *because you were slain,*
> *and with your blood you purchased for God*
> *persons from every tribe and language and people and nation.*
> *You have made them to be a kingdom and priests to serve our God,*
> *and they will reign on the earth."*
>
> *I looked and heard the voice of many angels, numbering thousands upon thousands, and ten thousand times ten thousand. They encircled the throne and the living creatures and the elders. In a loud voice they were saying:*

---

[452] Richard Bauckham, *The Theology of the Book of Revelation* (Cambridge: Cambridge University Press, 1993), 74.

[453] Sigve Tonstad, "Video Lecture 17," Revelation, Vision of Healing, May 2013, accessed August 17, 2013, http://www.youtube.com/watch?v=SfcggURm9YI.

> *"Worthy is the Lamb, who was slain,*
> *to receive power and wealth and wisdom and strength*
> *and honor and glory and praise!"*

*Then I heard every creature in heaven and on earth and under the earth and on the sea, and all that is in them, saying:*

> *"To him who sits on the throne and to the Lamb*
> *be praise and honor and glory and power,*
> *for ever and ever!" (Revelation 5:6, 9-13).*

*"The kingdom of the world has become the kingdom of our Lord and of his Messiah, and he will reign for ever and ever." (Revelation 11:15).*

## Bibliography

Bauckham, Richard. *The Theology of the Book of Revelation.* Cambridge: Cambridge University Press, 1993.

Boyd, Gregory A. *God at War: The Bible and Spiritual Conflict.* Downers Grove: InterVarsity Academic, 1997.

Kovacs, Judith. "'Now Shall the Ruler of This World Be Driven Out': Death as Cosmic Battle in John 12: 20-36." *Journal of Biblical Literature* 114, no. 233 (1995): 227-47.

Ling, Trevor. *The Significance of Satan.* London: S.P.C.K., 1961.

McLaughlin, Bruce. "From Whence Evil." *Perspectives on Science and the Christian Faith* 56, no. 3 (1976): 237.

Myers, Bryant. *The New Context of World Missions.* Monrovia: MARC, 1996.

Newbigin, Lesslie. *Signs Amid the Rubble: The Purposes of God in Human History*, ed. Geoffrey Wainwright. Grand Rapids: Eerdmans, 2003.

Rees, D. Ben. *Vehicles of Grace and Hope: Welsh Missionaries in India 1800–1970.* Pasadena: William Carey Library, 2002.

Stetzer, Ed. *Subversive Kingdom: Living as Agents of Gospel Transformation.* Nashville: B&H., 2012.

Tonstad, Sigve. *Saving God's Reputation: The Theological Function of* Pistis Iesou *in the Cosmic Narratives of Revelation* (Library of New Testament Studies). London: T&T Clark, 2006.

Wink, Walter. "The World Systems Model." In *Understanding Spiritual Warfare: Four Views*, edited by James Beilby and Paul Eddy, 66. Grand Rapids: Baker Academic, 2012.

Winter, Ralph D. *Frontiers in Mission.* 4th ed. Pasadena: William Carey International University Press, 200

# Index

Africa/African 1, 4, 5, 43, 45, 46, 47, 49, 51, 57, 58, 59, 60, 87, 88, 89, 90, 91, 93, 94, 95, 96, 100, 101, 102, 110, 111, 148, 153, 155, 157, 158

Asia/Asian 1, 5, 46, 48, 49, 88, 90, 91, 93, 101, 113, 114, 115, 116, 117, 118, 119, 120, 123, 124, 126, 144

Assemblies of God 147, 151, 155, 156, 157, 159, 160, 162, 163, 194, 195, 196, 197, 198, 199, 200, 201, 202, 203, 204, 205, 206, 207, 208, 210, 212

Bible/biblical 13, 14, 15, 25, 26, 27, 28, 31, 32, 34, 35, 36, 37, 40, 44, 51, 53, 56, 57, 71, 87, 88, 90, 91, 101, 106, 109, 116, 117, 118, 123, 125, 126, 127, 128, 129, 130, 131, 132, 133, 134, 135, 136, 137, 138, 139, 140, 141, 142, 143, 144, 145, 146, 150, 152, 154, 155, 162, 167, 169, 170, 172, 201, 202, 215, 216, 217, 218, 219, 220, 221, 225, 228, 233, 235, 236, 238, 239, 241, 243, 244, 245, 246, 247, 249, 254, 255, 260, 261, 262, 266, 271

Bible School(s) 157, 194, 195, 196, 197, 200, 203, 204, 205

Buddhism/Buddhist 4, 50, 54, 123

Catholic/Catholicism 14, 20, 31, 35, 39, 46, 53, 57, 65, 90, 134, 142, 148, 149, 150, 197, 199, 208, 257, 259, 262

charismatic 3, 34, 35, 36, 114, 115, 116, 117, 122, 124, 157, 196, 197, 198, 199, 200, 202, 205, 211, 213

China/Chinese 3, 51, 58, 113, 114, 115, 116, 119, 121, 122, 123, 124, 154, 155, 265, 266,

Christendom 52, 53, 54, 106, 147, 148, 149, 150, 151, 152, 153, 154, 156, 163

Christian(s)/Christianity 1, 2, 3, 4, 5, 6, 10, 11, 12, 13, 17, 19, 24, 26, 28, 29, 30, 31, 32, 33, 34, 35, 36, 37, 38, 39, 41, 42, 43, 44, 45, 46, 47, 48, 49, 50, 51, 52, 53, 54, 55, 56, 57, 58, 59, 60, 61, 65-86, 87, 88, 89, 90, 91, 92, 93, 95, 96, 97, 98, 99, 101, 102, 103, 105, 106, 107, 108, 109, 110, 111, 112, 116, 117, 121, 122, 123, 124, 125-46, 147-66, 167, 168, 169, 170, 171, 173, 174, 177, 179, 181, 185, 187, 188, 190, 201, 215, 216, 217, 218, 219, 220, 221, 222, 225, 226, 227, 229, 233, 254, 255, 257, 259, 260, 261, 262, 263, 268, 270, 271

Church (of Jesus Christ) 4, 5, 6, 9-40, 41, 42, 43, 44, 45, 46, 47, 49, 50, 51, 54, 56, 57, 58, 59, 61, 68, 69, 87, 88, 91, 93, 94, 96, 97, 98, 102, 105, 106, 108, 109, 110, 111, 113, 114, 115, 116, 117, 118, 119, 121, 122, 123, 124, 132, 133, 135, 138, 141, 143, 144, 145, 146, 147, 148, 155, 162, 188, 217, 218, 221, 226, 243, 247, 259, 260, 261, 265, 268, 269,

church (congregations) 1, 2, 3. 4, 42, 47, 49, 50, 52, 53, 55, 58, 60, 87, 88, 89, 90, 94, 95, 97, 99, 101, 102, 106, 107, 108, 111, 113, 115, 116, 118, 119, 120, 121, 122, 123, 125, 126, 130, 131, 134, 137, 142, 143, 147, 148, 149, 150, 151, 153, 154, 155, 156, 157, 158, 159, 160, 161, 162, 167, 169, 170, 171, 178, 191, 193-214, 215, 218, 220, 225, 226, 227, 228, 231, 232, 233, 235, 259, 269

church growth 32, 50, 88, 117, 119, 163, 265

church history 42, 116, 123, 132, 141, 216

church planting 3, 50, 51, 59, 88, 155, 159, 160, 161, 201

communism/Communists 55, 65, 73, 91, 111, 163

connected(ness) 3, 6, 66, 144, 151, 239, 248

Constantine/Constantinian 12, 26, 44, 45, 154, 217

contextualization 134, 141, 142, 143, 144, 145, 215-24

cooperation 29, 58, 87, 88, 96, 100, 101, 102

273

culture/cultural 3, 4, 5, 6, 10, 15, 28, 40, 41-61, 65, 67, 69, 70, 71, 73, 75, 77, 78, 82, 85, 86, 89, 95, 96, 97, 101, 102, 103, 108, 109, 122, 123, 125, 126, 127, 132, 133, 134, 136, 137, 139, 140, 141, 142, 143, 144, 145, 146, 150, 155, 156, 160, 161, 163, 167, 169, 170, 172, 173, 189, 211, 215-22, 227, 233, 248, 261, 269, 270
devil 71, 78, 266, 267, 268, 269, 270
disciple(ship) 3, 4, 5, 16, 18, 19, 20, 24, 29, 30, 57, 88, 91, 93, 96, 215, 221, 254, 255,
Early Church 5, 12, 14, 22, 23, 25, 26, 28, 39, 41, 87, 88, 94, 96, 103
education(al) 4, 6, 58, 94, 106, 121, 126, 140, 144, 167-71, 193-207, 210, 212, 213, 214, 218, 220, 236, 258, 259
ekklesia 9, 18, 19, 23, 27, 172, 190
ethic(s)/ethical 6, 31, 37, 38, 39, 48, 53, 69, 74, 78, 83, 85, 86, 95, 96, 102, 105-112, 122, 134, 140, 143, 167, 170, 172, 173-77, 181, 182, 183, 185, 187, 188, 190, 198, 216, 218, 227, 228, 229, 231, 232, 233, 235-55, 260, 261, 268
Europe/European 3, 32, 39, 42, 46, 47, 48, 49, 53, 55, 57, 58, 61, 87, 89, 90, 91, 100, 110, 11, 125, 147-64, 168, 207, 214, 253, 265
evangelical(s) 2, 3, 9, 10, 12, 14, 15, 28, 30, 31, 32, 33, 35, 36, 37, 38, 39, 40, 41, 47, 55, 56, 57, 60, 61, 76, 90, 91, 106, 108, 125, 126, 127, 128, 131, 132, 138, 140, 141, 142, 144, 145, 147, 150, 152, 153, 154, 158, 161, 162, 168, 169, 197, 203, 205, 208, 215, 218, 257-263
evangelism/evangelize 4, 15, 31, 32, 36, 39, 40, 45, 53, 54, 59, 76, 88, 94, 119, 143, 150, 151, 153, 155, 161, 201, 202
evil/evil one 2, 16, 18, 33, 71, 72, 78, 79, 80, 81, 83, 93, 94, 106, 170, 220, 225, 227, 237, 238, 258, 265, 266, 267, 268, 269, 270, 271

faith 1, 2, 4, 6, 10, 11, 16, 17, 21, 22, 23, 27, 28, 29, 31, 32, 33, 37, 38, 41, 43, 44, 45, 46, 47, 48, 51, 52, 53, 54, 58, 59, 61, 65-86, 94, 95, 96, 98, 107, 108, 11, 116, 117, 118, 120, 121, 123, 127, 130, 132, 135, 137, 138, 139, 140, 148, 150, 1151, 152, 156, 167-91, 194, 200, 205, 215, 216, 219, 221, 222, 225, 226, 227, 228, 229, 230, 231, 232, 233, 234, 235, 236, 238, 242, 243, 244, 247, 251, 254, 255, 258, 257, 259, 261, 262, 263, 265, 269, 271
Global South 51, 60, 87, 88, 89,
globalization 1, 4, 47, 142, 144, 151, 163
good news 2, 6, 16, 17, 18, 26, 28, 30, 32, 33, 35, 43, 87, 147, 202, 219, 220, 221, 228, 244, 260, 263, 269
gospel 2, 4, 13, 15, 16, 17, 18, 19, 21, 22, 23, 24, 26, 33, 35, 36, 39, 40, 41-61, 88, 91, 92, 94, 96, 98, 99, 100, 101, 102, 106, 107, 108, 111, 113, 117, 118, 121, 123, 125, 127, 128, 131, 132, 134, 136, 137, 139, 141, 142, 143, 145, 146, 147-64, 167, 168, 169, 170, 171, 172, 173, 174, 175, 176, 177, 180, 181, 186, 188, 194, 201, 202, 215, 216, 218, 219, 220, 221, 225, 226, 227, 228, 229, 230, 231, 232, 233, 234, 238, 247, 254, 260, 262, 265, 268, 269, 271
Great Commission 19, 23, 131, 150, 151, 161, 221, 254
Greek(s) 5, 23, 27, 43, 44, 56, 61, 94, 97, 133, 134, 137, 150, 178, 191
hermeneutic(s) 27, 35, 101, 106, 125-46, 217, 222, 235, 254
Hindu/Hinduism 4, 42, 43, 47, 50, 51, 53, 54, 137, 154
history/historical 3, 4, 6, 11, 13, 14, 15, 18, 21, 22, 24, 25, 26, 27, 37, 38, 39, 40, 41, 42-50, 51, 53, 55, 56, 57, 59, 60, 61, 66, 67, 84, 94, 97, 99, 103, 106, 114, 116, 119, 121, 123, 126, 127, 128, 132, 133, 136, 137, 138, 141, 142, 147, 148,

149, 150, 151, 154, 155, 156, 157, 159, 160, 163, 172, 174, 183, 189, 193, 194, 195, 197, 198, 206, 207, 209, 210, 211, 213, 215, 216, 217, 218, 220, 222, 227, 228, 229, 233, 236, 237, 239, 245, 246, 247, 249, 250, 251, 253, 254, 259, 260, 261, 266, 270, 271

Holy Spirit/Spirit 5, 23, 24, 25, 29, 31, 33, 34, 35, 36, 37, 38, 90, 91, 92, 93, 100, 102, 107, 109, 115, 116, 117, 122, 123, 127, 131, 132, 133, 135, 140, 141, 143, 144, 147, 150, 151, 155, 156, 157, 158, 160, 161, 162, 163, 184, 185, 187, 197, 217, 218, 220, 227, 229, 230, 247, 267, 269

immigrant/immigration 3, 49, 58, 90-91, 108, 147, 152, 153, 154, 155, 157, 158, 161, 162

incarnation 11, 22, 30, 41, 143, 215, 217, 220

India 43, 48, 50, 51, 54, 57, 58, 125, 137, 155, 268, 271

injustice 72, 108, 237, 243, 257-263, 268, 270

integrate/integration 3, 125, 130, 161, 167-91, 228, 229, 269

intercede/intercession 22, 98, 242, 266

Islam(ic) 1, 6, 10, 42, 43, 37, 47, 53, 54, 61, 66, 69, 81, 84, 86, 125, 126, 128, 129, 130, 131, 132, 133, 134, 137, 139, 140, 143, 144, 145, 146, 147-64

Jews/Jewish/Judaism 5, 10, 12, 16, 17, 20, 21, 23, 26, 39, 43, 44, 45, 66, 67, 71, 81, 91, 92, 94, 95, 96, 97, 98, 99, 103, 128, 129, 132, 133, 137, 149, 151, 152, 173, 175, 177, 179, 181, 220, 227, 230, 238

judgment (divine) 18, 37, 225-34, 236-38, 250, 251, 266, 267

justice 2, 16, 35, 67, 83, 84, 86, 131, 134, 140, 144, 170, 172, 189, 190, 216, 221, 225, 230, 236, 237, 239, 241, 242, 243, 248, 250, 252, 253, 255, 261, 262, 268, 270

justification 172, 177, 178, 179, 180, 181, 182, 183, 191

Kingdom (of God/of heaven) 1, 2, 4, 5, 6, 9-40, 87, 88, 91, 98, 99, 101, 107, 108, 109, 110, 111, 119, 126, 131, 133, 142, 162, 169, 170, 172, 179, 189, 190, 217, 221, 222, 230, 231, 232, 245, 246, 249, 260, 265, 266, 267, 268, 269, 270, 271

Koran (see Qur'an)

Korea(n) 3, 9, 47, 50, 51, 57, 58, 67, 115, 117,

Kuzmič, Peter vii, 2, 6, 9, 55, 90, 100, 147, 149, 151, 156, 163, 193, 225, 267, 268

Latin America 46, 53, 57, 88, 89, 91, 101, 105, 106, 156, 157, 172, 191, 216, 219

leader(ship) 1, 2, 3, 4, 5, 6, 16, 20, 21, 24, 26, 30, 44, 55, 88, 89, 90, 91, 95, 96, 98, 100, 101, 106, 11, 117, 123, 125, 136, 140, 143, 147, 155, 156, 158, 159, 160, 161, 162, 167, 169, 170, 189, 194, 196, 197, 199, 200, 201, 202, 203, 204, 205, 206, 207, 208, 209, 210, 211, 212, 213, 220, 225

Lord/lordship (of Christ) 2, 3, 17, 21, 22, 23, 24, 25, 26, 27, 28, 29, 30, 31, 32, 35, 43, 54, 67, 88, 91, 94, 95, 97, 98, 99, 100, 108, 109, 120, 121, 127, 132, 135, 141, 150, 158, 162, 167, 168, 169, 184, 187, 188, 189, 201, 218, 221, 225, 226, 228, 229, 231, 232, 236, 237, 139, 240, 241, 242, 248, 251, 253, 254, 270, 271

Majority World 1, 49, 51, 53, 59, 108, 110, 111, 123, 217, 220

Missio Dei 1, 2, 92, 95, 100

missiology/missiological 43, 87-103, 125, 126, 132, 141,148, 150, 155, 163, 164, 225, 226, 234, 243, 267

mission(s)/missional 2, 4-6, 9, 10, 12, 13, 14, 16, 17, 18, 20, 23, 24, 25, 27, 28, 29, 30, 31, 32, 33, 34, 35, 36, 44, 46, 47, 56, 57, 58, 59, 60, 61, 87-103, 105, 106, 107, 111,

113, 114, 121, 123, 124, 127, 131, 142, 144, 145, 146, 148, 149, 150, 153, 151, 155, 156, 159, 160, 163, 164, 167, 171, 175, 178, 188, 201, 202, 215-22, 225, 226, 228, 233, 234, 235-56, 268, 269, 271
missionary/missionaries 1, 2, 3, 13, 24, 30, 41, 46, 53, 58, 59, 61, 87-103, 105, 107, 108, 111, 113, 116, 118, 121, 122, 132, 136, 137, 142, 151, 155, 156, 157, 158, 159, 160, 161, 162, 163, 194, 201, 215, 225-34, 268, 271
Muslim(s) 1, 4, 28, 42, 43, 53, 66, 67, 69, 70, 81, 125-46, 147, 149, 153, 154, 155, 158, 161, 162
new age/age to come 17, 18, 19, 20, 22, 23, 24, 184, 185, 189, 219, 230
New Testament 9, 10, 14, 15, 19, 20, 23, 24, 25, 27, 33, 38, 39, 40, 43, 52, 71, 86, 88, 92, 94, 96, 97, 102, 103, 106, 116, 133, 134, 135, 136, 137, 138, 139, 142, 143, 145, 146, 150, 156, 172, 173, 174, 175, 178, 181, 190, 216, 218, 230, 247, 254, 260, 261, 271
non-Western 1, 2, 4, 57, 59, 60, 89, 90, 101, 116, 123
North America(n)/United States 1, 3, 46, 48, 49, 53, 58, 87, 90, 107, 108, 109, 110, 111, 148, 153
obedience 10, 18, 22, 24, 30, 32, 92, 114, 131, 167, 174, 176, 180, 186, 187, 191, 216, 227, 232, 235-56, 267, 268, 269
Old Testament 16, 21, 23, 27, 38, 51, 91, 126, 127, 128, 133, 134, 142, 150, 152, 182, 235-56
Paul (the Apostle) 5, 22, 23, 26, 44, 69, 87-103, 106, 107, 111, 123, 134, 136, 157, 167-91, 213, 225-34, 235, 238, 242, 244, 247, 254, 266, 267
pentecostal(ism) 1, 3, 34, 35, 36, 47, 51, 60, 65, 90, 106, 115-17, 122, 123, 124, 142, 147, 150, 151, 152, 155, 156, 157, 158, 159, 160, 161, 162, 163, 193, 194, 197, 199, 200, 202, 204, 205, 206, 208, 210, 211, 213,
politics/political 1, 5, 6, 10, 12, 15, 16, 20, 21, 23, 28, 37, 48, 52, 59, 60, 61, 65, 67, 68, 69, 73, 75, 77, 78, 82, 83, 84, 85, 86, 89, 105, 130, 131, 140, 141, 149, 169, 171, 172, 173, 190, 207, 214, 217, 219, 225, 241, 251, 255, 257, 259, 260, 262, 263
post-Christendom 52, 53, 55, 60, 156
postmodern(ity) 52, 54, 55-57, 60, 61, 144
pray/prayer 3, 4, 5, 17, 23, 37, 38, 43, 93, 98, 99, 100, 109, 116, 117, 119-20, 122, 123, 130, 133, 135, 143, 152, 161, 162, 169, 189, 227, 231, 232, 251, 252, 253, 262, 266, 268, 270,
Protestant(ism) 13, 14, 20, 22, 31, 35, 39, 46, 51, 53, 57, 79, 117, 132, 148, 149, 200, 257, 258, 259, 262
Qur'an 42, 125, 128, 129, 131, 132, 133, 144, 152
reign (of God or of Christ) 11, 12, 17, 21, 25, 27, 31, 32, 57, 109, 111, 184, 193, 265, 266, 269, 270, 271
Reformation 13, 32, 33, 46, 49, 109, 134, 148, 149, 216, 259
religion(s) 1, 20, 42, 43, 47, 48, 49, 50, 51, 52, 53, 54, 57, 60, 61, 65, 66, 67, 68, 69, 70, 71, 73, 75, 78, 81, 82, 83, 84, 85, 86, 90, 123, 125, 130, 131, 132, 134, 139, 144, 145, 148, 150, 151, 152, 154, 155, 156, 157, 163, 169, 171, 172, 190, 198, 199, 200, 203, 206, 214, 215, 218, 220, 241, 248, 258, 259, 263
Resurrection 4, 11, 16, 21, 22, 23, 24, 135, 139, 141, 142, 150, 175, 184, 185, 186, 187, 188, 189, 218, 221, 228, 229, 268
righteousness 6, 28, 34, 92, 94, 180, 181, 182, 183, 184, 185, 186, 187, 189, 225, 236, 239, 241, 242, 243, 244, 252, 255, 268
Rome/Roman Empire 5, 23, 26, 41, 44, 45, 46, 57, 59, 71, 94, 106, 133,

137, 142, 149, 154, 163, 172, 177, 179, 180, 181, 188, 190
salvation  5, 11, 14, 17, 21, 22, 24, 28, 37, 39, 91, 93, 94, 103, 134, 137, 140, 147, 150, 151, 155, 171, 172, 180, 182, 183, 186, 188, 216, 227, 228, 229, 231, 232, 233, 241, 255, 260, 261, 270
Satan  93, 127, 201, 265, 267, 268, 269, 271
Scripture(s)  6, 10, 27, 31, 35, 51, 70, 71, 86, 125, 126, 127, 132, 133-39, 141, 142, 150, 162, 194, 215-21, 226, 237, 240, 254, 255
servant/servanthood/serve/service  2, 3, 11, 12, 22, 26, 28, 30, 31, 32, 34, 37, 38, 60, 67, 70, 72, 76, 86, 87, 90, 92, 94, 95, 97, 99, 100, 101, 102, 108, 111, 117, 142, 144, 150, 157, 158, 159, 169, 196, 200, 203, 204, 206, 215, 225, 226, 229, 232, 240, 247, 253, 265, 266, 270
social (issues)/society  1, 2, 3, 4, 5, 6, 10, 15, 19, 25, 28, 31, 34, 35, 38, 39, 40, 46, 48, 53, 54, 55, 65, 68, 70, 71, 72, 73, 74, 85, 93, 96, 100, 101, 105, 106, 108, 109, 112, 119, 121, 130, 131, 135, 136, 140, 141, 143, 144, 145, 149, 154, 156, 157, 158, 167, 169, 170, 171, 172, 173, 175, 176, 177, 180, 181, 188, 190, 193, 196, 197, 198, 199, 200, 201, 202, 203, 206, 207, 208, 209, 210, 211, 212, 213, 214, 215, 216, 217, 218, 219, 235, 238, 241, 246, 248, 249, 251, 252, 253, 255, 257, 258, 259, 260, 261, 262, 270
Spirit (see Holy Spirit)
spiritual(ity)  3, 4, 5, 6, 9, 10, 11, 13, 21, 33, 34, 36, 40, 45, 51, 53, 60, 71, 81, 88, 90, 92, 93, 98, 118, 119, 121, 122, 126, 132, 134, 135, 138, 148, 150, 154, 155, 156, 160, 162, 168, 169, 171, 172, 173, 200, 215, 216, 217, 218, 244, 259, 265, 266, 271
submission  6, 30, 32, 44, 66, 130, 152, 186, 187

theology/theological/theologian  2, 3, 4, 5, 6, 9, 10, 12, 13, 14, 15, 19, 23, 24, 25, 26, 27, 32, 33, 36, 38, 39, 40, 48, 50, 51, 54, 58, 59, 60, 61, 70, 71, 74, 76, 78, 79, 8485, 86, 91, 92, 94, 99, 101, 102, 103, 105, 106, 108, 109, 110, 111, 114, 115, 116, 122, 125, 126, 128, 129, 130, 132, 134, 135, 136, 137, 138, 139, 140, 141, 143, 144, 145, 146, 156, 163, 167, 168, 169, 170, 171, 172, 173, 174, 175, 176, 177, 178, 181, 183, 188, 189, 190,, 191, 198, 200, 203, 210, 214, 215, 216, 217, 218, 219, 221, 225, 226, 228, 232, 233, 234, 235, 236, 238, 239, 241, 242, 244, 251, 253, 255, 259, 260, 261, 262, 270, 271
transformation/transformative/transformed  2, 52, 60, 100, 106, 108, 111, 133, 134, 139, 143, 161, 167, 171, 172, 173, 182, 183, 186, 188, 189, 190, 199, 205, 206, 211, 215, 217, 218, 219, 220, 221, 226, 227, 229, 230, 244, 257, 258, 259, 261, 262, 269, 271
United States (see North America)
West/Western/Westerner  2, 3, 4, 10, 12, 28, 30, 35, 37, 42, 45, 46, 47, 48, 49, 51, 52, 53, 55, 57, 58, 59, 61, 66, 69, 74, 82, 85, 87, 88, 89, 90, 100, 101, 102, 107, 111, 114, 115, 116, 117, 121, 122, 123, 124, 136, 139, 142, 147, 148, 149, 150, 163, 215, 216, 217, 220
worldview  53, 55, 57, 58, 75, 93, 94, 102, 116, 125, 130, 131, 132, 136, 139, 141, 148, 171, 173, 175, 218, 226, 227, 229, 233, 269, 270

Made in the USA
Lexington, KY
02 March 2014